5/27

D1134700

Laughing at the Tao

LIVIA KOHN

Laughing at the Tao

Debates among Buddhists and
Taoists in Medieval China

PRINCETON UNIVERSITY PRESS
PRINCETON, NEW JERSEY

Copyright © 1995 by Princeton University Press
Published by Princeton University Press, 41 William Street,
Princeton, New Jersey 08540
In the United Kingdom: Princeton University Press,
Chichester, West Sussex

Library of Congress Cataloging-in-Publication Data

Hsiao tao lun. English.
Laughing at the Tao : debates among Buddhists and
Taoists in medieval China / Livia Kohn.
p.   cm.
Includes bibliographical references and index.
ISBN: 0-691-03483-4
1. Taoism—China. 2. Taoism—Relations—Buddhism.
I. Kohn, Livia, 1956–   . II. Title.
BL1910.H7313   1994   94-20924
299'.514—dc20

This book has been composed in Galliard

Princeton University Press books are printed on
acid-free paper and meet the guidelines for permanence
and durability of the Committee on Production
Guidelines for Book Longevity of the
Council on Library Resources

Printed in the United States of America

10   9   8   7   6   5   4   3   2   1

To my teacher,
Rolf Trauzettel

CONTENTS

ACKNOWLEDGMENTS

This work on the *Xiaodao lun* was begun in June 1982 when the text was first read in the research seminar on medieval Chinese thought at the Institute for Research in Humanities (Jimbun kagaku kenkyūjo) at Kyōto University. I was a participant in the seminar and remained so for the full duration of the reading, preparing a first English version as we went along.

When an extensive and corrected Japanese version appeared in print in 1988 (listed under "Kenkyūhan 1988" in the bibliography here), the time had come to revise and develop the English translation. Supported generously by the Japan Society for the Promotion of Science, I was able to do so in 1991–93. Both the English translation and annotation would have been impossible without the Japanese work or the inspiration and help of the Kyōto University group, especially their director, Prof. Yoshikawa Tadao.

Still, both are ultimately my own, and I am responsible for all misreadings and errors. More specifically, my English translation is based first and foremost on the Chinese original with the Japanese rendering used for suggestions and alternative readings. In most cases, I came to agree with the Japanese understanding, but there are still occasional passages where my reading differs.

The most important impact of the Japanese version lay in its ample annotation (1,148 notes). I relied heavily on it for the identification of passages and cross-references to other Taoist and Buddhist texts. Most notes that identify and compare *Xiaodao lun* citations with other Chinese sources are, therefore, based on the Japanese translation and are so marked in each case.

The more philological notes of the Japanese work, on the contrary, I did not include in the English version for the most part. I studied them carefully to deepen my understanding of the text and integrated their meaning in the rendition as much as possible. But I could not include them as separate notes because of space limitations and because they are highly specialized and would not be intelligible without characters in the text. I urge readers with a more philological interest to go to the Japanese work for an in-depth understanding of individual phrases and expressions in the *Xiaodao lun*.

Above and beyond the Japanese annotation, which remains largely in the realm of ancient Chinese materials, I developed my own notes by providing interpretations and comparative materials from secondary sources, analyses, and discussions of texts both of Western and East Asian provenance.

In addition, I gave the text a framework by supplying an introduction in the beginning and two appendixes in the end. The introduction raises the issue of the debates in the overall pattern of Buddhist adaptation to Chinese culture. The first appendix summarizes other texts of debates contained in the major Buddhist compendia, whereas the second on Taoist texts cited in the *Xiaodao lun* provides an analytical summary of the sources together with ample bibliographic information. This work again relies strongly on outstanding Japanese research in the field if not specifically on the Kenkyūhan translation.

Translations from other Chinese texts throughout the work are my own if only a reference to the original source is given. In cases when I consulted a previous Western translation, a reference to this work is added after the citation and introduced with the words *see also*. When earlier English translations are cited verbatim or with little alteration, I give the author, date, and page immediately without any further specification.

This work could never have been undertaken without the continued excellence of Japanese Taoist scholarship and the equally wonderful hospitality and helpfulness of Japanese scholars and the support of the Japanese Society for the Promotion of Science. In particular, I wish to express my heartfelt gratitude to Yoshikawa Tadao, who took many an hour to read and correct my work and made valuable suggestions on many parts of the manuscript.

Still, Western studies have played an important role, and I have profited much from the help of my colleagues. Most significantly, I have learned an enormous amount from a continued fruitful dialogue with Whalen Lai, who gave me much inspiration and guided me to a number of suggestive works in Buddhist studies, Western medieval history, and other areas. His questions and suggestions considerably shaped the introduction, and I am most deeply indebted to his help.

In addition, I am very grateful to Professors Kobayashi Masayoshi, Fabrizio Pregadio, Terence Russell, and Robert Sharf for reading parts of the manuscript and helping with criticism, bibliographic information, and suggestions on interpretation. They all gave their unfailing support and provided invaluable help in this difficult endeavor. I also thank Virginia Barker for her meticulous copyediting.

The translation of sections 13, 27, 29, 31, and 36, in an earlier version and with less-extensive footnotes, appeared in *Taoist Resources* 4, no. 1 (1993): 54–64.

ABBREVIATIONS

BZL	*Bianzheng lun* (T. 2210; 52.489c–550c)
DJYS	*Daojiao yishu* (*DZ* 1129, fasc. 762–63)
DZ	*Daozang,* Taoist canon as numbered in Schipper 1975c
fasc.	"fascicle," booklets of Taoist canon, 1925 Shanghai reprint
P.	Dunhuang manuscripts, Pelliot collection
repr.	reprinted in
S.	Dunhuang manuscripts, Stein collection
SDZN	*Sandong zhunang* (*DZ* 1139, fasc. 780–82)
T.	Taisho edition of the Buddhist canon
TPYL	*Taiping yulan*
trans.	translated
WSBY	*Wushang biyao* (*DZ* 1138, fasc. 768–79)
XDL	*Xiaodao lun* (T. 2103; 52.143c–152c)
YJQQ	*Yunji qiqian* (*DZ* 1032, fasc. 677–702)

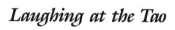

Laughing at the Tao

The *Xiaodao lun* in the Medieval Debates

The *Xiaodao lun* (Laughing at the Tao) is an anti-Taoist polemical text written by the official Zhen Luan and presented to Emperor Wu of the Northern Zhou dynasty in 570 C.E. Divided into thirty-six sections in mocking imitation of the division of the Taoist canon, the text concentrates on attacking Taoist mythology, doctrine, ritual, and religious practice. To do so, it cites heavily from Taoist scriptures and shows their inconsistency and absurdity by juxtaposing them with other Taoist texts and with Confucian classics, historical documents, and mathematical calculations. The *Xiaodao lun* is a highlight in an ongoing process of debate among Buddhists and Taoists in medieval China. Its origins, role, and special features are best understood in relation to the debates that both preceded and followed it.

Areas of Buddhist Adaptation to Chinese Culture

The medieval debates among Buddhists and Taoists from the fourth century to the early Tang dynasty formed an integral part of the adaptation of Buddhism into Chinese culture. During this period, Buddhism had to come to terms with the ways and worldviews of the Chinese aristocracy in three distinct areas. In all cases, this meant relating anew to its own heritage as well as reorganizing to fit the new environment.

The first area of Buddhist adaptation was the Confucian establishment of China. Here Buddhism was found unintelligible and problematic mainly because of its specific practices: shaving the head, leaving the family, living in celibacy. Many of these ways blatantly denied traditional Chinese virtues, such as filial piety, the inviolate state of the body, and proper worship for one's ancestors. In addition, a major issue at the time was the Buddhists' refusal to bow to secular authority on the grounds that the Buddha had left the world and his followers were thus no longer responsible to its rulers.[1]

[1] The demand that the monks should bow to secular authority and, especially, the emperor was first made by an official in 340 but met with opposition from other administrators who were more Buddhist in orientation. In 403, Huan Xuan, usurper of the Jin throne, again made the demand. At this time, Huiyuan answered in his famous memorial. See Ch'en 1954, 262. For more details, see Tang 1938; Zürcher 1959; Kimura 1962; Ch'en 1964; Schmidt-

Buddhist doctrine, also, was seriously questioned, especially the concepts regarding karma and rebirth (Lai 1993, 279). Whereas Buddhists proclaimed the doctrine of rebirth, the Confucian elite found it impossible to accept a new body after death. Moreover, the Chinese were utterly horrified by the notion of an ongoing responsibility and continued punishment. As Tsukamoto notes, "the reaction of the princes or nobles, told about reincarnation and the accompanying retribution, was a feeling of fright from which there was no escape." (Tsukamoto and Hurvitz 1985, 42). To explain how rebirth was possible, Huiyuan, in defiance of the doctrine of *anātman*, presented his thesis on the immortality of the spirit, often translated as "soul" in the literature.[2] These various discussions and confrontations helped to define the position of Buddhism within traditional Chinese society both as a social organization and as a system of thought.

A second area in which Buddhism had to compromise with Chinese beliefs was the Chinese sense of ethnic identity and cultural superiority. Buddhism originated among non-Chinese people, summarily called *hu,* or "barbarians," in the Chinese sources.[3] Although the teaching developed first in India, to the Chinese the main exponents and representatives of Buddhism were Central Asians. They were people of Hunnish or Turkish origin who may summarily be called "Turanians" (McGovern 1939, 7) or "Turko-Mongols" (White 1991, 124). Carried by these outsiders, Buddhism was presented in a strange language and with awkward practices and doctrines. To the Chinese mind, it was from the beginning associated with common prejudices regarding things non-Chinese, and its adaptation underwent phases that coincided closely with the changing fortunes of Chinese-Central Asian relationships.

The increasingly powerful domination of the northern part of China under Hun (Xiongnu and Xianbi) rulers fired the opposition of indigenous Chinese. In addition, the military prowess of marauding hordes who cruelly pillaged Chinese settlements caused the Chinese to associate their Central Asian neighbors with barbarianism of the worst sort. This image made its way into indigenous Chinese religion and literature. In the *Shenzhou jing* (Scripture of Divine Incantations), for example, the warriors of Central Asia were transformed into demons heralding the end of the world. In hosts of tens of

---

Glintzer 1976; Tsukamoto and Hurvitz 1985; Lai 1993. On the continuation of this debate in the Tang dynasty, see Tonami 1986, 479–88; Tonami 1988, 32.

[2] See Ch'en 1952; Ch'en 1964, 138; Liebenthal 1950, 1952, 1955; Schmidt-Glintzer 1976.

[3] There are various terms for *barbarian* in classical Chinese, denoting peoples in different regions beyond the Chinese borders. The Hu in this context are specifically the tribes to the north and northwest, with the Yi in the east, the Rong in the west, the Di in the north, and the Man in the south. The barbarians were frequently associated with animals as is shown in the graph for *man* with its *insect* radical and in the character for *di*, which follows *dog*. The Rong, moreover, are often called the "Dog-Rong," reflecting their dog-ancestor myth and their allegedly canine nature. For a detailed discussion of the traditional Chinese vision of the barbarians within a broader mythological and comparative context, see White 1991.

millions, they overrun helpless civilians, devour little children, and spread disease across the land. Fought with desperation, they can only be overcome by the heavenly host of the indigenous Taoist gods fortified by proper morals and ancient rites (Mollier 1990).

Anti-Buddhist sentiments did not, as a rule, go quite as far as this; still, the traditional prejudice against the Central Asian outsiders, who not only were the cause of military devastation, killing, and plunder but also lacked Chinese-ness and Confucian propriety, fueled the arguments again and again. Buddhism, from the beginning hindered by prejudices against all things other than Chinese, thus had to fight an uphill battle against the xenophobia and insecurity caused by the political situation of the time (Zürcher 1959, 305).

The third area of Buddhist adaptation and confrontation was its relation to Taoism as the indigenous tradition of Chinese thought and organized religious practice. This area included, first of all, philosophical Taoism and its development in the Lao-Zhuang tradition with which interaction overall was fruitful and exchange of ideas and terminology remained open.[4]

At the same time, however, the relation with Taoism also meant that Buddhism was compared with organized Taoist cults, with communal religious organizations and formal ritual practice as undertaken by the Tianshi (Celestial Masters) and their successors, especially the Lingbao (Numinous Treasure) school of the fifth century. In this respect, Buddhists tended to distance themselves decisively, not only to protect their self-identity but also to avoid the stigma of rebellion attached to organized Taoism since the Taiping (Tao of Great Peace), also known as the Yellow Turbans, rose against the Later Han in 184.

In these areas of adaptation and conflict, people referred to as Buddhists and Taoists were the exponents of the two major religions. In the south, they were aristocratic members of the ruling class who had personal inclinations toward one or the other teaching or whose family belonged to an organized group as, for example, the famous calligrapher Wang Xizhi who was a member of the Celestial Masters. In the north, they were political and church leaders, again of the upper classes, who sought to gain power as advisers to the emperor and representatives of organized religion. Here, however, the contestants were not only of Chinese origin; although still located in the upper classes, the division was also between Chinese and non-Chinese. As a general rule and in all parts of China, the debates were an upper-class phenomenon that had much to do with the establishment and reorganization of power at the time.

---

[4] In fact, the interaction with Lao-Zhuang was the one area in which Buddhism most easily influenced Chinese thought and through which it most swiftly entered the Chinese intelligentsia and aristocracy. In the long run, this fruitful association led to Chan Buddhism, the unique form Buddhism developed in China. See Fukunaga 1969; Knaul 1986; Kohn 1992a, 117–38; Lai 1993, 281.

Kinds and Phases of Debates

The formal debates, to which the *Xiaodao lun* belongs, expressed the confrontation of Buddhism with both Taoism and Chinese ethnic superiority. There were four major phases and types.

First was the theory of the "conversion of the barbarians" (*huahu*). Originally intended as a plausible and entirely unpolemical explanation for the appearance of Buddhism in the west, that is, Central Asia and India (Zürcher 1959, 293), it claimed that Laozi founded this new religion, so different yet so curiously similar to ancient Taoist thought and certain immortality practices, after he left China under the Zhou.

Later, around 300 C.E., the theory became more aggressive and was first formulated in a scripture of its own, the *Huahu jing*. In the centuries that followed, the text continued to grow both in volume and polemical harshness as its narrative became ever more fanciful. Buddhists in due course resorted to an anti-*huahu* theory of their own, claiming that Laozi was originally Kāśyapa, a disciple of the Buddha, who had been sent to bring an adaptation of Buddhism to China with his *Daode jing* (Scripture of the Tao and the Virtue) (Zürcher 1959, 308). The debate on the mutual conversion of Buddhism and Taoism continued in varying stages of intensity and publicity until the Yuan dynasty when it was finally proscribed and its texts burned (Wang 1934; Zürcher 1959; Ch'en 1945; Thiel 1961).

Second were the debates in South China in the fifth and sixth centuries. These, too, were carried by antiforeign sentiment. The gist of the anti-Buddhist position was that although Buddhism and philosophical Taoism might have much in common about basic teaching and access to universal truth, Buddhism was not suited for the Chinese because of its barbarian nature. Various single instances were cited in support of this claim and were refuted more or less ingeniously by fervent Buddhists.

The debates in the south took place in formal treatises and letters written among the Chinese aristocracy. They represent the process of the adaptation of the saṅgha to the reality of Chinese society and show how the Chinese came to accept the foreign beliefs in their midst. Here the discussions about the monks bowing to the emperor and about the immortality of the spirit were recorded. Throughout these organizational and doctrinal confrontations, however much Buddhism wrestled with the Confucian establishment, it yet showed a strong tendency to establish itself as a solid supporter of the Confucian state and an acceptable version of the Chinese indigenous worldview. Even in the debates with the Taoists, the ultimate argument was always the acceptability of some belief or practice within the Confucian system of rites and propriety. Thus, the *Hongming ji* (Record to Spread and Clarify [Buddhist Doctrine]) by Sengyou (445–518), which documents all these confrontations, was written expressly to justify the Buddhist faith and present it as an integral and worthy part of Chinese culture (Schmidt-Glintzer 1976).

Third were the confrontations between Buddhists and Taoists in North China. Here the role and position of organized religion, both Buddhist and Taoist, was closely linked with the government of the state. The north at this time was ruled by the Toba, a Xianbi-Hun people. They had increased gradually during the fourth century to extend their domination over all of northern China and had become quite sinicized in the process as they adapted Chinese administrative structures and governmental systems. Nevertheless, their rule was frequently shaken from within, both by rival chieftains arising in rebellion and by messianic cults spreading discontent and apocalyptic revolts (Eberhard 1949). To hold their rule together, the Toba keenly felt the need for an integrative orthodoxy that, supported by a network of institutions throughout the country, would hold the populace together and serve as an effective means of administration and supervision. Buddhist and Taoist clerics eagerly presented their respective teachings as candidates for the needed role.

For the most part, the Buddhists were successful in this venture. The establishment of so-called saṅgha-households under the Northern Wei gave them solid control over the local population and made their organization indispensable to the central administration (Sargent 1957; Lai 1987). But Taoists, too, had successes of this kind. Several northern rulers agreed to receive registers and thus become initiated Taoists (Seidel 1983). In addition, the Taoists built their own state religion under Kou Qianzhi, new Celestial Master, who had received divine inspiration from the deified Laozi in 415 (Yang 1956; Mather 1979).

The debates in the north were formally staged court affairs, a forum in which the two competing factions could vie for the emperor's favor. They were, in fact, power struggles disguised as doctrinal disputes yet often became hard-core polemics. In all cases, the factions tried to present their own teaching as of utmost usefulness to the ruler in active government while discrediting their rival's ability to be of equal service.

The *Xiaodao lun*, commissioned by and presented to Emperor Wu of the Northern Zhou in 569, in this context served to demolish Taoism as the ideal teaching with which to rule the Chinese. The debates at the time were part of the emperor's active search for a worldview that would not only keep his subjects content but could be combined with ancient Confucian ritual to supply an orthodoxy for a reunited China.

A fourth kind of debate took place in the first century of the Tang dynasty. Continuing the debates under the Northern Zhou, this set of confrontations, too, was concerned with the establishment of an orthodoxy for the newly unified empire. The Tang ruling house, because their surname Li was identical with that of Laozi, tended to favor Taoism. Pushing their luck, the Taoists Fu Yi and Li Zhongqing petitioned for a complete abolition of Buddhism. Buddhists, notably the monk Shi Falin, countered with attacks on Taoist theory and practice, compiling and developing much that had been said in earlier debates.

The dialogue flourished. All Tang emperors of the seventh century, concerned with social harmony and an integrated orthodoxy, convened conferences and opened forums for discussion between the two teachings. The debates only ceased with the ascension of Empress Wu, who clearly favored Buddhism (Tonami 1988, 41). Nor were they taken up again in the eighth century, when Emperor Xuanzong created an imperial version of Taoist orthodoxy (Benn 1987). Thereafter, the rebellion of An Lushan threw the country into disorder, and the various religious and political factions had to fight for survival rather than supremacy (Li 1981, 107). After the Tang, the debates flared up only once more, again clamoring for political influence under a foreign dynasty, the Yuan. They ended with a Buddhist victory and a serious proscription and massive persecution of all things Taoist (Ch'en 1945; Thiel 1961; Reiter 1990b).

The Barbarians

What the Chinese called "barbarians" (*hu*) were, in fact, people of the Central Asian steppes who were of Hunnish or Turkish origin. In ancient Central Asia, there were two groups of people: a western group of Indo-European descent and an eastern group of Huns, Turks, or Mongols. For lack of more exact information, the former are commonly called Scythians, as based on Greek sources, whereas the latter may be grouped as Turko-Mongols.

The two groups were quite distinct, as pointed out by McGovern (1939, 7). The Scythians were Caucasian, tall and bearded, red-haired and green-eyed. They spoke an Indo-European language and appeared on the horizons of history as wily warriors harrying the settled cultures of ancient Mesopotamia. They became the Aryan invaders of India, at this time having control over horses but not yet riding them, and later founded the Persian empires and opposed the eastern expansion of Rome under the name of Parthians.

The Turko-Mongols, too, as archaeological finds and Chinese sources suggest, were a Caucasian people, tall and hairy, with curly brown hair and brown eyes. They spoke an agglutinating language of the Turko-Altaic family and appeared first as a group of tribes on the northern and eastern borders of the ancient Chinese homeland. They were, at this time, not yet nomadic but practiced limited agriculture, moving on whenever the soil was exhausted and fighting on foot. From the beginning, they seem to have mixed continuously with people of ethnic Chinese origin, gradually changing their racial characteristics (McGovern 1939, 8).

The Turko-Mongols apparently learned their fabulous horsemanship from the Scythians around 400 B.C.E. as the result of improved contacts throughout North Asia. Chinese sources clearly describe battles with them fighting on foot in the sixth century B.C.E. By 350, however, they were riding and shooting their bows over their shoulders in characteristic steppe fashion (McGovern 1939, 101). They had given up their semisettled life in favor of the fully nomadic and highly specialized steppe culture they became so famous for.

Around the time China was unified in 221 B.C.E., they organized themselves into a larger political unit. Called Xiongnu by the Chinese, this became the first Hunnish empire, whose fortunes closely coincided with those of the Han dynasty to its south (McGovern 1939, 115). Relations between the two powers varied over the centuries, with especially Emperor Wu (140–87 B.C.E.) making serious inroads into Central Asia.[5] Nevertheless, the Xiongnu maintained their independence, and the two courts exchanged mutual gifts, "tributes" to the Chinese, and entered into regular marriage relationships. Never during this time was the supremacy of the Chinese seriously questioned. The statement of the *Lunyu* (Analects of Confucius) remained unchallenged that "barbarian tribes with rulers are inferior even to Chinese states without them" (3.5).[6]

After the downfall of the Han dynasty, the Huns, too, suffered from inner turmoil. Their empire was divided, and several small kingdoms took its place. Although some of them were heavily sinicized by then, they were still, in age-old fashion, content to remain on the fringes of Chinese politics. This changed, however, with the increased dissipation of the Western Jin rulers toward the end of the third century. A Xiongnu kingdom northwest of Chang'an, lead by members of the former Xiongnu ruling family, decided that they could rule China better than the Chinese. Claiming descent from the Han emperors through the female line, they adopted the family name Liu and founded their own dynasty, the Liu-Han, in 304 C.E.[7] For the first time, a foreign ruler was making claims to the Chinese throne. Expanding rapidly, the Huns thus struck terror at the Jin court but fell themselves victim to dissipation and indecision after a few victories had been won.

Two major generals of the Liu-Han, Shi Le and Liu Yao, rose in rebellion and defeated the Xiongnu emperor in 318 (McGovern 1939, 331). Turning against each other, they each founded an independent dynasty, Western Zhao and Eastern Zhao. After ten years of fighting, Shi Le of the Western Zhao emerged victorious and in 330 styled himself the new emperor of northern China (McGovern 1939, 337). His rule and that of his nephew and successor Shi Hu did not prosper. They lacked resources, were too military

---

[5] For a detailed exposition of the rise and fall, division and reintegration of the first great Hunnish empire, see McGovern 1939, 130–308.

[6] Throughout this time, myths of the canine nature of the barbarians and their dog-ancestor continued to flourish in China, keeping the outlanders well away from Chinese civilization and even the human community (White 1991, 126–28). The inherent anxiety of the Chinese in the face of things new, strange, and alien was thus expressed in the concrete fear of subhuman people threatening the northern borders and the integrity of Chinese culture (Trauzettel 1992, 315).

[7] See McGovern 1939, 320. For additional discussion, see also Wright 1948, 322; Zürcher 1959, 83. The article by Wright is reprinted in Wright 1990, 34–72.

in orientation, and suffered from ongoing racial conflicts. Their rule is described as one of pure terror in the Chinese sources (Wright 1948, 324). Nonetheless, the Xiongnu rulers made decisive changes in the role Buddhism played on Chinese soil.

Both Shi Le and Shi Hu used Fotudeng as their adviser. The first politically influential Buddhist in Chinese history, he established his authority by making rain, foretelling the future, and healing—all activities the Huns were used to from their native shamans (Wright 1948, 338). Once in power, Fotudeng managed to stay on the winning side in whatever conflict arose at court, thus exerting a strong influence on the politics of the day. Because of his efforts, Buddhism was for the first time accepted as a favored and official religion in China (Lai 1993, 285). He involved Buddhist monks in all activities of the court, created a popular Buddhist religion among the people with the support of the state, and acquired government sponsorship for translations, temples, and Buddhist art (Wright 1948, 327). Doing so, he developed the kind of state-centered Buddhism typical for the north.

At this time, Buddhism first extended to the ethnic Chinese, and Buddhist art and culture developed rapidly. Under Shi Hu (r. 334–349), moreover, official permission was granted to all his subjects not only to make offerings at Buddhist temples but to become Buddhist monks. As a result, "Buddhist temples and monasteries began to spring up in all parts of the country, and the monasteries were filled with thousands of devout monks of native Chinese origin" (McGovern 1939, 340).[8] Without this Turko-Mongol interference, which continued actively and eventually led to the massive translations of Buddhist texts under Kumārajīva and to the artistic marvels of the cave temples, Buddhism would not have played the active political role that it later did.[9]

Shi Hu was also the first non-Chinese ruler with the stated ambition to control all of China as the son-of-heaven. He even turned against his own compatriots to achieve this aim. Wily and ambitious, well-versed in Chinese statecraft and literature, he was no longer the primitive barbarian described in Chinese polemics, even though large numbers of those continued to be settled on Chinese soil. Shi Hu was a serious foe in the battle for the empire. His fortunes failed, however, owing to the instability of his own court. The flexible inheritance patterns of the Huns who, although much adapted to Chinese customs, never settled for undisputed primogeniture caused his dynasty to fail shortly after his death.[10]

---

8 For more details, see also Wright 1948, 327; Yoshikawa 1984, 463; Lai 1993, 286.

9 For more on the historical development of this time, see Franke 1934; Zürcher 1959; Eberhard 1965; Dien 1991; Lai 1993.

10 An adopted Chinese member of Shi Hu's family eventually emerged as emperor. He decided to throw in his lot with the Chinese and started a wholesale persecution of Huns,

Around the middle of the fourth century, northern China was divided among several kingdoms besides Shi Hu's Western Zhao in the northwest. Further into the Ordos region was a small Chinese kingdom known as Liang; in the northeast was the Yan kingdom under the Murong, a Hun-Xianbi tribe; in the center, finally, were the Toba, another Xianbi group, who called their state Dai (McGovern 1939, 347). Like the Liu-Han, the Toba were highly sinicized and from early on adapted Chinese administrative structures and techniques. They profited from the increased Hun-Murong hostilities and, over several decades, expanded their rule over most of northern Central Asia, ascending to imperial powers in 386 and holding North China for almost two centuries.[11]

The Conversion of the Barbarians

The theory of the "conversion of the barbarians" developed in this political context. It began, as Wang Weicheng (1934) and Erik Zürcher (1959, 288–320) have admirably demonstrated, in the second century C.E. and took its starting point with Laozi's biography in Sima Qian's *Shiji* (Historical Records). Here Laozi is said to have emigrated from China because of a decline in the virtue of the Zhou. He reached the border pass where the guard Yin Xi asked him to leave a record of his philosophy. He did so, transmitting the *Daode jing* in five thousand words, then left. "Nobody knows what became of him," the text concludes.[12]

Later works—a memorial by Xiang Kai of 166 C.E.,[13] the *Liexian zhuan* (Immortals' Biographies), Pei Songzhi's commentary to the *Sanguo zhi* (Record of Three Kingdoms), the *Xiyu zhuan* (Chronicle of Western Regions), and the *Gaoshi zhuan* (Biographies of Eminent Men)—developed the basic narrative to have Laozi continue his westward journey, either with Yin Xi or alone, and convert the barbarians of Central and South Asia in the name of Buddha.[14]

These documents referred mildly to a historical identity of Buddhism and

---

killing them by the tens of thousands (Wright 1948, 324). It is interesting to note that by this time Huns and Chinese were physically so close that they could not always be told apart (McGovern 1939, 350). Zürcher notes that "the infiltrated foreigners constituted one half of the population of Shensi" (1959, 81 and 307).

[11] The Toba were eventually supplanted in northern Asia by another Central-Asian tribe, known as Tujue, or Turks. For details, see Saunders 1971, 18–23.

[12] *Shiji* 63. See Fung and Bodde 1952, 1:170; Lau 1982, x; Kohn 1991a, 62; Kohn 1992a, 41–42.

[13] For a translation and analysis of the memorial, see Pelliot 1906, 386–90; Crespigny 1976, 29; Petersen 1989.

[14] For a detailed discussion of all these texts and their references to the conversion legend, see Wang 1934 and Zürcher 1959. On the role of the conversion in the Laozi legend, see Kohn 1989a. For its application as a framework narrative in other Taoist scriptures, see Seidel 1984a; Kohn 1991a, 64–70.

Taoism, treating the barbarians with indulgence.[15] Although different and culturally inferior, the Central Asians were known and could be dealt with (Nakajima 1985, 254). The inhabitants of India, in particular, were seen as "kind and full of love towards men, they adore the Buddha and therefore do not attack others, they are weak and afraid of war" (Zürcher 1959, 304, based on Han sources). The new teaching was a curiosity but not threatening, just as the Huns beyond the borders were clearly distinct and politically and culturally inferior.

This situation changed around the year 300, when a full-fledged conversion scripture, the *Huahu jing*, was compiled by Wang Fou. This event is recorded in Huijiao's and in Pei Ziye's *Gaoseng zhuan* (Biographies of Eminent Monks), in the *Jinshi zalu* (Miscellaneous Records of the Age of Jin), and in the *Youming lu* (Record of Darkness and Light) (Zürcher 1959, 294). In this "Conversion Scripture," the originally innocuous theory for the first time was used against Buddhism as a means to belittle and denigrate the newly arrived teaching. By polemical means it established the cultural superiority of the ethnic Chinese. Zürcher relates this change to the "atmosphere of fear and suspense and the awareness of acute danger" in the light of massive immigration of foreigners and more military activity of the Huns (1959, 307). In addition to this sense of danger and the strong presence of non-Chinese in the country, the fact that at this time a Xiongnu ruler laid first claims ever to the Chinese imperial throne tilted the precarious Chinese-Central Asian balance. No longer a clearly defined and outside entity, the "barbarians" suddenly were part of Chinese interior politics, worthy foes in all respects who might, and eventually did, conquer large parts of the country and establish themselves as rulers.

Whereas the conversion theory before had been used only to explain the appearance of a new religion in Central Asia, now it fulfilled the function of bolstering Chinese ethnic superiority. The Huns and Indians were no longer curious and strange yet ultimately predictable and culturally inferior peoples. Suddenly they appeared as equals and were threatening Chinese imperial integrity with their own means and on their own level. Far from uncouth barbarians, the Huns at this time and the Toba shortly after were aspiring to be the equals of the Chinese in culture and social structure and their superiors in military craft.

Before, the "conversion of the barbarians" had been a logical continuation of the well-known Laozi legend and a plausible explanation not only for the appearance of Buddhism but also for its welcome in China where the theory justified its place among the higher teachings. Now, under the impact of a

---

[15] The tendency to identify the two teachings also appears in early Buddhist texts of the time such as the *Mouzi lihuo lun* (Mouzi's Correction of Errors; T. 2102; 52.1a–7a), which describes Buddhist attainment in terms taken from the *Daode jing* and the Buddha like the deified Laozi. See Yoshioka 1959, 32.

threatening new political force, it was turned into a vivid expression of xenophobia and the helpless aggression generated against an overwhelming foe. The strangeness of culture and customs that once allowed the Central Asians to overrun China but had increasingly been replaced by Chinese cultural traits was now unearthed and turned against them, marking them as despicable and lowly. Buddhism, the teaching associated with the west (India), at this point became a vehicle for the expression of something entirely political and ethnic. As in the later debates, religion here was used as a means to political aims.

The original *Huahu jing* is lost today. Erik Zürcher has identified certain passages cited in the *Bianzheng lun* (In Defense of What Is Right) and in the *Xiaodao lun* as part of the old text:

> When the barbarian king did not believe Laozi, Laozi made him submit with his divine power. Eventually, the king begged [for mercy] and regretted his transgressions. He agreed to shave his head and cut off his beard and profusely apologized for his errors and sins. The Venerable Lord showed great compassion and sympathized with his ignorance and delusion. For the king he then revealed admonitions and teachings, giving him precepts and restraints fitting for all circumstances.
>
> He ordered all [barbarians] to become recluses and beg for their food thereby to control their murderous and greedy minds. He made them wear brown robes that were open at the shoulder thereby to suppress their fierce and aggressive inner natures. He had them cut and mutilate their bodies and faces thereby to show their personal status as branded and amputated [criminals]. He also strictly prohibited marriage and sexual intercourse among them thereby to exterminate their rebellious and contrary seed. (*BZL* 6; T. 2110, 52.535a; see also Zürcher 1959, 298–99)

Here, Buddhism is no longer a curious new philosophy and alternative way to long life as it had been received during the Later Han, but a radical means to stamp out the harsh nature, criminal activities, and even continued existence of the uncouth barbarians.[16] Their character has changed accordingly from harmless and slightly effeminate to primitive and criminal. The outsiders, threatening peace and cultural superiority, are turned into dog-men, only half-human and utterly despicable, linking polemic debates with ancient mythology.[17] The teaching they follow, still basically good because it

---

[16] The notion that a deity appears as the founder of a rival religion with the expressed purpose of destroying its followers is also found in the *Puranas* of Hindu mythology. Here Viṣṇu becomes the "magic deluder" and descends as the Buddha to destroy the demons under Hrāda, producing total confusion and corrupting them with many sorts of heresy (O'Flaherty 1975, 234). I am indebted to Whalen Lai for this reference.

[17] Many peoples have myths depicting their less-cultured neighbors as half-animals, particularly dogs. The complex of dog-men myths seems to have originated in Central Asia and, linked with the belief in a state of Amazons, spread both to ancient Greece and China. For details, see White 1991.

originated with Laozi, is nothing but an expression of criminal law, a way to restrain primitive fierceness and exterminate the "rebellious seed."

The second passage Zürcher places in the context of the first *Huahu jing* goes one step further and lays the responsibility for all Chinese misfortunes at the door of Buddhism.

> Buddhism first arose in the barbarian countries. Because the western region belongs to the energy of metal, people there are harsh and lack proper rites. Later the Chinese imitated their observances and established Buddhism. Everywhere people offered it special veneration, turning their backs on their original tradition and pursuing the newly arrived. Their words were empty and careless and lacked harmony with the wondrous teaching [of the Tao]. They adorned scriptures and carved images, deluding kings and ministers alike.
>
> Thus, all over the empire floods and droughts, rebellions and insurrections began to succeed each other. In less than ten years [after the transmission of Buddhism], disasters and strange phenomena came to be common occurrences. The five planets deviated from their course, mountains tumbled, and rivers ran dry. Ever since the royal rule has been at peace no longer. This is because Buddhism brought disorder. Emperors and kings no longer pay obeisance in their ancestral temples; the common people no longer sacrifice to their forefathers. Because of this the ancestral spirits and the earth god, the Tao and the primordial energy can no longer recover their proper way. (*Xiaodao lun* 21; see also Zürcher 1959, 305)

Linked with the cosmology of the five phases, Buddhism here is defined as part of the cosmic energy of the west, that is, metal, and is accordingly associated with decline, harshness, and killing. If a product of such localized special cosmic force enters the center, where it has no part, major upheavals are the result. These appear in natural catastrophes, such as floods, droughts, and locust plagues; in social unrest, as rebellion, regicide, and the fall of dynasties; and in disturbed relationships both among humanity and between humans and the gods. Buddhism, the representative of an alien energy, is thus held responsible for every disaster in the universe, the cause of all misfortunes that have befallen the Chinese oikumene.

The "Conversion" in Taoism

Once available, the theory of barbarian conversion took hold and became general knowledge among the literati, both in the south and the north. Within Taoism, it was closely linked to the hagiography of Laozi, the Highest Venerable Lord and personification of the Tao (see Kohn 1989a). By the early fifth century it was integrated into the Taoist doctrine of the reorganized Celestial Masters of the southern Liu-Song dynasty. (see Kobayashi 1992).

The *Santian neijie jing* (Scripture on the Esoteric Explanation of the Three Heavens) (*DZ* 1205, fasc. 876) of the year 420 mentions it three times. First it records how

> the Venerable Lord created three ways to teach the people of the world. First, the Middle Kingdom was of yang energy, pure and orderly; he gave it the Great Way of Non-Action to worship.
>
> Next, the eighty-one barbarian countries on the periphery were of yin energy, aggressive and awesome. He made them worship the Great Way of the Buddha and imposed strict regulations on them to control their yin energy.
>
> Third, the southern countries of Chu and Yue were of both yin and yang energies. He duly gave them the Great Way of Clear Harmony for their worship. (1.3a)

Then again, the *Santian neijie jing* records how Laozi converted the barbarian king and composed Buddhist scriptures for him so that he and his people would be civilized and learn the proper way (1.4a). Although the first passage uses the more cosmological discussion of the ancient *Huahu jing,* the later section integrates its mythological narrative.

Going beyond this, however, the *Santian neijie jing* also develops the myth of Laozi by having him order Yin Xi to become the Buddha.

> Then Laozi ordered Yin Xi to stride on a white elephant and change into a yellow sparrow. In this shape he flew into the mouth of Queen Qingmiao [Māyā]. To her, his shape appeared to be a shooting star coming down from heaven.
>
> In the following year, on the eighth day of the fourth month, he split open her right hip and was born. He dropped to the ground and took seven steps. Raising his right hand toward heaven, he exclaimed: "Above and under heaven, I alone am venerable! The Three Worlds are suffering. What can be pleasant in them?" He later realized that all birth is essentially suffering and became the Buddha. From that time onward, the Buddhist way flourished anew in these areas. (1.4ab)

This integrates, almost verbatim, the *jātaka* of the Buddha's birth as translated in the *Taizi ruiying benqi jing* (Sūtra of the Original Endeavor of the Prince in Accordance with All Good Omens) (T. 185; 3.471b–83a).[18] The same story, in a version in which Laozi himself entered the queen's womb and became the Buddha, is also dated to the fifth century and is found in the *Xuanmiao neipian* (Esoteric Record of Mystery and Wonder). Like the *Huahu jing,* this text only survives in citations but seems to have been a

---

[18] For a more extensive discussion and translation of the relevant passages, see Kohn 1989c. On the life of the Buddha and its Chinese adaptation, see Karetzky 1992. On the Taoist text, see Schipper 1978; Kobayashi 1990, 108–10.

record of Laozi's transformations and deeds, including his establishment of the Buddhist teaching (see app. 2).

One century later, the theory of Laozi becoming the Buddha was exploited in the court debates under the Toba-Wei by the northern Celestial Masters of Louguan, a Taoist center in the Zhongnan mountains (see n. 69). In the disputes of the year 520, Taoists used it to claim greater antiquity for their teaching and integrated it into the *Kaitian jing* (Scripture on Opening the Cosmos), now lost (Kusuyama 1976; Kusuyama 1979, 373). To replace this text, destroyed after a Buddhist victory, they then compiled the *Wenshi zhuan* (Biography of Master Wenshi), the esoteric biography of Yin Xi, the recipient of the *Daode jing,* called Wenshi xiansheng (Master at the Beginning of the Scripture) and Laozi's companion in the barbarian lands. This text, a detailed narrative development of the *Huahu jing,* dates from the mid-sixth century and is partly contained in the *Sandong zhunang* (Bag of Pearls from the Three Caverns; *DZ* 1139, fasc. 780–82), a Taoist encyclopedia of the seventh century (see app. 2). The same collection also holds a fragment of the *Huahu jing* then current. Both texts together represent the remainder of the second version of the text, detailing the narrative of Laozi's emigration, his meeting with Yin Xi, and the miracles he used to convert eighty-one barbarian kingdoms.[19]

Buddhist Reactions

Buddhists reacted to the theory in two ways, as Erik Zürcher has pointed out: by rational refutation and by applying their opponent's method (1959, 308). Both ways are apparent first in the *Zhengwu lun* (Rectification of Unjustified Criticism) of the fourth century (see Link 1961) and then in the debate on Gu Huan's *Yixia lun* (On Barbarians and Chinese) of the year 467 (see app. 1). Gu Huan claims that Buddhism is inferior because of its barbarian origins. His Buddhist opponents, for the most part, counter this assumption by pointing out the usefulness and positive aspects of the religion. Some of them, however, also use the Taoists' own method and mention the so-called counter*huahu* theory. This theory was first formulated in the *Qingjing faxing jing* (Sūtra on Practicing the Dharma in Purity and Clarity), one of the earliest Chinese Buddhist apocrypha.[20]

Mentioned in several early catalogs of Buddhist scriptures, the *Qingjing faxing jing* was thought lost until a full copy of the text was recently discovered in the Chōfukuji Temple (Nanatsudera) in Nagoya. It was among a set of five thousand scrolls of scriptures copied in the twelfth century upon or-

[19] The third version of the *Huahu jing* dates from the mid-Tang and has survived in Dunhuang manuscripts. For references and a description, see appendix 2. For an analysis and summary of the *Sandong zhunang,* see Reiter 1990a.

[20] On the phenomenon of Buddhist sūtras written in and by Chinese, see Buswell 1990.

ders of a high official who wished to improve the postmortem destiny of his daughter (Ochiai 1991; Ishibashi 1991).

The text now consists of two parts. The first deals exclusively with precepts for lay Buddhist practice: how to handle Buddhist images, how to store the scriptures, how to maintain the premises of Buddhist sanctuaries, and so on. The second part contains the counter*huahu* theory. Here, Laozi is described as a follower of the Buddha and a bodhisattva. Together with Confucius and his disciple Yan Hui, he is sent to China to awaken the people there. Laozi is the Elder Kāśyapa, Confucius is Rutong (Confucian Lad; Mānava), and Yan Hui is the bodhisattva Guangjing (Radiating Purity).[21] The three sages are messengers of the Buddha who teach the true faith to the Chinese. After accomplishing his mission as ordered by the Buddha, Laozi duly leaves China for the west. Rather than setting out for India to convert the people there, he is, in fact, returning home after having converted China.

The two theories were first clearly set against each other but later intermingled to create a state of utter confusion. The *Xiaodao lun*, in particular, shows the intricate and complex mixture of theories current in the sixth century. Using the confusion to fullest polemical advantage, Zhen Luan points out that, taking all the different versions of the conversion together, five Buddhas must have appeared simultaneously (sec. 5); Laozi, being both the Buddha and his disciple Kāśyapa, must have created his own body (sec. 18).

The Debates in the South

The debates in the south took place within the limited circle of the great ruling families. In many ways, they continued the Pure Talk conversations of the third century: they were philosophical rather than political, theoretical rather than practical. Their aim was to understand the doctrines and come to terms with the reality of aristocratic Buddhism in Chinese society. They were carried by "eminent monks" (Zürcher 1959, 97) and aristocratic administrators, genteel in tone and concerned primarily with theoretical issues.

Within this framework, the debates were characterized by two main features: they were based on the assumption that there was only one universal truth to which Confucianism, Buddhism, and Taoism had equal access at least in their original form (Lai 1979, 24), and they were intricately linked with the question of the position of the saṅgha in relation to the Chinese upper class and administration.[22]

The position of the saṅgha was a matter of dispute among the Buddhists

[21] See Ishibashi 1991, 80. For further references to this scheme in other Buddhist texts, see Zürcher 1959, 317. In other works of the same kind, even ancient Chinese sage kings and mythological figures are identified as bodhisattvas (Zürcher 1959, 318).

[22] For a summary of these debates from the point of view of Buddhism, see Ch'en 1964, 121–44; Magnin 1979, 143–50; Lai 1993, 278–84.

themselves. Huiyuan, with his pronounced refusal to bow to the emperor and his self-isolation on Mount Lu, presented the position of withdrawal. He saw the saṅgha as an otherworldly agent, an independent organization, entirely unbound by and, therefore, not responsible to anything above and beyond itself. Huilin, however, campaigned for an integrated saṅgha, a Buddhist organization that took an active role in the affairs of society and the state, a lay-style community that provided easy access to all believers and concerned itself with this world as much as with the next (Schmidt-Glintzer 1976, 6; Nakajima 1985, 241).

In terms of the monastic organization of Indian Buddhism, both had equally valid points. As Sukumar Dutt notes, "Isolation from society was never the cue of Buddhist monachism" (1962, 25), and most of the saṅgha's wealth and institutions were supplied by lay donors. The monks' main service was to be accessible to society, to spread the Buddha's teaching to whomever was willing to listen. The saṅgha leader was the spiritual counterpart to the "righteous ruler," the king who represented worldly authority with moral responsibility (Tambiah 1976, 41).[23] At the same time, as Dutt says, "India never had anything analogous to 'state religion': It is a concept totally foreign to the Indian mind" (1962, 27). The saṅgha was always a self-governing body, protected by the state against disruption but never actively interfered with.

Because, however, the Chinese state, at least ideally, did not recognize any religious authority other than itself and would formally accept no independent organizations on whatever terms (Overmyer 1990) nor wished for any semiforeign institution to interfere with its population, conflict was inevitable. Monks living in society and building temples disturbed the picture of an integrated and harmoniously controlled society. Monks living in seclusion and entirely beyond any means of supervision presented an active threat to imperial authority. To secure its survival under these conditions, the saṅgha eventually developed the image of a stout supporter of the Confucian state. It presented itself as an alternative form of state-controlled religion, a different and semi-independent version of the emperor's mediation between divinity and humankind.

Still, for some time in the south, it followed Huiyuan's leadership and stayed aloof, presenting itself as foreign and independent. This, coupled with the xenophobic sentiments and frustrations of people either driven out of their homeland by Central Asian armies or pushed into the political back-

---

[23] I thank Whalen Lai for this reference. He also points out that "the pattern of the debates in the North and South, which went with the two styles of Buddhism usually called 'state Buddhism' and 'gentry Buddhism' (Zürcher), may be based on two preexistent patterns in Buddhist kingship, . . . the Northern Path (Kaniṣka Kingship) and the Southern Path (Aśokan Kingship). So the North/South difference is not just a debate of politics versus culture, it is also a debate of two types of political culture already envisaged in Buddhism itself" (personal communication, December 1993). For more on notions of Buddhist kingship, see also Strong 1983.

ground by northern emigrés, provoked severe anti-Buddhist feelings. Buddhism destroyed the state, the opponents said, it usurped imperial authority, it was responsible for the shortened duration of dynasties, it encouraged people to leave their proper functions in society, it was bad for the family, it withdrew men and women from production, and was, in general, a hypocritical and immoral teaching.[24]

Sengyou, too, in his *Hongming ji*, an apologetic Buddhist compilation aimed at showing the integration of Buddhism into Chinese culture, lists the major Confucian objections to the teaching as the basis for dispute and eventual reconciliation.

1. Buddhist writings are vague and extensive.
2. Death is final; there can be no rebirth.
3. Buddhism is useless for governing the people.
4. None among the rulers of antiquity knew of the Buddha.
5. Buddhism is of barbarian origin, unfit for the Chinese.
6. Buddhism is untraditional and had no impact before the Jin.[25]

Consequently, the aim of the Buddhist argument at that time was to create a sinicized, Confucianized Buddhism acceptable as a firm authority within the state. It proposed to assimilate Buddhism to the Confucian vision of history, morality, and cosmic order and agreed to philosophical Taoist positions as much as they were in line with this goal. In all cases, however, the Buddhist position strongly rejected any association or even similarity with organized Taoist cults. Not only were they beyond the emperor's religious monopoly, they were also touched by the stigma of rebellion. The *Bianhuo lun* (To Discriminate Errors; see app. 1) shows the polemical length to which Buddhists were willing to go to secure their proper distance.

Although apparently concerned with doctrinal and practical issues between Buddhism and Taoism, the debates between the two teachings in the south thus were ultimately concerned with the social and political position of the saṅgha. Their primary aim was to accept or reject Buddhism in the Confucian orthodoxy, to secure or question the role of the saṅgha within the boundaries of the Chinese state.

The double aim of the saṅgha, to remain independent and yet prove itself part of the Confucian orthodoxy, led to the other main characteristic of this phase of the debates. Buddhism was obviously at odds with Confucian morality and family-centeredness and did not want to be aligned with organized Taoism. Therefore, to find an acceptable position within existing Chinese

---

[24] This summary of the position follows Xun Ji's memorial on Buddhism submitted to Emperor Wu of the Liang. See Ch'en 1952, 192.

[25] See the postscript to the *Hongming ji* (T. 52.95a–96a), translated and discussed in Schmidt-Glintzer 1976, 35–45; Yoshikawa 1984, 518–23; Nakajima 1985, 251–53. A complete and annotated Japanese translation is found in Kenkyūhan 1975.

philosophy it claimed that there was only one universal truth, equally accessible to all the teachings originally but expressed differently owing to circumstances of time and place. This position allowed Buddhists to claim special forms of filial piety and state support for themselves. Yet the argument also supported Taoism. Seeing Buddhism gain more popular support, Taoists also laid claim to the original identity of all and thus attempted to establish themselves on an equal footing.

The assumption of one single universal truth was quite in line with the traditional Chinese understanding of religion, including the state's monopoly on mediation between the divine and the human. It had made the first conversion theory plausible and allowed the Chinese emperor to worship the Buddha alongside Laozi (Seidel 1969). It had also led to first attempts to "harmonize the three teachings," a tendency that would come forcefully to the fore again in the Song dynasty. Sun Chuo (ca. 310–390), for example, combined Confucian social responsibility, the Lao-Zhuang ideal of contemplation, and Buddhist enlightenment in one organized system (Link and Lee 1966).

In the first southern debates on the *Menlü* (Instructions to My Followers) by Zhang Rong and the *Yixia lun* (On Barbarians and Chinese) by Gu Huan (see app. 1), the argument that "Buddhism and Taoism are fundamentally one" formed the basis of the discussion. Opponents still agreed with each other, Taoists and Buddhists, Chinese and Central Asians, were not yet completely separate, however much their actual behavior might have differed. The philosophical distinction between substance and function, origin and ends, was used to explain how an originally unified teaching could develop such different forms (Lai 1979, 24). The claim to underlying oneness represented a state of the debates in which reconciliation seemed still possible and peaceful coexistence of the teachings was the primary goal.

As the debates proceeded, however, the underlying identity was shaken, the "honeymoon of Neo-Taoism and Prajñāpāramitā Buddhism was breaking up" (Lai 1979, 38). First, Zhou Yong, in his letter to Zhang Rong, seriously questioned the search for any invisible roots and insisted on judging the teachings by their practices and outer appearances. Whereas Xie Zhenzhi, Zhu Zhaozhi, and Zhu Guangzhi, arguing against Gu Huan, still adhered to an overall unity of truth and human nature, Yuan Can in his answer to the *Yixia lun* emphasized differences rather than identity.[26]

The tendency was unmistakably toward confrontation. In the early sixth century, when the debate centered on the *Sanpo lun* (On the Threefold Destruction Caused By Buddhism), Taoists bluntly accused Buddhists of

---

[26] For a summary of these documents, see appendix 1. Most of them are translated and discussed in Schmidt-Glintzer 1976. Lai 1979 contains an analysis of the doctrinal issues involved in the debate between Zhou Yong and Zhang Rong together with an English translation of their letters.

subversive activities—destroying the state, the family, and the individual—
and no longer allowed for Buddhist access to universal truth (see app. 1).
Buddhists, hitting back equally sharply, justified their teaching with reference to Confucian moral codes and historical traditions while criticizing
Taoist exorcism and talismanic practice. In the mere fifty years documented
in the texts, a profound shift occurred away from philosophical theory to
practical application, away from possible oneness in the depth of the origins to massive confrontation in active religious practice.

The *Xiaodao lun* inherited this tendency toward confrontation. Among
the texts of the south, it followed especially the *Bianhuo lun* with its massive attack on Taoist practice and description of Taoist rites. To a lesser
extent, it also continued the standard arguments of Confucian orientation:
Buddhism supports the state, Taoism is rebellious; Buddhism is morally
pure, Taoists practice sexual orgies: Buddhism brings forth pure sages,
Taoist worthies rank second-best. The increasing sharpness in the southern
debates reflects a consolidation of saṅgha power in this period and the
support of Buddhism under the Liang dynasty, during which Taoism was
suppressed, even though Emperor Wu supported Tao Hongjing.[27] The
Xiaodao lun similarly in its harshness shows the degree to which the Zhou
emperor already favored Taoism. It reflects the outcry of the Buddhist
establishment against a newly developing orthodoxy with Taoist doctrine
at its center.

Buddhism and Taoism in the North

The situation of organized religion under the foreign dynasty of the Toba-
Wei in the north was significantly different from that in the south and so was
the nature of the debates. In the south, the discussions helped the ruling
aristocracy come to terms with a foreign religion in its midst. They took place
among the gentry and were in many respects a continuation of the aristocratic
Pure Talk tradition. In the north, on the contrary, all debates were court
affairs. There all things religious were first and foremost matters of state as
determined by the state-Buddhism created first under Fotudeng and the
Xiongnu dynasty of the Western Zhao (Tsukamoto 1974, 2:536; Magnin
1979, 5) and defined in Liangzhou through the work of Dharmakṣema (Hurvitz 1956, 57).

The society in the north at this time consisted of three distinct groups: the
conquerors; the Chinese upper class, that is, landowners and officials; and the
lower classes, that is, merchants and peasantry.

The conquerors, the Xianbi Toba, like their Xiongnu neighbors originally

---

[27] See Strickmann 1978c on the suppression of Taoism. Strickmann 1979 contains a discussion of Tao Hongjing's activity under imperial sponsorship.

had a shamanistic form of religion, which made them susceptible to the magic and exorcism wrought by practitioners of various denominations. At the same time, they were strongly inclined toward Buddhism, which had become the dominant religion of Central Asia. Monks to a large extent had replaced the shamans of old: they traveled into the heavens, prayed for rain, divined the future, and so on (Eberhard 1949, 228; Lai 1993, 285). The same affinity with shamanistic practices was also responsible for the Toba's fascination with Taoism. There was a court office called Scholar of Immortality and a laboratory for the concoction of elixirs given to prisoners for experimental purposes (Mather 1979, 106; Ware 1933, 224).

As they adapted more to Chinese statecraft, however, the foreign rulers were concerned increasingly with questions of state doctrine and orthodoxy. Throughout their rule, they felt a need for an integrative teaching, not only to keep Chinese officialdom under control but also to maintain stability within the various tribes and clans that made up their own population. The Toba rule of North China was continuously rattled by minor insurrections and rebellions of chiefs and local kings, very often of Xiongnu origin, against the central rule (Chen 1954, 268; Eberhard 1949, 240). Thus, the rulers had a sustained interest in finding working models to stabilize the state and give the country a solid theoretical and administrative framework.

The second major group in northern society was the Chinese aristocracy. Under the Toba, they were divided into cliques and factions that had more to do with economic and political power than with worldviews but can still be identified according to the major traditions of ancient China: Confucians, Taoists, and Buddhists, plus the leaders of the Taoist and Buddhist church organizations. The Taoism and Buddhism of individual aristocrats represented their general philosophical outlooks and was an addition to their classical erudition. Both teachings supplemented the standard Confucian worldview. They were philosophical ways of looking at the world, including fine arts, mathematics, medicine, astronomy, and the like (see Eberhard 1949, 236–37).

The Taoism and Buddhism of the church leaders, however, was a form of obtaining political influence and secure administrative power for themselves as individuals and also for their organizations at large (Ren 1990, 227). Following the model established under Fotudeng, church leaders and church organizations under the Toba were imperially sponsored. The Buddhist saṅgha, for example, was led by a head monk, or "comptroller of śramaṇas" (Hurvitz 1956, 85), who was appointed to a quasi-imperial office by the emperor, an unheard-of infringement on saṅgha status in Indian Buddhist terms. The practice of the religion, the status of the monasteries, the position of both lay and monastic communities depended entirely on the court influence of the religious leaders. Famous monks, such as Daoan, Kumārajīva, and Dharmakṣema, all worked closely with the government (Ch'en 1954, 267–70). Tanyao, head monk in the mid-fifth century, set up government-sponsored sangha-households and Buddha-households for the population.[28] In the same vein, the prime minister Cui Hao eagerly accepted Kou Qianzhi's Taoist state-religion and sponsored its installation throughout the country (Yang 1956; Mather 1979), while the Louguan monastery in the Zhongnan mountains became an active center of politically supportive Taoism (Qing 1988, 430–44; Ren 1990, 219–36; Zhang 1991).

The northern debates represent the competition among the different groups within the Chinese aristocracy. Their central issue was to find favor with the foreign rulers, to offer the best service in building the most efficient administration and the most harmonious society. Unlike in the south, the debates were not so much evidence of cultural adaptation but attempts to present working models of statecraft, orthodoxies, and administrative structures for the sake of a better empire.

The lower classes, finally, stood in opposition to both the conquerors and the Chinese upper classes. They were followers and believers of the widely popular messianism of both Buddhist and Taoist coloring led by what Eberhard calls the "free monks" (1949, 231), that is, unregistered and often wandering monks who eluded the control of the administration. As long as the salvational religions made the peasants hope for a better life in the future and kept them content with their lot, the state and the official churches supported them heartily. As soon as their messianism cried out for changes in the here and now, however, for more food and less taxes in this life, they came into open conflict not only with the government but also with the state churches.

Numerous rebellions under Toba rule were sparked by messianic and salvational ideas—often of Buddhist rather than Taoist origin.[29] At such times, the church leaders were hard pressed to keep their hands clean of any association with the rebels—something they not always succeeded in doing. The famous first persecution of Buddhism in 446, for example, was possibly sparked by the discovery of a huge cache of weapons in an imperially sponsored monastery in Chang'an. Assuming these weapons to be in support of a Xiongnu rebellion that had started in the previous year, the emperor reacted

[28] Sangha-households were families who paid taxes in the form of grain to the sangha but were exempt from all other state duties. The sangha stored the grain for redistribution during famine or sold it to satisfy their own needs. Buddha-households consisted of freed criminals or slaves who did manual work in the monasteries. See Ch'en 1964, 153–58; Hurvitz 1956, 73; Sargent 1957; Lai 1986, 1987.

[29] The first messianic revolt under unregistered Buddhist monks occurred in 473 (Eberhard 1949, 248). Ch'en lists altogether ten Buddhist-inspired uprisings in the fifth and sixth centuries (1954, 271). Eberhard describes all rebellions in detail (1949, 240–65). See also Tsukamoto 1942, 247–85.

with a general persecution of the religion (Eberhard 1949, 229–30; Hurvitz 1956, 65). Not the result of Buddhist-Taoist rivalry, this persecution was the outcome of the association of state Buddhism with popular movements.

Many arguments in the northern debates can thus be understood as a continued effort by the official religions to distance themselves from the popular—messianic and, therefore, often rebellious—movements in their names while claiming primary state-supporting status and reaping the benefits of imperial power.

The Court Debates

Only one major court debate is known before the controversy under the Northern Zhou of which the *Xiaodao lun* forms a part. In 520 C.E., the Taoist Jiang Bin and the Buddhist Tanmuzui argued the seniority of their teachings in the presence of the emperor. They concentrated on the problem of dating. If Laozi went west to convert the barbarians and become the Buddha, he must have left China earlier than the recorded birth of the Buddha in India. To begin with, the Taoists claimed that Laozi was born in 605 B.C.E. and converted the barbarians in 519. Buddhism was thus Laozi's second-hand teaching, developed to control the barbarians. Its presence in China could do nothing but harm.

The Buddhists countered this allegation by dating the birth of the Buddha back to 1029 B.C.E. This particular date was allegedly reached with the help of the *Mu tianzi zhuan* (Biography of King Mu of Zhou) which recorded certain celestial phenomena observed in the west indicative of the birth of a great sage. The Buddha consequently entered nirvāṇa in 949 B.C.E.[30] This dating was again bettered by the Taoists in the *Kaitian jing,* which is not identical with a text of this title still extant in the Taoist canon today. Showing that this scripture was a forgery and not a revealed text, the Buddhists emerged victorious in this phase of the debate and thereby gained influence at court (see app. 1).

This debate is not well documented in the literature, and its background is not clear. Tang Yongtong links it with an internal power struggle among senior ministers and comments that, although the Taoists were penalized for presenting a faked scripture as evidence, the Buddhists used much the same means (1938, 537). Wang Weicheng sees it as just one of the things emperors did at the time (1934, 44), just as Tsukamoto, in a slightly different context, notes that the debates often were a fashionable parlor game in which the aristocracy matched their wits (1974, 556). The debate of 520 may have had something to do with the impending division and destruction of the Toba

---

[30] For a discussion of the various dates of the Buddha's *parinirvāṇa* in early Chinese Buddhism with particular reference to the doctrine of declining, or semblance, dharma, see Lai 1986, 67–71. I am indebted to Whalen Lai for sending me an offprint of his work.

state. It may also have been related to struggles about the position of a lay-oriented saṅgha in the capital of Luoyang.[31]

The court debates of 568–70 under Wudi of the Northern Zhou, however, are much better known and more extensively documented. There is, in fact, a rather detailed description by Buddhist historians.[32]

TRANSLATION

How the Zhou Assembled Monastic and Lay Disputers
to Destroy the Buddhist Teaching

[52.135c] Gaozu, Emperor Wu of Zhou [Yuwen Yong], was of a cunning and suspicious mind, easily given to an ill temper in the face of obstruction. His cousin Yuwen Hu, prime minister and Duke of Jin,[33] competently managed the various affairs and handled the government with decision. The emperor secretly envied him and feared that he might usurp the throne. [52.136a] Eventually, he summoned him to the palace, killed him with his own hands,[34] and had all six leading ministers [loyal to Yuwen Hu] put to death together with their families. Doing so, the emperor imposed his sole will on the empire and had nothing left to worry about.[35]

Now, however, he began to believe in popular prophecies, and soon his mind was influenced by them. An ancient prediction had said that "black will win," meaning that someone of a black appearance would attain the empire. This was just like the false prophecy circulated at the end of the Han dynasty that "someone in yellow garb would become ruler," representing in symbolic terms the transition of power from the red to the yellow.[36]

[31] On the Buddhism of this time and place, see Ch'en 1964, 158–63; Jenner 1981; Wang 1984; Kamata 1984, 434–40; Lai 1990. The debates of 520 can be also relevant in the dating of apocryphal Buddhist texts as documented in Whalen Lai's dating of the *Xiangfa jueyi jing* (Sūtra to Allay Doubts during the Age of Semblance Dharma; T. 2870; 85.1335c–38c). According to him, the text must have been compiled before 530 because it remains entirely silent about Tanmuzui's "defense of faith" and does not mention the fall of Luoyang in the same year. See Lai 1986, 71.

[32] The following translation is based on *Guang hongming ji* 7 (Expanded Record to Spread and Clarify [Buddhist Doctrine]; T. 2103; 52.135c–36b). It was prepared with the help of the Japanese translation and annotation in Kenkyūhan 1988, 484–93.

[33] For Yuwen Hu's biography, see *Zhoushu* (History of the Northern Zhou Dynasty) 11. For details on him and his rule, see Franke 1936, 244.

[34] When Wudi ascended the throne in 560, the government was firmly in the hands of his cousin Yuwen Hu, an able but rather brutal character, whom he eliminated in 572. Asking him to the empress dowager's quarters in the palace on the eighteenth day of the third month, Wudi hit him with a jade tablet so that he fell down unconscious. The emperor then ordered an eunuch to kill him. The eunuch, however, was too frightened, so Yuwen Hu was eventually killed by a palace guard. See *Zhoushu* 11; Franke 1936, 243–44.

[35] The events are also recorded in *Zhoushu* 5 (Record of Wudi) and *Guang hongming ji* 6 (T. 2103; 52.125b–c). See Kenkyūhan 1988, 487 n.8.

[36] On popular prophecies and apocryphal interpretations of the classics and their political impact, see Dull 1966. On their role in Taoism, see Seidel 1983. The idea of colors indicating

The prophecies about the color black current under the Zhou were just like this. Because of them, Taizu [Yuwen Tai, who established the dynasty] had all garments and banners changed to black when he moved west to Chang'an to protect the royal house of the Toba-Wei. In his reliance on silly popular ditties, he can be described as following the model of Emperor Guangwu of the Later Han.[37]

Formerly, when Gao Yang [Emperor Wenxuan] established the Northern Qi dynasty, there were similar ditties current among the people. Yang then interpreted "black" to refer to the [Buddhist] Master Chou who would become emperor dressed in black. Therefore, he resolved to kill him. But Master Chou possessed powers of foresight, sensed the emperor's intention, and took flight. More details of these events can be found elsewhere.[38]

Emperor Wu of the Zhou originally venerated the Buddhist teaching and treated the religious community with humble formality. Still, even at that time, he only allowed the monks to wear yellow garments, strictly prohibiting the use of black.[39] Then, however, the Taoist Zhang Bin ap-

---

the change of mandate between dynasties is related to the theory of the five phases and their cycle of mutual overcoming. The cycle was fixed in the early Han. The Han themselves, succeeding the Qin who ruled under the sign of water and the color black, first saw themselves as ruling under yellow then changed it to red (see Bauer 1956). The Yellow Turbans at the end of the Later Han, then, believed they were destined to take over from the red and establish the rule of the yellow (see Eichhorn 1954, 1957).

[37] Yuwen Tai was the protector of the Northern Wei rulers. Since the division of the Wei rule, he was the de facto dictator of the Western Wei. As such, he began to see himself as the destined unifier of China. To realize his dream, he reorganized the administration in 541, conquered parts of Sichuan from the Liang in 553, and set up a new provincial order in 554. After his death in 556, his son Jue, then fourteen years old, inherited the position and became the first emperor of the Northern Zhou in 557. His cousin Yuwen Hu, then forty-one years old, was his guardian. Hu held the power through various succeeding rulers until his death in 572 (Franke 1936, 228–36). A detailed study of Yuwen Tai's rule and reforms is currently being prepared by Scott Pearce in an article entitled "Form And Matter: Archaizing Reform in Sixth Century China." I am indebted to the author for sending me a copy of this important work.

The change in official colors was installed by Wudi when he ascended the throne in 560. Even Yuwen Tai, later venerated as the founding emperor and known as Wendi or Taizu, however, was said to have been born with a black emanation, and one of his names contained the character "black" (*Zhoushu* 1). Omens and popular ditties were important in all dynasties, but especially flourished under Guangwu, the first emperor of the Later Han, in response to Wang Mang's ample use of them (Dull 1966, 183).

[38] Gao Yang was the first ruler of the northern Qi. He was the oldest son of Gao Huan, the Yuwen Tai of the Eastern Wei, who also began as protector and moved up to dictator. In 550, Gao Yang accepted the abdication of the Toba ruler and founded his own house. The history of the short-lived Qi dynasty is complex and rather unsavory, involving killings, intrigues, orgies, excesses, and even madness. For an overview, see Franke 1936, 236–42. For details, see Holmgren 1981, 1982, 1991.

[39] The emperor was first a pious and serious follower of Buddhism. He constructed temples, supported the ordination of monks, had sutras copied and images made. In 563, he even ordered the compilation of a Buddhist canon. See Magnin 1979, 159; Tsukamoto 1974, 2:532–35. See also Kenkyūhan 1988, 488 n. 20, citing *Lidai sanbao ji* (Record of the Three Jewels through the Ages.) 11 (T. 2034; 49.100a).

peared on the scene and with artful flattery deceived the emperor.[40] He and his lobby denounced the black-robed Buddhists as a danger to the state while praising the yellow-clad Taoists as good political omens. The emperor lent an ear to their words, began to believe in the Tao and no longer cared about the Buddha. He even received Taoist talismans and registers and dressed in their ceremonial robe and cap.[41]

Then there was the former monk Wei Yuansong, one of Zhang Bin's closest allies. They stuck together like lips and teeth. Treacherously, they aroused the emperor's feelings, maintaining that "most monks are lazy and greedy fellows, interested only in money and food, without even the slightest respect for their superiors."[42]

In response, the emperor summoned one hundred monks to the palace and made them practice the Buddhist way for seven days and nights.[43] The monks were very much aware that he had bidden them with a particular purpose in mind. Acting himself as a monk, the emperor personally slept and rose with them to see for himself the advantages and shortcomings of their practices. He chanted the sūtras with them and prayed with them for the forgiveness of sins. Because all the monks were afraid of him, none voiced any suspicions that the emperor had joined them in disguise. When the set period was over, the practice was brought to an end without incident.

On the fifteenth day of the third month of the fourth year of Heavenly Harmony [569], the emperor summoned meritorious monks, renowned Confucians, Taoist masters, and various civilian and military officials to the palace. All in all, more than two thousand people were present.[44]

Emperor Wu received them in the Great Hall to evaluate their presentation of the three teachings. In the end, he judged Confucianism to be

[40] For information on Zhang Bin, see Tsukamoto 1974, 2:573. He is mentioned in the biography of Jing'ai in *Xu gaoseng zhuan* (Further Biographies of Eminent Monks) 23 (T. 2060; 50.626b). Kenkyūhan 1988, 488 n. 23.

[41] Wudi was formally initiated as a Taoist in 567, probably by the ritual master Wei Jie, also known as a philosopher and mystical thinker. For details on the initiation, see Lagerwey 1981, 19. For more on Wei Jie, see Kohn 1991a, 167–88.

[42] Wei Yuansong was a native of Sichuan with a great predisposition toward the occult. He joined the Buddhist order as a young man, then moved to the capital where he was disgusted by the impious and commercial activities of the saṅgha. Impressed at the same time with the emperor's vision for a unified orthodox teaching and practice for all of China, he presented a memorial in 567, criticizing the actual state of Buddhism and proposing the establishment of a unified church that would encompass the Chinese empire.

In the literature, Wei Yuansong's memorial is linked not only with the debates of 568 and 570 but also with the persecution of organized religion in 574–77. His name was accordingly blackened, and he was described as a power-hungry charlatan who only wanted to sell his own magic and would easily walk over the corpses of harmless, honest monks and nuns to do so. See Kenkyūhan 1988, 489 n. 28 citing *Xu gaoseng zhuan* 25 (T. 2060; 50.657c). For a translation of the remaining version of this memorial, see Appendix 1. For discussions, see Yu 1931; Wright 1951; Tsukamoto 1974, 2:541–50; Ch'en 1964, 187–89; Magnin 1979, 160–62.

[43] This is also mentioned in the biography of Jing'ai in *Xu gaoseng zhuan* 23 (T. 2060; 50.626b). See Kenkyūhan 1988, 489 n. 33.

[44] See *Lidai sanbao ji* 11 (T. 2034; 49.101b), cited in Kenkyūhan 1988, 490 n. 44.

first and Buddhism last. But as the highest of all, Taoism was acknowledged because it alone went beyond even the nameless, transcending the ultimate of heaven and earth.[45] The dispute at this conference was rather confused, however, and participants tended to become agitated in defense of their personal preferences. Thus, in the end they parted without reaching any definite conclusions.[46]

On the twentieth of the same month, the emperor reconvened the earlier assembly for discussion. Right and wrong were once again broadly evaluated. But the results did not satisfy the emperor. He said, "Confucianism and Taoism have been venerated in this country for a long time, but Buddhism is relatively recent. It seems to me that it cannot be placed [along with the other two]. What do you think of this matter?"

At this time, all debate participants reiterated their various views, but none would advance the abolition of Buddhism. The emperor said, "The three teachings are indeed being followed in the world, but they cannot be practiced together."

On the first day of the fourth month, newly convening a similar assembly, the emperor asked participants to present exhaustively the rights and wrongs of their various teachings. Still, no conclusion was reached.

After this, the emperor ordered the metropolitan commandant Zhen Luan to prepare an analytical comparison of the two teachings, Buddhism and Taoism, settling once and for all which was superior and which was inferior, which was true and which was false.

In the fifth year of Heavenly Harmony [570], Zhen Luan submitted his work "Laughing at the Tao" in three scrolls to the throne. [52.136b] Its division was meant to ridicule the Taoist classification of the Three Caverns.

On the tenth of the fifth month, Emperor Wu assembled a large crowd of officials and had them critically examine Zhen's presented discussion. They thought that it harmed and wronged the Taoist teaching. Because the emperor had personally received [Taoist registers], he was thwarted in his original intention and had the text burnt then and there.

Around the same time, the Buddhist Daoan also submitted an essay, entitled *Erjiao lun* (The Two Teachings).[47] The "two teachings" were the

---

45 These two characteristics refer back to *Daode jing* 32 and 25. See also the first chapter of the *Huainanzi* (Writings of the Prince of Huainan), trans. in Morgan 1934; Larre, Robinet, and Rochat de la Vallée 1993. For a collection of analytical essays on this text, see Le Blanc and Mathieu 1992.

46 These events are also mentioned in the biography of Daoan in *Xu gaoseng zhuan* 23 (T. 2060; 50.628b) and in the *Fodao lunheng* (Balanced Discussion of the Buddhist Way) (T. 2104; 52.372a). See Kenkyūhan 1988, 491 n. 52.

47 Daoan was one of the senior leaders of the saṅgha at this time. His biography is contained in *Xu gaoseng zhuan* 23 (T. 2060; 50.628b). The text of the *Erjiao lun* is found in *Guang hongming ji* 8 (T. 2103; 52.136b–143c). For a summary, see appendix 1. For an annotation, see Hachiya 1982. On his role in the debates, see Tsukamoto 1974, 2:566–69.

inner and the outer. The methods of purifying the spirit as represented by the three vehicles of Buddhism were the inner teaching. The various techniques of nourishing the body as set forth in the writings of the nine traditions that developed after Confucius were the outer teaching.[48]

Taoism in this scheme was not ranked as a separate teaching but subsumed under the Confucian tradition. It was, in fact, what the *Yijing* [Book of Changes] calls the "most humble."[49] The emperor glanced through Daoan's work and asked his courtiers about it. When none of them had any objections to it, the matter was not pursued any further.

Five years passed. In the third year of Established Virtue [574], on the seventeenth day of the fifth month, the teachings of both Buddhism and Taoism were proscribed. Buddhist monks and Taoist practitioners had to return to the laity. The prosperity and wealth of the Three Jewels was distributed among the state officials. Buddhist and Taoist institutions—monasteries, temples, local sanctuaries, and pagodas—were given to the local aristocracy. And so on. Further details are found elsewhere.[50]

At that time, the Duke of Wei could not bear it any longer. He entered the palace district and set the Qianhua Gate on fire in rebellion against the emperor. Without success, he had to retreat to Hulao where he was taken captive and brought to the capital. Twelve members of his family along with a great many other participants in the plot were put to death.[51]

END OF TRANSLATION

The Emperor's Vision

The debates under the Northern Zhou, therefore, began with the memorial by Wei Yuansong, presented in 567, in which he criticized the commercial activities and loose morals of the saṅgha and proposed the establishment of an encompassing Buddhist church with the people as the flock, the saṅgha as administrators, and the emperor as *tathāgata*.[52] Because this meant the disso-

[48] The nine traditions are the Confucians, Taoists, Yin-yang Cosmologists, Legalists, Nominalists, Mohists, political theorists, miscellaneous thinkers, and agriculturists. See Kenkyūhan 1988, 492 n. 74, citing the bibliographical section of the *Hanshu* (History of the Han Dynasty) (100B).

[49] This refers to the hexagram *qian*, "modesty" (no. 15). See Wilhelm 1950, 75.

[50] See Kenkyūhan 1988, 493 n. 79, citing *Zhoushu* 5; *Guang hongming ji* 10 (T. 2103; 52.153c); *Xu gaoseng zhuan* 23 (T. 2060; 50.626c). For discussions of the prosecution, see Franke 1936, 244–45; Tsukamoto 1948; Tsukamoto 1949; Tsukamoto 1984, 2:580; Ch'en 1964, 190–94; Magnin 1979, 162; Lagerwey 1981, 19–20.

[51] The duke of Wei, Yuwen Zhi, has a biography in *Zhoushu* 13 (Kenkyūhan 1988, 493 n. 80). Hulao is in modern Henan. This unsuccessful palace revolt, although it occurred soon after the persecution of Buddhism, had its root in more general discontent and was linked with the religion primarily in Buddhist documents.

[52] Whalen Lai points out that Wei's vision closely mirrors the ideas of the *Xiangfa jueyi jing*, a Chinese apocryphon of the early sixth century. He notes this in an unpublished manuscript, "The *Hsiang-fa chüeh-i ching* and the Economy of Salvation," which he kindly sent me.

lution of an independent Buddhist organization and the return of all clerics to the laity, Buddhist leaders argued heatedly against it. The emperor, however, was so pleased with its general drift that he honored Wei Yuansong with the title Duke of Shu. Although an actual answer to the memorial was not compiled until 579,[53] the arguments presented in the debates and, in particular, the *Xiaodao lun*, can be seen as a discussion and refutation of its ideas.

Emperor Wu was so very pleased with Wei Yuansong's concept because of the vision he had inherited from his father Taizu, Yuwen Tai. Taking over the rule from the Toba-Wei, Yuwen Tai had seen himself as the new unifier of China. To this end, he had conquered part of Sichuan from the Liang in the south, reorganized the imperial administration, and established a new provincial order. Moreover, he had begun to develop ideas for a new orthodoxy, a worldview that would support his unification. Yuwen Tai was very much taken with the ancient rules and organizational patterns found in the *Zhouli* (Rites of the Zhou), and both his choice of dynastic color (black, like the unifying Qin) and his dynastic name (Zhou, like the longest of all Chinese dynasties) indicate his strong preoccupation (Franke 1936, 228–35; Tsukamoto 1974, 2:532–35).

When Wudi, Yuwen Yong, took over the government in 560, he continued along the same lines. Although he moved between various religions and worldviews—he was a devout Buddhist in the beginning, became an initiated Taoist in 567, and always supported Confucian principles of government—his ultimate concern was the creation of an orthodoxy for unification. To this end, he wished to see a model that would integrate the various teachings and beliefs of China into one whole. He searched for an "equalization of the three teachings," a worldview that would, in combination with the ancient rites of the Zhou, give his state the stability necessary for the conquest and reorganization of all China.

Wei Yuansong presented Buddhism as the best vehicle for the emperor's dreams. The Taoist Jiang Bin, however, handed him Taoism for the same purpose. In this, he continued the tradition of Kou Qianzhi whose revelations of the Tao had given the early Toba-Wei an integrative teaching and practice, both religious and administrative, to support their rule. Just as Jiang Bin continued the tradition of Kou Qianzhi, so Wei Yuansong, in his own way, was a successor of the head monk Tange, who had first declared that Emperor Taizu of the Northern Wei was the Maitreya of the present age. He also followed the example of Tanyao and radicalized his idea of saṅgha households. Wudi, in his turn, not only adhered to the ideas developed by his father but also continued an age-old tradition of Chinese rulers, the search for a unified and integrative teaching that would not only allow them to remain at the pinnacle of society but to extend their influence powerfully throughout all of China.

---

[53] By Wang Mingguang, see *Guang hongming ji* 10 (T. 2103; 52.157a–60a).

The use of Taoism as a unifying teaching is also documented from later periods. The Tang emperor Xuanzong, especially, developed a "program to make Taoism, both as a philosophy and as a religion, a state doctrine, to propagate it as a dynastic, monarchical, and bureaucratic ideology" (Benn 1987, 128). To this end, he established state-sponsored Taoist temples throughout the empire, inaugurated a state-run Taoist examination, elevated Taoists to the status of imperial relations because his surname was that of Laozi, and spread a barely concealed personality cult in the name of Taoism to enhance his own image as the chosen ruler of the Tao.

Several centuries later, Huizong of the Northern Song attempted a similar project under the guidance of his adviser Lin Lingsu. Identifying himself with the Lord of the Tao, Sovereign of Life Everlasting, who originally resided in a heavenly sphere known as Shenxiao (Divine Empyrean), Huizong had temples of this new Taoist dispensation set up all over the empire. "In them were to be installed images of the Great Sovereign, Emperor of Life Everlasting, and his younger brother, now reigning in heaven, the Sovereign of Qinghua" (Strickmann 1978a, 346). In many cases, Buddhist facilities were taken over and Buddhism in general was persecuted or at least had to adapt Chinese, that is, Taoist, patterns for its institutions. Monasteries were renamed, icons were altered, ritual forms changed to suit indigenous models. The effort ended with the departure of Lin Lingsu in 1119 (Strickmann 1978a, 348).

Emperor Wu of the Northern Zhou had something very similar in mind. For him, the debates were an organized effort to find a unifying doctrine or general consensus that would satisfy his leading subjects. He wished to either pull the various factions into a generally acceptable mixture of teachings or to gain their submission to one superior doctrine. As Tsukamoto points out, for the officials, literati, and high clergy, the discussions remained highly speculative and theoretical. The emperor, however, not only had an eminently practical aim in mind but also looked to the teachings for their concrete setting and administrative usefulness. Where the gentry, in other words, discussed Taoism as the teaching of Laozi and Zhuangzi, Wudi saw the actual religion with its universalist claims as it was propagated and practiced by religious Taoists (Tsukamoto 1974, 2:569–73).

For Wudi, the chosen teaching, whether Buddhist or Taoist, had to be compatible with an overall Confucian framework and with the model set down in the *Zhouli*. This model, however, demanded not only smooth cooperation between church and state but also their complete identity. There was no room for any independent religious organization of whatever denomination. The Chinese state, from its beginnings in the Shang dynasty, had always seen religious activity as its monopoly, claiming its own unique right to represent the cosmic order (Overmyer 1990, 192). Wudi's later persecution of both Buddhism and Taoism in their monastic forms was a necessity not only because the ancient Confucian code did not allow for anyone to refuse the social duty of marriage and procreation but also because, to realize his unification under the orthodoxy chosen, he had to radically destroy all rival organizations and eradicate all possible infringements on the state's central monopoly.[54] At the same time, he promoted Taoism as the main teaching, set up the Tongdao guan (Monastery of Reaching to the Tao; see Yamazaki 1979) under the leadership of the Louguan Taoist Yan Da (Qiug 1988, 436; Ren 1990, 223; Zhang 1991, 81), and sponsored the compilation of the *Wushang biyao* (Esoteric Essentials of the Most High; *DZ* 1138, fasc. 768–79), the first Taoist encyclopedia and an integrated vision of the world according to the Tao (Lagerwey 1981, 8–13).

The *Xiaodao lun*

The *Xiaodao lun* in this context was not so much an answer to Wei Yuansong's memorial as a reaction to the emperor's growing conviction that Taoism might serve his purposes best. What Zhen Luan, in fact, says is: "It won't work. Taoism can't do this job. It's too confused, too disorganized, too immoral, too dishonest, and too much at odds with the Confucian tradition. It is a plagiate and poor imitation of Buddhism, it defies common sense and mathematical calculation, it does not lead anywhere. Taoism is not the orthodoxy you want." The text, in other words, is not an attack on Taoism as such nor a defense of Buddhism or Confucianism in their own right. Rather, it aims to demolish the emperor's vision of a unified orthodoxy built with Chinese indigenous means. To that end it attacks most viciously the Taoist claim to universality, to overall integration of all current teachings—the very trait that was most important to the emperor's vision. Small wonder that His Majesty had the treatise burned then and there and never hesitated to reduce the document that destroyed his vision to ashes.

No wonder, either, that he accepted the *Erjiao lun,* prepared four months after the demise of the *Xiaodao lun,* without much comment. Here, only two teachings were accepted: Confucianism with all its offshoots on the outside and Buddhism on the inside.[55] Taoism in its philosophical form was subsumed as one of the nine traditions of Confucianism. The text as a whole, although it did not preach the full integration of the three teachings, at least admitted that the combination of Confucianism and Taoism would serve the state—as long as Taoism was not tainted by the organized cults with their fancy talismans and vulgar longevity techniques. The *Erjiao lun,* although

[54] In addition, the members of the saṅgha-households by this time numbered several million, and the movement threatened to become a serious independent administrative force. The persecution weakened it considerably, and it disappeared completely during the Tang. See Lai 1987; Lai 1993, 323.

[55] The same classification according to an inner (Buddhist) and an outer (Taoist) teaching is also found in Jizang's *Sanlun xuanyi* (Mysterious Meaning of the Three Treatises) (T. 1852; 45.2a). See Lai 1979, 39–40.

more agreeable than the *Xiaodao lun,* still fell short of the emperor's vision, and he decided not to follow its advice.

But why did the emperor commission Zhen Luan to write the *Xiaodao lun* to begin with? Why did he choose Zhen Luan rather than anyone else? The official order to compare and evaluate the teachings came in the fourth month of 569, after a major debate. At this time Taoism came out highest, but the arguments were difficult and rather confused, which is not surprising with more than two thousand people in attendance. Various subsequent meetings could not satisfy the emperor nor determine the preferences of his leading subjects and the possibilities for an overall consensus. He then turned to Zhen Luan.

Zhen Luan, also known as Shuzun, was originally from Wuji district in modern Hebei.[56] At the time of the debates, he was metropolitan commandant, holding powers of investigation and impeachment over all officials in the area of the imperial capital. This was a very central post and included great supervising power over the capital area (Hucker 1985, 451). In addition, Zhen Luan was well known for his work in mathematics, astronomy, and calendar sciences, areas in which he had been active since at least 535. The *Siku tiyao* (Catalog of the Four Storehouses) mentions him as the author of various mathematical works: *Jiuzhang suanshu* (Calculation in Nine Sections) (107.2198), *Shushu jiyi* (Record of Mathematical Arts) (107.2200), and *Wujing suanshu* (Calculation Arts of the Five Classics) (107.2203).

The emperor may have respected Zhen Luan for his work on the calculation of the Northern Zhou calendar, which was in active operation from 566 to 578, as well as for his services as overseer of officials in the metropolis. Maybe he saw in him a man of common sense, one who not only dealt with cosmic phenomena and could calculate and measure correctly but one who also, because of his official role, was familiar with the problems involved in holding the empire together and controlling its subjects and officials. On the one hand, it may have been, as Tsukamoto suggests, that the emperor wished Zhen Luan to judge the antiquity and, therefore, indigenous value of the teachings on the basis of his astronomic calculations, thereby continuing the earlier debate on dating (1974, 2:557). On the other hand, the emperor may have selected him among all his ministers because he thought him a potential ally, one who well understood the need for an overall Chinese orthodoxy.

Zhen Luan was not a devout Buddhist, yet he preferred its teachings to those of Taoism. He was a stout Confucian and servant of the state while a member of the mathematical tradition of cosmic and divinatory calcula-

---

[56] See *Xiaodao lun,* preface. Wuji is also the place of origin of one of his known descendants, Zhen Dan, for whom Zhang Yuezhi of the Tang wrote a memorial inscription, which is contained in *Zhang Yuezhi wenji* (Collected Works of Zhang Yuezhi) 18.

tions, which was also adapted into Taoism.[57] In addition, he knew enough of the religious Taoism of his time to cite its scriptures at some length and had personal experiences with Taoist training as described in section 35 of the text. When he was about twenty years old, he says, he participated in a ritual of "harmonizing the energies," which he found so shameless and immoral that he could only turn away in disgust.

Not an outspoken champion of Buddhism nor an easy man to please in terms of a valid worldview, he was maybe the closest medieval China came to a neutral, dispassionate scientist. The emperor's choice reflects his respect for mathematical and cosmic calculations and his preoccupation with the ancients; in the *Zhouli,* divination, astronomy, and the calendar are the heart and soul of an integrated, harmonious, and well-functioning universe. His choice, though, turned out to be a disappointment. Zhen Luan, with the sharpness of a trained observer and with the ruthlessness of practical common sense, heartlessly and fearlessly proceeded to demolish the emperor's cherished vision. He uncovered the flaws and inconsistencies in his chosen teaching and pointed out the insuperable difficulties of establishing Taoism as the valid orthodoxy for a unified China.

The Tang Debates

A fourth kind of debate took place in the first century of the Tang dynasty. Continuing the debates under the Northern Zhou, this set of confrontations, too, was concerned with the establishment of an orthodoxy, now for the newly unified empire. Unlike the Sui who saw Buddhism as the best teaching to bind the empire together, the Tang strove for a compromise. In accordance with the overall tendency of the gentry, they instituted an official examination system based largely on the Confucian classics but left the Buddhist beliefs and affiliations of their subjects untouched (Wright 1951, 36).

Beyond that they felt a particular affinity for Taoism because of the identity of their surname Li with that of Laozi, allowing and supporting its practice (Hendrischke 1993, 113). This compromise, however, remained shaky for several decades during which the religious factions at court contended with each other for the emperor's favor. Each wished a larger share of the empire's good fortune and prosperity, and so they engaged in mutual attempts to oust each other. On the whole, no faction really won and none suffered lasting harm despite the edict of 637 that secured the formal precedence of Taoists over Buddhists (Li 1981, 102).

The first major debate took place under Gaozu in the 620's when the Taoists Fu Yi and Li Zhongqing in a series of memorials petitioned for a complete abolition of Buddhism. Little is known about Li Zhongqing whose

[57] Zhen Luan appears as an *Yijing* (Book of Changes) cosmologist in Taoist works of the Song dynasty (Knaul 1981, 48). See also A. Volkov in *Extrême-Orient, Extreme-Occident* 16 (1994): 72.

"Ten Differences and Nine Errors" are cited in Shi Falin's *Bianzheng lun* (In Defense of What Is Right; T. 2110). Fu Yi, however, in both position and background was not unlike Zhen Luan.

Born in 555 into an influential south Shensi family, Fu Yi had joined Emperor Wu's academy, the Tongdao guan, as a young man. Here he not only became a Taoist by conviction but also acquired the skills that earned him a high office later on: astronomy, mathematics, calendar sciences. In 593, he requested permission from the Sui emperor to practice as a Taoist scholar, and, in 597, was appointed chief diviner to a provincial governor, who also happened to be a royal prince of the Sui. Dissuading his employer from insurrection against his imperial brother, Fu Yi fled when the prince rose in rebellion despite his advice. In 618, he came to the Tang court, where he was appointed Grand Astrologer. In this position, he developed a different way to measure time with the water clock, a new system that was generally adopted in 620.[58]

In 621, he first presented his memorial on reducing Buddhist institutions and recluses to enhance the state and benefit the people (*Jiansheng sita sengni yiguo limin shi*; see app. 1). In eleven points, he emphasized the uselessness of Buddhist institutions, the parasitic nature of the clergy, the otherworldliness of Buddhist doctrine, and its overall harm for the Confucian state. He argued from economic, political, and nationalistic points of view and suggested that all monks and nuns be returned to the laity and the Buddhist teaching be sent back whence it came.[59]

The memorial, repeated in essence six more times, triggered an outcry among the Buddhist clergy. The monk Shi Falin, especially, wrote a lengthy rebuttal, the *Poxie lun* (To Destroy Heresy; T. 2109), which he followed up with the *Bianzheng lun*. The monk Shi Minggai also presented a "Strong Rebuttal," contained in *Guang hongming ji* (Expanded Record to Spread and Clarify [Buddhist Doctrine]) 12 (T. 2103; 52.168b–75c), and Li Shizheng answered with his *Neide lun* (On Inner Virtue; T. 2103; 52.187b–95a). There was no immediate imperial reaction to the memorials. Only in 626, shortly before his son's coup d'état, Gaozu issued an edict that ordered the purge of both Buddhism and Taoism, not unlike the measures taken by his predecessor of the Northern Zhou. Taizong, after rising to power, rescinded the edict.[60]

---

[58] On Fu Yi, see especially Wright 1951. This article is reprinted in Wright 1990, 112–23. See also De Groot 1903, 36–43; Michihata 1957, 329–34; Lagerwey 1981, 11–13; Li 1981, 100; Weinstein 1987, 7–8; Twitchett 1989, 180; Tonami 1992. Fu Yi's biography is found in *Jiu Tangshu* (Old History of the Tang Dynasty) 79, *Tangshu* (History of the Tang Dynasty) 107. See also *Guang hongming ji* 7 (T. 2103; 52.134a).

[59] The text of the memorial is contained in *Guang hongming ji* 7 (T. 2103; 52.134–35b) and in Fu Yi's biography in *Jiu Tangshu* 79. It is translated by De Groot (1903, 39–41) and summarized according to arguments by Wright (1951, 40–45).

[60] The text of the edict is found in *Zhenzheng lun* (To Examine What Is Right) 3 (T. 2112; 52.568ab). Although most documents date Fu Yi's memorial to 621, the *Poxie lun* to 622, and the *Bianzheng lun* to 626, the *Fozu lidai tongzai* (Comprehensive Account of Buddhist Patri-

The debates under Gaozu were the most extensive and best documented, but lesser skirmishes between the religions occurred under succeeding rulers. Taizong, in the four main phases of his life—youth, consolidation of power, glorious success, and gradual decay (Wright 1973)—had a varied and rather contradictory relation to Buddhism. He founded a monastery as part of the Buddhist observances after the death of his mother, he greatly honored the monk Xuanzang when he returned from the west in 645, but he also issued the famous edict of 637 that gave Taoist priests formal precedence over Buddhist monks. This may have had to do with his preoccupation with genealogy and the belief that his family was related to Laozi. It may also have been part of a larger attempt to limit the growing economic and social power of the clergy.[61]

Not willing to accept the edict, the Buddhists, especially the monks Falin and Zhishi, memorialized their protests. When Taizong impatiently repeated his orders and they still refused to obey, he had Zhishi flogged in his audience hall, defrocked, and sent into exile.[62] Around the same time, the Taoists accused Falin of treason. His *Poxie lun,* they claimed, contained slander against the imperial lineage. Accused of lèse-majesté, Falin was given a seven-day reprieve during which he was to invoke Guanyin to make him invulnerable, a power he had claimed for the deity in his earlier work. He used the time, however, to invoke not Guanyin but Taizong himself, claiming that the emperor was, in fact, one with the bodhisattva. Pardoned to exile, he died on the road.[63]

The Taoists, in this phase, remained victorious and the edict was repealed only in 674 when Empress Wu came to power. Taizong also issued a set of strict regulations for all clergy in an attempt to purge their conduct and exercise control over their activities. The regulations were based on the apocryphal *Yijiao jing* (Sūtra of Testamentary Teachings), allegedly issued by the Buddha immediately before he entered nirvāṇa. The text massively restricted the behavior of his followers, condemning especially the four major crimes of fornication, murder, theft, and pretense of enlightenment. It placed offenders under worldly authority. As a governmental measure, the regulations were set to guarantee a tame, docile, otherworldly clergy with no room for zealots like Falin and Zhishi, for monk entrepreneurs and capitalist monasteries, nor for the kind of unregistered, free monks who inspired the peasantry with messianic ideas and rose in revolt (Wright 1973, 261–62; Weinstein 1987, 17–22).

---

archs through the Ages) has Fu Yi's work in 625 and the two works by Falin in the same year, 626 (T. 2036; 49.564ab).

[61] See *Zhenzheng lun* 3 (T. 2112; 52.569c–70a). See also Wright 1973, 258; Li 1981, 101; Weinstein 1987, 16–17; Tonami 1992, 259.

[62] See *Fozu tongji* 39 (T. 2035; 49.364b). The edict is contained in *Quan Tangwen* (Complete Tang Literature) 6; *Guang hongming ji* 25 (T. 2103; 52.283c).

[63] *Xu gaoseng zhuan* 24 (T. 2060; 50.638aB); *Quan Tangwen* 6; *Falin biezhuan* (Special Biography of the Monk Falin) (T. 2051; T.50.198a–213b). For a discussion, see Wright 1973, 259–60; Weinstein 1987, 17.

Minor debates continued under the rule of Taizong's successor, Emperor Gaozong. No full texts of the arguments and contentions survive, but traces are found in Buddhist histories. There were, for example, several debates in 658, 660, and 663, in which the Taoist philosopher and poet Li Rong participated. Points of discussion were highly theoretical, such as the creation of the world, the question of whether or not the Tao were conscious of the meaning of the Three Caverns, the notion of original time, and so on. According to the Buddhist sources, the Taoists were regularly reduced to helpless anger and thoroughly defeated. Nevertheless, Gaozong remained firm in his support of Taizong's edict and even demanded, after a set of debates in 662, that the monks kneel before their parents and pay them filial respects.[64]

Gradually, the heat was going out of the contest. Empress Wu, as is well known, favored the Buddhist side;[65] Xuanzong, in the eighth century, was a fervent Taoist. Under his rule, a number of edicts regulated the behavior of monks and nuns of all persuasions, and they were ordered to pay respects to their parents and to secular authority (Tonami 1986, 497). Still, Xuanzong did not attempt to abolish any of the religions but used their institutions to promote his own orthodoxy and a tighter rule over the empire (Tonami 1988, 45). The formal debates, so frequent during the period of division and so important for the gradual integration of Buddhism into Chinese culture and society, were losing their momentum.[66] Factional strife and mutual polemics continued in different ways, but serious debates at court and among the gentry were only held again under the Mongol rulers of the Yuan dynasty (Ch'en 1945; Thiel 1961; Reiter 1990b).

The great medieval debates among Buddhists and Taoists with their lengthy expositions and convoluted arguments thus ended in the seventh century with works like Falin's *Bianzheng lun*. This extraordinary summary and masterful integration of everything that had happened before was like a last long, loud shout at the end of the drama. Then the lights gradually dimmed over the scene that had formed an important aspect of the religious and political life in medieval China.

Main Anti-Taoist Arguments

The arguments in the debates among Buddhists and Taoists, as Leon Hurvitz has pointed out, tended to be petty and rather confused (1961, 29). Often,

[64] For the various debates, see *Fozu lidai tongzai* 12 (T. 2036; 49.575c–78a). On Li Rong and his involvement, see Kohn 1991a, 196–99. For Gaozong's policy toward Buddhism, see Weinstein 1987, 27–37. On the debate concerning the monks' bowing to authority, see Tonami 1986, 488–96.

[65] Nevertheless, she did not agree to the proposal by the monk Huicheng, in 696, to have the *Huahu jing* destroyed completely. The petition, together with the remonstrations in favor of the text by various learned courtiers, is described in *Hunyuan shengji* (Sage Record of Chaos Prime) 8.17b–20b (DZ 770, fasc. 551–53).

[66] For later developments under the Tang, see Li 1981; Tonami 1986.

questions that seem obvious were never asked, much basic common ground was concealed, and vast historical excuses hid more essential issues. The standard arguments against Buddhism focused on its foreign nature and the harm it did to society and persons in China.[67] Arguments against Taoism, by contrast, were of two fundamental kinds: they either expressed a defense of Buddhism or gave vent to an active attack.

The most commonly offered defense of Buddhism can be divided into four distinct lines of reasoning. First was the emphasis on difference. This argument countered the idea that Buddhism, Taoism, Confucianism and all other possible teachings were originally one and shared the same common ground (Hurvitz 1961, 30). The notion of equality was dangerous to Buddhism because it could open the way for an integration into Chinese culture so intense that Buddhism as a teaching of its own would be lost altogether. Equality of the teachings, argued by Taoists especially in the very early phases of the debates, would allow a free mixture of doctrines and practices, which, in turn, might contaminate if not estrange Buddhism's inner heritage. To defend their teaching, Buddhists strongly insisted that their creed was fundamentally different from Taoism and other Chinese worldviews and practices.

Second, Buddhists claimed the superiority of their teaching because of its transcendent and otherworldly nature. Buddhism was the one teaching that was truly permanent, while Confucianism dealt only with the world here and now, and Taoism laid claim to an immortality that was spurious at best. Comparing the religious goals, nirvāṇa and immortality, Buddhism was the higher, more constant, eternal, and truly transcendent teaching. On the grounds of this superiority and otherworldliness, then, Buddhists did not need to bow to parents and secular authority and were exempt from taxes and military service. For their position both within the Confucian state and the intellectual traditions of China, the argument of inherent superiority was essential and continued to be much repeated throughout the debates (Hurvitz 1961, 30). The argument did not openly attack Taoism but implicitly relegated it to a secondary position.

Third, Buddhists insisted on the participation and usefulness of their teaching in the Confucian state. Although in blatant contradiction to the first two positions, this stance argued that Buddhism was known to the Chinese sages of antiquity and was, in fact, the teaching that had inspired their work. The new form of the religion was, therefore, nothing really new to China (Hur-

---

[67] In a separate study on the symbolism of evil in ancient China, I conclude that much of the anti-Buddhist reaction in medieval China might have had to do with the Chinese rejection of individual guilt as a valid symbol of evil. That is, Buddhism with its precepts and doctrine of karma and retribution placed the cause of all evil firmly in the individual, giving him predominant status and singular authority and responsibility. This view went against every communal and cosmic ideal ancient (and more recent) Chinese society held high and holy. As a result, there was strong resistance, which led to the continued affirmation of cosmological and social symbols of evil (defilement and sin). See Kohn, forthcoming (b).

vitz 1961, 37). Despite their insistence on a separate organization and exemption from state duties, Buddhists maintained that their presence was useful to the Confucian state owing to the merit they gained for the entire population. This merit was superior to the Confucian efforts toward political order or the Taoist rituals for protection against demons. In this line of argument, Taoism appeared as the secondary form of an originally Buddhist teaching. It was depicted as a fickle and unreliable way to support the state. Buddhism, on the contrary, was both more original and more politically effective.

Fourth, Buddhists defended themselves against the various accusations by developing the counter*huahu* theory. This position took the above position one step further. The sages of ancient China not only received vague inspiration from Buddhism but were in fact disciples of the Buddha sent on purpose to proselytize in the eastern countries. Buddhism, from a new addition to the Chinese intellectual and social scene, was thereby turned into its very foundation. It was the ultimate teaching that lay at the root of all order and intellectual progress. Doing away with the stigmatized position of being "barbarians," Buddhists with this argument established themselves in the very center of power. They laid claim to the root and origin of all and made the Chinese look ignorant and uncultured. Taoism again appeared secondary because Laozi was identified with Kāśyapa, a senior disciple of the Buddha.

In a different track, Buddhist argumentation against Taoism took on a more aggressive form. Again, the main positions can be divided into four. First, one argument contrasted philosophical and religious Taoism. Taoist practice, it said, claimed the heritage of the ancient philosophers but did nothing even remotely like it. The *Daode jing* itself was a worthy and venerable classic, but the actual practice of Taoists was strange and fraudulent. Neither spells nor talismans, exorcism nor shamanistic trances were ever mentioned or intended in the great classic of old. Taoists by this inherent contradiction of their teachings showed their dishonest nature, their vulgar and dishonest ways of dealing with the world.

The argument developed variously. Sometimes the *Daode jing* was used expressively to support and confirm the Buddhist position. Then again, the *Daode jing* itself was described as confused and obscure and contrasted effectively with the clarity and openness of Buddhist sūtras. In a third line, religious Taoist scriptures were contrasted with the ancient classic and their imitations of Buddhist sūtras pointed out.[68] The argument thus claimed

---

[68] There is no question that religious Taoism developed under heavy influence from Buddhist religious organization and doctrine. Kamata Shigeo, especially, has presented a number of illuminating studies on this process and the specific forms it took in Taoist scriptures. See Kamata 1963, 1966, 1968. He also compiled an impressive selection of Buddhist texts reprinted with minor alterations in the Taoist canon as Taoist scriptures (Kamata 1986). A recent Western study that focuses on borrowing from Buddhism in the Lingbao scriptures is found in Zürcher 1980.

Buddhist superiority as opposed to the fraudulent, dishonest, and confused nature of Taoism.

Second, Buddhists demolished the political usefulness of Taoism. Far from just performing harmless exorcisms and playing around with demons, they argued, Taoists had always, from the very beginning of their religion, associated themselves with betrayal and rebellion. The *fangshi*, magicotechnicians, at the courts of the Qin and Han dynasties, had tricked emperors to make them believe in physical immortality and the possibility of communicating with the dead. The early Taoist movements, moreover, had resulted in the insurrection of the Yellow Turbans under the Later Han, causing the downfall of this dynasty. Taoism not only lay at the root of political instability but was an inherent danger to any dynasty in power. Taoist revelations were a potential source of illegal and improper activities, a danger to state security and to the people's virtue. Referring to the Chinese belief in the interdependence of social, natural, and cosmic phenomena, Buddhists made out that Taoism was the weakest and most destructive link in the fine equilibrium of forces. It was, in fact, a danger that had to be banished.

Third, Buddhists invoked Confucian morality and common sense to move against specific Taoist ideas and practices. Especially sexual practices, the symbolic and ritual interaction between yin and yang, were part of Taoism since the Celestial Masters' movement. These, as experienced by Zhen Luan himself, went against traditional Confucian morality, according to which women could only be approached by their immediate relatives and even the appearance of a lady in public was scorned, let alone the swapping of wives that apparently was part of the ritual. In addition, Taoists unlike Buddhists did not abstain from alcohol but drank it during their ceremonies. These occasions might turn boisterous, which, especially when associated with the dead, caused the scorn of the morally righteous. Thus, morality as defined in the Confucian code was cited repeatedly against the practices of religious Taoists (see app. 1, *Bianhuo lun*).

Another argument against Taoism was the application of common sense to Taoist doctrines, a line taken frequently in the *Xiaodao lun*. Most commonly, this argument appeared in one of two forms. First, it confronted Taoist doctrines with basic common sense, including the logic of chronology, mathematical calculation, the standard Confucian vision of history, and the traditional understanding of Chinese culture. Taoism with its claim to sacrality and the universality of the Tao, stood in frequent contradiction to all of them.

A different line of this argument confronted different Taoist scriptures and practices with each other. A text stating that Laozi left China after he had served King You of Zhou as a historian, for example, was matched with one that had Laozi reborn as the son of the King before he set out for the west. The nine heavens of one text were contrasted with the twenty-eight in another, and so on. As a result of the multiplicity of Taoist revelations and scriptural traditions, the contradictions were numerous and could be continued forever. Taoism in all cases was made to look far inferior to the powerful theoretical structures of Buddhism. It was branded not only fraudulent and dishonest, immoral and rebellious, but also confused and nonsensical.

A fourth argument against Taoism criticized its claim to universality. An extension of the other lines taken, this went specifically against the possibility that Taoism might serve as the Chinese orthodoxy and be promoted to imperially sponsored doctrine. Both the *Bianhuo lun* and the *Xiaodao lun* emphasized this point. Believing themselves members of the celestial hierarchy, according to these texts, Taoists claimed to have control over the events of this world. Because the Tao was both the creative foundation of all existence and a recurrent force that maintained and developed the world, it was ubiquitous and omniscient. With the Tao as the key to understanding and controlling the world, Taoism thus represented the totality of all teachings and was the most powerful way to govern the empire. This attitude, Buddhists pointed out again and again, was folly and arrogance. It could only lead to an overbearing manner and might even cause the death of innocent people. Power over life and death was nothing to the Taoists, and Laozi thought little of killing the seven sons of the barbarian king. This tendency was dangerous and subversive; it could harm the state and ruin the empire.

Argumentation in the *Xiaodao lun*

The *Xiaodao lun* uses all these positions. It confronts descriptions of Taoist doctrines and practices with contradicting statements in other texts; it measures Taoist ideas against common sense and orthodox visions of history; and it reveals the antagonism between Taoism and Buddhism.

Zhen Luan presumes that Taoism is the best teaching to serve a unification orthodoxy, the declared position of Emperor Wu. He then challenges this position by pointing out that Taoism is not fit for such a role because it is absurd and nonsensical and that it frequently imitates Buddhism, which is much better suited to the task.

He proceeds to furnish proof for his challenge by citing a large number and variety of Taoist scriptures and ritual manuals, sometimes at considerable length. Unlike most polemical texts, which concentrate on raising philosophical issues and supporting them with citations of generally known and accepted materials, Zhen Luan uses specialized and even esoteric sources to make his point. Focusing on issues of Taoist myth, worldview, and practice, he discloses the inner inconsistencies of the Taoist teaching, using its very own sources and confronting it with historical sources and common-sense calculations.

Altogether, Zhen Luan cites forty-two Taoist texts, a detailed list and analysis of which are found in appendix 2 here. Among these scriptures, the vast majority belong to the Lingbao group (sixteen texts), followed by Louguan texts relating to the conversion of the barbarians and the hagiography of Laozi (eight texts).[69] Six further scriptures belong to the environment of the Celestial Masters, two are related to Ge Hong and the *Baopuzi* (Book of the Master Who Embraces Simplicity), and one forms part of the Sanhuang (Three Sovereigns) group. References to an early catalog of Taoist scriptures and eight unidentified sources complete the picture (see table 1).

Not all these texts survive in independent editions. Materials associated with the Lingbao and Sanhuang schools and those related to the *Baopuzi* and the hagiography of Laozi for the most part are found separately either in the Taoist canon or in Dunhuang manuscripts. Passages from these texts can be largely identified although many *Xiaodao lun* citations are shorter than or different from the texts available today. This is either the result of intentional alteration by Zhen Luan, as Kusuyama suspects in the *Chuji* (Record of Beginnings; Kusugama 1979, 432) or possible later reediting of Taoist scriptures. By the early Tang, partly as a result of the debates, many Taoist texts were found to be too close to their Buddhist counterparts and were changed to sound more indigenous (Bokenkamp 1991). The version cited by Zhen Luan might represent a more original variant than the later editions.

Works from the Celestial Masters are partly known from independent editions, but here, as in the *Laozi baibashi jie* (Eighty Precepts of Laozi), unidentified passages occur. Sexual manuals such as the *Huangshu* (Yellow Book) have not survived intact and can often be correlated only to other citations in

[69] Louguan is a monastery southwest of Chang'an at the foot of the Zhongnan mountains. It is allegedly the old home of Yin Xi, where Laozi transmitted the *Daode jing* to the Guardian of the Pass. A place of seclusion for immortality practitioners, it came to imperial attention first under the leadership of Yin Tong, a putative descendant of Yin Xi, in the 420s.

Toward the end of the fifth century, the Taoist Wang Daoyi removed there from the capital with a group of disciples and a host of craftsmen. He built the center up and established a formal Taoist community in the wake of Kou Qianzhi's new Celestial Masters. Wang also had Taoist scriptures collected from all over the country, paving the way for the fruitful integration of the northern and southern forms of the religion.

In the sixth century, Louguan Taoists were the leading representatives of the religion in the north, both as active participants in the debates and as compilers of new scriptures and commentaries (Wei Jie), textual catalogs (Wang Yan), and imperially sponsored encyclopedias (Yan Da).

Louguan belief centered around the hagiography of Laozi and placed strong emphasis on Yin Xi and the conversion of the barbarians. Its practice focused on *Daode jing* recitation in conjunction with a variety of immortality techniques and spiritual methods adopted from Shangqing and Lingbao. See Qing 1988, 430–44; Ren 1990, 219–36; Zhang 1990, 1991.

Table 1
Taoist Scriptures according to Schools

Schools	Scriptures
Lingbao	*Dayou jing, Duming miaojing, Duren benxing jing, Duren miaojing, Fuzhai jing, Jiku jing (= Yundu jieqi jing), Jiutian shengshen zhangjing, Sanyuan pin, Shijie jing, Wufu jing, Wulian jing, Zuigen pin, Zhutian neiyin, Ziran jing.*
	To these can be added two scriptures of the Shangqing corpus, the *Dajie wen* and the *Dongfang qingdi song*, both cited as from the Lingbao or Dongxuan group.
Huahu	*Chuji, Huahu jing, Laozi xiaobing jing, Laozi xu, Miaozhen jing, Shengxuan jing (= Xisheng jing), Wenshi zhuan (= Yuanshi zhuan), Xuanmiao neipian.*
	Among these, three texts are part of the tradition of the *Daode jing* (*Laozi xu, Miaozhen jing, Xisheng jing*); the others are conversion scriptures written particularly to present the anti-Buddhist position at court.
Celestial Masters	*Huangshu, Laozi baibashi jie, Nüqing wen, Santian zhengfa jing*
	Two additions, the *Daolü* and the *Zhenren neichao lü*, are unidentified and used in section 35 on ritual sexual practices.
Baopuzi	*Jinye jing, Shenxian zhuan*
Sanhuang	*Sanhuang jing*
Unclear	*Daozhai jing, Xuanzhong jing, Xuanzi.* These Taoist texts use Buddhist concepts and moral codes.
	Du guowang pin, Dushen pin, Guangshuo pin, Nanji zhenren wenshi pin, Youwu shengcheng pin. All these end in *pin*, which might indicate chapter titles. They contain Buddhist doctrine in Taoist guise.
Catalog	*Xuandu jingmu*

Buddhist polemics. The same holds also true for all early catalogs of Taoist scriptures.

Most complex is the identification of Louguan conversion texts (Qing 1988, 439). Banned several times because of their defaming contents, these materials have only survived in citations and Dunhuang manuscripts. Some of them, such as the *Xuanmiao neipian,* are cited several times in the literature with the same passage so that an identification of sorts is possible. Then again, some texts such as the *Chuji* or the *Laozi xiaobing jing* (Laozi's Scripture of Melting Ice) are unknown except for their appearance in the *Xiaodao lun*. Both the most central texts of the conversion, the *Huahu jing* and the *Wenshi zhuan*, are cited several times with passages entirely unknown outside the *Xiaodao lun* and other Buddhist polemics.

Unidentified materials are of two kinds: first, three texts cited in regard to proper Taoist behavior and Buddho-Taoist cosmology; second, five documents with titles ending in the suffix *pin*, which might refer to chapters of texts. In content, these contain Buddhist doctrines in a Taoist framework, focusing on descriptions of Buddho-Taoist myth and cosmology, but some also deal with formal Taoist rules. Where the Buddhist content is obvious, one might suspect that the texts were lost in the same way as the conversion materials—too-explicit adaptations of Buddhist myth and doctrine, they were either edited out of longer scriptures or destroyed altogether. It remains unclear, however, why texts like the *Xuanzhong jing* (Scripture of Central Mystery) or the *Xuanzi* (Writings of Xuanzi), which focus on Taoist formal activities and emphasize morality, should not be extant.

The two most frequently cited sources are the *Huahu jing* (eleven times) and the *Wenshi zhuan* (fourteen times), documenting the centrality of the conversion theme and Louguan Taoism in the *Xiaodao lun*. In both cases, only a few citations could be identified in other editions or citations. Furthermore, because the *Xiaodao lun* citations are not only numerous but also quite long, this text has become an important source for the reconstruction of the early conversion texts (Zürcher 1959, 305).

Next in frequency are citations of Taoist codexes of rules and precepts, showing Zhen Luan's concern for the actual behavior and religious regulations of Taoists. Independent of their sectarian background, all major Taoist scriptures on precepts are cited often: the *Dajie wen* (The Great Precepts; five times), the *Sanyuan pin* (Precepts of the Three Primes) and the *Zuigen pin* (The Roots of Sin; four times each), the *Shijie jing* (Scripture of the Ten Precepts) and the *Laozi baibashi jie* (once each).

The third most frequently cited texts deal with cosmology and are of both Lingbao and Celestial Masters provenance. They focus particularly on the numbers and sizes of the heavens and the events at the end of a kalpa cycle: the *Santian zhengfa jing* (Scripture of the Proper Laws of the Three Heavens) and the *Yundu jieqi jing* (Scripture on Kalpa Revolutions) four times each, the *Zhutian neiyin* (Esoteric Sounds of All Heavens) and the *Duren benxing jing* (Scripture of the Original Endeavor of Universal Salvation) three times each, the *Duren jing* (Scripture of Universal Salvation) two times, and other Lingbao texts once.

Altogether, the choice and frequency of Taoist scriptures in the *Xiaodao lun* shows that Zhen Luan's prime interest was to demonstrate that Taoism consisted merely of a bad imitation of Buddhist sūtras, precepts, cosmology, and myth. He concentrates particularly on texts on the conversion because they represent the clearest confrontation between the teachings and prefers to cite from the Lingbao group because these texts were most strongly influenced by Buddhism.

Zhen Luan uses his materials by pitting different texts against each other, either taking texts from different groups that deal with similar topics and citing them against each other, using conversion texts against Lingbao (sec. 10, 17, 21, 23) or Lingbao against materials of the Celestial Masters (sec. 3, 4), or by taking texts from the same groups and using them in confrontation (sec. 1, 5, 9, 18, 19, 22, 27, 30, 33). He thereby shows the inconsistency of the Taoist teaching not only between different traditions but also within the same group of texts or even in the same text.

In a next step, he confronts the resulting picture of Taoist confusion with (1) historical sources like the *Hanshu* and with respectable Taoist texts, such as Ge Hong's *Shenxian zhuan* (Biographies of Spirit Immortals) and the *Liezi* (Writings of Liezi) (sec. 1, 2, 14, 16, 22, 34); (2) reason and common sense (sec. 9, 12, 15, 17, 20, 25); and (3) his own personal experience (sec. 6, 31, 35). In doing so, Zhen Luan establishes a hierarchy of credibility. Anything to do with the conversion of the barbarians and with Buddho-Taoist cosmology is most unreliable and absurd, closely followed by anything coming from the Lingbao texts. Most trustworthy are facts and data documented in historical records or arrived at through mathematical calculation, reason, and common sense.

In technique, Zhen Luan frequently uses rhetorical questions. He first presents contradictory evidence on a specific subject, then poses different possible interpretations. How, if the Tao was unknowing and pure, can there be good and evil? How, if it knew what it was doing, can there be evil at all? Why not create a world all good? And so on. The questions lead the reader around in circles. They expose the inherent contradictions in Taoist thinking and open the path for its condemnation.

Then Zhen Luan follows up the insecurity he has created with three kinds of judgment. First, he openly condemns, judging Taoism as foolish, treacherous, rebellious, unworthy, and immoral. On occasion, he even expresses his rage and freely states how much he detests and despises the Taoist teaching, which is worthless and should be erased from the world. Second, he remains calm and rational. Certainly, he seems to say, faced with all this evidence of contradiction, with the fact that Taoists have no answers to even the most obvious doctrinal issues, every reasonable person must realize that it is not a suitable teaching, that it is unfit to serve state and salvation.

Third, he brings out the ridiculous, absurd, and abstruse, following a well-known traditional rhetorical device of ancient China (Kao 1974, xix). Having created insecurity, he again reassures the listener by making him laugh. Many sections thus end with the appeal to mock: "Ridiculous indeed!" or "What a laugh!" Zhen Luan points out incoherences and contradictions, then turns them into something easy to sweep away as simply foolish and absurd. By making Taoist ideas a target for ridicule, Zhen Luan places Taoism in a position of irrelevance where it can be easily dismissed. Taoism is no serious opposition to Buddhism that needs to be threatened, nor is it a doctrine even worth a rational challenge. Taoism becomes a nonteaching, an absurd conglomeration of ideas to be brushed aside without further thought.

The argumentation of the *Xiaodao lun* inherits all the various anti-Taoist positions and uses them to their best advantage. Not only a summary and development of the arguments preceding it, the text represents the most developed and sophisticated form Buddhist demolition of Taoism took in medieval China. It cites large numbers of Taoist texts and pokes its rhetorical spears into many different aspects of the Taoist teaching. Twisting and turning, it raises rhetorical questions, then takes the built-up insecurity and laughs the opponent thoroughly out of all competition. Reading the *Xiaodao lun*, the various myths, doctrines, and practices of Taoism seem utterly foolish and unable to stand up to their Buddhist counterpart, unfit to serve the orthodoxy of a newly reunited China.

ZHEN LUAN

Laughing at the Tao

*Translated and annotated in cooperation with
the research seminar on medieval Chinese thought at
Kyōto University*

Preface

[143c20][1] Your servant, Zhen Luan, humbly offers this memorial. By imperial decree, I was ordered to examine the two teachings, Buddhism and Taoism, in order to settle their precedence, their relative value, and their differences. Because this humble servant is not sufficiently experienced to judge the quality of the teachings, I reverently present the following concrete record to gracious imperial hearing.

In private, I think there are considerable differences between the visible traces of Buddhism and Taoism.[2] Their respective rise and decline, appearance and withdrawal, and their overall transformations are not alike at all.[3] In either case, however, the inner subtleties and esoteric mysteries are not easily understood.[4]

Yet upon comparing them one finds that although the Buddhists consider karma and retribution as the main doctrine,[5] the Taoists venerate natural spontaneity as their major principle.[6] Natural spontaneity is constituted by nonaction;[7] karma and retribution, on the other hand, are manifest in the accumulation of deeds.[8] When one holds

[1] The translation follows the text of the *XDL* as found in the *Guang hongming ji* (T. 3102; 52.143c–52c). The page and line number of this edition are noted at the beginning of every section.

Immediately after the title, the *Guang hongming ji* editor adds the note, "Because the text is rather extensive, I edited it to include only the funny parts." The text here is, therefore, an abbreviated reedition of the *XDL*, burned after incurring Emperor Wu's displeasure. Additional fragments of the text are also found in the *BZL* and are supplied at the appropriate place in the notes here.

[2] This phrasing is taken from Sengzhao's reply to a letter by Recluse Liu. See *Zhaolun* (Treatises of Sengzhao), T. 1858; 45.155c (Kenkyūhan 1988, 521 n. 5). The mention of the "visible traces" refers to the distinction between the origin and the traces, the original root and intention of a teaching and its later practice. This distinction was used to introduce Buddhism as a new variant of universal truth already accessible to the Chinese. It also played a role in the early debates around Zhang Rong and Gu Huan (see appendix 1).

[3] These are variant expressions for the visible traces. For a study of the subtler meanings of "overall transformations" (*biantong*), see Sivin 1991.

[4] The same phrase is also used in the historical record of the debates, translated in the introduction. It goes back to Zong Bing's *Mingfo lun* (T. 2102; 52.12c) and the Liang Emperor Yuan's *Neidian beiming jixu* (T. 2103; 52.244c). See Kenkyūhan 1988, 521 n. 8.

[5] The doctrine of karma and retribution is also described as the core of the Buddhist teaching in the "Treatise on Buddhism and Taoism" of the *Weishu* (chap. 114). See Hurvitz 1956, 32.

[6] For a discussion of spontaneity and nature as understood in the Taoism of this time, see Nakajima 1982; 1985.

[7] This connection is made in *Daode jing* 37 and in *Liji* 26 ("Zhongyong"). See Kenkyūhan 1988, 522 n. 12.

[8] The same distinction is also made in section 30 of the text. In the earlier debates, it plays a role in the *Ronghua lun* (On Barbarians and Chinese; T. 2102; 52.47c).

onto the origin,[9] all affairs will be tranquil and principle will be well balanced. But when one deviates from the main doctrine, one's intention will go astray and the teaching will be perverted. Only with principle in perfect balance can beginning and end be in complete harmony.[10] But when the teaching is perverted, then there is nothing that is not done.[11]

For me, Laozi's *Wuqian wen* (Text in Five Thousand Words) is venerable and lofty both in style and in meaning.[12] It should be valued very highly. By righting the self and ordering the state, the ways of the ruler are enriched.[13] For this purpose, the Taoists have the practices of writing talismans and reciting spells,[14] whereas the Buddhists prohibit all arts that rely on extrasensory powers or are contrary to the ideal of compassion.

Placing the outer appearances of both side by side, the average person is easily confused about which is true and which false. How could this be the meaning of the Great Tao with its natural spontaneity, emptiness, and nonaction? It can only be explained in that later generations turned their backs on the origins and erroneously brought forth specious ideas.

Then again, there are all those Taoist magical arts by which one supposedly can ascend to the immortals as a spirit. They all brought forth nothing but deception, doubt, and betrayal. In antiquity, for example, Xu Fu used such ideas to cheat [the First Emperor of the Qin] and enter the country of the eastern barbarians; later Li Shaoweng and Luan Da bewitched and betrayed Emperor Wu of the Han.[15] Then the

[9] This expression is taken from *Zhuangzi* 36/13/63 (ed. Harvard-Yenching Sinological Index Series, supplement no. 20). See Kenkyūhan 1988, 522 n. 14.

[10] This adopts the phrasing of *Xunzi* 72/19/43 (ed. Harvard-Yenching Sinological Index Series, supplement no. 22). See Kenkyūhan 1988, 522 n. 16.

[11] This is a rather denigrating use of the famous saying of *Daode jing* 38 and 48, also found in *Zhuangzi* 57/22/10.

[12] This refers to the *Daode jing*. This variant title goes back to Laozi's biography in *Shiji* 63, where it is said that he transmitted his teaching in five thousand words.

[13] See Kenkyūhan 1988, 522 n. 20. The close relationship between personal cultivation and the stability of the state is clearly expressed in the "Great Learning" (Daxue) chapter of the *Liji*, in the *Xiaojing* (Classic of Filial Piety), and in Heshang gong's commentary to the *Daode jing*. For the former, see Chan 1964; on the latter, see A. Chan 1991.

[14] These are the central practices of the early Celestial Masters. See Levy 1956; Stein 1963; Kabayashi 1992. For Chinese references, see Kenkyūhan 1988, 522 n. 21.

[15] Xu Fu was the envoy sent by Qin Shihuang to find the isles of the immortals. The others were magicians at the Han court. See *Shiji* 28; Watson 1968b, 2:13–69. For more on Emperor Wu, see Schipper 1965; Smith 1992. For Chinese references, see Kenkyūhan 1988, 524 n. 32–33.

three Zhangs caused disorder in the west, in Liang, and later Sun En raised the banner of rebellion in the east, in Yue.[16]

Terrible disturbances of this kind have always been condemned, even in antiquity. Most certainly, any government applying such behavior can only be a government of falsehood and corruption. A people guided along such lines will surely be deluded and confused.

In addition, the examination of Taoist scriptures reveals contradictions from scroll to scroll, whereas the analysis of their doctrines shows they have neither head nor tail.

Traditionally, one judged the quality of a person's filial behavior from the way he behaved toward his ruler. Seeing a man who served his lord with exhaustive ritual formality, one would honor him like a filial son caring for his parents. Seeing a man who served his lord without ritual formality, one would persecute him like an eagle chasing a sparrow.[17]

Confucius said, "The gentleman serves his lord in such a way that, approaching him, all his thinking is of loyalty; withdrawing from him, all his concerns are about making up his shortcomings. He strives ardently to emulate his lord's good characteristics and works hard to correct his bad traits. Only thus can ruler and minister treat each other like kin."[18]

The *Zuozhuan* (Mr. Zuo's Commentary to the *Spring and Autumn Annals*) says, "Whenever in what the lord says there is some part acceptable and some part unacceptable, one should relate to what he can accept and dismiss what he cannot."[19]

Now, although I am not quite like that, having been asked for my judgment by Your Majesty, I yet do not dare to answer fully. [I will freely admit that] the *Daode jing* in two scrolls can easily be accepted by an orthodox Confucian. Still, what I consider questionable is that it does not go with the extreme other end of the Taoist teaching. I, therefore, pray you judge and evaluate my opinions.

The *Daode jing* says,

---

[16] The "three Zhangs" indicates the first three generations of the Celestial Masters, Zhang Ling, Zhang Heng, and Zhang Lu. For more details on their activities, see section 7. Sun En led a rebellion against the Jin in 399 C.E. On him, see Eichhorn 1954; Miyakawa 1979. See also Kenkyūhan 1988, 524 nn. 34–35.

[17] This passage is taken from *Zuozhuan*, Wen 18. See Kenkyūhan 1988, 525 n. 44.

[18] The passage is taken from *Hanshu* 12. The latter part refers back to *Xiaojing* 8. See Kenkyūhan 1988, 525 n. 45.

[19] *Zuozhuan*, Zhao 20. See Kenkyūhan 1988, 525 n. 46.

When the highest kind of people hear of the Tao, they diligently
practice it.
When the medium kind of people hear of the Tao, they half
believe in it.
When the lowest kind of people hear of the Tao, they laugh
heartily at it.
If they did not laugh at it, it would not be the Tao.[20]

Your servant has taken the liberty to follow the attitude of the lowest
kind and has written a treatise called "Laughing at the Tao" in three
scrolls and thirty-six sections. The three scrolls laugh at the Taoist classification of the Three Caverns; the thirty-six sections laugh at the
thirty-six divisions of scriptures.[21]

Cold sweat on my forehead, my heart trembling to distraction, I
venture to present this to Your Majesty.

On the fifteenth of the second month, fifth year of Heavenly Harmony under the Great Zhou [570].

With deepest respects,

Zhen Luan

Metropolitan Commandant
Native of Wuji District
Earl of Opening the Country

[20] Chapter 41.
[21] On the division and development of the Taoist canon, see Liu 1973; Ōfuchi 1979b;
Thompson 1985. See also Kenkyūhan 1988, 526 n. 56.

1

The Highest Lord of the Tao
Created Heaven and Earth

[144b13] The *Chuji* (Record of Beginnings) says:[1]

"Because the virtue of King You of Zhou [r. 781–771 B.C.E.] was
declining, Laozi wanted to cross the pass for the west. There he agreed

[1] This text is lost in other editions. Down to "Then Laozi changed his shape," the passage
represents an abbreviated but substantially correct description of the conversion of the barbarians as recorded in the *Huahu jing, Wenshi zhuan,* and Laozi's hagiography. For more

with Yin Xi to meet again after three years at a [stall selling] liver of black sheep in the market of Chang'an.[2]

"Laozi was then reborn in the womb of the empress. When the appointed time came, Yin Xi indeed found a person selling black sheep's liver.[3] He then asked to see Laozi, who just at this time emerged from his mother's chest. His hair and temples were white, and he was sixteen feet tall. He wore the cap of heaven and held a staff of gold.[4]

---

details on these texts and others used, see appendix 2. The passage cited here has also been translated in Zürcher 1959, 299–300.

[2] Laozi left China, met Yin Xi, the Guardian of the Pass, and transmitted the *Daode jing* to him. First recorded in *Shiji* 63, this is part of the classical hagiography of Laozi. For further documentation, see 2 n. 7, that is, note 7 of section 2. (Cross-references to notes will henceforth be abbreviated in this manner.) On the emigration, see Kusuyama 1979; Kohn 1989a; Kohn 1991a, 60–70. Laozi's meeting with Yin Xi after three years is part of the conversion of barbarians. See Wang 1934; Zürcher 1959, 290–320; Kusuyama 1978; Reiter 1990b; Seidel 1984a.

[3] This episode summarizes the second and later version of the reunion of the two sages studied in Kusuyama 1978; Kusuyama 1979, 423–36. The first version is found in the *SDZN* extracts of the *Wenshi zhuan* (9.8b–14b) and the *Huahu jing* (9.14b–20b). Here Laozi meets Yin Xi in Chengdu, the capital of Shu (Sichuan) while visiting with a local dignitary. The sale of a black sheep in the market is the sign of recognition.

The second version appears in a lost text variously cited as *Benji* (Original Record), *Hunyuan benji* (Original Record of Chaos Prime), or *Tangji* (Tang Record), which is probably a Laozi hagiography by the Tang Taoist Yin Wencao (Kusuyama 1979, 428–29). It is mentioned first in Le Penggui's *Xichuan qingyang gong beiming* (Inscription at the Black Sheep Temple in Sichuan; *DZ* 964, fasc. 609) of the year 884, then in *Youlong zhuan* 4.1a–2a (Like onto a Dragon; *DZ* 774, fasc. 555), to make its way eventually into Xie Shouhao's *Hunyuan shengji* 3.25a–29b (Sage Record of Chaos Prime; *DZ* 770, fasc. 551–53). Here, Laozi ascends back to heaven and is reborn in the family of the prefect of Shu. (Only the *XDL* locates the story in Chang'an.) He cries so loudly and pitifully that a Taoist is summoned who decrees that only the milk of a black sheep will calm the child. A servant is sent to the market to buy one, thus giving Yin Xi the divine sign. The sheep's "liver" mentioned in the *XDL* may well be a corruption of "milk" of this version (Kusuyama 1979, 430). The sheep is renowned in Taoist legend. Its statues still grace the entrance to the Qingyang gong (Black Sheep Temple) in Chengdu (Yūsa 1986, 88).

In addition, "black sheep" is also a form of mica, a classical immortality drug (see Schafer 1955). The *Baopuzi* (Book of the Master Who Embraces Simplicity; ed. *Zhuzi jicheng*; index Schipper 1975b; trans. in Ware 1966) describes black sheep as a sign of long life, based on the shape visible in pine trees older than one thousand years: "A pine tree of a thousand years has branches sticking out in all four directions, but the tips of its twigs are not long. Looking up into it, it seems like a slanted canopy with something in it, something that looks like a black ox, a black sheep, maybe a black dog, or even a black person. They are all a thousand years old" (3/8/20; see also Ware 1966, 55–56).

The word translated here as "black," *qing*, is the color associated with the spring and the east. It is commonly rendered as "green" or "blue" and indicates the fresh color of vegetation in the spring (see Porkert 1961; Baxter 1983). It means also the shimmering black in the skin of very old yet vigorous animals or people. Accordingly, Laozi left China astride a *qing* ox, symbolizing his longevity.

[4] Laozi's miraculous birth and wondrous signs are first recorded in the *Shenxian zhuan* (Biographies of Spirit Immortals; trans. in Güntsch 1988, 36; Kohn forthcoming a). See Yoshioka 1959; Kusuyama 1979. The tale is later merged with the hagiography of the birth of the Buddha. See Kohn 1989a; 1989c, 75. In particular, Laozi's white hair indicates his old age

"Together with Yin Xi he set out to convert the barbarians. They withdrew to Mount Shouyang,[5] always protected by a purple cloud.[6]

"The king of the barbarians suspected they were evil sorcerers. He threw the Venerable Lord into a cauldron with boiling water, yet he did not even become hot.[7] Instead, he got very angry and resolved to kill the king's seven sons and a portion of the country's population. They all died.

"The king finally surrendered. He ordered all the people of his kingdom to convert to Laozi's teaching. They shaved their heads, stayed celibate, and began to observe 250 precepts.[8] They also made images of the Venerable Lord, burned incense, and paid obeisance to him.[9]

"Then Laozi changed his shape. His left eye became the sun; his right eye, the moon. His head became Mount Kunlun;[10] his hair, the

---

and wisdom; his size, a characteristic inspired by Buddhist sources (*Mouzi lihuo lun*, T. 2102; 52.1c; *Shier youjing* [Sūtra of the Twelve Wanderings], T. 195; 4.146c) and statues (see sec. 7), shows his superhuman stature; the cap of heaven is part of the formal dress of the perfected (*Taiqing zhonghuang zhenjing* [Perfect Scripture of Central Yellow of Great Clarity] 2.9b; *DZ* 817, fasc. 568; also in *YJQQ* 13); and the staff of gold is a sign of old age and divinity (*Guishan xuanlu* [Mysterious Record of Turtle Mountain] 1.19a; *DZ* 1394, fasc. 1048). See Kenkyūhan 1988, 527 nn. 63–67.

    5 This is the mountain where the famous recluses Boyi and Shuqi withdrew in the beginning of Zhou (*Shiji* 61). Here the mountain seems located farther west of China proper. According to Zürcher, this part of the story takes place in India (1959, 300).

    6 The purple cloud is the sign by which Yin Xi recognizes the sagely nature of Laozi when he ascends the western frontier pass. See *Shenxian zhuan* 1.

    7 Kenkyūhan 1988, 528 nn. 71–72. An earlier example of such a feat is recorded in *Soushen ji* (In Search of the Supernatural) 11. Immersion in boiling water is a standard punishment in hell. See *Jiuku jing* 4a (*DZ* 373, fasc. 181); Doré 1914–38, 7:266, 288.

    8 These are the classical practices of a Buddhist monk, with the number of precepts equaling those of the *Pratimokṣa*. See Dutt 1962.

    9 This passage recounts the central story of the conversion of the barbarians as found in all related texts. See the discussion in the Introduction and "*Huahu jing*" in appendix 2. See also Kenkyūhan 1988, 529 nn. 75–78. A translation of the first chapter of the *Huahu jing* is found in Kohn 1993a, 71–80. A similarly abbreviated description of the events is found in *BZL* 5 according to the *Huahu jing* (T. 52.522b).

    10 Kunlun is the name of a mountain range in Central Asia and of a Taoist paradise that first gained prominence under the Han. It is a mountain surrounded by water, just like its maritime counterpart of Penglai in the eastern sea. The water surrounding Kunlun is "weak water," too weak to float anything, not even a feather. Crowned by three major peaks, the top of the mountain is said to be wider than its base. Here the Queen Mother of the West (Xiwangmu) has her palaces, pond, hanging gardens, and peaches of immortality. In a traditional worldview, Kunlun symbolizes the mythical and cosmological center of the universe. For details on the mountain, see Yuan 1985, 235–36; Liu 1988, 76–81; Sōfukawa 1981; Tetsui 1990, 227–43; Robinet 1984, 1:135; Stein 1990, 223–46. On the Queen Mother, see Loewe 1979; Fracasso 1988; Kominami 1991; Cahill 1993.

    In Taoist meditation, Kunlun is the head as explained in *Huangting waijing jing* A 38 (Outer Radiance Scripture of the Yellow Court; *YJQQ* 12.34b; Schipper 1975a; Kenkyūhan 1988, 529 n. 80). For a discussion of the Taoist image of the body, see Asano 1982; Homann 1971; Schipper 1982; Kohn 1991b. Laozi's head becoming Kunlun is linked with both the cosmological centrality of the mountain and its role in Taoist meditation.

stars. His bones were dragons; his flesh, wild beasts; his intestines, snakes. His belly became the ocean; his fingers, the five sacred mountains. The hair on his body turned into grass and trees; his heart, into the Flowery Canopy.[11] Last, his testicles joined to become the true father and mother of humankind."[12]

I laugh at this and say:

The *Hanshu* (History of the Han Dynasty) states:[13] "Chang'an was originally called Xianyang. When Han Gaozu [r. 206–194 B.C.E.] unified the empire, he thought to move the capital to Luoyang. But after Lou Jing's remonstration, he sighed and said, 'Well, then I will establish my long peace [*chang'an*] here.' Thus, the city came to be named Chang'an."

Under King You of the Zhou the city, therefore, did not exist with this name. How could Laozi have foreseen its later existence and agreed to meet Yin Xi there?

In addition, the *Santian zhengfa hundun jing* (Scripture of the

---

[11] Kenkyūhan 1988, 529 n. 81. The Flowery Canopy is the constellation Cassiopeia in the sky and the lungs in the human body. See *Huangting neijing jing* 9.1 (Inner Radiance Scripture of the Yellow Court; *YJQQ* 11.25a).

[12] This creation myth is usually associated with the cosmic giant Pangu and as such is cited in the *Poxie lun* (T. 2109; 52.486c). See Erkes 1942; Maspero 1981, 340; Yuan 1960, 36–38; Yuan 1979a, 20; Yuan 1979b 1–15; Yuan 1985, 258; Liu 1988, 199–206. Earlier it is recorded in the third-century text *Sanwu liji* (Chronological Record of the Three and Five; *TPYL* 78.1b); *Yiwen leiju* (Clarified Collection of Artistic Writings 1.2a) and in the *Shuyi ji* (Record of Marvels) of the Liang dynasty (see Kenkyūhan 1988, 529 n. 79).

In a Taoist context, the myth is found in the *Yuanqi lun* (On Primordial Energy; *YJQQ* 56.1b–2a). On occasion, Pangu is also identified with Yuanshi tianzun, the Heavenly Venerable of Primordial Beginning (see Wang 1989). For more on Taoist creation myths in general, see Grube 1896; Erkes 1931; Schipper 1978; Girardot 1983; Kohn 1993a. The body of Laozi, too, is described as the world. See *Laojun benqi jing* (Scripture on the Original Endeavor of the Venerable Lord; *YJQQ* 10.7b–8a). In Taoist practice, moreover, the mediator places himself at the center of the universe, visualizing his body unified with it. See *Neiguan jing* 6b (Scripture on Inner Observation; *DZ* 641, fasc. 342; Kohn 1989d), *Daode zhenjing xujue* (Introductory Explanation to the *Daode jing*; S. 75, P. 2370; Ofuchi 1979, 509–11; Takeuchi 1978, 6:222).

Zhen Luan's linking of the creation myth with the conversion story is unusual. A possible model may be found in a *Huahu jing* passage:

Laozi thereupon changed into a great man of gold and diamonds, brilliantly radiating in five colors. He was sixteen feet tall and endowed with the seventy-two auspicious signs. His face and eyes glittered in purple, and he could be seen floating freely in midair. Left he appeared, right he disappeared; up he went, and down he came. This was his true body of the emptiness of the ten directions. (*SDZN* 9.19ab)

Still, the relation between the two parts of the passage remains spurious and may well be a combination of different Taoist scriptures. Kusuyama even believes that Zhen Luan intentionally arranged the *Chuji* in this way to serve his own purposes (1979, 432).

[13] Kenkyūhan 1988, 503 n. 83. This is a mixture of three sources: *Hanshu* 34, biography of Lu Guan; *Hanshu* 1, Record of Emperor Gaozu, fifth year; and *Sanfu huangtu* (Yellow Chart of the Three Mainstays), Introduction. The three mainstays are administrative centers (see Hurvitz 1956, 62).

Proper Law of the Three Heavens in Original Chaos) says:[14] "In the beginning of chaos, light energy rose and formed heaven, turbid energy sank and formed earth. Then the seven luminants and the myriad images took shape."[15] [Thus, we know that] these things already existed for a long time [before Laozi went west]. How could Laozi turn into the sun and moon, mountains and streams, and so on, only after he had converted the barbarians?

If these statements were true, then before King You of Zhou heaven and earth had not yet given life to the myriad beings. Why, then, do Taoist scriptures speak of the Three Sovereigns, the Five Heavenly Emperors, and the Three Kings?[16] If the text used above is true, however, heaven and earth only began under King You.

Furthermore, the *Zao tiandi ji* (Record of the Creation of Heaven and Earth) says:[17] "Mount Kunlun is 4,800 miles high. On its top there are the mountain of Jade Capital and the mountain of Grand Network. They, too, are 4,800 miles high. The three mountains together thus measure 14,400 miles."[18]

The *Guangshuo pin* (Chapter of Broad Explanations) states, how-

---

[14] This passage is found in a different version in the *Santian zhengfa jing* today (*DZ* 1203, fasc. 876; *YJQQ* 21.1ab):

> The Perfected King of the Nine Heavens and the Heavenly King of Primordial Beginning both were brought forth before the first energy. At that time, the radiance of heaven was not yet bright, the thick accumulation was not yet clear, the watery expanse was without shore. Chaos it was and great emptiness, vast openness and eternally flowing darkness!
>
> After more than seven thousand kalpas, darkness and light first divided. Then the nine energies arose. Each energy was separated from the next by 99,990 years. The clear energy rose up to be pure; the turbid chaos sank down to be spread out. The Perfected King of the Nine Heavens and the Heavenly King of Primordial Beginning were endowed with the quality of spontaneity and established in the names of the nine heavens. The nine energies coagulated in darkness and formed these deities according to the true plan of the nine heavens. Thereupon, the sun and the moon, the stars and the chronograms began to shine forth. (1a)

[15] These astrophysical notions are first spelled out in chapter 3 of the *Huainanzi*. See Major 1993.

[16] These mythical rulers stand for the prehistory of Chinese culture. The Three Sovereigns are the first creators of the civilized Chinese world and commonly identified as Fu Xi, Shennong, and Nügua. The Five Heavenly Emperors, associated with the five phases, are Huangdi, Zhuan Xu, Di Ku, Yao, and Shun. The Three Kings refer to the founders of the three oldest Chinese dynasties, Yu of the Xia, Tang of the Shang, and Wuwang of the Zhou. See De Groot 1918; Haloun 1925; Guy 1936, 127; Yuan 1984, 1985. In Taoist scriptures, this sequence of rulers is described in *Kaitian jing* 4a–6a (*DZ* 1437, fasc. 1059; *YJQQ* 2; trans. in Kohn 1993a, 35–43). For more Chinese references, see Kenkyūhan 1988, 53 n. 90.

[17] This text is the same as the *Chuji* cited previously. Its full title is *Taishang laojun zaoli tiandi chuji* (Record of the Beginning of Heaven and Earth as Created by the Highest Venerable Lord). For more details, see appendix 2.

[18] The same quotation is also found in the *Shijia fanzhi* (Record of Śākya; T. 2088; 51.949c). See Kenkyūhan 1988, 53 n. 91.

ever:[19] "Heaven and earth are one hundred million and five thousand [100,005,000] miles apart."

If we now calculate that the Palace of Purple Tenuity is on the five billionth layer of heaven, it comes out several million miles higher than the top of Mount Kunlun.[20]

Now, the heart of the Venerable Lord turned into the Flowery Canopy, his liver became the Palace of the Green Emperor, his spleen changed into Purple Tenuity, while his head became Mount Kunlun. I really do not know what crime the Venerable Lord might have committed that he must hang upside down, with his head below and his liver above.[21]

Could it be that, because of such a twisted position, his vision is upside down as well? Maybe that is why he believes that Chang'an already existed when he went across the pass. Perhaps that is why he thinks that the universe was created under King You of Zhou. How, with such crooked ideas, can one ever expect to transform all beings?

Measurements of Mount Kunlun are also found in the *Huainanzi* (Major 1993, 150–56) and in the *Shizhou ji* 10b–11b (Record of the Ten Continents; *DZ* 589, fasc. 330; *YJQQ* 26; trans. in Smith 1990, 110–14; Smith 1992, 555–59). For a general description of the mountain, see *WSBY* 4.5b (Lagerwey 1981, 75). The relation of Mount Kunlun and Grand Network is described in the *YJQQ*: "The *Dadong yin zhujing* (Annotated Scripture on the Secrets of Great Persuasion) says: 'Above Mount Kunlun, the nine energies came together and formed a wheel around the Jade Sighting Sphere. In the midst of the Great Void, the center of the Dipper is right above Mount Kunlun. Here are the towers of the Heaven of Grand Network, located on the Mountain of Jade Capital'" (21.4b).

The Jade Sighting Sphere is one of the central stars in the Dipper. It is named after an astrological instrument not unlike an armillary sphere. See Needham 1958, 238, 334–39; Schafer 1977. Again, the text emphasizes the cosmic centrality of Kunlun.

[19] The text and citation are unclear. For more on the distance between heaven and earth, see section 9.

[20] Kenkyūhan 1988, 531 n. 94. Traditionally, the Palace of Purple Tenuity is the highest residence of the gods in Mystery Metropolis on the Mountain of Jade Capital. As the *Daomen jingfa* (Scriptural Methods for Taoist Followers; *DZ* 1128, fasc. 762) has it: "The highest heaven of all is called the Heaven of Grand Network. It is on the Mountain of Jade Capital with its Mystery Metropolis. There are the golden towers of [the Palace of] Purple Tenuity with its soaring trees of the Seven Treasures" (1.3ab). This is also where the divine scriptures are stored. See *Duren jing* 1.3b (*DZ* 1, fasc. 1–12). On the layers of heaven, see section 32. For a discussion of Taoist heavens, see Robinet 1984, 1:131–33; on Taoist cosmology, see Lagerwey 1981, 38–48.

[21] Kenkyūhan 1988, 532 n. 96–97. Hanging upside down is an ancient form of punishment mentioned in *Hou Hanshu* (History of the Later Han Dynasty) 39 and applied in Buddhist hells. See *Apitan piposha lun* 56 (Abhidharma-vibhāsā-śāstra; T. 1545; 28.267c). According to Doré, it is applied in the eleventh hell of both the third and the seventh courts (1914–38, 7:270, 288).

2

Fictitious Reign Titles

[144C16] The *Daode jing xujue* (Introductory Explanation to the Scripture of the Tao and the Virtue) says:[1]

"In the first year of the reign period Highest Sovereign,[2] *dingmao,* Laozi descended and became the teacher of Zhou.[3] In the first year of the reign period Nonultimate, *guichou,* he left the Zhou and went to cross the pass."

I laugh at this and say:

In antiquity, emperors and kings did not use reign titles. They were only introduced by Emperor Wu of Han [140–86 B.C.E.] when he named his reign Established Prime [140 B.C.E.].[4] Later rulers followed his example, and the practice has been continued to the present day. [In the light of historical fact,] reign titles like Highest Sovereign are absurd and utterly ridiculous.

---

[1] This is shorter than its counterpart in section three of the *Daode zhenjing xujue* as it has survived in Dunhuang (S. 75, P. 2370; Ōfuchi 1979, 509–11). It reads:

> In the first year of the reign period Highest Sovereign, on the twelfth day of the first month (*bingwu*), with the year star in *dingmao,* Laozi descended and became the teacher of Zhou. When the first year of the reign period Nonultimate was reached, with the year star in *guichou,* on a *renwu* day of the fifth month, he left the Zhou, went west, and crossed the pass. (Takeuchi 1978, 6:221)

The same passage is also cited in the *Xuanyan xinji minglao bu* (Iluminated and Venerable Sections in the New Record of Mysterious Words; P. 2462; Ōfuchi 1979b, 502, lines 13–15) as well as in *SDZN* 8.28b (*DZ* 1139, fasc. 780–81). The latter dates Laozi's departure to the twenty-fifth of the twelfth month.

[2] Kenkyūhan 1988, 536 n. 129. Celestial reign titles originally date events in the heavenly realm at the beginning of the universe. As the *SDZN* explains it, citing the *Erjiao yaolu* (Essential Record of the Two Teachings): "Highest Sovereign, first year, refers to a reign title under the Human Sovereign. It is a period seventeen dynasties before the Zhou. Quite possibly, the Zhou adapted this reign title in imitation of the earlier age. It might also be that they wished to relate themselves to a reign title of heaven" (8.29). The same reign title also occurs as the name of a kalpa. See *Zuigen pin* 1.2a–3a (The Roots of Sin; *DZ* 457, fasc. 202). For more details on kalpas and their cycles, see section 27.

[3] This title is applied to Yu Xiong, the author of a philosophical volume mentioned in the bibliographic section of the *Hanshu* (chap. 30). See Kenkyūhan 1988, 533 n. 103.

[4] Reign titles were only introduced under the Han, but not by Emperor Wu. The first one historically known is "Later Prime" established in 163 B.C.E. by Emperor Wen (Franke 1930, 98). For details on the reign titles used by Emperor Wu, see *Shiji* 12, *Hanshu* 6 as cited in Kenkyūhan 1988, 533 n. 106.

Furthermore, the *Wenshi zhuan* (Biography of Master Wenshi) states:[5] "Ever since the Three Sovereigns, Laozi in every age has been the teacher of the dynasty." In addition, the *Huahu jing* (Scripture of the Conversion of the Barbarians) says:[6] "In the time of King Tang of Shang [1766–65 B.C.E.], he was Xishouzi (Master of Granting Longevity); in the beginning of the Zhou dynasty [1122 B.C.E.], he was Guoshuzi (Master of Regions Adjusted)."[7]

Now, if Laozi really appeared in antiquity, he should be mentioned in official records. Why is he not mentioned anywhere? Why do we only hear of Yi Yin, Fu Yue, Lü Wang and Kang Shao?[8] The chronicles only record that Laozi was a historian under the Zhou.[9] But the Taoists say that he was the teacher of Zhou. An imperial adviser is a secular official, so why do the histories and chronicles not speak of him?

In addition, as for "the first year of Highest Sovereign with the year star in *dingmao*," in more than seven hundred years of the Zhou dynasty, there is no such reign title to be found. According to all histories

[5] This citation is not found in the text as it survives today. On the text, see appendix 2.

[6] Kenkyūhan 1988, 534 n. 111. This passage is contained in the *SDZN* as from the *Huahu jing*: "In the time of King Tang of Shang, he emerged and became the imperial teacher. He was then called Xizezi (Master of Granting Rules). He brought forth the *Daoyuan jing* (Scripture of the Prime of the Tao). In the time of King Wen of the Zhou, he emerged and became the imperial teacher. He was then called Xieyizi (Master of Adjusting the Towns)" (9.7a).

[7] The passage refers to the myth of the transformations of Laozi, according to which he appeared in each generation under a different name. See Yoshioka 1959; Kaltenmark 1969; Seidel 1969; Kusuyama 1979. He served as the "teacher of the dynasty," an especially virtuous and influential minister of state or an imperial adviser. The expression occurs first in *Hanshu* 99 (Kenkyūhan 1988, 534 n. 110).

Laozi's exploits in this role and his various names are found, with variants, in *Laozi bianhua jing* (Scripture of the Transformations of Laozi; S. 2295, Ōfuchi 1979b, 686–88); *Shenxian zhuan* 1 (*Daozang jinghua* 5.11); *Huahu jing* (*SDZN* 9.6b–7b); *Kaitian jing* (*DZ* 1437, fasc. 1059); *Miaomen youqi* (Entrance to the Gate of All Wonders; *DZ* 1125, fasc. 760); *Santian neijie jing* (*DZ* 1205, fasc. 876). The complete list, following the *Santian neijie jing*, is also contained in *Daode zhenjing guangsheng yi* (Wide Sage Meaning of the *Daode jing*; *DZ* 725, fasc. 440–48), *Hunyuan zhenlu* (Perfect Account of Chaos Prime; *DZ* 954, fasc. 604), *Youlong zhuan* (*DZ* 774, fasc. 555), *Hunyuan shengji* (*DZ* 770, fasc. 551–53), *Laozi shilue* (Brief History of Laozi; *DZ* 773, fasc. 554), and *Laojun nianpu* (Chronology of the Venerable Lord; *DZ* 771, fasc. 554).

[8] Yi Yin was the founding minister of the Shang dynasty under King Tang. Fu Yue served the second Shang king, Muding (see Chan 1968). Lü Wang is better known as Taigong wang. He was a master of military strategy and the teacher of the early Zhou kings, whom he helped to defeat the Shang (Allan 1972). Kang Shao was a son of King Wen of Zhou, who greatly helped his father. For Chinese references, see Kenkyūhan 1988, 534 nn. 113–17.

The imperial adviser is an important mythological theme in Confucian historiography. On the early myths, see Allan 1981. for later developments, see Bauer 1956 (on Zhang Liang), Yoshikawa 1990 (on Wang Yuanzhi), Knaul 1981 and Kohn 1990b (on Chen Tuan), and Chan 1968 (on Liu Ji).

[9] Among non-Taoist sources, only the *Zhengyi* (Right Meaning) commentary to the *Liji* (7.16) cites the *Shiji* to the effect that Laozi was a "historian." His biography in *Shiji* 63 has him serve as an "archivist." See Kenkyūhan 1988, 535 n. 118.

and chronicles, Laozi went west across the pass under King Jing [544–519 B.C.E.].[10] Confucius died in the sixteenth year of Duke Ai of Lu [479 B.C.E.], which corresponds to the time of King Jing [519–475 B.C.E.].[11] He was the son of King Jing, who, in turn, was a descendant of King You of more than ten generations. On the one hand, there is the claim that Laozi and Confucius were contemporaries.[12] On the other hand, the *Huahu jing* says that "Laozi went across the pass in the days of King You."[13] I have never heard that Laozi returned again, so how was he able to meet Confucius?

Again, the *Huahu jing* has:[14] "Laozi served as historian of the Zhou for seven hundred years." Calculating the time from the beginning of the Zhou [1122 B.C.E.] to the reign of King You [781–771 B.C.E.], only about three hundred years passed. How could they have gotten it so utterly wrong? Really, the reign title Highest Sovereign must be a Taoist fabrication![15]

In the same vein, the *Lingbao* (Scripture of Numinous Treasure) has Laozi say:[16] "In the first year of Highest Sovereign, halfway through

[10] For the problems surrounding the dating of Laozi's life and emigration, see Kusuyama 1976; Kusuyama 1979, 373–82. The dates given here represent the Buddhist assumption that Laozi was born in 605 B.C.E., that is, 345 years after the nirvāṇa of the Buddha in 950 (see Lai 1986, 67–71). For similar statements in other Buddhist texts, see *Fodao lunheng* (T. 2105; 52.403a) and *Poxie lun* (T. 2109; 52.478b). On the early development of the Laozi legend, see Fung and Bodde 1952, 2:170–77; Kaltenmark 1969; Graham 1990; Seidel 1969b, 1978a, 1978b.

[11] Kenkyūhan 1988, 535 n. 124. This date is based on the biography of Confucius in *Shiji* 47. See also Creel 1949.

[12] Laozi's meeting with Confucius is mentioned in *Shiji* 63 as well as in several passages of the *Zhuangzi* (35/13/45, 38/14/44, 55/21/24, 58/22/28). On the role of this meeting in the Laozi legend, see Graham 1990.

[13] As cited in *SDZN* 9.14b.

[14] This is an interpretation of what the *Huahu jing* actually says. It has:

In the time of King Wu, he emerged and became the imperial teacher. He was then called Guoshuzi (Master of Adjusting the Regions). He was also called Xuchengzi (Master of Continued Perfection). He served as historian.

In the time of King You, he emerged and became the imperial teacher. He was then called Tianlao (Old Man from Heaven). He was also called Laozi (Old Master). He served as historian. (*SDZN* 9.7b)

[15] The title Highest Sovereign occurs first in the *Zhuangzi:* "The ruler will shine mirrorlike over the earth below, and the world will bear him up. He may be called the Highest Sovereign" (36/14/5; Watson 1968a, 154–55).

[16] Kenkyūhan 1988, 536 n. 131. This passage is found in a different version in the *Zuigen pin,* a Lingbao scripture in the Taoist canon (*DZ* 457, fasc. 202).

The Heavenly Venerable said: " . . . By the time of Highest Sovereign, people's minds gradually became more decadent. I feared that, because of this development, the true teaching might no longer be complete. Thus, I wandered around many countries and distributed heavenly scriptures in many places. I made people join the divine law and perfect it in their minds. When the kalpa was half over, I allowed for a gradual decline. People's life spans were then reduced to a mere eighteen thousand years." (1.3a)

the kalpa, I saved humanity. Human beings then lived for eighteen thousand years."[17] Now, how could he see beyond half a kalpa into the future and know already what reign title would be used then? This is truly ridiculous.

Reign titles such as Highest Sovereign and Nonultimate are uninformed and specious. Authors probably wanted to give their work a divine touch and thus added reign titles and specific dates, hoping that some believers would accept them.

Again, let us look the statement that "Laozi came to be the teacher of the dynasty in every age." Ge Hong, in the introduction to his *Shenxian zhuan* (Biographies of Spirit Immortals), already finds it strange.[18] If Laozi had appeared in the world as a sage, his foremost concern would have been the establishment and preservation of peace. Yet King Jie of Xia was a cruel tyrant who oppressed the people, whereas Kings Tang and Wuding of Shang sought worthy men as if they were dying of thirst.[19] Why, then, did Laozi not become the helper of these wise monarchs or the teacher of the cruel ruler?

Instead, all he ever did was to cultivate his person, nourish his inner nature, and preserve himself.[20] When he was about to reach a hundred years of age, he knew that he would die soon.[21] Thus, he left the country incognito via the western pass. Only when directly ordered by Yin Xi did he transmit [the *Daode jing*]. He himself did not care to pass it on to others. He died on the pass where his tumulus can still be found. Qin Shi went to mourn him, cried three times and left again.[22]

---

[17] A similar idea of declining life spans is also found in Buddhism. According to the *Dīghanikāya*, people will live as long as eighty thousand years when Maitreya lives on earth. See Lamotte 1958, 777.

[18] Kenkyūhan 1988, 537 n. 141. In his biography of Laozi, Ge Hong explains his position,

For my part, I think that if Laozi was a spiritual being of celestial origin, he should indeed have appeared in some form in each successive generation, exchanging his honorable rank for a humble condition, sacrificing his ease and freedom to subject himself to toil. . . . Most certainly, the arts of the Tao have existed ever since there were heaven and earth. . . . They were there in every generation—yet why should they all have been only forms of [the single figure] Laozi? (*Shenxian zhuan* 1; see Kohn, forthcoming a)

[19] These rulers are among the classical examples for the tyrannical and depraved last ruler as opposed to the virtuous founder of a new dynasty. For a detailed mythological analysis of this traditional theme, see Allan 1981. For Chinese references, see Kenkyūhan 1988, 537 n. 144.

[20] All these are expressions for Taoist self-cultivation, which includes methods such as gymnastics, breathing, meditations, and so on. See Kohn 1989a; Sakade 1988.

[21] "A hundred years of age" is referred to by the expression "chin period." This goes back to an ancient physiognomic method, according to which every part of the face corresponds to a particular period of one's life. See Hou 1979; Kohn 1988.

[22] Kenkyūhan 1988, 538 n. 153. The location of Laozi's tomb is reported in *Shuijing zhu* (Annotated River Classic) 19. The story about Qin Shi is contained in the *Zhuangzi* (8/3/14–15;

Studying the chronicles and scriptures, all works of later people are mere foolish talk. They claim to honor and elevate the Tao, yet in fact they only disgrace it.

Watson 1968, 52). Both pieces of information have been variously used in anti-Taoist polemics. See *Erjiao lun* 5 (T. 2103; 52.139a) and *BZL* 5 (T. 2110; 52.522c).

3

Primordial Energy Turned into Heavenly Beings

[145a18] The *Taishang sanyuan pin* (Highest Precepts of the Three Primes) says:[1]

"The heavenly office of the first rank of Highest Prime. When primordial energy[2] first coagulated and the three luminants [sun, moon, stars] began to shine, the green and yellow [and white] energies[3] combined and established the three offices of Highest Prime.[4]

"The first among them is called the Palace of Purple Tenuity of Primal Yang and Sevenfold Treasure in Mystery Metropolis. It is the green

[1] Kenkyūhan 1988, 539 n. 160. This passage is almost identical with *Sanyuan pin* 1.1a (*DZ* 456, fasc. 202). Only the last sentence is not found here.

[2] According to Taoist cosmogony, primordial energy is the first material form of the Tao, the initial bridge between the Tao as the Great Ultimate (see Robinet 1990) or the One (see Kohn 1989b) and the development of the universe. It is the ground of all life—breath, lifeforce, pneuma, vitality, and so on. See Porkert 1961, 1974; Onozawa 1978; Ishida 1987, 1989; Engelhardt 1987; Sivin 1988.

[3] Kenkyūhan 1988, 540 n. 163. The green, yellow, and white energies are the three basic energies of the cosmos, mysterious, primordial, and beginning. See *Daomen jingfa* 1.16b (*DZ* 1128, fasc. 762); *Santian zhengfa jing* 1b (*DZ* 1203, fasc. 876).

[4] The Three Primes are

First, the prime of the great nonbeing of Coagulated Pervasion; second, the prime of the great nonbeing of Red Chaos; third, the prime of the mysterious thoroughfare of Dark Obscurity. From the first, the prime of the great non-being of Coagulated Pervasion, developed the Lord of Heavenly Treasure. From the second, the prime of the great non-being of Red Chaos, developed the Lord of Numinous Treasure. From the third, the prime of the mysterious thoroughfare of Dark Obscurity, developed the Lord of Spirit Treasure. In the traces of great overall pervasion, these were transformed into separate entities. They rule the Three Clarity Heavens. (*Daojiao sandong zongyuan*, *YJQQ* 3.4b–5a; Kohn 1993a, 66)

See also *Jiutian shengshen zhangjing* 1ab (Stanzas of the Vital Spirit of the Nine Heavens; *DZ* 318, fasc. 165; *WSBY* 24.1ab). For a discussion of the historical development of Taoist heavens, see Miura 1983; Kobayashi 1990, 482–510; Miyakawa 1991.

primordial energy of beginning yang. It rules absolutely over the spontaneity of highest perfection, the highest sovereigns of Numinous Treasure of the jade palace, and the emperors and kings of all the heavens and all the great gods of superior sageness. This palace consists of 555,555 billion layers of green yang energy.

"All the spirit immortals, government officials, and heavenly beings here are ranked in as many layers.[5] They were all formed from spontaneous green primordial energy.

"The layers and inhabitants of all the Nine Palaces are just like those of Purple Tenuity."[6]

I laugh at this and say:

The *Santian zhengfa jing* (Scripture of the Proper Law of the Three Heavens) has:[7] "The radiance of heaven was not yet bright, the thick accumulation was not yet clear. After more than seven thousand kalpas,

---

[5] For more on the organization and structure of the celestial administration, see section 11.

[6] These are the three palaces of each of the Three Primes, not to be confused with the nine palaces in the head (Homann 1971; Robinet 1979; Miyazawa 1986; Yamada 1989a; Kohn 1991b) or with the nine palaces in the stars (see Gu 1936, 139–51; Gu 1963, VII, 2:189–203; Kalinowski 1985). They are, in particular:

Highest Prime
  1. Purple Tenuity (green energy)
  2. Left Palace of the Great Ultimate (yellow)
  3. Right Palace of the Great Ultimate (white)

Middle Prime
  4. Palace of Clear Numinosity
  5. Palace of Southern Pervasive Yang
  6. Palace of the Northern Hill

Lower Prime
  7. Palace of Pervading Source
  8. Palace of Clear Iciness
  9. Palace of Fengdu in the North (*Sanyuan pin*, DZ 456, fasc. 202; Kenkyūhan 1988, 540 n. 167)

On the ninefold division of Chinese cosmology, see Maspero 1924; on the nine continents on earth, see Major 1978, 1984. For details on the original ninefold division of the Shang cosmos, see Allan 1991.

[7] Kenkyūhan 1988, 540 n. 168. This version is shorter than its counterpart in *Santian zhengfa jing* 1ab (*DZ* 1023, fasc. 876; *YJQQ* 21. 1ab). The first part of the passage is translated in 1 n. 10 above. The last paragraph in the Taoist canon is divided into text and commentary:

Duly there were the emperors of the nine perfections. NOTE: Lord Green Lad says, "The nine perfections are the pure energies of the nine heavens. They coagulated and formed the positions of the nine palaces." . . .
Once the names of the three heavens had become clear, the Ladies of the Three Primes were brought forth from their energy. Heaven was their father; energy was their mother. Thus, they are called the three goddesses of Great Simplicity. They each took energy of spontaneity and became with child. Three gods were duly born to the three goddesses, who were all properly named with women's names. . . . NOTE: There were three thousand

darkness and light first divided and nine energies arose.[8] Each energy was separated from the next by 99,999 miles.

"The clear energy rose up and was pure; the turbid chaos sank down and descended. The Perfected King of the Nine Heavens and the Heavenly King of Primordial Beginning were brought forth in the midst of the nine energies. The energies coagulated and gave them form.

"Duly there were the Emperors of the Nine Perfections. They all coagulated from the pure energies of the Nine Heavens and were established in the positions of the Nine Palaces. Then the Ladies of the Three Primes were brought forth from pure energy to reside in the Cavern Chamber. Three thousand jade lads and three thousand jade maidens waited upon them. Heaven was their father; energy was their mother. They were born to the Lords of the Three Primes."

Again, the *Lingbao zuigen pin* (The Numinous Treasure Scripture on the Roots of Sin) has:[9]

"The Highest Lord of the Tao paid obeisance to the heavenly Venerable of Primordial Beginning and asked him about the ten good deeds and other aspects of the divine law.[10] Thereupon the Heavenly Venerable summoned the spirit immortals to speak on karma and retribution. People as numerous as the sands of the Ganges have obtained the Tao and proceeded to become *tathāgata*s. But those who have not yet reached there are also as numerous as the sands of the Ganges."[11]

---

jade lads of golden morning light and three thousand jade maidens of western fluorescence. They waited upon the goddesses of the Three Primes in the palace of the Cavern Chamber. (1b)

On the gods of the Cavern Chamber and their role in Taoist meditation, see Yamada 1989b.

[8] The nine energies develop through the triplication of each of the original three energies: mysterious, beginning, and primordial. See *DJYS* 7.5b (Kenkyūhan 1988, 541 n. 172).

[9] Kenkyūhan 1988, 541 n. 176. This passage appears in various separate sentences in *Zuigen pin* 1.1a, 1.2a, and 2.1a (*DZ* 457, fasc. 202). The text explains that the Heavenly Venerable had to take different measures to help living beings to salvation as kalpas declined.

[10] The ten good deeds consist of avoiding the ten evil ways: killing, stealing, sexual misconduct, lying, speaking double-tongued, slander, ornamented speech, craving, ill-will, false views. See Mochizuki 1933–36, 2284b; Hurvitz 1962, 342; Bokenkamp 1989. In Buddhism they are detailed in *Mohe zhiguan* (Great Treatise of Śamatha-Vipaśyanā; T. 1911; 46.36a); in Taoism, in *DJYS* 3.6a.

The *Zuigen pin* has a list of its own. Here, Taoists should guard the life of all beings, help the sick, support those in need, serve their teacher properly, pay obeisance to the scriptures, maintain the fasts, be withdrawing and yielding, teach the ignorant, spread the teaching, and always remain within the rules of the teaching (1.4ab). For more on Taoist precepts, see Yoshioka 1961; Kusuyama 1982, 1983; Kohn 1994.

[11] Kenkyūhan 1988, 542 n. 177. The metaphor of the sands of the Ganges indicating the countless number of bodhisattvas, believers, or stūpas, is common in Buddhist sūtras. See, for example, *Miaofa hualian jing* (Saddharmapuṇḍarīka sūtra; T. 262; 9.2b, 3a). hereafter cited as *Lotus Sūtra*. See also Murano 1974, 6, 10, 17.

Moreover, the *Yuanshi zhuan* (Biography of Master Yuanshi) states:[12] "The heavenly halls lie opposite the earthly prisons. The good ascend into heaven; the bad enter the earth."[13]

If we take these accounts into consideration, the above description cannot be true. Why is that? The text says that the Heavenly King of Primordial Beginning, the Highest Lord of the Tao, and all the divinities of the heavens originally developed through the coagulation of spontaneous and pure primordial energy. They did not attain [their heavenly state] by cultivating themselves and obeying the precepts. If they themselves did not originally follow the precepts to attain their heavenly state, how can they order us to perform good deeds and thereby hope to find attainment?

Again, the *Duren benxing jing* (Scripture of the Original Endeavor and Universal Salvation) says:[14] "The Highest Lord of the Tao said: 'I have saved innumerable people through countless kalpas. Because of this karmic merit, the Heavenly Venerable of Primordial Beginning bestowed the title "Highest" upon me'."

Following this, some doubts arise. For example, the *Youwu shengcheng pin* (Chapter on Being and Nonbeing, Birth and Completion) has:[15] "Emptiness is the mother of the myriad beings; the Tao is their father."[16]

This means that the Tao was there first, then the myriad beings emerged. Consequently, this Tao that is the father of all beings is not something created by living beings. Given this, the Tao is there anyway. So why should all beings cultivate goodness in order to attain it?

Moreover, [the texts say that] the Tao gave birth to the myriad beings.[17] When beings were first born, that was the beginning of all. Therefore, when "I" first emerged, there could be neither impurity nor defilement. How, then, can there be six ways of sentient existence, four forms of rebirth, and the differences between suffering and bliss?[18] It really makes no sense!

[12] This citation is unclear. The text may be identical with the *Wenshi zhuan*. See appendix 2.

[13] Kenkyūhan 1988, 542 n. 179. The juxtaposition of the heavenly halls and the earthly prisons is first found in Xi Chao's *Fengfa yao* (Essentials in Worshiping the Dharma; T. 2102; 52.86c). For this, see Zürcher 1959, 164–76; Ch'en 1963; Tsukamoto and Hurvitz 1985, 1010–28.

[14] Kenkyūhan 1988, 542 n. 182. This passage is shorter than the version in the *Duren benxing jing* as it survives in P. 3022 (Ōfuchi 1979b, 54–55), *YJQQ* 101.2a–3a, *BZL* 8 (T. 2110; 52.543a). For a translation of the full passage, see section 27.

[15] The text and citation are unclear.

[16] More common is the idea of the Tao as the mother of all creation (*Daode jing* 1) or of heaven and earth in this role (*Zhuangzi* 48/19/6).

[17] Such a statement is first found in *Daode jing* 42.

[18] The six ways of rebirth are hell, hungry ghosts, giants, animals, humanity, and gods

They say, also, that all beings are naturally endowed with spirit and consciousness yet claim that these were not created by the Tao. Still, the Tao had already brought forth the myriad beings. Could it be that spirit and consciousness are not beings? It is all quite absurd!

(Mochizuki 1933–36, 5071c). The four forms of sentient existence are those born from womb, egg, water, and by transformation (Mochizuki 1933–36, 1842b).

4

Humanity Was Created from Earth

[145b24] The *Santian zhengfa jing* says:[1]

"When the nine energies divided, the Heavenly Kings of the Nine Perfections, the Divine Ladies and Lords of the Three Primes, and the Highest Lord of the Tao took shape.

"When the age of the Sovereign Emperor arrived,[2] humankind was first created. The Sovereign Emperor formed images from earth in vast wilderness.[3]

---

[1] Kenkyūhan 1988, 543 n. 193. This passage appears somewhat altered in the *Santian zhengfa jing* today (*DZ* 1203, fasc. 876).

When the age of the Yellow Emperor arrived, humankind was first created. NOTE: People living in the later age first developed under the Yellow Emperor. The Yellow Emperor formed images from earth and set them into the vast wilderness. Over three hundred years the five colors kept on transforming. Then they could speak and form words. Each was placed in one direction. Thus, there are the different groups of Tibetans and Chinese, of northern and southern barbarians. The five families, joined in virtue, are therefore patterned on pure spontaneity. They received the energy of highest perfection and only thus became human. (2a)

[2] The *DZ* here has "Yellow Emperor." According to Yang (1963), both expressions, *huangdi* and Huangdi, were commonly exchanged. According to Allan, the "Yellow Lord" was originally the ruler of the netherworld and quite distinct from the ruler of humanity (1991, 64–67). For more on the Yellow Emperor, see Yasui 1958; Yü 1964; Lewis 1990; Yuan 1960, 98–140; Yuan 1979b, 101–27; Yuan 1979a, 64; Yuan 1984, 164; Yuan 1985, 347; Liu 1988, 673–731; Tetsui 1990, 326–78.

[3] Kenkyūhan 1988, 543 n. 192. This is an adaptation of the classical Chinese myth according to which Nügua shaped human figures from earth. As the *Fengsu tongyi* (General Account of Popular Customs) has it,

When heaven and earth first split open, there were not yet any human beings. Then Nügua molded yellow earth and made human beings; she exerted herself in the great effort and did not rest in her toils. Then she pulled a thread through variegated mud, making human beings from that, too. As a result, all those wealthy and noble were originally made from

"After three years, they could speak.[4] Each was placed in one direction. Thus, there are the different groups of Tibetans and Chinese, of northern and southern barbarians.[5]

"Then the five emotions were harmonized in virtue, and the five laws were followed naturally.[6] People received the energy of highest perfection and only thus became human.

I laugh at this and say:

The *Sanyuan pin* has:[7] "The karmic retribution of good and evil comes from one's very own self."

In addition, the *Yuanshi zhuan* states:[8] "When one commits debauchery, robbery, or unfilial acts, one will go to the earthly prisons after

---

yellow earth. All those poor and humble were originally made from variegated mud. (*TPYL* 78.5a)

The same story, in a Taoist version, is found in *Shengxuan jing* 8 (Scripture of Ascension to the Mystery):

Emerging from the darkness and entering obscurity, the Tao moved along with all without bent. Thus, it created heaven and earth, brought forth the various gods, set up the five phases, the sun, the moon, and the chronograms. It divided yin and yang and established the distinction between winter and spring. Concluding all, it set up continents and countries. Then it molded the earth and formed human beings, patterning them on heaven and earth and establishing rulers and vassels among them. (P. 2474; Ōfuchi 1979b, 264)

On the classical myth of Nügua, see Eberhard 1942a, 279; Karlgren 1946; Yuan 1954, 25; Yuan 1960, 54; Yuan 1979b, 16–41; Yuan 1979a, 23; Yuan 1984, 103–10; Yuan 1985, 46; Liu 1988, 500–509; Tetsui 1990, 366–78. For an interpretation of this figure in relation to other goddesses and dragon ladies, see Schafer 1973; Chan 1990.

[4] According to the *DZ*, this took three hundred years.

[5] According to *Kaitian jing* 2ab (*DZ* 1437, fasc. 1059), the Venerable Lord created humanity by mixing the energies of heaven and earth. The *Santian neijie jing* (*DZ* 1205, fasc. 876), in addition, has him place people in different sections of the world. "The Venerable Lord then harmonized the three energies [of heaven, earth, and water] and formed the nine countries. In each country he placed nine people, three men and six women" (1.2b). The *WSBY* (50.9b) also records forms of the Venerable Lord appearing in the various directions (Kenkyūhan 1988, 544 n. 198).

[6] The five emotions are anger, joy, worry, sadness, and fear, corresponding to the five inner organs of Chinese medicine. See *Huandi neijing taisu* 2.4; Porkert 1974, 117–52. In the context of Buddhism, see Mochizuki 1933–36, 1178b. The five laws are the five Confucian virtues: benevolence, righteousness, ritual propriety, wisdom, and faithfulness. See *Dadai liji* 66 (8.5a). The *DZ* version replaces "five emotions" with "five families." See the translation in note 1, this section. For more Chinese references, see Kenkyūhan 1988, 544 nn. 199–200.

[7] Kenkyūhan 1988, 544 n. 202. This passage corresponds to a section of the *Sanyuan pin* (*DZ* 456, fasc. 202) that introduces a series of scriptural statements on one's karmic responsibility. "Good and evil each have their karmic retribution; the sin or fortune of life and death all have their roots of destiny. Like this, there is always the proper reward; the karmic retribution of good and evil in all cases goes back to one's very own self" (32b).

[8] The source of this citation is not clear. The title *Yuanshi zhuan* usually refers to the *Wenshi zhuan*. Similar punishments are mentioned in *Shier shangpin quanjie* 5b, 6a, 9b (Twelve High-level Precepts, *DZ* 182, fasc. 77).

death. One will be punished with the five kinds of suffering and put in the eight difficult conditions.[9] Later one will be reborn as one of the six domestic animals or among barbarians on the fringes."[10]

Taking these words into account, the contradictions are simply too much! For example, from the day the Sovereign Emperor molded the images from earth it took three years and the infusion of the energy of highest perfection, and only then the figures could speak.

Now, this energy of highest clarity comes from the same source as the Highest Lord himself. The text states that formerly there was neither good nor evil. But then—how did good and evil enter into the earth images, so they would fall into the eight difficult conditions and be turned into barbarians?

Moreover, there was no karmic cause when the earth was first molded. Therefore, I ask: Why, after their completion, was there the distinction between the center and the fringes [Chinese and barbarians]?[11]

[9] Kenkyūhan 1988, 545 n. 206. These are Buddhist concepts. The five sufferings are (1) birth, old age, sickness, death; (2) parting from one's beloved; (3) meeting with the disliked; (4) inability to obtain the desired; (5) the sufferings caused by the five skandhas (Mochizuki 1933–36, 1132a).

The eight difficult conditions are situations in which it is difficult to meet a buddha or hear of the dharma: in the earth prisons, as an animal, in the northern continent, in the heavens of longevity, when deaf, when blind, when dumb, when a philosopher of the world between one buddha and the next. See *Zengyi ahanjing* 36 (Ekottarāgama; T. 125, 2.747ab); Mochizuki 1933–36, 4221c. In Taoism, these are changed and integrated into the concepts of rebirth and hell. The *Santu wuku jing* (Scripture of the Three Bad Rebirths and Five Sufferings; *DZ* 455, fasc. 202) has,

The five sufferings [in the deepest hells] are

    1. the mountain of knives;
    2. the tree of swords;
    3. the hot iron pillar;
    4. the boiling caudron;
    5. the endless pool with deep waves;

These are the five sufferings.

The eight difficult conditions [to attain] are

    1. to attain life as a human being;
    2. to leave womanhood behind and become a man;
    3. to have a whole and healthy body;
    4. to attain life in the Middle Kingdom;
    5. to have access to a Taoist lord or father;
    6. to be endowed with grace and benevolence;
    7. to live in a state that has Great Peace;
    8. to encounter the Three Treasures. (4a)

[10] Kenkyūhan 1988, 544 n. 207. The six domestic animals are horse, ox, sheep, chicken, dog, and pig. See *Zuozhuan,* Zhao 25, commentary. To be born among the barbarians on the fringes means that there is no dharma one can hear. See *Chuyao jing* (Dharmapada; T. 609; 4.653a).

[11] The worldview that the center is the most blessed of all places, whereas the fringes are barbaric and abandoned, is part of the universal symbolism of the center (Eliade 1961, 27–56).

In addition, that energy of highest perfection—Was it stupid or was it smart? If it was stupid, it could not have endowed earth with the ability to speak. If it was smart, it should have known about the five kinds of suffering and the eight difficult conditions. Why, then, did it not let people enjoy goodness and happiness but desired to make their lives full of suffering and difficulties?

Considering all these contradictory statements, I cannot but laugh out loud!

In the Chinese worldview, it is explicit in ancient cosmology, which placed China in the center of the world (Major 1984). In Buddhist doctrine, too, the Buddha is born in the very center of "the three thousand suns and moons, the twelve thousand galaxies" of the universe (*Taizi ruiying benqi jing*; T. 185; 3.473b). On Buddhist cosmology, see Beal 1871, 100–25; Lamotte 1958, 759–61. The question about the karmic cause for the creation of humanity echoes the "Heavenly Questions" chapter of the *Chuci*: "Nügua had a body. Who fashioned it?" (Hawkes 1959, 51).

5

Five Buddhas Appear Simultaneously

[145c11] The *Wenshi zhuan* says:[1]

"In the first year of the reign period Highest Sovereign, Laozi descended and became the teacher of Zhou. In the first year of Nonultimate, he climbed into a flat wagon drawn by a black ox and crossed the pass.[2]

"There he recited the Text in Five Thousand Words for Yin Xi. He told him: 'I wander freely between heaven and earth. But you have not yet realized the Tao and so cannot follow me. First, you must recite these five thousand words ten thousand times. Then your ears will gain

---

[1] This comprises the basic story of the conversion as it is told in the *Wenshi zhuan* (*SDZN* 9.8b–14b; *DZ* 1139, fasc. 780–82). The passage does not include any dialogue and marginal episodes, such as the incident with Xu Jia, Laozi's retainer, the reunion in Chengdu, and the banquets with the barbarian king. The first two sentences are also cited in section 2. For another translation, see Zürcher 1959, 300, 302. According to Zürcher, a very similar narrative, cited from the *Huahu jing* in *BZL* 5 (T. 2110; 52.535a), constitutes one of two remaining passages of the original fourth-century conversion scripture (1959, 298).

[2] See *SDZN* 9.10a. The standard hagiography has Laozi ride to the pass on a black ox, a motif frequently found in pictures of the sage. See 1 n. 3.

pervasive hearing; your eyes will develop penetrating sight.[3] Your body will be able to fly,[4] and you will attain the six supernatural powers[5] and four attainments.'[6]

"They agreed to meet again in Chengdu. Yin Xi followed Laozi's instructions and attained the powers. Then he went to Chengdu to meet Laozi, and together they went to Mount Dantaloka in Kashmir.[7]

"Later the local king tried to kill Laozi by burning him in fire and drowning him in water. But Laozi remained seated in the lotus posture and continuously recited his scripture. Thereupon, the king pleaded for mercy and deeply regretted his error.

"Laozi chose Yin Xi to be the barbarians' teacher. He told the king, 'This teacher of mine is called Buddha. Through him you can served the Highest Tao.'[8]

"The king was converted, and all men and women of his kingdom cut their hair and abstained from marriage.

"Thus, the Highest Tao used the majestic divinity of the Buddha and made Yin Xi the Buddha of Kashmir. He was, thenceforth, known as the Learned Youth of Sparkling Light.'[9]

---

[3] Kenkyūhan 1988, 547 n. 222–23. "Pervasive hearing" is mentioned as one of the skills of the sage in *Lunheng* 26.1a (Balanced Discussions) (trans. in Forke 1907). "Penetrating insight" occurs in *Baopuzi* 2/4/9 (trans. in Ware 1966).

[4] Kenkyūhan 1988, 547 n. 224. See *Liexian zhuan* 6 (Kaltenmark 1953, 53) and *Baopuzi* 19/98/5 on this art of the immortals. For other classical immortals' techniques, see Robinet 1979b, 1986. The Buddha, too, is said to be able to fly. See *Mouzi lihuo lun* (T. 2102; 52.4c–5a); *Mingfo lun* 2 (To Clarify Buddhism; T. 2102; 52.12b).

[5] The powers of a Buddha in the fourth *dhyāna*: (1) universal vision; (2) universal hearing; (3) knowledge of other minds; (4) seeing former lives; (5) multilocation; (6) knowing the end of vicious propensities (Mochizuki 1933–36, 5060a). See also *Yudao lun* 3 (To Illustrate the Way; T. 2102; 52.17c); *Huayan jing* 40 (Avataṁsaka Sūtra; T. 278; 9.655a); *Dafang guangfo huayan jing* 57 (Buddha Avataṁsaka Sūtra; T. 279; 10.300b) as cited in Kenkyūhan 1988, 547 n. 225.

[6] These are the powers of the spirit as described in the *Zhuangzi:* "Pure spirit reaches in the four directions, flows now this way and that; there is no place it does not extend to. Above, it brushes heaven; below, it coils on the earth. It transforms and nurses the myriad beings, but no one can make out its form" (40/15/18; Watson 1968a, 169). According to Zürcher, the expression is a mistake for "three attainments," that is, the three kinds of wisdom a Buddha attains upon enlightenment (1959, 435 n. 55).

[7] Kenkyūhan 1988, 547 n. 226. The name of the mountain is not mentioned in the *Wenshi zhuan*. It is originally the place where Prince Sudana went to practice the Buddhist teaching. See *Da Tang xiyu ji* 2 (Record of Western Regions of the Great Tang Dynasty).

[8] The *Wenshi zhuan* has, "At that time, he selected Yin Xi to be their teacher and ordered the king and all the people of his land to serve him" (*SDZN* 9.14a).

[9] Kenkyūhan 1988, 549 n. 235. The Youth of Sparkling Light is a disciple of the Buddha. See *Erjiao lun* 8 (T. 2103; 52.140a); *Poxie lun* 1 (T. 2109; 52.478c). The identification recalls the counter*huahu* theory with its linking of Yan Hui and the bodhisattva of Radiating Purity, discussed in the Introduction.

I laugh at this and say:

The *Guangshuo pin* (Chapter of Broad Explanations) has,[10] "When the King of [the country of] Original Longevity first heard the Heavenly Venerable expound the Law, he at once became a stream enterer[11] together with his wife and children.[12] When the King of [the country of] Pure Harmony heard of this, he at once took his courtiers and subjects and went to the palace of the Heavenly Venerable. All together they ascended to heaven in broad daylight.[13]

"The king then became the chief of the Brahma Heavens[14] and was given the title Preceptor of Mysterious Center.[15] His wife, who had also listened to the law and ascended with him, became the ruler of the Wondrous Brahma Heaven.[16] Later, she was reborn in Kashmir as King Puṇḍarīka, a cruel and violent ruler who was entirely without the Tao.

"The Preceptor of Mysterious Center thereupon descended to save the cruel king. By transformation he entered the womb of Mother Li. After eighty-one years, he split open her left armpit and was born, having white hair.[17] Three months later, he rode on a white deer[18] and, together with Yin Xi, went west to live in seclusion on Mount Dantaloka.

"Three years later, King Puṇḍarīka came across them when hunting

---

[10] Citation unclear. For an earlier translation, see Zürcher 1959, 300.

[11] *Srota-āpanna*, the first stage of Buddhahood. Mochizuki 1933–36, 2485a.

[12] Kenkyūhan 1988, 549 n. 237. This story is found in the *Hunyuan shengji* (DZ 770, fasc. 551–53), recording Laozi's deeds in the kalpa Dragon Country, before the time of the Three Sovereigns. "The King of [the country of] Original Longevity practiced the Tao together with his wife, children, and subjects. Altogether they were over five thousand people. They all became earth immortals" (2.12b).

[13] This is the most desirable form of ascension to immortality in Taoism. See Kohn 1990b.

[14] In Taoist cosmology, these are four heavens reserved for true believers, located beneath the Three Clarities and above the Three Worlds (*YJQQ* 3.6b; Kohn 1993a, 69). On the Brahma heavens in their original Buddhist setting, see *Jinglü yixiang* 1 (The Extraordinary World of Sūtras and Rules; T. 2121; 53.3a) as cited in Kenkyūhan 1988, 549 n. 240.

[15] This is Laozi's name in the era of the Three Sovereigns. See *Shenxian zhuan* 1; *Hunyuan shengji* 2.13a, cited in Kenkyūhan 1988, 550 n. 241.

[16] According to the *Hunyuan shengji*, the king himself became the ruler of this heaven. He was later banished to India and converted by Laozi to become the Buddha (2.12a).

[17] This follows the standard Laozi hagiography with the variant of seventy-two years of pregnancy. See Kusuyama 1979; Kohn 1989c, 69–71. See 2 n. 6 for documentation. For Chinese references, see Kenkyūhan 1988, 550 n. 245.

[18] Kenkyūhan 1988, 550 n. 246. The white deer is first mentioned as Laozi's animal in the *Laozi bianhua jing* (see Seidel 1969b, 68). The *Shuijing zhu* (chap. 19) cites the *Shenxian zhuan* as saying that Laozi ascended to heaven on a cloud carriage drawn by white deer. The same is also recorded in the *Yongcheng jixian lu* 1.8b (Record of the Assembled Immortals in the Heavenly Walled City; DZ 783, fasc. 560–61; Kohn 1989c, 103).

in that region. He tried to kill them by burning and drowning. But Laozi did not die. The king thereupon submitted to him, shaved his head, and took the monk's robe. He accepted the surname Shi [Śākya], the personal name Dharma [Teaching], and the sobriquet Śramaṇa [Monk]. He attained the fruits of Buddhahood and became the Buddha Śākyamuni. In the Han dynasty, his teaching spread east and reached the country of Qin [China]."

In addition, the *Wenshi zhuan* says,[19] "When Laozi converted the barbarians, he chose Yin Xi for their teacher, and thus effected a successful conversion."

The *Xiaobing jing* (Scripture of Melting Ice), however, has,[20] "Yin Xi chose Laozi as their teacher."

Yet the *Wenshi zhuan,* as cited previously, states: "This teacher of mine is called Buddha. Through him you can serve the Highest Tao." And, "Thus, the Highest Tao used the majestic divinity of the Buddha and made Yin Xi the Buddha [of Kashmir]."

Taking all these statements together, there is enormous confusion over the question who is master, who disciple. How could any serious teaching be found in them?

The *Huahu jing* and the *Xiaobing jing* both claim that Laozi, when he converted Kashmir, personally became the Buddha.[21] The *Guangshuo pin,* on the contrary, describes King Puṇḍarīka as Laozi's wife. This person then attained the Tao and was called Buddha Śākyamuni; her teaching was later transmitted to China under the Qin and Han.

Now, the *Xuanmiao pian* (Record of Mystery and Wonder) states:[22] "Laozi crossed the pass and went to the country of Kapilavastu in India. There he entered the mouth of Queen Māyā. On the eighth day of the fourth month of the following year, he split open her left armpit and emerged. Raising his hands, he exclaimed, 'In heaven above, on

---

[19] This is found in the *Wenshi zhuan* as cited in *SDZN* 9.14a.

[20] The text *Xiaobing jing* has not been identified. The citation is found in the *Wenshi zhuan.*

[21] On this reference and the related problems of who became the Buddha when and where, see Zürcher 1959, 302.

[22] Kenkyūhan 1988, 551 n. 256. For details on this text, see appendix 2. The birth story here is based on the birth of the Buddha as recorded in the *Taizi ruiying benqi jing.* "On the eighth day of the fourth month, at night when the stars were just beginning to shine, the bodhisattva emerged from his mother's right hip. Scarcely having touched the ground, he walked seven steps, raised his hands to his face and exclaimed: 'The chief I am above and under heaven. The Three Worlds are nothing but pain; what is there enjoyable?'" (T. 185; 3.437b). For a comparison between the two passages, see Zürcher 1959, 433 n. 68. A recent study of the life of the Buddha is found in Karetzky 1992.

the earth below, I alone am venerable. The Three Worlds are nothing but pain. How could one take pleasure in it?'"

Taking all this evidence together, I find that in the single country of Kashmir five Buddhas appeared simultaneously:

1. Yin Xi, also known as the Learned Youth of Sparkling Light;
2. Laozi who converted Kashmir;
3. Laozi's wife, King Puṇḍarīka, later the Buddha Śākyamuni;
4. Laozi as the Buddha in Kapilavastu, also called Śākyamuni;
5. Prince Siddhārta, son of King Śuddhodana, also called Śākyamuni.

According to the *Wenshi zhuan*,[23] "in five hundred years there is only one wise man; in one thousand years, there is only one sage." But here we have five Buddhas appearing all at the same time. Is this not a nuisance?

One may now say that a sage can multiply his body to save and transform living beings. But such a sage by necessity would leave behind various different doctrines and scriptures. How is it that Laozi's transformations were so numerous, whereas his writings consist of a mere two scrolls that never changed?

In addition, to the present day, I have never heard of any Buddhist sūtra originating from the Learned Youth, Yin Xi, or King Puṇḍarīka. There is only the teaching of King Śuddhodana's son.

If we base our analysis on this, the falsehood of all these reports on Laozi and Yin Xi becoming the Buddha is quite evident. At the same time, the claim that other scriptures of Laozi were transmitted secretly and have never been accessible to the public contradicts the known facts and is entirely far-fetched.[24]

But then, if Laozi really could become the Buddha, they are, in fact, one and the same person. Yet Taoists are so terribly deluded that they do not even know how to worship him as the Buddha! If the father is a Taoist and the son is a Taoist, too, how is it that the son cannot recognize his own father?[25]

---

[23] Citation unclear. The notion that great sages appear only rarely is found in *Mengzi* (Writings of Mencius) 2B.13; *Shangshu kao lingyao* (Numinous Radiance in Analyzing the Book of History; *TPYL* 401.4a); *Shiyi ji* (Collected Records of Things Inherited) 3. See Kenkyūhan 1988, 552 n. 263.

[24] Kenkyūhan 1988, 552 n. 268. The bibliographic section of the *Hanshu* (30.19b) mentions a *Laozi fushi jingshuo* (Mr. Fu's Explanations to the *Laozi*) in 37, and a *Laozi xushi jingshuo* (Mr. Fu's Explanations to the *Laozi*) in six sections.

[25] Following Kenkyūhan 1988, 553 n. 273, this reading omits the four-character phrase *shi qi yi dao* from the original.

6

Revival of the Dead through Fivefold Purification

[146a25] The *Wulian jing* (Scripture of Fivefold Purification) says:[1]

"Bury the deceased with dyed silk. For the emperor use one bolt [14 m]; for a king or lord, one fathom [3.50 m]; for a commoner, five feet [1.75 m].[2] In addition, forge dragons from five pounds of pure gold, iron in the case of commoners. Then take five pieces of colored stone and inscribe them with jade writing.[3] After leaving the body outside for one night, bury it three feet deep."

The *Nüqing wen* (Nüqing's Writ) has:[4] [Through the proper purification] the souls of one's ancestors up to nine generations can leave their abode of perpetual night and enter the heavens of radiant light.[5]

---

[1] Kenkyūhan 1988, 553 n 275. This passage appears differently in the *Wulian jing* as it survives in *DZ* 369, fasc. 181.

The Spirit Man of the Flying Heavens said: "As regards the observances of the luminous perfected, for the emperor, use about one bolt as a pledge; for a king, a lord, or the ruler of a country, use about one fathom. Always employ careful drawings and pure gold so that heaven is properly represented. For a commoner, use about a foot and iron instead of gold. Proclaim it loudly to the celestials in all the heavens! Make it widely heard!" (18ab)

The context is a ritual that helps the dead in their journey through the underworld. It is described in more detail in the *Mingzhen ke* (Rules for the Illustrious Perfected; *DZ* 1411, fasc. 1052; see Bokenkamp 1983, 481; Kenkyūhan 1988, 554 n. 279):

First, take the *Danshu lingbao zhenwen wupian* (Perfect Text of Numinous Treasure in Cinnabar Writing and Five Tablets). In the courtyard, set up five tables in the five directions. On each of them place one tablet of the text. Then take five pounds of pure gold and from one each cast a dragon—five dragons in all. Then place these next to the tablets of the text. In addition, take [silk] painted in five colors as a pledge to settle the five emperors. (25b)

The offering of dragons in Taoism is best known from the Tang dynasty. At this time dragons, representative messengers to the otherworld, were cast from metal and thrown into flowing streams to carry prayers to the gods. See Chavannes 1919; Kamitsuka 1993.

[2] The measurements are: 1 foot (*chi*) = 10 inches (*cun*) = 35 cm; 1 fathom (*zhang*) = 10 feet = 3.50 m; 1 bolt (*pi*) = 40 feet or 4 fathoms = 14 m.

[3] Kenkyūhan 1988, 554 n. 280. Jade writing is the kind of script used in the originals of the sacred scriptures stored in the Heaven of Grand Network. See *Wulian jing* 4a; Bokenkamp 1991.

[4] Kenkyūhan 1988, 554 n. 282. This passage corresponds closely to the Dunhuang version of the *Wulian jing* (P. 2865; Ōfuchi 1979b, 75). The Dunhuang text only adds that, after the souls have arrived in the heavens, "the Three Bureaus delete their records and their names are recorded in the heavenly halls." The *Nüqing wen* is a text of the early Celestial Masters better known as *Nüqing guilü* (Nüqing's Statutes against Demons). See appendix 2.

[5] The "abode of perpetual night" is an expression for the grave and, by extension, for the underworld. *Mingzhen ke* 18b contrasts it with "radiant light," the heavens of immortality

There they feast.[6] After thirty-two years, they return to their former bodies and come back to life."[7]

I laugh at this and say:

The *Sanyuan pin* says,[8] "In the 3 offices of heaven, earth, and water,[9] there are 9 departments and 9 palaces with 120 offices, whose conscientious officials record all crimes, events of good fortune, and meritorious actions. There are no lacunae or errors. The life span of someone who does good is accordingly lengthened; the years of one who does evil are properly shortened."[10]

How could one, therefore, disregard karmic retribution and just use five feet of dyed silk to make the souls of one's ancestors up to nine generations enter the heaven of radiant light, and then, after thirty-two years, return to their former bodies? Obviously, this is entirely absurd!

From this, however, one can see that the text on the fivefold purification comes from a period before the separation of heaven and earth.[11] If it were still applicable today, then the dead would all dig open their graves and come back to life after thirty-two years.[12] Everyone would surely notice such an event with their eyes and ears.

(Kenkyūhan 1988, 555 n. 284–85). On light as a symbol of pure spirit and its importance in ancient concepts of the ancestors, see Vandermeersch 1985. Taoists at the time were very concerned with the salvation of their ancestors (see Kenkyūhan 1988, 554 n. 283; Strickmann 1985). This concern is also evident from the inscriptions on Taoist statues, which often implore the Venerable Lord to grant entry into the heavenly halls to the donor's ancestors up to seven generations (Matsubara 1961, plate 307b). For more on Taoist art, see section 7.

[6] Feasting is not only one of the major occupations of the celestials but also the key ritual process for union with the Tao. See Stein 1971; Saso 1972; Lagerwey 1987. For further details on Taoist ritual, see Schipper 1981, 1985a, 1985b, 1985c; Maruyama 1986, 1987, 1991.

[7] On Taoist rituals for transferring the souls of the dead to the heavens of the immortals, see Strickmann 1985b; Bokenkamp 1989. On the problems of the relation of death and immortality, see Loewe 1979; Seidel 1982. For Chinese references on the return to life, see Kenkyūhan 1988, 555 n. 287.

[8] Kenkyūhan 1988, 555 n. 288. This passage is slightly different from *Sanyuan pin* 20b (DZ 456, fasc. 202). The text here leaves out the reference to people's life spans and instead says that "those who study immorality accumulate good merit; those who commit evil are punished for their sins." The precepts contained in the *Sanyuan pin* are translated in Kohn 1993a, 100–106.

[9] This reflects the basic cosmology of the early Celestial Masters. See Stein 1963; Ōfuchi 1985a, 1991.

[10] On the celestial administration, see section 11. On divine record keeping, see Hou 1975; Seidel 1978a.

[11] Kenkyūhan 1988, 556 n. 296. This claim is made in the text itself, stating that it "emerged before the kalpa Dragon Country" (19a).

[12] Kenkyūhan 1988, 556 n. 297. A story about someone who did, in fact, dig up his grave is found in the *Soushen ji* (see DeWoskin 1977). "In the fifth year of Eternal Peace (261 C.E.) under Wu Sunxiu, a man from Wu named Chen Jiao came back to life seventy days after his death. He dug open his grave and came out" (chap. 6).

Why, then, is it that in all the time since Fu Xi no one ever heard of any Taoist whose ancestors of nine generations have risen from the dead and stepped out of their graves? Such absurdity! One can only laugh!

These days, I hear, somewhere in the country an old mound opened. Should it not it be some Taoist's forefather coming back to life? That is worth a good laugh, too!

7

Avalokiteśvara Serves on the Tao

[146b12] Taoists sometimes make statues of the Venerable Lord with two bodhisattvas in attendance.[1] One is Vajragarbha, the other, Avalokiteśvara.[2]

In addition, the Taoists wear yellow cloth that they wrap around their bodies as a robe. In this they plagiarize the Buddhist monks' for-

[1] Statues like these are indeed known from Zhen Luan's lifetime. They show Lord Lao in the center flanked by two smaller attendants on the right and left (see Matsubara 1961, plates 307a and 307c; Kamitsuka 1993, 238). Comparable Buddhist statues of the same period show the Buddha accompanied by two bodhisattvas (see Matsubara 1961, plates 190b, 190c, and 191a; Ōmura 1972, 378–80). While the Taoist figures are more heavily clad and show a Taoist hairstyle and long beards, they also have two lions at the foot of the central seat as do their Buddhist counterparts. Similar statues continue to be found in late centuries (Ōmura 1972, plates 722–25 and 834–50).

Zhen Luan here implies the plagiarism of Taoist art, which indeed developed in the wake of Buddhist inspiration. Although there seem to have been no visible depictions of the Tao in early Taoism, in accordance with the doctrine that the Tao is invisible and inaudible (Chen 1975, 296; Kamitsuka 1993, 226), detailed instructions on the production and veneration of statues are found in the *Fengdao kejie* (Rules and Precepts for Worshiping the Tao; *DZ* 1125, fasc. 760–61) of the midsixth century (see Akizuki 1965; Reiter 1988).

The earliest Taoist statues are associated with Kou Qianzhi and Lu Xiujing in the early fifth century (Kamitsuka 1993, 228), but the earliest surviving samples date from a century later (Matsubara 1961, 215; Ōmura 1972, 158; Kamitsuka 1993, 229). Inscriptions frequently are Buddhist on two or three sides and Taoist on the remainder, indicating a thorough mixture of the religions in the popular mind at the time (Kamitsuka 1993, 240). A central figure with two acolytes is most common, but there are also statues of two venerables sitting side by side, who are identified either as Laozi and Yin Xi or as Laozi and the Buddha (Seidel 1984a, 332). A complete list of extant statues and a detailed study of their history and inscriptions is found in Kamitsuka 1993.

[2] Vajragarbha is the bodhisattva in the *Laṅkāvatāra Sūtra* (trans. in Suzuki 1978). Avalokiteśvara (Guanyin) is the main bodhisattva of the *Lotus Sūtra* (trans. in Kern 1963; Murano 1974; Hurvitz 1976; Soothill 1987). For studies of Guanyin in the Far East, see Soper 1959, 141–77; Chamberlagne 1962; Getty 1962, 55–87; Tay 1976; Stein 1986; Yü 1990.

mal garb, the *kaṣāya*. That they wear yellow robes accords with the style of dressing of the wise men of old.[3] But their way of wrapping the cloth around themselves horizontally, fastening it in front, and using a double belt, shows that they have abandoned the ways of old in favor of imitating the monks' *kaṣāya*.[4]

I laugh at this and say:

The *Zhutian neiyin bazi wen* (Esoteric Sounds of All Heavens in Eight Character Verses) says:[5] "Brahma descends from emptiness, the Ninefold Numinous One reckons what is before." The Sovereign of Heavenly Perfection explains:[6] "Brahma is the name of the Heavenly Venerable of Primordial Beginning during the kalpa Dragon Country. In the kalpa Red Radiance, he was called Avalokiteśvara."

The *Shuji* (Record of Shu) states:[7] "When Zhang Ling went into the

[3] Kenkyūhan 1988, 558 n. 311. The same point is raised in *BZL* 6. "The Ninth Heresy: The demeanor of the followers of Laozi is imposing and formal; they bow with submission and yield to others. They wear a dark kerchief and a yellow gown, hold a ritual tablet, and drag their feet. In all this, they give expression to the patterns and images [of heaven and earth] and, in general, continue the ancient system of the Xia" (T. 2110; 52.529a).

[4] For more details on Taoist dress, see section 33.

[5] Kenkyūhan 1988, 558 n. 314. This corresponds to the eight character verses from *Duren jing* 4.11a (Scripture of Universal Salvation; *DZ* 87, fasc. 38–39), including the commentary by Li Shaowei (on the text and its commentators, see Sunayama 1984). Zhen's version matches it except for his punchline: where he reads *Guanyin* (Avalokiteśvara), Li has *wuming shi* (Mr. Anonymous). Guanyin, however, is mentioned in *Zhutian neiyin yuzi* (*DZ* 97, fasc. 49) 3.18b–19a.

[6] A more detailed explanation of the esoteric sounds by the Sovereign of Heavenly Perfection is contained in the *Zhutian neiyin yuzi*. It runs:

"Brahma" is the Heavenly Venerable of Primordial Beginning. He opened the kalpa Dragon Country. During the course of Red Radiance, he was called simply Primordial Beginning. In the course of Opening Sovereign, he was called the Elder of Primordial Beginning. Going along with the [cycles of the] world, he transformed and came to life, unifying his spirit.

"Descends from emptiness" means that whenever Primordial Beginning emerges out of emptiness, there are heaven and earth, the sun and the moon, and the three luminants. Thus, we know that there is perfect script in emptiness.

The "Ninefold Numinous One" is the Perfected of Ninefold Florescence. He resides in the upper southern palace and rules over the ninefold darkness [of the underworld], guiding the souls of the dead. "Reckons what is before" means that he calculates the merit and virtue of life and death. (3.18b)

[7] Kenkyūhan 1988, 558 n. 315. The *Shuji* is lost. *Erjiao lun* 9 (T. 2103; 52.140a) cites it with almost the same passage as by Li Ying, who is mentioned as the author of a *Yizhou ji* (Record of Yi Province) in *TPYL* 34.2b and has a biography in *Nanshi* 55. He lived in the first half of the sixth century. The *Erjiao lun* also has a longer citation of the text:

Zhang Ling entered Crane Cry Mountain and called himself Celestial Master. In the last year of Splendid Peace [177 C.E.], he was devoured by a python. His son Heng rushed to search for him but could not find him. Fearing that he would be heaped with general ridicule, he set up faked circumstances that showed the traces of a numinous transformation. He produced scattered traces of crane's feet and erected a steep pile of rocks. In the hills to avoid the plague, he learned the technique of exorcising demons.[8] He produced his own talismans and bewitched the common people. Later, he was devoured by a big snake. His disciples were ashamed of this and claimed that he had ascended to heaven in broad daylight. Ling's son, Heng, succeeded him as Celestial Master. Heng's son, Lu, in due turn inherited the title.[9] With his grandfather's methods of sorcery he brought rebellion and disorder to all under heaven."

The *Hanshu* has:[10] "Liu Yan gave Zhang Lu the post of a provincial supervisor. Zhang then killed Su Gu, grand prefect of Hanzhong, and seized his territory. He taught the people to worship demons."[11]

In those days, a rumor went around that someone wearing a yellow robe would become ruler. Accordingly, Lu ordered all his followers to dress in yellow robes and wear yellow kerchiefs on their heads as a sign that they would replace the Han.[12] Ever since, Taoists have never stopped wearing yellow robes.[13] It is most regrettable that they imitate the monks' way of dressing.

Now, among the principles of moral self-cultivation, loyalty and filial piety are foremost. If the father waits upon an image of the son, heaven and earth will not stand up.[14]

---

first year of Radiant Harmony [178], he announced, "On the seventh day of the first month, the Celestial Master has ascended to Mystery Metropolis." Rice farmers and mountain hunters were equally deceived. People often exploit the dead to get advantage for the living—but none as bad as this! (T. 2103; 52.140c)

The argument is of long standing in the debates. It appears first in the *Bianhuo lun* of about the year 500 (T. 2102; 52.48b).

[8] Kenkyūhan 1988, 559 n. 316. This is an important activity of the Celestial Masters. One of their earliest remaining documents contains long lists of spells to summon spirits and get rid of demons. See *Zhougui jing* (Scripture of spells against Demons; *DZ* 1193, fasc. 875); Kenkyūhan 1988, 559 n. 319. Similar attacks on the Celestial Masters are also found in *Bianhuo lun* 8 (T. 2102; 52.49a) and *Poxie lun* 2 (T. 2109; 52.486ab).

[9] On the early history of the Celestial Masters, see Levy 1956; Stein 1963, 1979; Seidel 1969a, 1984b; Schipper 1982; Robinet 1991, 61–83; Kobayashi 1992 (in Western languages); and Miyakawa 1954; Ōfuchi 1964, 1985b, 1991; Chen 1975, 308–70; Zhang 1990; Ren 1990, 42–42 (in Chinese and Japanese). For the biography of Zhang Daoling, see Imbault-Huart 1884; Doré 1914–38, 9:69–88; Franke 1930, 16–21.

[10] Kenkyūhan 1988, 559 n. 322. This passage is taken from the biography of Liu Yan in *Hou Hanshu* 65 except for the last sentence, which is from Zhang Lu's biography in *Sanguo zhi* 8.

[11] "Worship demons" is literally "the way of the demons" (*guidao*). This expression is interpreted to mean a primitive form of shamanism current in ancient Asia. See Fukunaga 1987a.

[12] On the Yellow Turban rebellion, see Eichhorn 1955, 1957; Levy 1956; Michaud 1958; Miyakawa 1980. For dynastic associations with specific colors, see Bauer 1956. On apocryphal prophecies and popular ditties in conjunction with dynastic changes, see Dull 1966; Seidel 1983; Yasui 1966, 1979.

[13] Kenkyūhan 1988, 487 n. 13. The same connection to the rebellious Yellow Turbans is emphasized in *Erjiao lun* 9 (T. 2103; 52.140a).

[14] Kenkyūhan 1988, 559 n. 329. This statement reflects *Xiaojing* 7: "Filial piety is the warp

Avalokiteśvara, in particular, holds an elevated position among the great, but Laozi does not even rank as a worthy.[15]

Making the grandfather serve upon his children and grandchildren is surely not filial behavior. Continuing to dress in the rebellious garb of Zhang Lu is certainly no sign of loyalty. If they embrace such disloyal and unfilial ways, how could they be worthy of being followed?

---

of heaven, the rightness of earth, the proper conduct of the people. It is the basic fabric of heaven and earth, and the people must follow it."

[15] This is an exaggeration. The *Hanshu* has, "Confucius belongs to the highest category of the top group. Thus, he is called a sage. Laozi belongs to the middle category of the top group. Thus, he is called a worthy" (chap. 20). A similar evaluation is also found in Sun Zheng's *Lao Dan fei daxian lun* (Lao Dan Was Not a Great Worthy; T.2103; 52.119b–20a) and his *Laozi yiwen fanxun* (A Critical Examination of Doubtful Questions about Laozi; T.2103; 52.120a–21b). Here, too, Laozi is compared with Confucius, who is praised for having inherent wisdom and not just the immortality techniquest of the Taoists. The same criticism is also used in *BZL* 6 (T. 2110; 52.525b) and in *Erjiao lun* 3 (T. 2103; 52.140b).

8

The Buddha Was Born in the West, in Yin

[146c2] The *Laozi xu* (Introduction to the *Laozi*) says:[1]

"The Tao of yin and yang brings forth the myriad beings.[2] Taoism originated in the east and corresponds to the realm of wood and of yang. Buddhism originated in the west and corresponds to the realm of metal and of yin.

"Taoism is thus the father; Buddism is the mother. Taoism is heaven; Buddhism is earth. Taoism is life; Buddhism is death. Taoism is the cause of things; Buddhism is their effect. Together they form a couple of yin and yang and cannot be separated.[3]

[1] This passage is not contained in the *Daode zhenjing xujue* as it has survived separately. A similar citation is found in section 34. The passage is translated in Zürcher 1959, 306.

[2] According to Chinese traditional cosmology, yin and yang are the two basic forces of the universe from which first the five phases and then the myriad beings develop. For a survey of their interpretation, see Fung and Bodde 1952, 1:159–69, 2:7–30. For an analysis, see Porkert 1974, 9–34; Henderson 1984. For Chinese references, see Kenkyūhan 1988, 560 n. 336.

[3] Yin/yang cosmology works through lines of inductive associations (Porkert 1974, 1–3). The various items mentioned here belong into this scheme. According to the system of the five phases, east represents rising yang and belongs to the phase wood, whereas west represents rising yin and belongs to the phase metal. East is then associated with life as it grows in the springtime, whereas west signifies the reaping of grain and death of vegetation in the fall. See *Chunqiu fanlu* (Variegated Remarks in the Spring and Autumn Annals) 11.3a. The asso-

"Buddhism originated from Taoism. As its greater vehicle, it guards the benevolent.[4] Taoism, by contrast, exists spontaneously and does not originate from anything else.[5]

"When Buddhists assemble, they sit 'big,' patterning themselves on the squareness of earth.[6] When Taoists assemble, they sit 'small,' patterning themselves on the roundness of heaven.[7]

"Buddhist monks do not serve as soldiers, which is another indication of their closeness to yin energy and the female principle. Thus, they are not conscripted at all. Taoists, on the contrary, serve in the army.

"In addition, Buddhist monks do not bow before the emperor or a feudal lord.[8] This, again, is an expression of their imitation of women, who usually stay in the depth of the palace and do not interfere with political affairs.

"Taoists, however, bow whenever they present themselves before the emperor or an imperial administrator. This clearly demonstrates their policy-sharing role as ministers and officials.

"In Taoist assemblies, the consumption of wine is not a sin.[9] In Bud-

---

ciations have a long history in ancient Chinese thought, as documented in Kenkyūhan 1988, 560 n. 337.

[4] Kenkyūhan 1988, 561 n. 340. The usual Taoist distinction is between Buddhists as the lesser and Taoists as the greater vehicle. The *Santian neijie jing* has, "The śramaṇas pursue the lesser vehicle. They sit quietly and count their respiration, beginning again when they have reached ten. . . . The Taoists pursue the greater vehicle. They constantly meditate on the images of the gods residing in their bodies" (2.4b). According to Zürcher, the sentence is a copying error (1959, 435 n. 94).

[5] Kenkyūhan 1988, 561 n. 341. This statement recalls the worldview of philosophical Taoism: "The Tao patterns itself on spontaneity" (*Daode jing* 25); "Heaven and earth are not born from anything at all, they exist spontaneously" (Zhang Zhan's commentary to *Liezi* 1.2b).

[6] Kenkyūhan 1988, 561 n. 342. To "sit big" or "square" means to sit with crossed legs in the lotus posture. The expression occurs variously in Buddhist literature. See, for example, *Shisong lü* (Sarvāstivāda vinaya) 40 and 41 (T. 23.291a and 300b); *Da zhidu lun* 7 (Mahāprajñā-pāramitā-śāstra; T. 1509; 25.111b); *Hongming ji* 12 (T. 2102; 52.77c). Earth is square, whereas heaven is round. See *Lüshi chunqiu* 3.5.

[7] Kenkyūhan 1988, 561 n. 344. Taoist gatherings for burning incense and offering worship are described in *Laojun yinsong jiejing* 20b (Scripture of Precepts Recited by the Venerable Lord; DZ 785, fasc. 562). See Yang 1956. "Sit small" is the kneeling position, the subject's posture during official occasions. A description is found in the *Liangshu* (History of the Liang Dynasty). "If one's inner nature is even and correct, though one may be in a small hall or dark chamber, one will yet maintain one's gown and cap in good order, sit small, and keep the folds of the robe properly arranged. Even in the hottest months of summer, one will never lift the robe or bare the skin" (3.30a).

[8] There was an extended debate, led especially by Huiyuan, on the monks' right to remain upright in front of civil authority. See Liebenthal 1950, 1952; Kimura 1962; Zürcher 1959, 231–39; Chen 1964, 76; Schmidt-Glintzer 1976, 53; Tsukamoto and Hurvitz 1985, 828–44. For Chinese references, see Kenkyūhan 1988, 562 n. 349.

[9] Kenkyūhan 1988, 562 n. 353. The role of wine in Taoist ritual banquets is specified in the *Laojun yinsong jiejing*: "The Venerable Lord says: "The way to hold banquet meetings is to prepare three courses: first a light meal, then wine, and finally rice. People today often cannot

dhist meetings, drinking is strictly prohibited.[10] The reason for this is that, when women drink, they tend to commit the seven reasons for divorce.[11]

"Taoists conduct no fasts because they attach importance to life, and to live is to eat. Buddhists, by contrast, observe fasting periods[12] because they are concerned with death, and the dead need no food.[13] In addition, they fast because women are moderate in their eating.

"Buddhists sleep alone; like women they are supposed to remain faithful to one only.[14] Taoists, on the contrary, live in matrimony and have no restrictive regulations."

I laugh at this and say:

The *Wenshi zhuan* has,[15] "Taoism originated in the east and corresponds to the realm of wood and the male. Buddhism originated in the west and corresponds to the realm of metal and the female."

If we now pursue this issue in terms of the five phases, we see that metal overcomes wood; it is the governor and ancestor of wood, whereas wood is its subject and wife. Consequently, Buddhism is the governor and ancestor of Taoism, whereas Taoism is Buddhism's subject and wife.[16]

Moreover, the statement of the *Wenshi zhuan* that "the Tao brought forth Buddhism" is logically impossible. In terms of the principles of

---

prepare all three courses, so they may only have wine, but no more than five pints" (8ab). See also Stein 1971b, 435. For more on the question of meat and wine, see section 20.

[10] Abstention from all intoxication is one of the five central precepts of Buddhism, the other precepts being abstention from killing, stealing, lying, and sexual activity. See Warder 1920, 191; Lamotte 1958, 60; Dutt 1962; Wijayaratna 1990, 73–74.

[11] Kenkyūhan 1988, 562 n. 356. The traditional seven reasons for which a man could divorce his wife are sterility, lewdness, disobedience to the parents in-law, loquacity, stealing, jealousy, and a repulsive disease. See *Kongzi jiayu* (Kong Family Annals) 7.11b; *Dadai liji* (Historical Record of the Elder Dai) 13.6a. See also van Gulik 1961, 266. In addition, there are seven rules of decency and good behavior put forward by Lady Ban (van Gulik 1961, 98).

[12] Kenkyūhan 1988, 562 n. 358. Buddhist fasting periods are specified in the *Fengfa yao* (T. 2102; 52.86b). See Zürcher 1959, 164–76; Tsukamoto and Hurvitz 1985, 1010–28. See also *Fayuan zhulin* 18 (Pearl Garden of the Dharma Forest; T. 2122; 53.417c). On this text, see Teiser 1985.

[13] The same division of "Taoism = life" versus "Buddhism = death" is also made in *Santian neijie jing* 1.9b (see Kenkyūhan 1988, 562 n. 357).

[14] Literally "guard the One." As a precept for women's faithfulness, see Lady Ban's instructions (van Gulik 1961, 98). In a more religious context, the expression refers to a meditation technique of exclusive concentration and fixation on one object (see Kohn 1989b).

[15] Citation unclear. Translated also in Zürcher 1959, 306.

[16] Kenkyūhan 1988, 563 n. 363. This statement reflects the theory of the five phases, as outlined in Xiao Ji's *Wuxing dayi* (Great Meaning of the Phases; trans. in Kalinowski 1991): "The overcoming agent is the lord, the husband, the governor, the offical, the ancestor. The agent that is overcome is the minister, the wife, the subject" (2.6ab).

yin and yang and the five phases, how could wood ever bring forth metal? Therefore, we know that the Tao could not possibly have brought forth Buddhism.

Buddhists sit big, in the lotus posture, because they are the governors and supervisors of the Taoists. Taoists always kneel because they bow deeply to their governors and supervisors.

Again, Buddhist monks do not serve in the army or pay taxes because their lineage goes back to a royal house.[17] Therefore, they are exempt. Taoists, by contrast, are lowly and common folk. As such, they have to serve in the army and pay taxes as a matter of course. Even their sacred scriptures state that evading the draft or the payment of taxes is contrary to the Taoist teaching.

In addition, the *Lingbao dajie* (The Great Precepts of Numinous Treasure) says:[18] "Taoists should not drink wine or deal in valuables." How is it, then, that they constantly violate their own major prohibitions? All later pronouncements appear entirely confused; they are completely without direction or target.

The text also says, "To the Taoists, fasting is a rite for the dead. Therefore, they do not fast." Why, then, do they not eat their fill all their lives[19] and nourish their bodies well?[20] Why do they, instead, propagate abstention from all grain and absorption of energy as techniques of extending life?[21]

I cannot see an end to the confusion! Their words are like discussions on how to catch a shadow.[22]

Then, again, the text says that "monks sleep alone, whereas Taoists live in matrimony." But consider: They also have the rite of harmonizing the breaths and the methods of the *Huangshu* (Yellow Book).[23] Their claim is surely false!

---

[17] Kenkyūhan 1988, 563 n. 367. The royal lineage of the Buddha is emphasized also in *Fayuan zhulin* 8 (T. 2122; 53.334a).

[18] Kenkyūhan 1988, 564 n. 371. This sentence refers to the *Dajie wen* (DZ 1364, fasc. 1039): "Students of the Tao must not drink wine" (1b); "Students of the Tao must not crave for or enjoy worldly honor and valuables" (3a). Similar prohibitions are also found in the *Yibai bashi jie* (nos. 22, 24; *YJQQ* 39.4a); *WSBY* 45.1a, 6a; and *Laojun jinglü* 6a (Scriptural Rules of the Venerable Lord; *DZ* 786, fasc. 562).

[19] This is a citation of *Lunyu* 17.20 See Kenkyūhan 1988, 564 n. 376.

[20] Nourishing the body is of central concern in Taoism. See Maspero 1981, 443–554; Kohn 1989.

[21] Taoists abstain from grain because they believe that it will feed the three worms and thus cause death. They absorb pure cosmic energy for nourishment instead. See Maspero 1981, 443–554; Lévi 1983; Engelhardt 1987. For more on Taoist diet and grain, see section 17.

[22] Kenkyūhan 1988, 564 n. 380. This expression is taken from *Huainanzi* 17.11a. Zhen Luan uses it again in section 28.

[23] See section 35, which is dedicated entirely to sexual practices.

9

The Size of the Sun and the Moon

[147a1] The *Wenshi zhuan* says:[1]

"Heaven and earth are 409,000 miles apart.[2] The diameter of the sun and the moon is 3,000 miles each; their circumference is 6,000 miles. The far north and south ends of the universe are 900 billion miles apart. So are its east and west ends, all the four corners of the universe."

In addition, the *Zhuanxing jiku jing* (Scripture on Rescue from Suffering in the Rebirth Cycle) states,[3] "Mount Kunlun is 15,000 miles high."

I laugh at this and say:

The *Jiku jing* states that "heaven and earth are one hundred million and five thousand [100,005,000] miles apart."[4] This is in obvious contradiction to the information given in the *Wenshi zhuan*. Here we learn that the "circumference of both the sun and the moon is six thousand miles, while their diameter is three thousand miles." Mathematically,

---

[1] Kenkyūhan 1988, 565 n. 383. The *TPYL* cites a similar passage from the *Guanling neizhuan* (Inner Biography of the Guardian of the Pass), an alternative title of the *Wenshi zhuan*: "The extreme north and south ends of heaven and earth are ninety million miles apart. So are their extreme east and west ends, thus causing all the four corners of the universe to be ninety million miles apart. Heaven and earth, furthermore, are four hundred million miles from each other" (2.6a). A Chinese mile is about 440 m or one-fourth of an American mile.

[2] Kenkyūhan 1988, 565 n. 385. The earliest measurements of heaven and earth are given in the *Huainanzi* (see Major 1993, 147–49).

Within Taoism, the *Daobao jing* (Scripture of the Treasure of the Tao; *DZ* 1353, fasc. 1036–37; 2.11b) contains a similar description with the same measurements. Usually, however, the numbers differ from text to text. For example, the *Tiandi yundu jing* (Scripture on the Revolutions of Heaven and Earth; *DZ* 322, fasc. 166) has, "Heaven is distant from earth by ninety thousand miles" (1a). The *Tianguan jing* (Scripture of the Heavenly Pass; *DZ* 987, fasc. 618) states, "Heaven and earth are forty-eight thousand miles apart. Their east and west, north and south ends are one hundred million and nine thousand [100,009,000] miles from each other" (2ab). The *Yundu jieqi jing* (Scripture on Kalpa Revolutions; *DZ* 319, fasc. 165) has, "Heaven and earth are one hundred million and five thousand [100,005,000] miles apart" (10b).

Comparable Buddhist measurements are found in the *Lishi apitan lun* (Lokaprajñāptyabhidharma; T. 1644; 32. 181c). See Kenkyūhan 1988, 565 n. 384.

[3] Kenkyūhan 1988, 565 n. 386. The same title and passage are also cited in *Shijia fangzhi* 1 (T. 2088; 51.949c), but the *DZ* version of this text (*DZ* 375, fasc. 181) does not contain any cosmological information. On mount Kunlun, see section 1.

[4] This line is not contained in the DZ edition of the text. The measurement given corresponds to that found in the *Guangshuo pin* (see sec. 1) and in the *Yundu jieqi jing* (see n. 2).

however, the circumference should be nine thousand miles, or triple the diameter. How is it they are only six thousand miles?[5]

Moreover, the roundness of heaven and squareness of earth are an integral part of Taoist worldview. But because the measurements given here of the four far ends and the four directions are the same, heaven and earth must both be round.

The *Huahu jing* says:[6] "The Buddhist teaching reaches only to the Heaven of the Thirty-Three Devas,[7] it does not reach to all eighty-one heavens of the Tao."[8] It also has, "Mount Kunlun consists of nine layers. Each layer is nine thousand miles from the next. The mountain has four sides; each side has one heaven. Thus, four times nine makes thirty-six heavens. Emperor Śakra resides on the first layer."[9]

If we now calculate all this, Mount Kunlun is supposed to be fifteen thousand miles high yet consists of nine layers. If each of these is nine thousand from the next, their total height should amount to eighty-one thousand miles. Yet the Taoists maintain that Kunlun reaches only up to fifteen thousand miles. The discrepancy is excessive and highly ridiculous.

[5] On the mathematical law that the circumference is triple the diameter, see *Jiuzhang suanshu* 1. For earlier calculations on the size of the universe, see *Jinshu* 11 (Kenkyūhan 1988, 565 n. 382).

[6] Kenkyūhan 1988, 566 n. 394. The following two passages are not contained in any of the extant versions of the *Huahu jing*. The same sentence on the layers and size of Mount Kunlun, however, is also cited as from the *Huahu jing* in *Shijia fangzhi* 1 (T. 2088; 51.949c).

[7] Commonly called Daoli tian (Trayastriṃśās), this is the second of the six *devaloka*, or heavens of the gods. It is the heaven of Indra, the Svarga of Hindu mythology, located on the summit of Mount Sumeru. See *Zhidu lun* 9 (Prajñāpāramitā-śāstra; T. 1509; 25.123a, cited in Kenkyūhan 1988, 566 n. 392); Nakamura 1981, 472. On its role in Chinese Buddhism, see also Soymié 1977, 9.

[8] Although Taoists usually have thirty-six heavens, the *Yundu jieqi jing* mentions eighty-one. "Mount Kunlun is located in the very center of the earth. It consists of eighty-one layers, which are also known as the eighty-one heavens. Kunlun has four sides, duly called the four 'realms under the heavens.' Each is ruled by a heavenly king while above governs the Emperor of the One" (10b–11a). See Kenkyūhan 1988, 566 n. 393.

[9] Kenkyūhan 1988, 566 n. 395. Emperor Śakra is the god Indra, who resides in the Daoli Heaven. See *Niepan jing* 33 (Nirvāṇa Sūtra; T. 374; 12.563c); *Zhidu lun* 56 (T. 1509; 25.458ab); Nakamura 1981, 904. The same passage is also found in the *Shijia fangzhi* (T. 2088; 51.949c) after the *Huahu jing*.

10

The Floating of Mount Kunlun

[147a16] The *Wenshi zhuan* says:[1]

"Every quatrillion (10^{24}) years, there is a deluge during which Mount Kunlun begins to float.[2] At that time, flying immortals take the kings of heaven and all good people to safety on the mountain.[3]

"Again, every ten billion (10^{16}) years, there is a great fire.[4] At that time, the sages fly up to take the kings of heaven and people to safety on the mountain."

I laugh at this and say:

The *Jiku jing* says:[5] "In the great disasters at the end of a kalpa, heaven and earth are incinerated to mere emptiness and vastness.[6]

---

[1] Kenkyūhan 1988, 566 n. 398. The same passage is cited again in section 25. It is found in *TPYL* 38.5b as from the *Zhenren guanling Yin neizhuan* (Inner Biography of the Perfected Yin, Guardian of the Pass), an alternative title of the *Wenshi zhuan*. The sole variation here is that twice 10,000 years are left out, making the flood occur once in 10^{16} years.

[2] The *Daobao jing* (DZ 1353, fasc. 1036–37) describes it: "After several million years, heaven brings forth rains and increases the waters. Above, they reach up to the eleventh heaven; below, all four regions of the earth are covered by the deluge" (2.1a). See Kenkyūhan 1988, 567 n. 399.

[3] "Good people" are those who are properly initiated. Only they survive at the end of a kalpa because of celestial interference. See *WSBY* 6.4a; *SDZN* 39.1b; *YJQQ* 2.4b–5a (Kenkyūhan 1988, 567 n. 401) For the end of the world in Taoism, see Zürcher 1982; Mollier 1990; Kobayashi 1990, 403–81; Kamitsuka 1988a, 1991.

[4] There are three great kalpa disasters: fire, water, and wind. According to the *Daobao jing*, when fires arises, "four or five suns emerge simultaneously, the rivers and streams dry up, even the ocean is exhausted. Then a sixth sun comes up, and all living beings must die" (2.1a).

[5] Kenkyūhan 1988, 567 n. 403. Parts of this passage are also cited in sections 15 and 25. Not contained in today's *Jiku jing*, it is found in the *Yundu jieqi jing* (DZ 319, fasc. 165). The full text goes:

> In the great disasters at the end of a kalpa, even the trigrams of heaven and earth are incinerated and the myriad beings are reduced to scattered ashes. Above, there is no longer the brightness of heaven; below, there is no more the depth of the earth. Above and below crash with a bang, and there is mere emptiness and vastness. Wild winds blow without stopping; red glowing energy fills and stretches everywhere.
> Then only will he [the Lord of the Tao] order the record-keeping wise ones to take control of the stove and forge a new key. Opening and expanding the world with it, they again bring forth the trigrams of heaven and earth. Then once again pure energy will rise up to form heaven; turbid energy will sink down to form the earth. The pure will spread the Tao of yang; the turbid will spread the Tao of yin.
> Pacing heaven and measuring the earth, he will bring forth the four mainstays of east and west, north and south, set up above and below and the center. Then he will commission the gods Juling and Huhai to create mountains and rivers—the five sacred mountains and four great rivers, in particular. (10ab)

[6] Kenkyūhan 1988, 567 n. 404. The same phrase is found in the *Weimo jing* (Vimalakīrti-nideśa Sūtra; T. 475; 14.550a).

Thereafter, once again pure energy will form heaven; turbid energy will form the earth. Then the gods Juling and Huhai will again form mountains and rivers,[7] and the sun and the moon will be there just as they were before."

Now, according to the Taoists, at the end of the world Mount Kunlun begins to float and serves as a refuge for humanity. If, however, heaven and earth are destroyed completely, this mountain, too, should be consumed by the flames. Its lone survival does not make sense. How, then, could the immortals take the kings of heaven and good people to safety on the mountain?

In addition, the *Duren miaojing* (Wondrous Scripture of Universal Salvation) states:[8] "On the five hundred millionth layer of heaven is the Heaven of Grand Network with its Mountain of Jade Capital. Kalpa disasters never affect it."

Considering the unlimited compassion of the Highest Lord, why is it that he does not give all people shelter in his Jade Capital? If he watches people die without helping them, he cannot be called compassionate. And if he is not able to help them, well, then he is nothing but a big cheat.

In this context, the *Duren benxing jing* says:[9] "The [Lord of the] Tao said: 'I go along with the kalpas, being born and dying alternatively'."

Now, the Highest Lord of the Tao resides in the Heaven of Grand Network where kalpa disasters never reach. Yet he maintains that he follows along with the kalpas and is being born and dies alternately. If even he dies, how could the flying immortals ever be able to give refuge to the kings of heaven and good people on the mountain and thus save them from certain death?

The whole thing is full of incomprehensible nonsense. Utterly laughable indeed!

---

[7] Juling and Huhai are the sons of Hundun (chaos) and the gods of rivers and mountains (Yuan 1954, 34; Yuan 1985, 51). The *Kaitian jing* (DZ 1437, fasc. 1059) describes their emergence.

In the time of Hundun, there were consciousness and language. With Hundun, there were two men. The elder was Huchen; the younger was Huling. The elder died and became the god of the mountains. The younger died and became the god of the rivers. They gave names to the five sacred mountains, the four great rivers, and to all the mountains and rivers, high and low (3ab; *YJQQ* 2.11a; Kohn 1993a, 39)

[8] Kenkyūhan 1988, 568 n. 410. This passage is not contained in the *Duren jing* today. It is cited in *BZL* 8 (T. 2110; 52.543a) and in section 27 as from the *Duming miaojing* (DZ 23, fasc. 26). Here, it is indeed found, describing the fate of the sacred scriptures, but no mention is made of "five hundred million layers." The text has: "At the end of a great kalpa, all the sacred texts return to the Mystery Terrace of the Seven Treasures on the Mountain of Jade Capital in the Highest Heaven of Grand Network. Here kalpa disasters never reach" (15a).

[9] This passage is found in *YJQQ* 101.2b–3a and in P. 3022 (Ōfuchi 1979, 54). For more details, see section 27.

11

Taoist Heavenly Bureaucracy

[147b3] The *Wufu jing* (Scripture of the Five Talismans) says:[1]

"The Lord of the Central Yellow[2] said, 'Heaven brings forth the myriad beings.[3] Humanity is highest among them. The human body contains heaven and earth.[4] There is nothing that it is not patterned on.[5]

Moreover, there are an emperor, three dukes, nine ministers, twenty-seven high officials, and eighty-one secretaries inside.[6] It also contains 9 provinces, 120 prefectures, and 1,200 districts.[7]

[1] Kenkyūhan 1988, 569 n. 418. This passage is somewhat shorter than the version in *Wufu xu* 1.19b–20a (*DZ* 388, fasc. 183). The same passage is also contained in *BZL* 6 (T. 2110; 52.536ab).

[2] This is the official heavenly title of Huangdi, the Yellow Emperor. See *YJQQ* 3.19a (Kenkyūhan 1988, 569 n. 419). For details on the Lord of the Central Yellow in Taoist meditation, see Yamada 1989.

[3] This sentence is taken from *Daode jing* 42.

[4] The *DZ* text adds here:

> . . . the sun and the moon, the Northern Dipper, the Jade Sighting Tube, the Equalizer, the five sacred mountains, the four great rivers, mountains and streams, rivers and oceans, the Wind God, the Rain Master, the Star Lords, the Earth God, unicorns and phoenixes, dragons and tigers, turtles and snakes. There are also the five grains, mulberry and hemp, the six domestic animals, oxen and horses. There are birds and beasts, fish and tortoises, bamboo and trees, and the hundred plants. (1.19b)

[5] For studies of the body in Taoism, see Asano 1982; Homann 1971; Schipper 1982; Kohn 1991b. Cf. also *WSBY* 5.8a–15b (Lagerwey 1981, 79–80).

[6] This bureaucratic structure corresponds to the ancient Chinese ideal as it is already formulated in *Liji* 5.10 (Kenkyūhan 1988, 570 n. 424). For further details in Taoism, see Ware 1933, 222; Rao 1956, 77–78; Ishii 1983; Kubo 1986.

[7] Here, the *DZ* text continues:

> . . . 18,000 counties, 36,000 communities, and 180,000 villages. In addition, there are palaces and towers, homes and residences, doors and windows, wells and stoves, cauldrons and jars, rice and grains, barley and millet, so that the various gods can live and eat. When people know this, they can live long.
>
> The human head is round in imitation of heaven; the feet are square, patterned on earth. The hair represents the stars and chronograms; the eyes are the sun and the moon. The eyebrows are the Northern Dipper; the ears are the gods of soil and grain. The nose represents mountains and hills; the mouth is like the streams and rivers. The teeth are jade and minerals; and the four limbs correspond to the four seasons.
>
> The five orbs, moreover, are patterned on the five phases. They are also the five emperors and the five officials. Above, they are linked to the five planets; below, to the five sacred mountains. On the inside, they are the five kings; on the outside, the five virtues. More than that, they are also the five clouds, which turn into the five dragons.
>
> The five orbs are the lungs, heart, liver, spleen, and kidneys. The six viscera relate to each of them: the gall to the liver, the stomach to the spleen, the large intestine to the lungs, the small intestine to the heart, and the bladder to the kidneys. The navel, finally, is the central administration of them all. (1.19b–20a)

"'The gall is the emperor, the Great Lord of the Tao; the spleen is the empress. The heart is the defender-in-chief; the left kidney is the minister of education; the right kidney is the minister of public works.[8]

"'The eight gods [of the eight trigrams] together with the navel are the nine ministers.[9] The twelve gods of the throat and the twelve [counseling] officials of the stomach [spleen][10] together with the three gods of the three burners[11] are the twenty-seven high officials.

"'In addition, the gods of the four limbs are the 81 secretaries.[12] All in all, there are 120 deities inside the body, matching the number of the prefectures.

"'Moreover, the lungs are the administration of high officials [grand secretariat], whereas the liver is the administration of the orchid terrace [historical archives]'."[13]

I laugh at this and say:

Examining the names of prefectures and districts in Taoist scriptures, one finds that they sound very much like those of today. In antiquity, however, districts were large, whereas prefectures were small. This can easily be verified with the help of the *Chunqiu* (Spring and Autumn

---

[8] These are the so-called three dukes, that is, heads of the three major offices of the imperial administration under the Later Han. See Hucker 1985, 450, 458, 485. In Taoism, the same description is found in *Laozi zhongjing* (Central Scripture of Laozi) 2.7b (*DZ* 1168, fasc. 839; also *YJQQ* 19.7b–8a; Kenkyūhan 1988, 570 n. 426). On this text, see Schipper 1979; Maeda 1988.

[9] These deities as well as the gods of the throat are also listed in *Huangting neijing jing* 23 (*DZ* 402, fasc. 190; 2.25ab). See Kenkyūhan 1988, 570 n. 427.

[10] On these gods, their organization and their functions, see *Laozi zhongjing* 20 (1.14b–15a; *YJQQ* 18.15ab). See Kenkyūhan 1988, 570 n. 429.

[11] On these deities, see *Huangting neijing jing* 1.8 (*YJQQ* 11.24ab; Kenkyūhan 1988, 570 n. 430).

[12] Here the DZ adds,

The upper energy secretaries serve as continuous messengers. The lower energy secretaries serve as far-reaching runners. In the upper section, they correspond to the nine transformations. In the middle section, they correspond to the nine orifices. In the lower section, they correspond to the nine names. The 3 dukes, 9 ministers, 27 high officials, and 81 secretaries all in all make 120 deities inside the body. (1.20b)

A similar discussion is also found in *Laozi zhongjing* 14 (*YJQQ* 18.11a).

[13] The DZ version details this information.

The lungs are the administration of high officials, the Palace of Jade Hall. The heart is the administration of primordial Yang, the Red Palace. The liver is the administration of the orchid terrace, the Palace of Pure Yang. The gall is the administration of Nonultimate, the Palace of Purple Tenuity. The spleen is the administration of great simplicity, the Central Palace. The kidneys are the administration of great harmony, the Palace of Dark Splendor. (1.20b–21a)

The same offices and palaces are also named in *Huangting neijing jing* 2.22 (*YJQQ* 11.54b–55a) and *Laozi zhongjing* 2.7b. See Kenkyūhan 1988, 571 n. 431.

Annals) or the *Zhoushu* (Book of the Zhou).[14] Today, it is exactly the other way round, and prefectures are larger than districts.

Yet do not Taoists claim that their scriptures originated in an age even before the Spring and Autumn period? The whole thing is so absurd it is not even worth discussing! It only merits a hearty laugh!

[14] Kenkyūhan 1988, 571 n. 432. See *Zuozhuan*, Ai 2: "A higher minister receives a district to govern; a lower minister rules in a prefecture." Commentary: "A district contains four prefectures." The same argument is also made in *BZL* 6 (T. 2110; 52.536b).

12

The Appellation "Nanwufo"

The *Huahu jing* says:[1]

"When Laozi went to convert the barbarians, their king would not at first accept his teaching.

"Laozi said, 'If you won't believe [in my teaching], I will go south to India and convert all the kingdoms there. My teaching will come to flourish greatly, and from here on south (*nan*) there will be no (*wu*) deity more venerable than the Buddha (*fo*).'

"The barbarian king still did not believe. Instead he said, 'If you go south and convert India, I shall knock my head to the ground and call you "Nanwufo," No Higher Buddha South.'[2]

"Again, on the frontier of the flowing sands, there was the kingdom of the Jiayi,[3] whose people had always been plunderous. The king of the barbarians dreaded them and sent out men to guard the frontier pass. These, however, were continuously frightened and in due course came to be called Youpose, 'frightened on the pass.'[4] Their wives, too,

[1] This passage is not contained in any extant *Huahu jing* fragments. For a translation of the first part, see Zürcher 1959, 301.

[2] *Nanwu*, literally "none south," is the transliteration of Sanskrit *nama*. See Nakamura 1981, 1029. The expression originally means "I submit" and is used frequently in incantations and liturgy as a formula of faith. The entire passage is based on reading the Sanskrit transliterations literally with their Chinese meaning. A similar form of anti-Buddhist argumentation is also found in the *Sanpo lun*. See appendix 1.

[3] Kenkyūhan 1988, 572 n. 441. This is one of several names of Kapilavastu. See *Fanyi mingyi ji* (Collection of Translated Terms and Meanings; T. 2131; 54.1096c–97a).

[4] *Youpose* originally is a transliteration of Sanskrit *upāsaka*, meaning "one who sits at another's feet" (Hurvitz 1956, 36). The term indicates a Buddhist layman who observes the five precepts. See Mochizuki 1933–36, 1800a.

greatly feared to be raided by the Jiayi and shivered lest their husbands be harmed by them. Thus, they were called Youpoyi, 'frightened of the Yi'."[5]

I laugh at this and say:

Nanwu is really a barbarian word, which translates into Chinese as "I take refuge with my life!" or "Save me!"[6] The barbarian word *youpose* really means "male believer of good faith," whereas *youpoyi* refers to a "female follower of good faith."[7]

Yet according to these words of Laozi, the Buddha was called Nanwu because he first emerged in the south. Had he first appeared in the west, would he then have been called Xiwufo, No Higher Buddha West?

In addition, they argue that the men guarding the frontier pass were suffering from fear and, thus, were known as "frightened on the pass." Their wives, sharing their fear and worrying about their husbands, were duly called "frightened of the Yi." That may make sense, but it still leaves the word *po*, "ancestress," unaccounted for. Or is it that they were particularly frightened of their old grandmothers?

Translating and interpreting terms literally like this is disgraceful and foolish. Distressed and embarrassed, one can only laugh.

[5] *Youpoyi* transcribes Sanskrit *upāsikā*, lay female follower. For a Chinese discussion of both male and female lay followers, see *Jinglü yixiang* 38 (T. 2121; 53.198a–205c).

[6] This is explained in *Fahua yishu* 4 (Commentary to the Lotus Sūtra; T. 1721; 34.509b). See Kenkyūhan 1988, 572 n. 44.

[7] The title "follower of good faith" (*shanxin nan/nü* is adapted in Taoist ordination as "faithful follower" or "follower of pure faith" (*qingxin dizi*). It is given to Taoists of lower ranks, both lay and monastic, who have taken refuge in the Tao and vowed to observe the ten precepts and fourteen principles of self-control. See Yoshioka 1959, 123; Kusuyama 1992, 114–35; Benn 1991, 74–75.

13

Birds' Tracks as the Earliest
Form of Writing

[147c2] The *Dongshen sanhuang jing* (Spirit Cavern Scripture of the Three Sovereigns)[1] says:[2]

"The West Country Immortal[3] said, 'What is called august writing is the earliest written material. It comes from a time before the Three Sovereigns and was patterned on birds' tracks'."

Again the text says:[4]

"The Three Sovereigns are the venerable gods of the Three Caverns,[5] the ancestral energy of great existence.[6] The Heavenly Sovereign presides over energy; the Earthly Sovereign rules over spirit; and the Human Sovereign governs life. All three combine their virtue and the myriad beings are created."

---

[1] The *Sanhuang jing*, or *Sanhuang wen* (Text of the Three Sovereigns), is a collection of ancient talismanic texts. These were the sacred materials with which the Three Sovereigns of high antiquity ruled the world. As the *Sanhuang jing* itself says:

> In the old days, when the Heavenly Sovereign ruled, Heaven bestowed upon him a celestial scripture in one scroll. He governed all-under-heaven with it for twenty-eight thousand years.
> Then the Earthly Sovereign succeeded him. On him, too, Heaven bestowed a sacred scripture in one scroll, and he governed all-under-heaven with it for twenty-eight thousand years. Then the Human Sovereign succeeded him. He, too, was given a celestial scripture in one scroll, and he governed all-under-heaven with it for twenty-eight thousand years.
> The scripture revealed to the Three Sovereigns thus consist of three scrolls altogether. Ever since, they have been known as the "Three Great Works" or as the "Scriptures of the Three Sovereigns." (*YJQQ* 4.10ab)

Lost rather early, the *Sanhuang jing* today survives only in citations (see appendix 2). On the Three Sovereigns in traditional Chinese mythology, see Gu 1936. For more on them within Taoism, see *WSBY* 25.1a–10b (Lagerwey 1981, 106). On their revelation to Bao Jing, see 31 n 13.

[2] Kenkyūhan 1988, 573 n. 452. This passage is also found in *Badi jing* (Scripture of the Eight Emperors) 16a (*DZ* 640, fasc. 342), *WSBY* 49.5b and *YJQQ* 6.5b.

[3] Kenkyūhan 1988, 573 n. 452. The *Badi jing* has "Lord King of the Western City." This is the celestial title of the immortal Wang Yuan, also known as Wang Fangping. See *Shenxian zhuan* 2; trans. by Güntsch 1988, 74.

[4] This passage is slightly shorter than the *Sanhuang wen* as quoted in *WSBY* 6.5ab. See Kenkyūhan 1988, 573 n. 454.

[5] The Three Caverns are the major division of the Taoist canon, developed in the fifth century. See Ōfuchi 1979a; Mollier 1990. On the history of the canon and its divisions, see Fukui 1952; Yoshioka 1955; Chen 1975; Yamada 1984a; Liu 1973; Thompson 1985b; Boltz 1987.

[6] The *WSBY* version of the text adds here:

> The Lord of Heavenly Treasure is the head prime of Great Cavern of great primordiality and jade mystery. The Lord of Numinous Treasure is the beginning prime of Mystery

I laugh at this and say:

The *Nanji zhenren wenshi pin* (Chapter of Questions Asked by the Perfected of South Culmen) states:[7] "The perfect text of the Lingbao scriptures in thirty-six scrolls is stored in a jade chamber on Mystery Terrace on the Mountain of Jade Capital.[8] The huge characters of this perfect text fill the entire chamber. Heaven and earth may be destroyed, they may rise and fall ten thousand times, yet the perfected text will shine forth in eternity."[9]

Now, this perfect text is the writing of the Three Caverns. The Three Sovereigns are the venerable gods of the Three Caverns. This being so, they cannot possibly have been brought forth later than the text.

In addition, in those days there were no birds or beasts. How, then, can they speak of "the earliest written material that comes from a time before the Three Sovereigns and was patterned on birds' tracks"?

If, however, we assume that Fu Xi was one of the Three Sovereigns,[10] the statement of the *Huainanzi* applies. It says, "the Sovereign [Yellow] Emperor ordered Cangjie to study birds' tracks and create writing."[11] But this definitely took place under the reign of a sovereign,

---

Cavern, of great simplicity and chaos perfected. The Lord of Spirit Treasure is the wondrous energy of Spirit Cavern, of shining numen and great emptiness.

When these three primes coagulate and transform, they are called the Three Caverns. The energy of the Caverns is high and void, it reaches as far as Grand Network. Thus, Great Cavern is located on Jade Clarity, Mystery Cavern is in the realm of Highest Clarity, and Spirit Cavern, with its combined appellations, is in the Great Ultimate.

The energy of Great Cavern is the Heavenly Sovereign. The energy of Mystery Cavern is the Earthly Sovereign. The energy of Spirit Cavern is the Human Sovereign. (6.5ab)

[7] Citation unclear. *YJQQ* 4.9b–10a mentions thirty-one scrolls of texts revealed at a meeting of the Lord King with the Perfected of South Culmen. See Kenkyūhan 1988, 574 n. 459.

[8] Kenkyūhan 1988, 574 n. 460. That the Lingbao scriptures consist of thirty-six scolls, or wrappers, is mentioned by Lu Xiujing in his *Lingbao shoudu yibiao* 5b (Memorial on Transmission and Ordination in Numinous Treasure; *DZ* 528, fasc. 294) and in *YJQQ* 4.4b.

[9] A similar statement is found in *WSBY* 21.1a. For more details on the scriptures and their survival of cosmic disasters, see section 27. On sacred texts and their role in Taoism, see Robinet 1979a, 1984.

[10] The classical list of the Three Sovereigns includes Fu Xi, Nügua, and Shennong. See 1 n. 12.

[11] Kenkyūhan 1988, 575 n. 466. Such a citation is not found in the *Huainanzi* today. It mentions Cangjie in chapter 19 and relates birds' tracks to writing in chapter 16. The *Shuowen jiezi zhu* (Annotated Character Dictionary), however, has a similar statement in its introduction. "Cangjie, a minister under the Yellow Emperor, observed the tracks left by birds and beasts. He realized that they could be divided according to their similarities and differences. Thus, he first created written signs and tallies." This story, which is also recorded in the *Diwang shiji* (Chronological Record of Emperors and Kings; *TPYL* 235.4b), is the classical Chinese myth on the origin of writing. For a scholarly discussion, see Chaves 1977.

so how can they claim that writing began with birds' tracks before the Three Sovereigns?

14

Zhang Qian Acquires Buddhist Sūtras

[147c15] The *Huahu jing says:*[1]

"The bodhisattva Kāśyapa[2] said, 'Five hundred years after the nir-vāṇa of the Tathāgata, I went east and gave the Tao to Han Pingzi. Then I ascended to heaven in broad daylight.

"'Two hundred years after this, I revealed the Tao to Zhang Ling. Another two hundred years later, I transmitted it to Jian Pingzi. After two hundred more years, I gave it to Gan Shi.[3]

"'Nevertheless, around that time, at the end of the Han dynasty, the world grew more and more decadent and people no longer venerated my Tao.[4]

"'However, the seventh year, *jiazi,* of Everlasting Peace under Emperor Ming of the Han arrived [64 C.E.]. The year star shone brightly, illuminating the western night like day, and the emperor dreamed of a spirit man sixteen feet tall and with a halo of sunlight.[5]

---

[1] This passage is not found in the extant *Huahu jing.* Zürcher translates it, interpreting it as a prophecy and using the future tense (1959, 320). I follow the Japanese translation, which places it in the past.

[2] Kāśyapa, or Mahākāśyapa, was among the senior disciples of the Buddha. In anti-Taoist polemics, he is an incarnation of Laozi (see Introduction). Kenkyūhan 1988, 575 n. 468, citing *Hongming ji* 7 (T. 2102; 52.47b); *Erjiao lun* 9 (T. 2103; 52.140a); *Poxie lun* (T. 2109; 52.162b). See also section 18.

[3] Kenkyūhan 1988, 575 n. 469. Among the four recipients of the Tao mentioned here, only Zhang Ling and Gan Shi, or Gan Ji, are known historically. The former received the Tao in 142 C.E. and became the first Celestial Master (see sec. 7). The latter was associated with the revelation of the *Taiping jing* (Scripture of Great Peace) in the first century C.E. On this text and its tradition, see Kaltenmark 1979; Kandel 1979; Mansvelt-Beck 1980; Petersen 1989, 1990a, 1990b, 1992; Hendrischke 1991 (in English); Wei 1981; Wang 1982; Tanaka 1984; Harada 1984; Maeda 1985b; Kamitsuka 1988 (in Chinese and Japanese). The *Taiping jing* as it survives today is found in DZ 1101, fasc. 746–55 and edited in Wang 1960.

[4] Kenkyūhan 1988, 575 n. 469. A similar passage is found in Cheng Xuanying's *Daode jing kaiti xujue yishu* (Supplementary Commentary and Topical Introduction to the *Daode jing*; P. 2353; Ōfuchi 1979, 463; trans. in Robinet 1977, 105). It is also cited in *BZL* 6 (T. 2110; 52.525c).

[5] This is the classic story of the first official introduction of Buddhism into China. It occurs first in the *Mouzi lihuo lun* (T. 2102; 52.4c–5a). It is entirely legendary because just at this time wars in Central Asia sealed off all roads to and from China. The *XDL* is the oldest literary work to cite the story. See Tsukamoto and Hurvitz 1985, 41–50. For a complete list of

"'In the morning, the emperor asked his ministers [what the dream meant]. Fu Yi[6] said: "It shows that the crown prince of the barbarian king in the west has realized the Tao and is now called the Buddha."

"'Emperor Ming duly sent out Zhang Qian with a small force to explore the sources of the Yellow River [in Ferghana]. He traveled through all thirty-six countries[7] until he finally reached Kapilavastu. The Buddha had already entered nirvāṇa, so Zhang only copied the 605,000 words of the sūtras.[8] He returned home in the eighteenth year of Everlasting Peace [75 C.E.]'."[9]

I laugh at this and say:

The *Hanshu* says,[10] "Zhang Ling lived under Emperor Xun of the Later Han [126–45 C.E.]. He went to Shu to study and retreated to Crane Cry Mountain. There he was devoured by a snake."

Now, Emperor Xun was Emperor Ming's grandson of the seventh generation. Zhang Ling, therefore, cannot have lived more than one hundred years before Emperor Ming.

Again, the text says: "Emperor Ming sent Zhang Qian to explore the

---

early references, see Tsukamoto 1974, 1:76–77. See also Hurvitz 1956, 28; Zürcher 1959, 22; Ch'an 1964, 29–31.

[6] Fu Yi, also known as Wuzhong, served as a minister under Zhangdi, the successor of Mingdi. See *Hou Hanshu* 80A.

[7] Kenkyūhan 1988, 576 n. 476. Thirty-six is the traditional number for Central Asian countries as mentioned in *Hanshu* 96.

[8] According to the *Huahu jing* as cited in the *SDZN*, Laozi "composed scriptures in 640,000 words" to instruct the barbarians (*SDZN* 9.20a).

[9] The activities of Emperor Ming are also, at somewhat greater length, described in the introduction to the *Sishier zhangjing* (Sūtra in Forty-two Sections) as it is found in *Chu sanzang jiji* (Collected Records from the Tripitaka) 6 (T. 2123; 55.42c; Kenkyūhan 1988, 575 n. 467). The same account is again cited in Tao Hongjing's (456–536) *Zhengao* (Declarations of the Perfected; DZ 1016, fasc. 637–40).

Emperor Ming of the Later Han dreamed that he saw a divine personage who was sixteen feet tall and had a halo surrounding his brow. He was flying into the emperor's halls. Joyful and delighted at this vision, the emperor asked everyone in his court what it might mean.

Fu Yi, a perceptive man, answered: "Your servant, I have heard that in India there is a man who has attained the Tao. He is called the Buddha. According to what I have heard, he can fly and his body is surrounded by a white radiance. Perhaps this is the spirit your majesty saw?"

The emperor understood. He consequently sent out Zhang Qian as the leader of a group of fourteen men, including the gentleman of the palace guard Qin Jing and the eminent scholar Wang Zun, to go to the country of the Greater Yuezhi and copy Buddhist sūtras in forty-two sections. He was then to store the texts secretly in the fourteenth section of the historical archives. (9.19b–20a)

On the *Zhengao* and its author, see Strickmann 1978b, 1979, 1981; Robinet 1984, 2:313–45; Mugitani 1976; Ishii 1980; Kamitsuka 1986–87.

[10] Kenkyūhan 1988, 576 n. 480. *Hou Hanshu* 64, biography of Liu Yan. For details on the controversy over Zhang's fate, see section 7.

sources of the Yellow River." This is equally foolish. According to the *Hanshu*, Zhang Qian set out to explore the sources of the Yellow River on behalf of Emperor Wu of the Former Han [140–86 B.C.E.].[11]

How, I ask, could Emperor Ming of the Later Han send Zhang Qian out again? Indeed, I never realized that Zhang Qian was such a long-lived immortal! Sent on missions generation after generation—what terrible hardships he must suffer![12]

All this foolishness! I can only laugh!

[11] See the biography of Zhang Qian in *Hanshu* 61 (Kenkyūhan 1988, 577 n. 482). For discussions, see Hirth 1917; McGovern 1939, 131–35.

[12] As if in anticipation of Zhen Luan's criticism, Tao Hongjing adds the following note to his description of the events in the *Zhengao*: "I would like to note that the Zhang Qian mentioned here is not the well-known traveler of the Former Han. Rather, he is a different person who happened to have the same name. Fu Yi is also known as Zhongwu, as can be learned from the *Hanshu*. Qin Jing, Wang Zun, and the other members of the mission are not clearly identified" (9.20a).

15

Suns and Moons Assembling

[148a3] The *Zhutian neiyin* (Esoteric Sounds of All Heavens) in its third section, under the heading "Eight-Character Spells of the Floating Ancestral Heaven," quotes the spell "*ze luo jue pu tai yuan da luo qian.*"[1]

The Sovereign of Heavenly Perfection[2] explains this spell:[3]

[1] Kenkyūhan 1988, 577 n. 488. This passage corresponds closely to *Zhutian neiyin yuzi* 3.19b and 20b (Esoteric Sounds and Spontaneous Jade Characters of All Heavens; *DZ* 97, fasc. 49), which has *ze luo jue pu, ti tai luo ying*. A similar spell, *ze luo pu tai lü luo da qian*, with nearly the same commentary is also found in *Duren jing* 4.11b (*DZ* 87, fasc. 38–39).

[2] This personage is quoted as the commentator in the *Zhutian neiyin*. A biographical account is found in *Lishi zhenxian tidao tongjian* 4.1a (Comprehensive Mirror through the Ages of Spirit Immortals and Those Who Embody the Tao; *DZ* 296, fasc. 139–48). Here he is described as a tall, hairy man who lived under the Yellow Emperor on Mount Emei, always surrounded by spirit lads and jade maidens. The Yellow Emperor received the Lingbao scriptures from him.

[3] The full text in the *DZ* version runs:

Ze is the mountain in heaven where the dragons have their lair. There is a yellow chamber on the mountain. It is also called the Terrace of Jade Glamor. *Luojue* is the esoteric name of the Lord of the Tao of Perfect Morning Light. He rules in the yellow chamber. Even in the chaos at the end of a great kalpa, he does not end but passes through to the initial kalpa Dragon Country and shines forth anew. Therefore, he brings great joy even in the midst of darkness. *Pu* is the secret appellation of the flying heavenly perfected. There are countless

"*Ze* is the mountain in heaven where the dragons have their lair. *Luo jue* is the esoteric name of the Lord of the Tao. *Pu tai* is the secret appellation of the Perfected.

"*Yu tai* [*yuan da*][4] is the Jade Terrace on the southern slope of Mount Ze. Thirty thousand suns and moons illuminate it from right and left. *Luo han* [*Luo qian*] is the Lady of the Moon.

"When the disasters at the end of a great kalpa strike, the suns and moons of all the heavens assemble on the Jade Terrace on Mount Ze. In all parts of the Great-Thousand World,[5] all under heaven is then changed into Great-Thousand Chaos."

I laugh at this and say:

The *Jiku jing* states:[6] "After the trigrams of heaven [Qian] and earth [Kun] have fallen into chaos, Juling and Huhai will newly create mountains and streams. From the darkness, suns and moons will be brought forth anew.[7]

"Thirty trillion (10^{12}) miles south of Mount Kunlun there is another Mount Kunlun. In the same way, there are a thousand Kunlun Mountains.

"One such system is called a Small-Thousand World. One thousand of these Small-Thousand Worlds is then called a Middle-Thousand World. One thousand of these Middle-Thousand Worlds in turn makes up one Great-Thousand World."[8]

---

numbers of them. *Yu tai* is the Jade Terrace located on the southern slope of Mount Ze. Thirty thousand suns and moons illuminate it from right and left. *Luoying* is the esoteric name of the celestial personage of the sun and the moon. She rules in the Sun-and-Moon Palace (3.19b).

The *Duren jing* version reads: "*Lüluo* is the Lady of the Moon. She is also called Luoying. Her complexion is like jade, and she wears a green skirt and pure robe. Thus, she is called Lüluo, 'green gauze.' She resides in the Sun-and-Moon Palace" (4.11b).

[4] The spell cited does not match the words explained in the commentary. Zhen Luan's original characters are noted in brackets.

[5] This reflects the chiliocosm theory of Buddhist cosmology:

One world = Mount Sumeru and its seven surrounding continents, together with the eight seas and the ring of iron mountains
1 small chiliocosm = 1,000 worlds
1 medium chiliocosm = 1,000 small chiliocosms
1 great chiliocosm = 1,000 medium chiliocoms

See Mochizuki 1933–36, 1598a; Beal 1871, 102. A Chinese outline is found in *Da zhidu lun* 7 (T. 1509; 25.113c). See Kenkyūhan 1988, 578 n. 493.

[6] Kenkyūhan 1988, 578 n. 496. There is no such passage in the *Jiku jing* of today's canon. A similar text, however, is found in *Yundu jieqi jing* 10b, 11b (DZ 319, fasc. 165).

[7] On this part of the passage, see 10 n. 5.

[8] The *Yundu jieqi jing* describes this cosmology as rather more complex:

Thirty quatrillion (10^{16}) miles south of Mount Kunlun, there is another Mount Kunlun.

In other words, in a Great-Thousand World, there must be ten billion (10^{10}) suns and moons altogether.

The text also says:[9] "When a great kalpa ends, heaven and earth collapse. There are no more suns, moons, or stars."

Let us now calculate this. All in all, there should be ten billion suns and moons assembling on the Jade Terrace. Why, then, does the Sovereign say that only thirty thousand arrive? If all the others do not come to the assembly, is it because they remain unaffected by kalpic disasters? Or is it that there are worlds entirely without any suns or moons?

If it is because these worlds do not have them, how can it be that, whereas here on earth every ordinary person is richly bathed in the light of the sun and the moon, the [beings in the] higher heavens above, supposedly fortunate and superior, are utterly without light?

Moreover, all that is beneath the sun and the moon is the World of Desire.[10] Lowly humanity that resides there cannot appeal to the higher world of Grand Network where cosmic disasters never strike. Could this be the reason why those distant suns and moons do not come to the gathering?

Or again, could it simply be that whoever compiled this scripture had just heard the expression "Great-Thousand World" and was confused about the exact numbers of its suns and moons and, thence, all these contradictions?

And another, and another, east and west, south and north, without end and utterly uncountable. One Kunlun established with one sun and one moon is called a four-corner universe, yet one cannot reach to all its ends. From one Kunlun to the next Kunlun, one reaches one thousand; this is one system. From one Kunlun to the next Kunlun, one reaches one thousand; this is a second system. From one Kunlun to the next Kunlun, one reaches one thousand; this is a third system. And so on, to one thousand systems, this is one small combination. From one small combination to one thousand, this is one Small-Thousand World.

From one Small-Thousand World to one thousand, this is one Small-Thousand World System. From one Small-Thousand World to one thousand, this is one Small-Thousand World System. From one Small-Thousand World again to one thousand, this is a second Small-Thousand World System. From one Small-Thousand World again to one thousand, this is a third Small-Thousand World System. When these three each reach to one thousand systems, then there are three thousand worlds or one Great-Thousand World. (11b)

[9] *Yundu jieqi jing* 12a.

[10] Kenkyūhan 1988, 578 n. 502. The lower twenty-eight of a total of thirty-six Taoist heavens constitute the Three Worlds. Among them the World of Desire, the *kāmaloka* of Buddhism, is found in the lowest six heavens. Here, beings still have desires for food, sleep, and sex. See *WSBY* 4.1a–3b; *DJYS* 7.1ab; *YJQQ* 3.6a.

16

The Highest Lord Is the Most Venerable

[148a23] The *Wenshi zhuan* says:[1]

"Laozi and Yin Xi traveled to heaven. Upon entering the white gate of the ninth layer,[2] the Emperor of Heaven received Laozi with proper respects.[3] Laozi thereupon ordered Yin Xi to also exchange formal greetings with His Majesty.

"Laozi said, 'The Highest Lord is the Most Venerable.[4] He regulates the sun and makes it shine. The Highest Lord resides in the Palace of the Seven Treasures on the Mountain of Jade Capital.[5] Above all the heavens, he is serene and obscure, pure and far distant'."

I laugh at this and say:

The *Shenxian zhuan* has:[6] "Shen Xi from Wu ascended to the immortals in broad daylight. After four hundred years, he came home and said:

"'When I first ascended to heaven, I wished to have an audience with

---

[1] Kenkyūhan 1988, 579 n. 506. This passage is not contained in the *Wenshi zhuan* as extant. The same passage is also cited in section 23. The *Wenshi zhuan* in the *SDZN* only mentions Laozi's ability to ascend to heaven (9.10b). The *Louguan benji* (Original Record of Longuan), another lost text on the exploits of Yin Xi cited in *Miaomen youqi* 7a, however, says that both sages went to heaven together. In the *Youlong zhuan,* Laozi and Yin Xi travel all around the earth then ascend to the nine heavens (4.2a–3b).

[2] On the nine layers of heaven in ancient Chinese cosmology, see Maspero 1924. On travels to heaven in Taoism, see Robinet 1976, 1989; Kroll 1985; Kohn 1992a, 96–116. Chinese references are found in Kenkyūhan 1988, 579 n. 507.

[3] On the historical relation of the Emperor of Heaven and the highest Taoist deities, see Fukunaga 1987b.

[4] Many titles are given to the Tao. As the *Shengxuan jing* has it, "The Tao said: 'I took the five energies and wandered around the eight ultimate ends of the universe. I was called Primordial Beginning or Venerable Lord or Highest Lord or Tathāgata. Sometimes I was the teacher of the world; sometimes I was the ancestor of the mystery'" (P. 2474; Ōfuchi 1979b, 264). On the various titles of Laozi, see also Yoshioka 1959, 153. On the relation of Laozi to the Heavenly Venerable, see Fukui 1952, 178–90.

[5] Kenkyūhan 1988, 579 n. 510. This information is also found in *Miaomen youqi* 2b (*DZ* 1123, fasc. 760). For details on this heaven, see section 1.

[6] Kenkyūhan 1988, 590 n. 513. This passage summarizes Shen Xi's biography in *Shenxian zhuan* 8 (*Daozang jinghua* 5.11, 8.33ab; *YJQQ* 109.6b–8a; *Taiping guangji* 5.36) For a translation, see Giles 1948, 31–33; Güntsch 1988, 243–46; Kohn 1993a, 326–28.

the Emperor of Heaven. But the Most Venerable could not be met. Therefore, I was first received by the Highest Lord. He was seated in the main hall surrounded by several hundred servants both male and female.'"[7]

This description leaves no doubt that the Highest Lord ranks beneath the Emperor of Heaven. The statement that the Highest Lord is the Most Venerable and rules above the manifold heavens is, therefore, false.

Now, let us look at the *Jiutian shengshen zhangjing* (Stanzas of the Vital Spirit of the Nine Heavens), which says:[8] "The Highest Lord resides in the palace of Mystery Metropolis. The Palace of Jade Clarity is above this."

How can there be another palace even above Jade Clarity? it must be two notches higher than Mystery Metropolis! Yet Laozi says, "The Highest Lord rules above the manifold heavens." How can there be a foolish mistake like this?

[7] The corresponding passage in the *Shenxian zhuan* says:

"Although I was not brought before the Emperor of Heaven himself, I did get to meet the Venerable Lord, who is his right-hand man. The attendants instructed me not to make any formal acknowledgments but simply to take my seat in silence. The celestial palace seemed composed of an insubstantial, luminous haze, shot through with an enormous variety of colors too fantastic to describe. There were hundreds of attendants, mostly female. In the gardens grew trees bearing pearls and jade; all sorts of immortality herbs and magic mushrooms sprouted in great profusion." (Kohn 1993a, 327)

In this version, the distinction is not between the Highest Lord and the Most Venerable but between the Emperor of Heaven and the Venerable Lord.

[8] Kenkyūhan 1988, 590 n. 517. The *Jiutian shengshen zhangjing* of today (DZ 318, fasc. 165) does not contain such a statement. Rather than ranking the gods, it describes the lords of the Three Treasures. The first, the Lord of Heavenly Treasure, is Jade Clarity; the second, the Lord of Numinous Treasure, is the Palace of Purple Tenuity in Mystery Metropolis (1ab; *WSBY* 24.1ab). Taken together, the two statements might be read to the effect that Jade Purity is higher than Mystery Metropolis.

17

The Five Grains Chisel Life Away

[148b8] The *Huahu jing* says:[1]

"When the Three Sovereigns cultivated the Tao, no human ever died. During High Antiquity, heaven brought forth sweet dew and earth produced springs of wine. People ate and drank these and enjoyed long life.[2]

"In Middle Antiquity, heaven brought forth the five energies and earth produced the five tastes.[3] People lived on these and prolonged their years.[4]

"In Lower Antiquity, the world declined. Heaven brought forth wind and rain, and earth nurtured the many species of wild animals. People caught and ate those.[5]

"I [the Venerable Lord] was grieved at their circumstances and, therefore, raised the various grains to feed the multitude of the people.[6] Consequently, the three sovereign [Celestial Masters] offered me five pecks of grain as a pledge of their faith.[7] They prayed that their descen-

---

[1] This passage is not found in the extant *Huahu jing*.

[2] Kenkyūhan 1988, 581 n. 519. This passage is found in the *Kaitian jing* (DZ 1437, fasc. 1059; *YJQQ* 2.9a–14b): "From Grand Antecedence to Grand Immaculate, heaven brought forth sweet dew and earth brought forth sweet wine. People nourished on these and attained long life. Upon death, they did not bury the dead but abandoned them in distant wilderness. This was High Antiquity" (3a; Kohn 1993a, 39).

Sweet dew and springs of wine are traditional signs of a golden age. See *Liezi* 5.9b, *Liji* 9.30 (Kenkyūhan 1988, 581 n. 522). In Taoism, swallowing the saliva to extend life is associated with nourishing on sweet dew. See *Baopuzi* 11/47/14 (Kenkyūhan 1988, 581 n. 523).

[3] Kenkyūhan 1988, 581 n. 524. The five energies are usually six: Yin and yang, wind and rain, darkness and light (*Zuozhuan,* Zhao 1). The five tastes are bitter, sour, sweet, pungent, and salty. For their role in relation to the five orbs, see Porkert 1974, 117–52.

[4] Again, the *Kaitian jing* reads: "The time from Chaos to the Great Lian is called Middle Antiquity. During this period, heaven brought forth the five energies, and earth produced the five tastes. People lived on these and prolonged their years" (4a; Kohn 1993a, 40).

[5] The *Kaitian jing* has this, too: "Fu Xi taught the people how to make nets and traps to catch birds and beasts. People ate those" (4b; Kohn 1993a, 41). The division into High (Fu Xi), Middle (Wenwang, the beginning of the Zhou), and Lower Antiquity (Confucius) is part of ancient Chinese historiography. See *Hanshu* 30 (Kenkyūhan 1988, 581 n. 521).

[6] Here, the *Kaitian jing* has, "The Venerable Lord taught Shennong about the hundred plants and gave him the five grains for the people to plant and reap. Consequently, they ate those instead of taking the lives of birds and beasts." (5a; Kohn 1993a, 41).

The first cultivation of grain through Shennong, the Divine Agriculturist, is part of classical Chinese mythology. It is mentioned in *Yijing,* "Xici" as well as in *Huainanzi* 19.1a (Kenkyūhan 1988, 582 n. 528). For more, see Mitarai 1971; Yuan 1979, 53; Yuan 1985, 299. Liu 1988, 276–99 contains a collection of relevant classical passages with explanations.

[7] The Celestial Masters collected five pecks of rice as a contribution from their followers

dants should live for generations unbroken and that the five grains would continue to grow in this Country of the Gods."[8]

I laugh at this and say:

The *Wufu jing* states:[9] "The third immortal king[10] told the Sovereign Emperor: 'People live long and reach old age because they do not eat the five grains.'

"As the *Dayou jing* (Scripture of Great Existence) says:[11] 'The five grains are chisels that cut away life. They make the five inner organs stink and shorten the life span. Once this food has entered the stomach, there is no more chance of longevity. If you aspire to complete avoidance of death, you must keep your intestines free of excrement'."[12]

Again, the *Wufu jing:*[13] "Yellow Essence is the energy of triple yang

---

(Kenkyūhan 1988, 582 n. 529). See Levy 1956; Stein 1963; Kobayashi 1992. For further bibliography, see 7 n. 9.

[8] The expression "country of the gods" as a name for China occurs first in the biography of Mencius in *Shiji* 74 (Kenkyūhan 1988, 582 n. 531).

[9] Kenkyūhan 1988, 582 n. 532. This version is much shorter than the corresponding text in *Wufuxu* today (*DZ* 388, fasc. 183). It has:

> The third immortal king also told the emperor, "In the old days I followed a dietetic regimen and attained immortality. My teacher made me increase the sweet spring in my mouth and swallow it in accordance with the following incantation:
>
> > The white stones, hard and rocky, are rolling on and on.
> > The gushing spring, bubbling and pervasive, becomes a thick juice.
> > Drink it and attain long life—longevity forever longer!
>
> "These twenty-two words—you should follow them! If you can actually do this and nourish on the True One without stopping, swallow from your flowery pond without interruption, then your inner energy will grow and remain strong, never to be weakened. You attain the Tao by avoiding all grains. You will never again have to follow the rhythm of the moon and plant or harvest. Now, the people of mysterious antiquity, they reached old age because they remained in leisure and never ate any grains." (3.21b–22a)

[10] This is a title in the heavenly hierarchy, which consists of immortal kings, dukes, ministers, and so on. See *Zhengao* 1.15a; *YJQQ* 3.6b (Kenkyūhan 1988, 582 n. 533). For more on the celestial administration, see section 11.

[11] Kenkyūhan 1988, 582 n. 535. This passage corresponds closely to the *Wufuxu* where it is introduced by "The Verse of Great Existence says" (3.22a). The same text is also cited as from the *Dayou jing* in *SDZN* 3.1b.

[12] On the efficacy of avoiding grains to attain long life, see *Zhuangzi* 2/1/29; *Baopuzi* 15/67/6 (Kenkyūhan 1988, 582 nn. 534, 538). For a general discussion of Taoist dietetics, see Lévi 1983; Engelhardt 1987.

[13] Kenkyūhan 1988, 583 n. 539. This is a shorter passage than that in the *Wufuxu:*

> Yellow Essence is the essence of highest yang. If swallowed, it makes people live long. . . . Yellow Essence as a plant enhances life. It is the energy of triple yang and enters the Palace of Great Clarity above. Its refined energy is mysterious and wondrous; it follows along with the changes in utmost purity. Its brilliance flows through the Nine Wilds; it spreads throughout the Six Harmonies. It may float with the clouds; it may lie hidden in mountains, ever changing with the flow of cosmic energy. Its stem is erect and strong; even its leaves are full of its essence. Its taste is sweet and fragrant. (2.18b–19a)

and enters the Palace of Great Clarity above. When eaten, it tastes sweet and is quite delicious. It also prolongs life."[14]

Considering this, I really do not understand why Laozi did not give people this essence but made them eat the five grains, which only rot the intestines. Moreover, the three sovereign [Celestial Masters] were all spirit men. Why, then, did they not make their descendants kings in the Country of Long Life?[15] Instead, they left them with those rules about offering five pecks of grain and prayed that they would become kings in the Country of the Gods, pursuing a shortened life span through the very foodstuff that chisels human life away and rots the intestines. Laughable, that!

[14] Yellow Essence (*huangjing*) is a plant. As the *Bowu zhi* (Record of Ample Things) says, "The herb of highest yang is called Yellow Essence. By eating it, one can attain long life" (5.4a). The *Baopuzi* also mentions it (11/45/2; Kenkyūhan 1988, 583 n. 542). Ware translates "knotgrass" and says: "It is also called hare bamboo, restorative, or pearl pendant. . . . It is better to eat its flowers than the fruit, better these than the root" (1966, 179). See also Stuart 1976, 339.
[15] Kenkyūhan 1988, 583 n. 545. The Country of Long Life is mentioned in the "Haiwai xijing" section of the *Shanhai jing* (Classic of Mountains and Seas; trans. in Mathieu 1983).

18

Laozi Became the Buddha

[148b24] The *Xuanmiao neipian* says:[1]

"After Laozi had crossed the pass and reached the kingdom of Kapila-vastu, he entered the mouth of Queen Māyā. Later he ripped open her left armpit and was born.

"He then took seven steps and exclaimed: 'In heaven above, on the earth below, I alone am venerable.'

"This was the beginning of Buddhism."

I laugh at this and say:

The *Huahu jing* states:[2] "When Laozi converted Kashmir, all its people began to worship Buddhism.

[1] The same passage is also cited in section 5. For details on the text, see appendix 2.
[2] Kenkyūhan 1988, 583 n. 548. This passage is not contained in any extant version of the *Huahu jing*. A somewhat similar passage, however, is found in the *Hunyuan shengji* (DZ 770, fasc. 551–53). It runs:

"Then Laozi said: 'One hundred years from now, there will be another, a true Buddha, who now dwells in the Tuṣita Heaven. He will then be born in Śrāvastī [Kapilavastu] as a son to King Śuddhodana.[3] At that time, I will send Yin Xi to be born and become the Buddha's disciple. His name will be Ānanda. He will compile the scriptures in twelve divisions.'[4]

"One hundred years after Laozi had left, a son was indeed born to the king of Śrāvastī. After six years of mortification, he perfected the Tao and was named the Buddha Śākyamuni.[5]

"Forty-nine years later, when he was about to enter nirvāṇa,[6] Laozi appeared again on earth. He was then called Kāśyapa.[7] Under a pair of sal trees, he asked the Tathāgata thirty-six questions on behalf of the great assemblies [of followers].[8] Then the Buddha entered nirvāṇa.

The Venerable Lord wished to return to the Middle Kingdom and bade farewell to the barbarians. But they seized his carriage, not wanting to let him go. He understood their good intentions and said, "I will now return to heaven for a short while to settle the registers of humans and demons. Thereafter, I shall descend again. Moreover, in about one hundred years, I shall send you the Buddha. He will be born on the soil of your country and spread the teaching among your descendants." (5.4ab) . . .

Thus, the Venerable Lord bade farewell to the barbarians. About one hundred years later, King Fanda [a former king of Kashmir] descended to Kapilavastu to be born as the son of the king. He was to become the Buddha and teach the people. In the ninth year of King Zhuang of the Zhou, with the year star in *guisi*, in the night of the seventh day of the fourth month, he was born through the right armpit of Queen Māyā. (5.11b)

[3] The various births of the Buddha are recorded in the Jātaka tales (trans. in Dutoit 1906; Aspinwall 1927). On his birth as the Buddha Śākyamuni, see *Taizi ruiying benqi jing* 1 (T. 185; 3.473b; Kenkyūhan 1988, 584 n. 553). For a discussion, see Karetzky 1992.

[4] Kenkyūhan 1988, 584 n. 555. On Ānanda and the compilation of the first Buddhist canon, see *Mohe moye jing* (Mahāmāyā sūtra) 3 (T. 383; 12.1013b). See Lamotte 1987, 30, for more details.

[5] This is part of the standard hagiography of the Buddha. See *Guoqu xianzai yinguo jing* (Sūtra on Cause and Effect in Past, Present, and Future) 3 (T. 189; 3.639a; Karetzky 1992, 129).

[6] Kenkyūhan 1988, 584 n. 558. At the time of his *parinirvāṇa*, the Buddha reportedly had been teaching for forty-nine years. See *Foban nihuan jing* 2 (Mahāparinirvāṇa Sūtra; T. 7; 1.171b). Hurvitz 1956, 59; Warder 1970, 43–54; Karetzky 1992, 191.

[7] Kenkyūhan 1988, 584 n. 559. Kāśyapa was a brahmin of Magadha who became one of the main disciples of the Buddha and the leader of Buddhist ascetics. After the Buddha's *parinirvāṇa*, Kāśyapa convoked and directed the first Buddhist council. Because of this, he is also known as the "chairman" and venerated as the first compiler of the Buddhist canon. See *Niepan jing* 3 (Nirvāṇa Sūtra; T. 374; 12.379b); Mochizuki 1933–36, 4721b. Laozi in the role of Kāśyapa is also mentioned in *Erjiao lun* 9 (T. 2103; 52.140a); *BZL* 5 (T. 2110; 52.524a). For more details on the emergence and development of this identification, see Zürcher 1959, 312; Ōzaki 1976, 109–10.

[8] A variant version of the same *Huahu jing* citation is found in *BZL* 5: "When Laozi realized that the Buddha was about to enter nirvāṇa, he appeared again in the world. He was then called Kāśyapa. He asked questions on behalf of the community [of followers in the wood of sal trees" (T. 2110; 52.524a). In terms of the history of Buddhism, this is an apocryphal tradition. Kāśyapa plays no role in the *Mahāparinirvāṇa Sūtra* (Warder 1970, 107–16). For later references to the questions of Kāśyapa, see commentaries to the text in *Daban niepan*

"After cremating the Buddha's corpse,[9] Kāśyapa assembled his relics, distributed them to different countries, and erected stūpas over them.[10] Later, King Aśoka also built eighty-four thousand stūpas."[11]

Following this account, Laozi cannot actually have become the Buddha. If he had indeed become the Buddha, would he not have had to cremate his own corpse and erect stūpas in his own honor? What a joke!

Yet many texts assure us that Laozi, in fact, became the Buddha, just as they say that he served as the teacher of dynasties. Really, must all the dynastic teachers and buddhas of the world inevitably depend on old Boyang? Must the salvation of humankind, the reform of the world, always be steered by Mr. Li Er?[12]

If you say that even the Buddha could not be himself without the Tao, does this mean that ever since the primordial beginning of things there was only one and the same Laozi? There never were any others allowed to realize the Tao and serve as dynastic teachers? If this is the case, then Laozi really puts himself ahead[13] as the only one on earth able to perform these tasks.

At the same time, Buddhist sūtras maintain that everyone can attain the fruits of Buddhahood by practicing the proper cultivation. Taoist scriptures do not speak of this. For them, there was and is only one, the

---

jingshu 7 (T. 1767; 38.76b; Kenkyūhan 1988, 585 n. 562); *Daban niepan jing jijie* 8 (T. 1763; 37.411b); *Fozu tongji* 4 (T. 2035; 49.164c).

[9] For the events surrounding the cremation of the Buddha's corpse, see *Fo suoxing zan* 5 (*Buddhacarita*, T. 192; 4.52a; Kenkyūhan 1988, 585 n. 563); Karetzky 1992, 197.

[10] According to the early records, the various states in which the Buddha had taught all laid claim to his ashes and a considerable quarrel arose. The claimants were pacified by a brahmin who gave them a share each; thus, eight shares were distributed and eight stūpas were built in various countries of northern India. In addition, the brahmin erected a stūpa in his own village over the urn in which he had first collected the ashes. A clan who came too late to receive anything, furthermore, built a stūpa over the charcoal embers of the Buddha's pyre. Thus, there were ten stūpas originally believed to contain actual physical relics of the Buddha. See Warder 1970, 227; Karetzky 1992, 198.

[11] According to Buddhist histories, which in substance seem confirmed by archaeology, King Aśoka, who reigned around the middle of the third century B.C.E., opened most of the original stūpas and removed the relics of the Buddha. He divided them into eight-four thousand parts and built as many new stūpas to distribute them over his empire, consecrating his land, as it were, for Buddhism. The classical record of the king's activity is the *Aśokavadāna* (Story of King Aśoka; trans. in Strong 1983). Its Chinese version is found in *Ayu wang jing* (Aśokarāja-sūtra; T. 3042; 50, 135a). See Kenkyūhan 1988, 585 n. 565. See also Warder 1970, 267; Bhandarkar 1955; Kern 1956; Lamotte 1987, 223–59; Strong 1983, 109–19.

[12] Boyang is one of the names of Laozi. It is first mentioned in *Liexian zhuan* 9 (Kaltenmark 1953, 60; Kenkyūhan 1988, 585 n. 567). Li Er is Laozi's personal name in the biography in *Shiji* 63. For a list of Laozi's various names, see Yoshioka 1959, 152; Seidel 1969, 65.

[13] According to *Daode jing* 22, this is precisely what the sage does not do (Kenkyūhan 1988, 585 n. 571).

Venerable Lord. How, then, is it that Buddhism is so generous while Taoism is so mean?

In addition, Taoist words are foolish and the tradition is hollow. One cannot make head or tail of its claims: just as the *Shuji* states that Zhang Ling was devoured by a snake, while the Taoists claim that he ascended to heaven in broad daylight;[14] just like the *Hanshu,* which says that Liu An was killed upon imperial order, whereas Taoist legends make him out to be an immortal who never died at all.[15]

Is it, therefore, any wonder that Taoist accounts lie about Laozi becoming the Buddha?

Moreover, the *Zao tiandi jing* says: "When he had converted the barbarians in the west, Laozi transformed his body and vanished. His left eye became the sun; his right eye became the moon."[16] Yet, according to the *Xuanmiao jing,* "Laozi strode on the essence of the sun and entered the mouth of Queen Māyā." This means that Laozi strode on the essence of his very own left eye to enter her mouth.

If we now assume that [Laozi as] the all-pervasive spirit of the Great Tao is present everywhere,[17] then why would he have to rely on one specific essence to enter the womb of the queen? If, however, he must make use of some essence, then this essence, in turn, has to depend on his head. Consequently, if he indeed strides on his own head to enter the queen, then both his eyes should be going in together.

But here he is—entering her astride on only one eye! Is there thus a single-eyed, lopsided Great Tao? How utterly ridiculous!

[14] This repeats the argument in sections 7 and 14.

[15] Liu An, the Prince of Huainan (d. 154 B.C.E.), was the compiler of the *Huainanzi* (see *Hanshu* 44; Kenkyūhan 1988, 586 n. 577). He is stylized as an immortal who ascended to heaven in broad daylight in *Shenxian zhuan* 4 (Giles 1948, 42–45; Güntsch 1988, 119–28). According to historical sources, however, he committed suicide after being accused of rebellion. See Kandel 1973.

[16] On this passage, see 1 n. 12.

[17] Such a claim is first expressed in *Zhuangzi* 59/22/44; Watson 1968, 240–41 (see Kenkyūhan 1988, 586 n. 584).

19

Gautama as a Messenger

[148c25] The *Laozi huahu ge* (Song on Laozi Converting the Barbarians) says:[1]

"When I was in Kapilavastu, I gave Gautama the following order: 'Together with the great bodhisattvas go out and bring [teach][2] the scriptures east to the country of Qin. Passing through the Country of the Gods, you will reach the Eastern Sea. Wherever you go, spread the [highest] world-honored teaching and use it to guide the ignorant masses. I give you this teaching of highest spiritual power, this Tao of transformation that will last a thousand years. When that time is up [ends], I shall return myself.[3] Be careful though that you do not grow attached to the central [eastern] land of Qin. Otherwise [lest] the Emperor [energy] of Heaven will be angry, and the Highest Lord will stamp [trample] the earth in rage'."

I laugh at this and say:

Gautama is, in fact, Śākyamuni. The *Huahu jing* states:[4] "In the reign period Original Initiation under King Zhuang of Zhou [696–681 B.C.E.], with the year star in *bingchen,* the son of King Śuddhodana attained full enlightenment. He was then called the Buddha Śākyamuni.[5]

"When Laozi saw that he was about to leave the world, he feared that humanity might fall into lax and lazy ways. Therefore, he descended to earth once more in Tārā village. He was then called Kāśyapa.[6]

---

[1] Kenkyūhan 1988, 586 n. 586. This passage corresponds closely to the tenth chapter of the *Huahu jing,* "Xuange" (Songs of Mystery), as found in P. 2004 (Ōfuchi 1979, 675; T. 2139; 54.1267c).

[2] Readings in brackets give the variants found in P. 2004. See also Kenkyūhan 1988, 587 nn. 590, 592, 596–99.

[3] Kenkyūhan 1988, 587 n. 595. The *Za ahan jing* (Samyuktāgama) 25 (trans. in Geiger 1925; Rhys-Davids 1950) has a similar prophecy.

Today, I shall take the true law and entrust it to people and celestials, so that all beings in the heavens and all people of the world receive the law. This law that I teach shall not change for one thousand years. . . .

After one thousand years have passed, the time will come when this law that I teach will perish. Then there will be no law, and I will again appear in the world. (T. 99; 2.177b–78c)

[4] Citation unclear. Translated in Zürcher 1959, 312.

[5] On the dating of Laozi's emigration in relation to the birth of the Buddha, see 2 n. 10; appendix 1.

[6] The birth of Kāśyapa in Tārā village is recorded in the *Mahāparinirvāṇa sūtra* (Warder 1970, 107–16). See *Niepan jing* 3 (T. 374; 12.379b; Kenkyūhan 1988, 588 n. 606).

"He became a close follower of the Buddha and, after the latter's demise, cremated his corpse and assembled his relics. Distributing them to various countries, he erected stūpas over them."[7]

Relying on the latter account, Śākyamuni had not yet been born, so Laozi could not possibly have ordered Gautama to go to the eastern lands. Even if we assume that he had already been born and become the Buddha, how could he have received a commission from Kāśyapa and served as his messenger for a thousand years?

In addition, how could a bodhisattva who personally served the Buddha possibly order the Buddha to become a messenger? On top of everything, King Zhuang of the Zhou ruled only for fifteen years. Because his reign began with the year star in *yiyou*, none of that period happened to be a *bingchen* year.[8] And, of course, the reign title Original Initiation is entirely fictitious.

Verily, it is enough to make one cover one's ears![9] It might even cause the Highest Lord to stamp the earth in rage!

[7] For Kāśyapa's activities, see section 18.

[8] Kenkyūhan 1988, 588 n. 612. A *bingchen* year would have been the thirty-second year of King Zhuang's reign. The backward calculation of the stems and branches relies on the record of the *Shiji*.

[9] This is a decisive and ancient way to show that one cannot bear to hear certain things. See *Zuozhuan*, Zhao 31 (Kenkyūhan 1988, 588 n. 613).

20

Offerings of Wine and Meat and Service to Deviant Spirits in Pursuit of the Tao

[149a12] The *Duren miaojing* says:[1]

"The demon kings of the Three Worlds each have their particular spells. Recite them one hundred times, and your name will be entered in the registers of life in the Southern Palace.[2] Recite them one thousand times, and you will be received by the demon kings. Recite them ten thousand times, and you will fly up and into the great void, go beyond the Three Worlds, and become a lord among immortals."

[1] Kenkyūhan 1988, 588 n. 615. This passage corresponds closely to *Duren jing* 1.18ab (*DZ* 1, fasc. 1–13).

[2] Demon kings, as opposed to the host of malevolent demons and nasty sprites, serve as powerful protectors of active Taoists. See Kamitsuka 1992b.

The Southern Palace is the place where the registers of immortal life are kept. Much of the

The *Xuanzhong jingjing* (Essential Scripture of Central Mystery) has:[3]

"Taoists receive precepts,[4] talismans,[5] and registers.[6] They erect altars in the direction of the five sacred mountains[7] and worship them repeatedly with offerings of wine and meat."[8]

I laugh at this and say:

The *Guanshen dajie* (Great Precepts of Self-observation) says:[9] "Students of the Tao must not offer sacrifices to demons and spirits. They must not pay obeisance to them."

These demon kings still belong to the World of Desire; they have not

---

meditative activity, especially of Shangqing Taoists, aims at traveling ecstatically into the heavenly realms and having one's name removed from the files of death and entered into the registers of life at the Southern Palace. See *Tianguan santu* (*DZ* 1366, fasc. 1040; trans. in Kohn 1993a, 257–67) for a detailed description. See also *Zhengao* 12.10b, 16.1b; *WSBY* 41.16b, 50.12b (Kenkyūhan 1988, 589 n. 617). For a discussion of the practice, see Robinet 1976, 1979, 1989.

[3] Kenkyūhan 1988, 589 n. 621. Citation unclear. The same text appears again in section 33 below and in *BZL* 2 (T. 2110; 52.497b). A different *Xuanzhong ji* is also cited by Du Guangting in connection with Laozi's lineage. See *Daode zhenjing guangsheng yi* 2.18b (*DZ* 725, fasc. 440–48).

[4] Taoist precepts, in general, are patterned on the basic Buddhist system, but different schools add various special rules and regulations. See Hackmann 1920; Yoshioka 1961; Akizuki 1964; Kusuyama 1982, 1983; Bokenkamp 1989; Ren 1990, 288–339; Kohn 1994.

[5] Taoist talismans are essential for proper protection from demons and free passage among the spirits. They go back to the tallies used in the administration under the Zhou and are inspired by ancient sacred charts, such as the *Hetu* and *Luoshu*. See Doré 1914–38, vol. 2; Kaltenmark 1960; Saso 1978; Seidel 1981, 1983; Schipper 1967; Yamada 1987.

[6] Registers are lists of deities' names that Taoists receive upon initiation. They identify bearers as members of the celestial hierarchy. See Ōfuchi 1985b; Ren 1990, 340–90.

[7] The five sacred mountains are Mount Tai in the east, Mount Song in the south, Mount Heng in the center, Mount Hua in the west, and Mount Heng in the north. Associated with the five phases, they are the mainstays of the world and represent the horizontal structure of the universe. Power over them with the help of talismans, especially the *Wuyue zhenxing tu* (Chart of the True Shape of the Five Sacred Mountains), leads to control over the world and approach to the Tao. See Schipper 1967. Their worship in Lingbao Taoism is described in *WSBY* 34 and 39 (see Kenkyūhan 1988, 590 n. 623).

[8] Offerings of wine and meat were part of ancient Chinese religious ritual as much as of sealing formal covenants between clans and political groups. See Eichhorn 1976; Bilsky 1975; Vandermeersch 1980; Lewis 1990.

In a Taoist context, the *Baopuzi* states that wine and meat should be offered in a pledging ceremony when the practitioner enters the mountains (17/82/1; Ware 1966, 285). See Kenkyūhan 1988, 588 n. 614. They were also part of communal feasts (*chu;* see Stein 1971b). The *Suishu* in its tract on Taoism mentions wine and meat as part of a *jiao* ceremony: "At night, under the stars and zodiacal signs, Taoists offer wine and meat, cakes and cookies, sacrificing them one after the other to the Heavenly Emperor of the Great One, to the five planets, and twenty-eight lunar mansions. They also prepare a written document like a formally presented petition to address the gods. This is known as performing the *jiao*" (35.12b; Ware 1933, 246).

[9] These two rules are contained in *Dajie wen* 9b (*DZ* 1364, fasc. 1039). See Kenkyūhan 1988, 590 n. 625.

yet gone beyond all existence. How, then, could the mere recital of their incantation for one hundred times cause one to reach the Southern Palace?

Besides, the practices of the three Zhangs contain special services to the earth god and the stove god at the spring and autumn equinoxes.[10] They also have ritual offerings just like those of the common people at the summer and winter solstices.[11] The military talismans and earth-god tokens [used in such offerings] speak of generals and soldiers [to fight against demons];[12] none of them contain even a word of precepts against evil or exhortations toward the good.[13]

Now, as regards all these gods—Are they popular deities or are they part of the Tao? If they are popular deities, Taoists should not venerate them. If they are part of the Tao, they should not offer them wine and meat.[14]

In any case, how could they ever go out of the Three Worlds by merely reciting some demon king's incantation and performing petty rituals? Is it not really pitiful?

[10] For such sacrifices as practiced by the Celestial Masters, see Stein 1964, 55; Gernet 1956, 253.
   On the earth god in ancient China, see Chavannes 1910. On the stove god, see Yuan 1960, 177–81; Stein 1971a. Their worship—still part of popular religion today, with the ancient god of the soil now merged with the lord of the community, Tudigong—is attested even before the Han. See *Liji* 6.35 ("Yueling"); *Fengsu tongyi* 8.61 (Kenkyūhan 1988, 590 n. 629).

[11] Kenkyūhan 1988, 590 n. 629. This practice is specified in *Daomen kelue* 1b (Abbreviated Rules for Taoist Followers; *DZ* 1127, fasc. 761) and in the *Santian neijie jing* (*DZ* 1205, fasc. 876): "On auspicious days in summer and winter, the people should worship their ancestors and deceased parents. In the second and eighth months, they should offer sacrifices to the god of the soil and the stove god" (1.6ab).

[12] Kenkyūhan 1988, 590 n. 631. The fight against noxious influences and demons was seen as a military enterprise. Every Taoist was equipped with registers of varying numbers of generals and soldiers to defend him. See *Zhengyi yuelu yi* 4a–6a (Arranged Observances of Orthodox Unity; *DZ* 797, fasc. 565); *Yaoxiu keyi* 9.8b (Essential Rules and Observances; *DZ* 463, fasc. 204–7); Ren 1990, 340.
   The connection between the supernatural and the military is also evident in the old myth of the battle between Huangdi and Chiyou. Here the Dark Girl descended from heaven and bestowed military talismans on Huangdi, which helped him to victory (*Shiji* 15). According to Du Guangting, the same feat is performed by the Western Queen Mother (*Yongcheng jixian lu* 1.10b–11a; *DZ* 783, fasc. 560–61). For references on Huangdi, see section 4.

[13] Kenkyūhan 1988, 590 n. 628. The same criticism is also voiced in *BZL* 2 (T. 2110; 52.497b).

[14] On the delimitation of Taoism versus popular religion in the Six Dynasties, see Stein 1971b, 1979; Fukunaga 1987a; Miyakawa 1974, 1979; Robinet 1991, 69–72.

21

Buddhist Deviant Teachings Disturb the Political Order

[149125] The *Huahu jing* says:[1]

"Buddhism first arose in the barbarian countries. Because the western region belongs to the energy of metal, people there are harsh and lack proper rites.[2] Later, the gentlemen of the Country of the Gods imitated their observances and established Buddhism.[3]

"Everywhere people offered special veneration [to Buddhism], turning their backs on their original tradition and pursuing the newly arrived. Their words were empty and careless and lacked harmony with the wondrous teaching [of the Tao].[4] They adorned scriptures and carved images, deluding kings and ministers alike.

"Thus, all over the empire floods and droughts, rebellions and insurrections began to succeed each other. In less than ten years [after the transmission of Buddhism], disasters and strange phenomena came to be common occurrences.[5] The five planets deviated from their course, mountains tumbled, and rivers ran dry.[6]

---

[1] Citation unclear. According to Zürcher, this is part of the original *Huahu jing* of the fourth century (1959, 305–6).

[2] The same argument is made in sections 8 and 34 and in the *BZL* (T. 2110; 52.178bc). Here the basic forces of yin and yang are mentioned along with their corresponding qualities of west and east, death and life, metal and wood, left and right, righteousness and benevolence, shallow and deep, the trigrams *kun* and *qian,* and so on. The barbarians' lack of civilization because of their "metal" energy is also emphasized in the *Miehuo lun* (T. 2102; 52.50c; Kenkyūhan 1988, 591 n. 639) and in the first chapter of the *Huahu jing* (S. 1857; T. 2139; 54.1267a).

[3] Kenkyūhan 1988, 591 n. 640. This echoes Gu Huan's *Yixia lun* (See app. 1): "Nowadays people change the nature of the central country of Xia [China] and imitate the practices of the western barbarians" (*Nanshi* 75; *Nan Qishu* 54).

[4] "Wondrous teaching" (*miaofa*) imitates the expression "wonderful law" as it occurs in the title of the *Lotus Sūtra.* See Kenkyūhan 1988, 592 n. 646.

[5] The text here seems to link the various natural calamities, wars, and insurrections of the first century C.E., which were indeed numerous, to the introduction of Buddhism under Emperor Ming. It may refer specifically to the epidemics and earthquakes of the year 76, the famines and fires of 77, the strange occurrences of 79 (Franke 1930, 388). On the lore of omens and their political interpretation in the Han, see Crespigny 1976. For references to such occurrences in earlier Chinese sources, see Kenkyūhan 1988, 592 nn. 649–51.

[6] According to ancient Chinese belief, all these are signs that the mandate of heaven is changing, that the world as currently known is coming to an end. Within the intricate mutual balance of heaven, earth, and humanity, this is the result of people's wrong behavior, in particular, the worship of inferior or deviant deities (see Bilsky 1975; Eichhorn 1976).

In Taoism, the idea is prominent in *Santian neijie jing* 1ab (*DZ* 1205, fasc. 876). The text here specifically echoes the *Hanshu* (see Kenkyūhan 1988, 592 n. 652): "Heaven above was

"Ever since, the royal rule has been at peace no longer. This is because Buddhism brought disorder. Emperors and kings no longer pay obeisance in their ancestral temples; the common people no longer sacrifice to their forefathers. Because of this the ancestral spirits and the earth god, the Tao and the primordial energy can no longer recover their proper way.[7]

I laugh at this and say:

The *Zuigen pin* (The Roots of Sin) says:[8] "The Heavenly Venerable of Primordial Beginning said, 'As the kalpa was half over, in the first year of Highest Sovereign, I liberated humanity and extended people's life spans to eighteen thousand years. After I left, people's minds became decadent, and there were orgiastic cults and deviant deities[9] with offerings that included blood sacrifices. People would even slaughter each other, bringing early death and harm upon themselves. Thus, their life spans had no fixed length'."

According to this account, orgiastic cults and deviant deities were the pleasure and delight of the myriad gods. The union of primordial

---

quaking in anger, disasters and strange phenomena descended below, the sun and moon were eclipsed, the five planets deviated from their course, mountains tumbled, and rivers ran dry" (chap. 85).

[7] The ancestral spirits, more importantly, those of the imperial house, were believed to control the forces of nature and had to be offered sacrifices regularly to ensure the timeliness of rain and sunshine and the fertility of the land (see Bilsky 1975, 37; Eichhorn 1976). The earth god symbolizes the land of the ancestors and is especially responsible for excesses of yin energy such as solar eclipses and floods (Chavannes 1910, 491–501).

The Tao and the primordial energy are the two fundamental forces of the universe, seen as closely related yet distinct principles in Taoist thought. The Tao is the metaphysical, ruling principle, whereas energy is the physical, governed force. Only through their interaction can beings come to life (Mugitani 1985, 76; Kohn 1991, 84–95). For Chinese references, see Kenkyūhan 1988, 592 n. 655.

[8] Kenkyūhan 1988, 593 n. 656. This passage is shorter than the version in the *Zuigen pin* today (*DZ* 457, fasc. 202). The first part is already cited in section 2. The full text runs:

As the kalpa was half over, I allowed for a gradual decline. People's life spans were then reduced to a mere eighteen thousand years.

After I had left, the course of heaven continued in its cycle and people's minds became decadent. They schemed against each other, jealously guarded their egoistic advantages, and struggled in their competition for merit and fame. They had no more faith in the scriptures and the teaching but were full of doubts regarding the truth of heaven. Their mouths would say "right" while in their hearts they thought "wrong." So they created their own personal teachings.

There were orgiastic cults and deviant deities with offerings that included blood sacrifices. In utter delusion and not responsible for their actions, people would even slaughter each other, bringing early death and harm upon themselves. Their destinies did no longer accord with principle and their life spans had no fixed length. (1.3ab)

[9] The expression also occurs in *Baopuzi* 9/38/17 (Ware 1966, 153). See Kenkyūhan 1988, 593 n. 659.

energy with the Tao ensured happiness and prosperity. Why, then, does the text say that those very practices led to cutting human life short and destabilizing it?[10]

Again, before the time of Emperor Ming of the Han [r. 58–76 C.E.], when Buddhism was not yet practiced,[11] the Tao and the primordial energy flourished greatly. Why, then, is it that in those times wars and insurrections occurred frequently, that floods and droughts succeeded each other? It rained blood, mountains tumbled, and famines and disasters succeeded each other.[12] Above all, the tyrants Jie and Zhou punished men by tying them alive to the iron pillar.[13]

It has now been five hundred years since the reign of Emperor Ming and the introduction of Buddhism. In this time, have there been any ominous disasters or cruel governments worse than before? Looking at old times from the standpoint of today, could anyone seriously falsify the facts? With all properly recorded on bamboo and silk, the truth cannot be denied.

Trifling as my opinion may be, I have tried to weigh the two teachings. Because Taoism is humble and withdrawing[14] and propagates false practices, the veracity of Buddhism is made clear. As Buddhism is pure and upright and accords with principle, it has the potential to develop the true inner nature of all beings. Not judging Taoism this way, one should certainly die with laughter.

[10] Taoists traditionally have understood themselves as protectors of life. Blood sacrifices, a common part of ancient Chinese ritual and the sealing of covenants (see Lewis 1990) were especially horrible to them. Taoism in its history has, thus, undertaken countless efforts to eradicate such practices or, at least, distance itself from them (see Strickmann 1980, 225, on the notion of "heterodoxy"). This has, however, always been a delicate task, since the Taoists' "own practices were basically, at least in large parts, the same as those of the popular specialists" (Stein 1979, 80). See also Stein 1971; Fukunaga 1987a. Taoist collections of precepts inevitably contain strong rules against killing, for example, *Laozi baibashi jie* 3a (*YJQQ* 39); *Dajie wen* 1b (Kenkyūhan 1988, 593 n. 660); *Sanyuan pin* 23b. See also *WSBY* 44–46; Lagerwey 1981, 143–49.

[11] On the introduction of Buddhism under Emperor Ming, see section 14.

[12] All these events are mentioned in pre-Han sources, such as the *Mozi* (Writings of Mozi), *Liji*, and *Shijing*. See Kenkyūhan 1988, 594 n. 671–72.

[13] Kenkyūhan 1988, 594 n. 673. These are the last rulers of the Xia and Shang dynasties, particularly cruel and wicked kings. Their atrocities caused instabilities in heaven and earth and eventually led to the downfall of their dynasties. See Franke 1930, 67, 92; Yuan 1979b, 384, 406; Allan 1981.

[14] Kenkyūhan 1988, 595 n. 681. These are the virtues of ministers of old. See *Lunyu* 11.20; *Shiji* 24.

22

Trees Wither upon Hearing the Precepts

[149b15] The *Laozi yibai bashi jie* (The One Hundred and Eighty Precepts of Laozi) says:[1]

"My precepts are very powerful. Pronounced over trees, the trees will wither. Pronounced over animals, the animals will die."

The *Lingbao jing* (Scripture of Numinous Treasure) has:[2] "When practiced by the people of antiquity, the Tao of mystery and simplicity ensured extended years. When practiced by people today, it lessens the years and decreases the life span."

In addition, Taoists receive the commanding general's method to control the three [forces] and five [phases].[3] Those harboring any grudge or hatred, however, will turn manic-depressive and slowly waste away.[4]

Moreover, the *Du guowang pin* (Chapter on Saving the Kings) states:[5] "The Eastern Lord of Opening Light[6] who summons the perfected is clad in a black cap and gown covered with mysterious writing. His feet are one hundred paces wide; his head is the pillar of heaven.[7] He de-

---

[1] Citation unclear. A text of this title is contained in *YJQQ* 39 and cited in other collections (see app. 2). It does not contain this passage. Still, a similar statement is found in the *Zhougui jing* (DZ 1195, fasc. 875) of the early Celestial Masters: "Just speak a spell over metal, and the metal will spontaneously melt. Just speak a spell over wood, and the wood will spontaneously be felled. Just speak a spell over water, and the water will spontaneously run dry" (3a).

[2] Citation unclear.

[3] For the various references and meanings of the "three and five," see Sivin 1991. Within Taoism, the *Taidan yinshu* (Great Cinnabar Secret Writings; DZ 1330, fasc. 1030) gives a variety of possible meanings. See Kenkyūhan 1988, 631 n. 1081. The military spell mentioned here also occurs in *Zhenzheng lun* 3 (T. 2112; 52.569ab; Kenkyūhan 1988, 596 n. 694). In a Taoist context, it is found in *Baopuzi* 17/79/16 (Ware 1966, 299).

[4] Kenkyūhan 1988, 596 n. 696. Manic depression is described in the *Nanjing* (Classic of Difficult Issues):

When mania first sets in, the patient sleeps little and does not feel hungry. He thinks himself great, believes himself wise, and revels in his own boldness. He laughs wildly and delights in song and music. Running about hither and thither, he never rests. When depression begins, however, the patient does not feel happy. He stares ahead blankly, lies down without moving. His pulse, in all three sections of the body, both in yin and in yang, is overflowing. This is depression. (2.34b; see also Unschuld 1986, 527)

[5] Citation unclear. A *Duwang pin* is cited in section 30.

[6] The Eastern Lord is commonly known as the Lord King of the East. Developed in the Han dynasty as a counterpart to the Queen Mother of the West, he was later identified with the Green Lad. See Kroll 1985; Kamitsuka 1990.

[7] Following Kenkyūhan 1988, 596 n. 700, I read "feet" for "body." The pillar of heaven is usually called Buzhou. Gonggong tore it down, and Nügua repaired it. Buzhou is in the

vours evil spirits with a mouth like a mountain.[8] He swallows these evil specters, garments and all—five hundred in the morning, three thousand at night, always in batches of five and ten."

I laugh at this and say:

The *Sanyuan dajie* (Great Precepts of the Three Primes) states:[9] "When the Heavenly Venerable explained the ten precepts, the ten good deeds, and other aspects of the divine law, innumerable people attained the Tao."

A precept says:[10] "Do not harbor an evil heart. If you accept the precepts yet give rise to slander, you are committing a sin."

Now, trees do not have feelings.[11] They could not possibly commit a sin or give rise to slander. Why, then, should the pronouncement of the precepts make them wither? If the trees really wither and die, they must have knowledge.[12] If they have knowledge, they can also hear the

---

northeast where the gate to the old country of the dead is, an area later associated with Mount Tai. See Eberhard 1942a, 258; Yuan 1954, 21; Yuan 1979a, 30.

[8] Kenkyūhan 1988, 596 n. 701. This part of the myth may be related to the ancient tradition about the warrior brothers Shenshu and Yulü, who were later deified as guardian door gods. The *Lunheng* (Balanced Discussions; trans. in Forke 1972) has the full story.

> In high antiquity, there were two brothers called Shenshu and Yulü. They could naturally control even powerful demons. They lived on Mount Dushuo on the coast of the Eastern Sea underneath a tall peach tree. There they inspected the various hundred demons. If any of them was found wanting for the proper morals or had foolishly caused bad fortune for mortals, the two warriors would bind him with reeds and throw him to the tigers. (22.15b–16a)

The story is mentioned in De Groot 1964, 2:954–55; Granet 1926, 1:302 n. 2; Bodde 1975, 130. A special study is found in Uehara 1951.

[9] Kenkyūhan 1988, 597 n. 703. Citation unclear. It possibly refers to the *Dajie wen* (DZ 1364, fasc. 1039), which is divided according to the Three Primes.

[10] Kenkyūhan 1988, 597 n. 705. This is similar to a precept found in *Dajie wen* 2b. See also section 24.

[11] Kenkyūhan 1988, 597 n. 708. This passage recalls the *Xinlun* (New Discussions) of Huan Tan (trans. in Pokora 1975).

> Liu Zijun believed the magician's lies and seriously believed that he could learn how to become a spirit immortal. At that time I saw a big elm tree in his garden, very ancient and already bent. I pointed it out to Liu and said, "That tree does not even have feelings. Yet it is withered and full of worms. Human beings have desires for love and nourishment. How could they ever be kept from decay?" (*Yiwen leiju* 88.14a)

[12] A lengthy discussion about the consciousness (lit. "knowledge") of ghosts and demons is contained in *Lunheng* 20 (trans. in Forke 1972). The *Shuoyuan* (Garden of Stories) also has the following discussion of the subject (see Kenkyūhan 1988, 597 n. 710):

Zigong asked Confucius, "Do the dead have knowledge or do they not?"

"If I were to say that the dead have knowledge," Confucius replied, "then I'm afraid that filial sons and obedient grandsons would be hindered in their lives because they would always be preoccupied with the dead. If, however, I were to say that they do not have knowledge, then I'm afraid that unfilial sons and grandsons would not even bother to bury their kin. So, if you want to know whether or not the dead have knowledge, you'll have to wait until you die yourself. Then you'll know for sure, and it will not be too soon, either." (18.26a)

teaching and attain enlightenment. But because this is not the case, what use is it to pronounce precepts over trees?

As is generally known, people today who actually practice the use of these spells will find their life spans harmed. Yet even now, as the poison of disaster is already at work, does the Great Tao in its forebearance notice it or does it not notice it? Does it, in fact, cause the misfortune to pass down to later generations and at the same time keep it from being entered in the records?

Again, among the arts of the three Zhangs there is the *Weigui ke* (Observances to Scare off Demons), which says:[13] "On the left, wear the seal of the Great Ultimate. On the right, wear the great sword Kunwu. Point the seal at the sun, and it will stop in midair. Turn the sword on demons, and they will be wounded even at a distance of ten thousand miles."[14]

Furthermore, Taoists claim that writing the Red Seal of Yellow Spirit will kill demons,[15] whereas the vermilion counterpart is deadly to humans. Then again, Taoists practice mud-and-ashes rites, smearing yellow mud on their faces, rolling in the dirt like donkeys and mules, hanging themselves from pillars head down, and flagellating themselves into a fever.[16]

In the reign period Righteous Splendor of the Jin dynasty [405–19

[13] Kenkyūhan 1988, 598 n. 717. Text and citation are unclear although they are frequently used in polemical works. See *Bianhuo lun* (T. 2102; 52.42c); *Erjiao lun* 9 (T. 2103; 52.140c); *BZL* 6 (T. 2110; 52.533c).

[14] Taoists in the pursuit of immortality acquire many magical powers. Some of them are similar to the abilities of shamans. They heal the sick, exorcise demons or beasts, make rain or stop it, foretell the future, prevent disasters, and so on. Other powers are reminiscent of those possessed by wizards. Taoists may be shape changers and appear in multiple bodies; they can become visible and invisible at will and travel thousands of miles in an instant; they can make rivers flow backward and mountains tumble; govern the life and death of plants, animals, and people. For more details, see Robinet 1979b, 1986; Kohn 1993a, 290.

[15] Kenkyūhan 1988, 598 n. 721. This passage is also found in the *Bianhuo lun* (T. 2102; 52.49b). The Spirit Seal is described in the *Baopuzi*. "When the seekers of antiquity entered the mountains, they always wore the All-Overcoming Yellow Spirit Seal. It was four inches wide and contained 120 characters." (17/89/12b; see also Ware 1966, 298).

Earlier, the seal is mentioned in a tomb inscription found in Shaanxi province and dated to 133 C.E. Its last sentence runs, "The divine medicine serves to satisfaction, sealed with the All-Overcoming Yellow Spirit Seal, in proper accordance with the statutes and ordinances." On Han tombs and their spiritual writings, see Ikeda 1981; Seidel 1985, 1987a, 1987b.

[16] The same argument is also presented in the *Sanpo lun*. See appendix 1. Mud-and-ashes rites were rituals of elaborate ceremonial punishment believed to ward off real calamities. They were performed in the posture of the condemned and imitated their actions. Small groups of participants fasted for several days, then assembled on the sacred ground to chant prayers of sin and repentance. Gradually the rhythm increased, excitement took over, and the participants rolled on the ground. Breaking the circle, the ritual master then calmed them and delivered a lecture on sins, to begin the same cycle again later. See Maspero 1981, 381–87; *WSBY* 50, Lagerwey 1981, 156–58.

C.E.], the Taoist Wang Gongqi proscribed flagellation and similar practices.[17] But a few years later, Lu Xiujing [406–77][18] especially applied
yellow mud to his forehead, trussed himself up, and hung himself upside down.[19] Lewd rites and mass orgies like these one can only laugh at!

Again, the "Record of Imperial Concubines" in the *Hanshu* says:[20]
"When the emperor suspected Lady Ban had cursed him, she defended
herself and said: 'If demons and spirits have knowledge, they certainly
will not accept senseless curses. If they do not have knowledge, what
meaning is there in a curse? Therefore, I would never engage in such
things'."

Evaluating the matter from this perspective, ordinary people can understand it perfectly. How much more so should demons understand it
with their spiritual intelligence and direct ways?[21] I have never heard
that such beings might accept any stupid oppression.

Thus, when we look at the various Taoist texts, we find that neither
words nor meaning make any impact. They are rather [senseless] like
popular shamans' songs or the ditties of street entertainers. How can

[17] This personage is not known from the literature. Efforts to reform overly ecstatic Taoist
practices and lascivious cults were made by the Celestial Master Kou Quianzhi around the
same time. See Yang 1956; Mather 1979; Qing 1988, 401; Ren 1990, 199.

[18] On this important Taoist and his works, see section 31. He conducted a great mud-and-
ashes rite in 468.

[19] Kenkyūhan 1988, 599 n. 728. Tethered securely, the dead are punished in hell. The biography of Liu Gen gives an illustration. Challenged by the local prefect to prove his powers,
he summons the prefect's dead parents from the underworld. "The prefect then saw an old
man and an old lady come in below, trussed up with stout ropes and led along as prisoners.
Their heads hanging down, they stood before the court. The prefect looked at them carefully;
they were indeed his deceased father and mother" (*Shenxian zhuan* 3; see Giles 1948, 57;
Güntsch 1988, 98).

[20] Kenkyūhan 1988, 599 n. 731. This passage is shorter than the text of the *Hanshu*. The full
story goes:

In the third year of Vast Joy [18 B.C.E.], Zhao Feiyan slanderously accused Empress Xu and
the Beautiful Companion Ban of resorting to sorcery to win favor. They supposedly put a
curse on the other women of the palace and extended their imprecations even to the
person of the ruler.

As a result of these charges, Empress Xu was removed from her position. But when
Lady Ban was cross-examined, she said: "I have heard that life and death are decreed by
destiny, that wealth and honor rest with heaven. Even when one follows correct behavior,
one cannot be certain of good fortune, so what could one hope for by committing evil? If
demons and spirits have knowledge, they certainly will not listen to the pleas of a disloyal
subject. If they do not have knowledge, what meaning is there in a curse? Therefore, I
would never engage in such things."

The emperor was impressed with her answer, took pity on her and awarded her a gift of
one hundred catties of gold. (97B; Watson 1974, 262–63)

[21] Kenkyūhan 1988, 599 n. 736. This is the power of spirits as described in the *Zuozhuan*
(Zhuang 32).

one expect any trace of the Great Tao in such utterances? How could anything put forth in such a mean way not be false?

I certainly have no wish to reel in lust and drunkenness or spend my years flushed with drink and debauchery. But how can I manage otherwise, if I rely only on reason in my search for truth?

23

In Worship, the North Is Venerated First

[149c14] The *Shijie shisi chishen jing* (The Scripture of the Ten Precepts and Fourteen Principles of Self-control) says:[1]

"Make obeisance once toward the north. Begin with the north,[2] then turn to the east, and from there to all the ten directions. In each case, visualize the true shape of the Highest Lord."

I laugh at this and say:

The *Wenshi zhuan* has:[3] "Laozi and Yin Xi traveled to heaven. Yin Xi wanted to see the Highest Lord, but Laozi explained: 'The Highest Lord resides on the Mountain of Jade Capital in the Heaven of Grand Network. This mountain is extremely obscure and very far away.[4] Therefore, we can only worship him from afar.' Thus, they returned from their travel without having seen the Highest Lord."

Following this description, the Mountain of Jade Capital in Mystery Metropolis is the residence of the Highest Lord.[5] Seen from our posi-

---

[1] Citation unclear. There is a text called *Shijie jing,* which also contains "fourteen principles of self-control" (*DZ* 459, fasc. 203), but it does not have this passage (Kenkyūhan 1988, 600 n. 759). Still, a similar statement appears in the *Fengdao kejie* (*DZ* 1125, fasc. 760–61): "Obeisance to the ten directions begins with the north. First take refuge in the Nonultimate Heavenly Venerable of Highest Numinous Treasure of the North. The procedures for all the ten directions are the same. After the north, move on to the east" (6.10b).

[2] Kenkyūhan 1988, 600 n. 743. The ritual sequence of worshiping the north first is mentioned in *Chishu yujue* 1.2b (Jade Instructions in Red Characters; *DZ* 352, fasc. 178) and *YJQQ* 11.10a. It is also the standard practice in the recitation of the *Dadong zhenjing* (Prefect Scripture of Great Pervasion; *DZ* 6, fasc. 16–17). See Robinet 1979, 154. Most commonly, however, worship begins with the east.

[3] See section 16 for this citation. It is not found in the *Wenshi zhuan* extant.

[4] Kenkyūhan 1988, 600 n. 748. This expression is used to describe the Tao in *Zhuangzi* 52/20/18.

[5] On this heaven, see 1 n. 20 and section 11.

tion, this is located straight above. Why, then, do Taoists not give utmost priority to the upward direction and instead begin their worship with the north?

In addition, the Tao is born in the east, in yang.[6] Why, then, do Taoists not begin their worship with the east? Buddhism, on the contrary, originated in the west, in yin. The north, too, belongs to yin. Why do Taoists first take great pains to humble this, then again venerate it with particular respect, placing the north at the very beginning of their rites?

Moreover, the *Zuigen pin* says:[7] "The Highest Lord of the Tao paid obeisance to the Heavenly Venerable of Primordial Beginning in the Hall of Pervading Yang. He asked about the ten good deeds and other aspects of the teaching. The Heavenly Venerable duly gave him the appropriate precepts."

Again, why do Taoists in their rites not pay respect to the Heavenly Venerable but persist in visualizing the Highest Lord? This really is losing the original roots and pursuing the extreme branches![8] Whose fault would it be?

[6] On the differentiation of Taoism and Buddhism in terms of yin and yang, see section 8.

[7] See 3 n. 9 for this citation of *Zuigen pin* 1.1ab (*DZ* 457, fasc. 202).

[8] Kenkyūhan 1988, 601 n. 756. This expression goes back to *Daode jing* 52. For a discussion of the historical development of the concept in Han and Dark Learning thought, see Lai 1979, 23.

24

Harming One's Kin to Pursue the Tao

[149c27] The *Laozi xiaobing jing* says:[1]

"Laozi said to Yin Xi: 'If you wish to study the Tao, your must first give up the five attachments. These are father and mother, wife and

[1] Kenkyūhan 1988, 601 n. 758. The citation is unclear. A similar passage is cited in *BZL* 6:

The *Huahu jing* says: "Yin Xi wished to follow Lao Dan, but the latter told him, 'If you have made up your mind perfectly to follow me, you must first cut off the heads of the seven members of your family—your father, mother, wife, and children. Only then can you go with me.'

"Yin Xi made up his mind and went to behead the seven members of his family, including his father and mother. But when he brought the seven heads before Lao Dan, they had changed into the heads of seven pigs." (T. 2110; 52.526b–c)

children, feelings and passions, wealth and material goods, and office and rank.[2] If you give up these, you can come with me to the west.'

"Yin Xi took this to heart. He duly cut off the heads of all the seven members of his family and brought them before Laozi.

"Laozi laughed and said: 'I have examined your heart. You did not really do this. What you killed were not your kin but merely wild animals.'

"When Yin Xi bent down to look more closely, the seven heads were indeed seven treasures,[3] and the seven bodies were the corpses of seven wild birds. Troubled, he returned home. The seven members of his family were all still alive."

In addition, the *Zaoli tiandi jing* states:[4]

"When Laozi converted the barbarians, their king at first refused to submit. Therefore, Laozi killed his seven sons and a portion of the country's population."

I laugh at this and say:

The *Sanyuan jie* says:[5] "A student of the Tao must not harbor an evil heart. He must not be disobedient to his father and mother. He must not be unloving toward his wife and children."

Now, if Yin Xi when killing his family already knew it was just an illusion, why was he so doubtful that he went back home to see for himself? If, however, he firmly believed that the killing was for real, then, according to the precepts, he was harboring evil and committed a grave sin. And what could be more terrible than cutting off one's parents' heads?

In addition, when the barbarian king did not submit to Laozi, Laozi killed his seven sons. Is this not terrible indeed? Then he proceeded to do away with a portion of the country's population. How can this not be the lowest inhumanity?[6]

If such behavior was the general model for later generations, it

---

[2] The five attachments usually refer to the feelings evoked through the five senses or the five emotions: anger, joy, worry, sadness, and fear. See 4 n. 6.

[3] The seven treasures in Buddhism are gold, silver, lapis lazuli, crystal, agate, pearls, and cornelian. See Nakamura 1981, 587. For Chinese references, see Kenkyūhan 1988, 602 n. 766.

[4] For this passage, see 1 n. 1.

[5] Kenkyūhan 1988, 602 n. 770. The *Dajie wen* (DZ 1364, fasc. 1039) has equivalent precepts: "A student of the Tao must not speak good while harboring evil in his heart" (2b). "A student of the Tao must not live in separate quarters or different buildings from his father and mother" (7b). "A student of the Tao must not encourage others to be disobedient to their fathers and mothers, older and younger brothers" (10a).

[6] The expression "inhumanity" occurs with a positive attribution in *Daode jing* 5. See Kenkyūhan 1988, 602 n. 776.

would demand that every aspirant to the Tao kill his father and mother, wife and children. And would they not also find it right always to exterminate half a country's population if just one king lacked the right submission?

Advance and retreat are utterly out of balance here.[7] Ridiculous really!

[7] "Out of balance" literally reads "two and three." The expression occurs variously in *Songshu* (History of the [Liu] Song Dynasty) 42 and 44. See Kenkyūhan 1988, 603 n. 779.

25

The Life-Giving Talisman

[150a14] The *Sanyuan pin* says:[1]

"In the Palace of Purple Tenuity, there is[2] a life-giving talisman. If this talisman is written in the eight directions, the eight energies will respond to it and form human beings.[3] If the talisman is destroyed by burning, people will dissolve into smoke and become pure energy. The text of this talisman appears only once in forty thousand kalpas."

[1] Kenkyūhan 1988, 603 n. 782. This passage is shorter than the *DZ* version of the *Sanyuan pin* (*DZ* 456, fasc. 202). The full text runs:

In the palace of Purple Tenuity, there is a life-giving talisman. If this talisman is written in the eight directions, their energies will arrive together. Echoing and responding to each other, they will form human beings. If the talisman is destroyed by fire, the people will accordingly dissolve into smoke and return to pure energy.

Unless one has attained the Tao and one's jade name is entered in the golden tablets [of immortality], one cannot work this magic. The text of the talisman appears only once in forty thousand kalpas. It is ruled by the fire officials of Great Yang and executed by the upper division of Great Mystery. (1b)

[2] Following Kenkyūhan 1988, 603 n. 783, I read "there is" for "green."

[3] Kenkyūhan 1988, 603 n. 784. The eight energies of heaven correspond to the eight winds on earth. As the *Hetu guadi xiang* (River Chart Patterns of the Earth) has it:

Heaven has five phases; earth has five sacred mountains. Heaven has seven planets; earth has seven far ends. Heaven has four mainstays; earth has four great rivers. Heaven has eight energies; earth has eight winds. Heaven has nine layers; earth has nine continents. (*TPYL* 36.5a)

The *Shi sanshijiu zhangjing* (Explanations to the Scripture in Thirty-Nine Sections) describes the eight energies as appearing through "the joining of clouds in different colors." (*YJQQ* 8.5a)

I laugh at this and say:

The *Wenshi zhuan* states:[4] "Every quatrillion (10^{24}) years, there is a deluge during which Mount Kunlun begins to float. At that time, flying immortals take the kings of heaven and all good people to safety on the mountain.

"For one hundred million (10^{8}) years from then on, heaven and earth are in a state of chaos, shapeless like the yolk in an egg.[5] This period is called the first kalpa."

Now, even in the days of a great flood, heavenly beings do not die. So there is no need to take them to the mountain.

Again, the *Jiku jing* says,[6] "After Qian [heaven] and Kun [earth] have dissolved into chaos, they are in a state of destruction, empty and desolate."

Considering this, in the first kalpa there are neither people nor other living beings. The life-giving talisman, however, only appears once in forty thousand kalpas. How can there be not even heavenly beings for a period of forty thousand kalpas? Shrouded in darkness and mystery,[7] is this not far-fetched indeed?

Now let us look at the calculation. Ten thousand (10^{4}) times ten thousand (10^{4}) makes one hundred million (10^{8}), or one *yi*. This multiplied by itself [$10^{8} \times 10^{8}$] comes to 10^{16}, or what we call one *zhao*. To number years in terms of *yi* and *zhao* is, therefore, within reason. But when it comes to years in the magnitude of ten thousand yi (10^{12}) times ten thousand yi (10^{24}), we really do need a new mathematics with classics of its own. I certainly cannot figure those numbers out.

---

[4] The citation is unclear. For the first part, see 10 n. 1.

[5] Kenkyūhan 1988, 603 n. 786. This image is also found in the Pangu myth as recorded in the *Sanwu liji* (*Yiwen leiju* 1.2a). The *Zongxian ji* (Collection of the Host of Immortals; *DZ* 166, fasc. 73) has a similar description: "The *Zhenshu* (Book of the Perfected) says: 'In the old days, when the two forces had not yet separated, all was dark and obscure, vast and endless. There was neither growth nor form; heaven and earth, the sun and the moon did not yet exist. The universe was like an egg, the dark and yellow mingled in chaos. Then there was Pangu the Perfected'" (12a).

[6] See 10 n. 5 and 15 n. 6.

[7] Kenkyūhan 1988, 604 n. 792. These terms are commonly used to describe the Tao. See *Zuigen pin* 1.2a (*DZ* 457, fasc. 202).

26

A Kalpa Lasts as Long as a Chun Tree

[150a27] The *Dongxuan dongfang qingdi song* (The Eulogy for the Green Emperor of the East, Contained in the Mystery Cavern) says:[1]

The nine energies[2] do not last forever.
Heaven and earth are bound to perish.
Even a great kalpa lasts only as long as a chun tree.[3]
One hundred and six[4]—the cycle revolves.

I laugh at this and say:

When the great flood soaks the earth, Mount Kunlun begins to float. Later the great fire comes, and even gold and iron melt. There are no plants left on the earth.[5]

Then, hundreds of millions of years later, heaven and earth are again like the yolk in an egg. This cycle is called one kalpa.

Even the long-lived chun tree is only a tree of this world. Ordinary fire will reduce it to ashes. Once set aflame with kalpic fire, it will perish

---

[1] This corresponds closely to *Shangqing zhuzhen zhangsong* 3b (*DZ* 608, fasc. 334).

[2] Reading "energies" for "five" on the basis of the DZ edition.

[3] Kenkyūhan 1988, 604 n. 795. This tree is described in the *Zhuangzi*. "The morning mushroom knows nothing of twilight and dawn, the summer cicada knows nothing of spring and autumn. . . . Long long ago, there was the *chun* tree that counted eight thousand years as one spring and eight thousand years as one autumn. It was long-lived" (1/1/12; Watson 1968a, 30).
   The link between kalpas and chun trees is also made in the *Duming miaojing* (*DZ* 23, fasc. 26):

> All the perfected and jade maidens in the highest palace of the north chant together to harmonize the energies of the five palaces. Their jade verses of spontaneity serve to put spirit at rest and save all living beings. . . .
>
>> Allow me to reside anew in the highest palace,
>> Erase my records from the halls of ninefold darkness!
>> Save me to live forever in the towers of Vermilion Hill,
>> And preserve me like the chun tree, through a billion kalpas! (18a)

[4] Kenkyūhan 1988, 604 n. 800. The number 106 signifies yin (earth) at its end. It is the opposite of 81, which that stands for true yang (heaven) at its beginning, and indicates the duration of a kalpa. The *Tiandi yundu jing* (*DZ* 322, fasc. 166) distinguishes a lesser and a greater 106, lasting 3,300 and 9,900 years respectively (see Kobayashi 1990, 403–30). Robinet suggests that the "hundred and six" may be an abbreviation for "three hundred and sixty," the number of earth based on the days of the year (1984, 2:87).

[5] Kenkyūhan 1988, 605 n. 802. For further discussion of kalpic disasters, see section 27. The particular features mentioned here are already mentioned in the *Zhuangzi*: "The great drought melts metal and stone. It scorches the earth and hills" (2/1/33; Watson 1968, 33).

completely.[6] Yet the text says that a great kalpa lasts as long as a chun tree. This is misleading and false. Ridiculous!

[6] Kenkyūhan 1988, 605 n. 804. The *Da zhidu lun* 27 says of kalpic fire: "When a great kalpa cones to an end, fire burns all the greater three thousand worlds. There is nothing left at all—so great is the power of this fire" (T. 1509; 25.260c).

27

Arising and Dying with the Kalpas

[150b6][1] The *Duming miaojing* (Wondrous Scripture on the Salvation of Life) says:[2]

"When a great kalpa comes to an end, heaven tumbles and the earth is submerged.[3] In the World of Desire, all perishes into nothingness.[4] Only the *Scripture of Great Peace*,[5] and the greater and lesser sections of the *Lotus Sūtra*[6] continue to circulate up and down throughout the eighteen heavens of the World of Form.[7]

[1] Kenkyūhan 1988, 605 n. 805. This entire section, with slightly longer citations, is also contained in *BZL* 8 (T. 2110; 52.543ab).

[2] Kenkyūhan 1988, 606 n. 806. This passage represents a shorter version of the *Duming miaojing* than is found in the Taoist canon (*DZ* 23, fasc. 26).

[3] Kenkyūhan 1988, 606 n. 807. On the situation at the end of a kalpa, see the selection of passages in *WSBY* 6.1a–5a, "Kalpa Revolutions" (Lagerwey 1981, 80–82), and in *YJQQ* 2.4b–9a under the same heading. For discussions of Taoist eschatology, see Zürcher 1982; Kobayashi 1990, 403–81; Mollier 1990; Kamitsuka 1988a, 1992b.

[4] The World of Desire (*kāmaloka*) is the lowest of the Three Worlds. In Taoism, it consists of the first six of the total thirty-six heavens. Above it are eighteen heavens of the World of Form, followed by four heavens of the World of Formlessness. Beyond the twenty-eight heavens of the Three Worlds, there are, furthermore, four so-called Brahma heavens for true believers, the Three Clarities, and the heaven of Grand Network. See *Daojiao sandong zongyuan* (*YJQQ* 3.5b–6a); *WSBY* 4.1a–3b (Lagerwey 1981, 74). For a description of Buddhist cosmology, see *Jinglü yixiang* (T. 2121; 53.1a–4a).

[5] On the *Taiping jing* (Scripture of Great Peace), see 14 n. 3.

[6] On the *Lotus Sūtra* and its adaptation in Taoism, see section 29. The notion that sacred scriptures vanish at the end of a kalpa was adapted into Taoism in the late fifth century. In Buddhism it is found in the *Mohe moye jing* (T. 383; 12.114a). See Zürcher 1982, 28 n. 49.

[7] The *DZ* version reads:

When a great kalpa comes to an end, heaven tumbles and the earth is submerged. The four seas are merged in darkness, and even gold and jade begin to melt. The myriad aspects of the Tao cease to exist, and only this scripture survives, its teaching never ending.

All writings on the various methods, on techniques such as gymnastics and nourishing life, change with the kalpas and are scattered among ordinary folk. They are tied to the Six Heavens, the World of Desire. When a small kalpa ends, these methods perish along with everything else and vanish completely.

"When a great kalpa comes to an end, these texts too cease to exist. The sacred scriptures of the Three Caverns, the perfect texts and jade characters of the highest Tao of Jade Clarity, however, originated in Primordial Beginning.[8] They rest above the twenty-eight heavens, beyond even the World of Formlessness. [When a great kalpa ends], they return to the Mystery Terrace on the Mountain of Jade Capital in the Heaven of Grand Network.[9] Here no disaster ever reaches.[10]

"Therefore, all the writings of spontaneity[11] appear and disappear with the cycles of time. By properly venerating them, you can cause your ancestors up to seven generations to be reborn in heaven.[12] As Sage Kings of Transmigration,[13] they will live on for generations unending."[14]

The transformative talismans and charts of Highest Clarity, the *Taiping jing*, the methods and techniques of the Tao proper, and the lesser sections of the scriptures continue to circulate up and down throughout the eighteen heavens of the World of Form. (14b–15a)

[8] Kenkyūhan 1988, 607 n. 812. The heaven of Jade Clarity is the third of the Three Clarities and, therefore, the thirty-second among the heavens. Sacred scriptures revolve in it. See *Zhengao* 1.15b–16a; *YJQQ* 3.4b–5a.

[9] For more details on this highest of all heavens, see 1 n. 20. For its immunity against kalpic disasters, see 10 n. 8.

[10] The *DZ* version reads:

When a great kalpa comes to an end, heaven and earth change completely. Then, these texts, too, cease to exist and there is nothing left. The highest Tao of Jade Clarity, as manifest in the sacred scriptures of the Three Caverns, the tiger script of divine perfection, as all writings in gold and jade characters, and the perfect texts of Numinous Treasure originated in Primordial Beginning. They rest above the twenty-eight heavens, beyond even the World of Formlessness.

At the time when a great kalpa cycle ends, these texts all return to the Mountain of Jade Capital in the highest heaven of Grand Network, to the Mystery Terrace of the Seven Treasures. Here, no disaster ever reaches because the heaven of Grand Network is above the 555,555 layers of heaven. (15a)

[11] Kenkyūhan 1988, 607 n. 813. The highest writings of Taoism are themselves the pure spontaneity of the Tao. They create the world and never perish, though they may, as the present text claims, disappear from view in the heavenly realm. See *WSBY* 24.2b–16a (Lagerwey 1981, 105); Robinet 1979a, 29–44; Robinet 1984, 1:112–16; Robinet 1993, 19–29.

[12] Kenkyūhan 1988, 607 n. 818. On the transfer of ancestors from the realm of the dead to the heavens of the immortals, see section 6.

[13] Kenkyūhan 1988, 607 n. 819. "King of Transmigration" (*cakravatī rāja*) is the title of one who has gone beyond the cycle of life and death. See *Taizi ruiying benqi jing* (T. 185; 3.473b); Nakamura 1981, 991.

[14] The *DZ* has here:

Therefore, all the writings of spontaneity, such as the perfected scriptures of the Great Cavern and the Numinous Treasure scriptures of the Caverns of Mystery, Emptiness, and Nonbeing appear and disappear with the cycles of time.

As a conscientious practitioner, you must cherish and properly venerate these scriptures as the original doctrine of the heavens and cultivate them continuously. Then you will attain spirit immortality, eternal life, and salvation from the world. In broad daylight you

I laugh at this and say:

The *Duren benxing jing* has,[15] "The Tao said: 'From the time when Primordial Beginning first opened the light to the first year of Red Radiance,[16] through more than nine hundred billion (10^{11}) kalpas, I have saved living beings as uncountable as the sands of the Ganges. By the first year of Highest Sovereign, those saved were utterly innumerable.

"'Following the kalpas, I arose and died for generations unending. Always, I emerged together with the Numinous Treasure.[17] At the end of one kalpa, when the nine energies revolved again,[18] I took refuge in the womb of Lady Hong for more than three thousand years.[19]

"'Then the cycle Red Radiance began. When the year star was in *jiazi*, I was born in the Heaven of Supporting Strength.[20] Again, I emerged together with the Numinous Treasure to save living beings. Because of my excellent karma, the Heavenly Venerable of Primordial

---

will fly off, galloping away on a dragon steed, to enter emptiness and nonbeing. Properly venerate them, nurture them along in deep reverence! Then you can cause your ancestors up to seven generations to be reborn in heaven. Sage Kings of Transmigration, they will live on for generations unending. (15ab)

[15] Kenkyūhan 1988, 607 n. 820. This passage is shorter than that in the *Duren benxing jing* in *YJQQ* 101 and P. 3022 (Ōfuchi 1979, 54). The first part reads:

The Tao said: "All heavens and primes revolve, ever changing, while following the kalpas. They arise and pass away; they die and are born again. They perish, yet never end; they fall into darkness, yet come back to light.

"Always the Numinous Treasure brings forth the law and, following the generations, saves human beings. Since Primordial Beginning first opened the light down to the first year of Red Radiance, through all ninety trillion (9×10^{14}) kalpas, I have saved living beings as uncountable as the sands of the Ganges. Before Red Radiance, in the time of Miaoming [chaos], I also emerged kalpa after kalpa—unfathomable, unimaginable.

"After Red Radiance, the first year of Highest Sovereign arrived. By following the rules of the great law, large numbers of people attained salvation; even if I continued to speak for the time of all the heavens, I could not exhaust the list." (101.2b)

[16] Kenkyūhan 1988, 608 n. 822. Red Radiance is the name of the second of the four major kalpas in the beginning of the world. See *Zuigen pin* 2a; appendix 2.

[17] Kenkyūhan 1988, 608 n. 827. For an analysis of the concept of Numinous Treasure, see Kaltenmark 1960.

[18] Kenkyūhan 1988, 608 n. 829. The role of the nine energies during kalpic revolutions is also described in *WSBY* 6.3a.

[19] The *YJQQ* version has:

Following the kalpas, I arose and died for generations unending. Always I emerged together with the Numinous Treasure. After I had passed through seven billion kalpas, I encountered the Green Emperor. At the end of that kalpa, when the nine energies dissolved, I took refuge in the womb of Lady Hong and coagulated my spirit in her jasper palace for 3,700 years. (101.2b–3a)

[20] This heaven, Fuligai, is written Fudaogai in the *YJQQ* and Dunhuang editions. Its location is not clear.

Beginning bestowed the title Highest Lord upon me. Since then, I have resided on the [Mountain of] Jade Capital in Mystery Metropolis'."[21]

According to this account, all perfected writings are on the Mountain of Jade Capital where no disaster ever reaches. Yet the earlier text also claims that "the writings of spontaneity appear and disappear with the cycles of time." Coming and going with time, how can they not be affected by diasters?

Again, the text says, "I emerged and perished together with Numinous Treasure," and "I arose and died following the kalpas." This means that with the cyclical end of the Numinous Treasure the Highest Lord also perishes. Yet the text insists that he lives forever and never dies. This is plainly false.

In addition, the Mountain of Jade Capital is above all the heavens. Here no disaster ever reaches. The logic of this statement is suspect. All things that have matter and form do not exist permanently. The Jade Capital and the Jade Terrace undeniably have form and so belong to the World of Form.[22] The World of Form is impermanent. How can the Jade Capital exist forever?

Finally, the name Red Radiance and its year, *jiazi*, are as unreal as the Yellow and the Han rivers are real.

---

[21] Here the *YJQQ* has:

Then the cycle Red Radiance began. When the year star was in *jiazi*, I was born in the Heaven of Supporting Knives in the Western Jade World on the Mountain of Floating Network. Again, I emerged together with the Numinous Treasure to save living beings. Because of my excellent karma, the Heavenly Venerable of Primordial Beginning bestowed the title Highest Lord upon me. He enfeoffed me as Lord Emperor of Heaven, ruler of the Glorious Jade Terrace and the Forest of Great Joy. Since then, I have ruled in the Jade Capital in Mystery Metropolis." (101.3a)

[22] Kenkyūhan 1988, 609 n. 838. See section 15: "The Jade Terrace is on the southern slope of Mount Ze."

28

Taking Cinnabar Brings a Golden Complexion

[150c1] The *Shenxian jinye jing* (The Spirit Immortals' Scripture on the Golden Fluid) says:[1]

"The golden fluid and reverted cinnabar were taken by the Highest Lord to become a spirit being.[2] When heated, cinnabar turns into mercury, then it reverts back to cinnabar.[3]

"Taking this, one attains immortality and ascends to heaven in broad daylight.[4] To aspire for immortality without attaining this method is to pain oneself for nothing.[5]

[1] Kenkyūhan 1988, 609 n. 842. In the *Baopuzi shenxian jinzhuo jing* (The Spirit Immortals' Scripture on the Golden Fluid As Transmitted by the Master Who Embraces Simplicity; *DZ* 917, fasc. 593) contained in the DZ today, this passage appears as text and commentary. It reads:

> The golden fluid and reverted cinnabar were taken by the Great One to become a spirit immortal and ascend to heaven in broad daylight. To aspire for immortality without attaining this method is to pain oneself for nothing. (1.1a; text)
> Mercury is originally cinnabar. When heated, it turns into mercury. Heat this mercury, and it will revert back to cinnabar. As cinnabar thus recovers its original form, one speaks of reverted cinnabar. (1.4a; commentary)
> Upon taking it, a golden complexion will radiate from the face. This is a firm proof that one has attained the Tao. This golden complexion, however, is not because one's body has become hard and solid like a statue of gold. (1.7b; commentary)
> Drinking it when facing the sun, one immediately becomes like a statue of gold (1.7b; text).
> To take it when facing the sun means to drink it at the first rising of the sun. In the old days, Han Zhong took it and his body instantaneously acquired a golden complexion. (1.7b; commentary)

There is no mention of the Buddha or the "diamond body." For more details on the history of the text and its alchemical method, see Wang 1964; Pregadio 1991, 574–78, app. 2.

[2] Kenkyūhan 1988, 609 n. 844. Both the *DZ* version of this text, the *Baopuzi shenxian jinzhuo jing*, (1.1a) and the *Baopuzi* (4/19/14; Ware 1966, 89) say that it was the Great One (Taiyi), not the Highest Lord (Taishang), who took the golden fluid and became immortal.

The *Baopuzi* by Ge Hong of the fourth century consists of an inner and an outer part, translated respectively by Ware 1966 and Sailey 1978. For an index of the entire text, see Schipper 1975b. For alchemy, its theory, history, and application, see Sivin 1968; Needham 1974, 1976, 1980. For the role of Ge Hong's thought in the history of Taoism, see Robinet 1991, 85–116.

[3] Kenkyūhan 1988, 609 n. 845. This is the basic premise of ancient Chinese alchemy. As the *Baopuzi* has it: "Cinnabar when heated produces mercury which, after a number of successive transformations, reverts to cinnabar" (4/13/4; Ware 1966, 72).

[4] Kenkyūhan 1988, 609 n. 846. The *Baopuzi* says: "Acquire any of the nine elixirs, and you will be an immortal. There is no need to prepare all nine. Which one is prepared depends entirely on your preference. After taking any one of them, if you wish to ascend to heaven in broad daylight, you can do so" (4/15/15; see also Ware 1966, 78).

[5] Kenkyūhan 1988, 610 n. 847. The *Baopuzi* has this, too: "Taking various herbal medicines,

"NOTE: When heated, cinnabar turns into mercury. Heat this mercury, and it will revert back to cinnabar. Thus, one speaks of reverted cinnabar.

"In antiquity, Han Zhong took it[6] and his complexion turned golden.[7]

"In addition, the radiant golden complexion of the Buddha developed because he used this method of the Tao. Only thereby did his body, inside and out, become as solid as gold. Therefore, it was called the gold-hard [diamond] body of the Buddha."

I laugh at this and say:

The *Wenshi zhuan* states:[8] "The highest Lord Laozi and the Primal Lord of the Great One—these two sages join to form one body."[9]

Yet the *Jinye jing* says:[10] "As regards the Great One, the Elder of Central Yellow[11] and the Lord of the Great One are the true rulers of

---

even as many as ten thousand pecks of them, can only give small benefit. In the end, it will not bestow eternal life on people. Therefore, the secret instructions of Laozi say: 'Unless you get hold of reverted cinnabar and the golden fluid, you pain yourself for nothing!'" (4/13/4; see also Ware 1966, 70).

[6] Kenkyūhan 1988, 610 n. 848. Han Zhong was an immortal in the time of the First Emperor of Qin. He is mentioned in *Shiji* 6 and in the "Far-off Journey" chapter of the *Chuci* (Songs of the South; Hawkes 1959, 81–87). His elixir is described in the *Baopuzi:* "Han Zhong's cinnabar method was to fry cinnabar with the resin of the lacquer tree. Taking it, he gained extended years and long vision. Even in broad daylight his body would throw no shadow" (4/19/12; see also Ware 1966, 89).

According to the Shangqing tradition, Han Zhong received the method directly from the perfected: "The lady was Huang Jinghua, daughter of Han Qiong, the minister of Public Works under the Han. Han Zhong received her elixir on Mount Min. He took it and attained immortality" (*Zhengao* 12.14b).

[7] Kenkyūhan 1988, 610 n. 849. A golden complexion as a sign of immortality is mentioned in the *Baopuzi*. It says, "When the golden fluid enters the mouth, the body develops a golden complexion" (4/19/15; see also Ware 1966, 89). Described also in *WSBY* 87–6a.13a (Lagerwey 1981, 186), it was one of the indications of Laozi's divinity (Yoshioka 1959, 142). The Buddha, too, is said to have "given off a lustre for a distance of ten feet in all directions" as one of his thirty-two divine marks (Hurvitz 1962, 353). For more references on the Buddha's radiant body, see Kenkyūhan 1988, 610 n. 852.

[8] This citation is unclear.

[9] Kenkyūhan 1988, 610 n. 854. The *Baopuzi* also links these two deities: "The Primal Lord was the teacher of Laozi" (4/15/16; Ware 1966, 79).

[10] This corresponds closely to the *Jinzhuo jing*. "Since the old days, all members of the celestial administration have been subject to the Elder of Central Yellow and to the Lord of the Great One. These two are the rulers of the immortals. They took the golden fluid and the reverted cinnabar and ascended to heaven. Ever since, they have served as celestial deities and harmonized yin and yang" (1.7b; commentary).

Kenkyūhan 1988, 610 n. 858. The *Baopuzi* characterizes the Primal Lord in same way: "The Primal Lord is the chief among gods and immortals. He harmonizes yin and yang, gives orders to demons and spirits, wind and rain" (4/15/17; see also Ware 1966, 79).

[11] This title is given to Baishi xiansheng, Master White Stone, in *Shenxian zhuan* 2 (Güntsch 1988, 70). The Perfected of Central Yellow is also a title of the Yellow Emperor (see 11 n. 2).

the immortals. They drank the golden fluid and ascended to heaven. There they became great gods and harmonized yin and yang."

According to this, Han Zhong never took the golden fluid but was just an ordinary person. The one who took it and ascended to heaven was, in fact, the Venerable Lord. Yet he is the Highest Lord anyway, the master of the myriad perfected. Why should he need to take the golden fluid and only then be able to harmonize yin and yang?

Moreover, how many have attained the high divinity of the Great One? How many must there be who are able to harmonize yin and yang? If everyone who takes cinnabar attains this high state, how numerous must they be?

Moreover, cinnabar and mercury can be found all over the earth. To heat them and obtain reverted cinnabar is not difficult at all. Why, therefore, do the Taoists not all take it and ascend to heaven in broad daylight? Why do they not all become rulers among the heavenly immortals[12] instead of bearing hardships and knocking their teeth together,[13] thus wasting all their lives? How very deplorable!

At the same time, the very fact that Taoists do not all take it shows clearly that the whole cinnabar thing is just a hoax. It is just like trying to catch one's shadow.

They also say that the Buddha's golden complexion came about through a concoction of cinnabar. Yet the truth is that he did not need even one heated cinnabar pellet to achieve this. Such a mass of wrong notions! It is really too sad!

[12] Heavenly immortals are the highest ranking group among the immortals according to the *Baopuzi* (Ware 1966, 47; see Kenkyūhan 1988, 611 n. 865). The others are earth immortals, that is, those who prefer to remain on the earth for an extended period before taking up their rightful residence in the heavens, and immortals delivered from the corpse, that is, those who have to leave a corpse or, at least, a substitute behind at ascension. See *WSBY* 87–88 (Lagerwey 1981, 186–89); Robinet 1979b; Kohn 1990b; Yoshikawa 1992b.

[13] Kenkyūhan 1988, 611 n. 866. Knocking the teeth together is a preliminary exercise in Taoist gymnastics and meditation and a protective measure against bad luck and nightmares. As the *WSBY* describes it:

The way to knock the teeth together is threefold. Knocking left on left is called 'beating the heavenly gong'; knocking right on right is called 'beating the heavenly music stone'; knocking central upper and lower teeth against one another is called 'sounding the heavenly drum.'

If you encounter bad fortune, evil, or inauspiciousness of any sort, beat the heavenly gong thirty times. If you pass through mountains and have to ward off evil specters, awe spirits, and cast a great spell, then ring the heavenly music stone. If you wish to practice visualization and recollection of the Tao, calling down the perfected and summoning numinous powers, then sound the heavenly drum. (66.9b)

29

Plagiarizing Buddhist Sūtras for Taoist Scriptures

[150c22][1] The *Miaozhen ge* (Song of Wondrous Perfection) says:[2]

> Even as many people as there are sands of the Ganges,
> Who have heard the teaching,
> Will not be able
> To measure the wisdom of the Tao,[3]
> Try though they may with their combined efforts.

I laugh at this and say:

This text is merely a plagiate of the *Lotus Sūtra,* changing "wisdom of the Buddhas" to "wisdom of the Tao."[4] Except for this minor change, the two texts are identical. Nor is this a unique example.

---

[1] Kenkyūhan 1988, 611 n. 872. The same argument, formulated slightly differently, is also found in *BZL* 8 (T. 2110; 52.544c). A similar criticism is, moreover, voiced in *Erjiao lun* 10 (T. 2103; 52.141b) and *BZL* 6 (T. 2110; 52.543b).

[2] This citation is unclear. The *BZL* cites the passage as from the *Lingbao miaozhen jing ge* (Song from the Scripture of Wondrous Perfection of Numinous Treasure). On this text, extant only in citations, see appendix 2.

[3] Kenkyūhan 1988, 612 n. 876. "Wisdom of the Tao" is one of three types of wisdom according to the *DJYS,* the others being "wisdom of reality" and "wisdom of exigency."

Wisdom of the Tao arises immediately from original nonbeing. It indicates the original and spontaneous arising and growth of everything and can transform naturally with the Tao as such.

Wisdom of reality is the wisdom that comes from observing the self and guarding the One. It indicates that the Tao itself is without form, that is, only has a body in following along with existence. Thus, this wisdom centers on self-observation and teaches the visualization of spirit.

Wisdom of exigency indicates the power of expedient means. Reaching out everywhere throughout the myriad mental states, it broadly opens the teaching of the law, giving the right medicine to all that suffer disease. (8.3b)

[4] Kenkyūhan 1988, 612 n. 874. A very similar passage is indeed found in the *Lotus Sūtra* (T. 262; 9.6a). It runs:

> Even as many people as can fill the world,
> Who are as wise as you, Śāriputra,
> Will not be able
> To measure the wisdom of the Buddhas,
> Try though they may with their combined efforts.
> (Murano 1974, 23; for other translations, see also Kern 1963; Soothill 1987)

Many medieval Taoist scriptures developed as adaptations of Buddhist sūtras. A collection of such Buddhist texts in Taoist guise is found in Kamata 1986. Doctrinal and terminological borrowings are further discussed in Kamata 1963, 1966, 1968; Zürcher 1980.

In the old days, the Taoist Gu Huan was confronted with the problem.[5] He countered: "The *Lingbao jing* (Scripture of Numinous Treasure) is written in heavenly script and with great characters; it was brought forth directly from spontaneity and was not originally based on the *Lotus Sūtra*. On the contrary, Kumārajīva and Sengzhao[6] copied our Taoist scriptures to compile the *Lotus*."[7]

Stealing the *Lingbao jing* from the *Lotus Sūtra* is an act that may deceive the eastern people of Xia [China]. But although the *Lotus Sūtra* is different from the *Lingbao jing,* it is identical to the texts of the western regions. All versions produced by translators even today never deviate from the original text of the sūtra. Seen from this angle, it is clear that the Taoists plagiarized the Buddhist text rather than vice versa.

In addition, Buddhist sūtras are learned and concise; their words and meaning are broad and deep. Although they make up a thousand scrolls and a hundred divisions, there is no superfluous repetition—not at all like the scriptures of Laozi's followers, which entirely lack special insight and have to rely on Buddhist sūtras to expand their volume.[8]

In addition, there is not a single reference to the Buddha in the *Daode jing.* Nor do the eight collections of Buddhist texts ever talk about the Tao.[9] All other Taoist texts were made up later, stolen from Buddhist sūtras. The case really is so self-evident, there is no need to go into it any further.

[5] Kenkyūhan 1988, 612 n. 877. The *BZL* (T. 2110; 52.544c) names Gu Huan's challenger as Mr. Xie of the Liu Song. In *Hongming ji* 6, a letter from Xie Zhenzhi to Gu Huan is preserved in which he indeed raises the issue of Taoist versus Buddhist scriptures (see app. 1): "The scriptures and documents of the Taoists are simple and vulgar, oftentimes containing nothing but the boring of empty holes. Worst of all are the *Lingbao* and *Miaozhen,* which are taken directly from the *Lotus sūtra,* changed for their purposes in the most foolish manner" (T. 2102; 52.42c).

[6] Kenkyūhan 1988, 613 nn. 883–84. These men are two important and famous Buddhist translators and authors of the early fifth century. On Kumārajīva (344–413; biography in *Gaoseng zhuan* 2 and *Jinshu* 95), see Zürcher 1959, 226; Ch'en 1964, 81–83; Tsukamoto and Hurvitz 1985, 869–87. On Sengzhao (374–414; biography in *Gaoseng zhuan* 6), see Tsukamoto 1955; Ch'en 1964, 86–88; Robinson 1967, 1968; Liebenthal 1968.

[7] Kenkyūhan 1988, 612 n. 880. This specific rejoinder is not found in Gu Huan's biographies in *Nan Qishu* 54 and *Nanshi* 75 or in the section of the *Hongming ji* dedicated to his work.

[8] Comparison of the literary quality and volume of the scriptures is a popular topic in the debates. See the Introduction and appendix 1.

[9] Kenkyūhan 1988, 613 n. 898. According to the *Chu sanzang jiji,* the eight collections were created by Ānanda after the *parinirvāṇa* of the Buddha and detail the main division of scriptures according to Mahāyāna, Śrāvaka, and Vinaya. The eight are (1) Collection of Transformation in the Womb; (2) Collection of Intermediate Existence; (3) Collection of Great Methods; (4) Collection of Rules; (5) Collection of the Ten Bodhisattva Stages; (6) Collection of Miscellanea; (7) Collection of the Diamond; (8) Collection of the Buddha (T. 2145; 55.4a).

One more point, though. Ever since antiquity, the wise and worthy have been chanting and reciting Buddhist sūtras.[10] To the present day, they have been handed down for generation after generation without interruption. If the Taoist teaching really were superior, why is it that their scriptures are not handed down through recital? Wherever you look throughout the whole country, who would ever recite a Taoist text?[11] Thus, we know that Taoist scriptures cannot possibly be of any authority.

[10] Chanting and reciting the scriptures in ancient India was a way to preserve them (Warder 1970, 205–6). The first text ever chanted ritually, at the beginning of Buddhist monachism, was the *Pratimokṣa* (see Dutt 1962; Wijayaratna 1990). Later, the very voicing of the Buddha's words became a sacred act that conferred much merit, and one of the main tasks of the saṅgha was to keep the scriptures alive.

[11] Taoists have been chanting scriptures from the very beginning, starting with the Celestial Masters' recitation of the *Daode jing* (see Stein 1963; Kobayashi 1992). Later schools, too, have placed a high emphasis on recital, claiming that the very voicing of the sacred words can transpose the practitioner into the heavens of the immortals (see *WSBY* 23.8a–15b; Lagerwey 1981, 141–43). Even today, the recital of scriptures forms an integral part of Taoist monastic practice (see Yoshioka 1959, 122).

30

Imitating the Buddhist Principle of Cause and Effect

[15.1a9][1] The *Duwang pin* says:[2]

"The Heavenly Venerable said to Cunda:[3] 'From the host of sages who have attained the Tao to the tathāgatas as numerous as the sands of Ganges, there is none who did not reach attainment on the basis of being an ordinary person and accumulating merit.[4]

[1] Kenkyūhan 1988, 614 n. 910. The same section, somewhat longer, is also contained in *BZL* 8 (T. 2110; 52.545ab).

[2] Citation unclear. The *BZL* cites it as from the *Du guowang pin*, used also in section 22. The passage is also translated in Bokenkamp 1990, 130–31.

[3] Cunda, a lay disciple and a smith by profession, gave the Buddha his last meal in the capital of the Southern Malla Republic (Warder 1970, 77). The story is originally contained in the *Mahāparinirvāṇa Sūtra* (Dīghanikāya 16; trans. in Warder 1970, 107–16); in Chinese, it is found in *Niepan jing* 2 (T. 374; 12.371c; Kenkyūhan 1988, 615 n. 912).

[4] Kenkyūhan 1988, 615 n. 915. This gradual approach is also supported in the *DJYS:* "Rising from an ordinary person, one accumulates merit and attains the Tao. Then, one first transforms into an immortal. From an immortal, one duly becomes a perfected; and from a perfected, one is transformed into a sage of heaven" (1.13b).

"'Similarly, among the innumerable immortals along the ten levels,[5] there are those who attained the first stage all at once and there are those who ascended gradually as their merit accumulated.[6] If one's merit is great, one is promoted at once; if one's merit is low, one has to progress through the ten stages.[7]

"'Altogether, there are ten stages. As one progresses from the Realm of Joy to the Cloud of the Teaching,[8] one's external signs develop to fullness.'

"All the kings who heard these words immediately attained the four karmic fruits."[9]

In addition, the *Dushen pin* (Chapter on Saving Oneself) says:[10] "When the mendicant[11] heard the Heavenly Venerable preach the teaching, he immediately attained the stage of stream enterer."[12]

The *Wenshi zhuan* has:[13] "When Laozi was in Kashmir, he snapped

---

[5] Kenkyūhan 1988, 615 n. 916. The *DJYS*, speaks of ten successive transformations during the attainment of highest immortality (1.13b).

[6] Kenkyūhan 1988, 615 n. 918. According to the *Zhengao*, one thousand merits are enough for the attainment of immortality (5.16b). According to the *Yongcheng jixian lu* of the tenth century, ten thousand good deeds are required for acension to the top (1.5a).

[7] The *Yundu jieqi jing* also makes this point:

The Heavenly Venerable said: "From the first stage of immortality to the tenth stage, there is a progression. One cannot make them all equal in a single cycle. Why is this? There are ordinary people who move to the tenth stage, and there are those who have heard of it but are not yet awakened and, thus, cannot make it even to the first stage. This is because in practice there are the adept and the clumsy; in understanding there are the nearsighted and the far-reaching. (7b–8a; Bokenkamp 1990, 131)

[8] Kenkyūhan 1988, 616 n. 921. This refers to the ten *bhūmi*, or bodhisattva stages, of the Mahāyāna. They are the Realm of Joy, Freedom from Defilements, Developing Radiance, Flaming Wisdom, Overcoming Ultimate Difficulties, Open Way Ahead, Proceeding Afar, Immobility, Discriminating Wisdom, and the Cloud of the Teaching. See *Huayan jing* 23 (T. 278; 9.542c–543a); Nakamura 1981, 1228. On the ten stages in Taoism, see Bokenkamp 1990.

[9] The karmic fruits (*phala*) are the four final stages of stream enterer, once returner, non-returner, and arhat, or enlightened one. See Nakamura 1981, 509. For a Chinese description, see *Apitan piposha lun* 35 (T. 1546; 28.252a; Kenkyūhan 1988, 616 n. 923).

[10] This citation is unclear.

[11] *Niqian zi* transliterates Sanskrit *nirgrantha*, which means "someone freed from all ties," a wandering ascetic or mendicant. See Mochizuki 1933–36, 2425c. See also Kenkyūhan 1988, 616 n. 926.

[12] The *BZL* adds two further citations from the same work:

It also says, "[The Lord of the] Mysterious Center cultivated [the Tao] on Spirit Vulture Peak. There he revealed the venerable scriptures in five sections and saved innumerable beings."

Again, the text says, "Together with the Master of Great Harmony [Yin Gui] he resided on Mount Dataloka. There he greatly saved the king and the people who were henceforth called *śramaṇas*. (T. 2110; 52.545a)

[13] This citation is unclear.

his fingers,[14] and all the heavenly kings and arhats [enlightened ones] and all the flying immortals of the five supernatural powers came.[15] He made Yin Xi their teacher. The enlightened bodhisattvas duly chanted a hymn in his honor."[16]

I laugh at this and say:

Buddhism and Taoism have not the same obvious teaching; their practices change over time. In Taoism, spontaneity is the most venerable; in Buddhism, the law of cause and effect is the central principle.[17]

Spontaneity is perfected through nonaction; the law of cause and effect is realized through the accumulation of practice. Thus, there are the four karmic fruits in the Lesser Vehicle and the ten bodhisattva stages in the Greater Vehicle.

Although [in Taoism] there are plenty of scriptures and discussions on the progress from an ordinary to a realized person, I have never understood how the Taoists structured [the process]. Even though they speak of the four fruits and ten stages with the same terminology as the Buddhists, I have never seen any relevant Taoist theory of cultivation or doctrine of cause and effect.

Rather, Taoists practice breathing exercises with the goal of soaring up into the sky; they drink special water to attain realization of the Tao;[18] hearing the teaching, they fly through the air; subsisting on herbs, they are delivered from the corpse.[19] As the practices of the two religions differ greatly, their respective theories must also vary.

---

[14] Kenkyūhan 1988, 616 n. 928. This scene imitates the actions of the Buddha as described in the *Lotus Sūtra* (T. 262; 9.51c).

[15] Kenkyūhan 1988, 616 n. 929. Literally, this translates as "the flying heavens," but is defined as "the flying celestial spirit beings of all the ten directions" in *Zuigen pin* 1.2a.

[16] The *BZL* adds:

The *Lingbao zhihui zuigen pin* says: "Celestial beings as numerous as the sands of the Ganges heard the teaching and attained the Tao. They all became tathāgatas."

Foolish talk like this is very frequent [in Taoist texts]; such slanderous remarks are all too common. This is because Buddhism and Taoism have not the same teaching. (T. 2110; 52.454a)

[17] This is one of the main arguments of the entire text already pointed out in the preface.

[18] This refers to talisman water. A sacred talisman is burned and the ashes are dissolved in water and drunk. See Engelhardt 1987.

[19] Kenkyūhan 1988, 617 nn. 938–39. These four practices and their attainments correspond roughly to the three types of immortals distinguished in the *Baopuzi*: "Those who collect red sand and turn it into gold, then take it and ascend to heaven are the highest kind. Those who live on fungi and practice gymnastics and breathing exercises to nourish life are the second kind. Those who take herbal medicines and live on plants, returning after a mere thousand years, are the lowest kind" (16/73/10; see also Ware 1966, 269). For discussions of the various practices, see Maspero 1981, 443–554; Sakade 1983, 1988; Kohn 1989e; Yoshikawa 1992b.

Then again, the Taoists say that there are five levels of heaven, or 3,600 heavens.[20] Sometimes there are 81 heavens, or 60 great Brahma heavens;[21] then they have 36 heavens, or even 550,000 layers of heaven.[22]

They also speak of the Nine Perfected Kings of Heaven, the Heavenly Lords of the Nine Energies,[23] the Lords of the Energies of the Four Directions, the Three Heavens of the Three Primes, the Heavenly Officials of the Nine Palaces, of [the Palace of] Great Existence in the Heaven of Jade Clarity, of [the Palace of] Purple Tenuity in the Heaven of Mystery Metropolis, of [the Palace of] the Great Ultimate in the Heaven of the Three Sovereigns, and so on.[24]

Things like these should have a reasonable foundation. Placed about emptily, they appear pretentious and strange. So, please explain to me: Are these heavens horizontal or vertical? Material or immaterial? Which elixir or herb will convey what kind of people to what kind of heaven? If these things cannot be explained clearly, they must be mere foolishness. I can only laugh.[25]

---

[20] I read "hundred" instead of the second "thousand." The *BZL* has "36,000 heavens" (T. 2110; 52.545a).

[21] Eighty-one Taoist heavens are also mentioned in 9 n. 8. Usually, there are four Brahma heavens for true believers located right above the Three Worlds. See 27 n. 4.

[22] The *BZL* has: "They have thirty-six heavens, or thirty-two emperors, or twenty-eight heavens, or twenty-four emperors, or eighteen heavens" (T. 2110; 52.545a). The *BZL* does not mention the 550,000 layers of heaven, which are the subject of section 32.

Shangqing Taoism has thirty-six heavens, arranged vertically and including the twenty-eight heavens of the Three Worlds (see Kenkyūhan 1988, 618 n. 946). Lingbao Taoism has thirty-two heavens, arranged horizontally (Robinet 1984, 1:131). The Celestial Masters knew of twenty-four annual energies, changing with every new and full moon and still a basic part of the Chinese calendar.

[23] The *BZL* here adds "the six heavens of the World of Desire" (T. 2110; 52.545a).

[24] Kenkyūhan 1987, 618 nn. 948–54. The Lords of the Energies of the Four Directions are otherwise unknown. On the Three Primes and the Nine Palaces, see 3 n. 6. The three last palaces mentioned refer to the Lords of the Three Treasures, described in *Jiutian shengshen zhangjing* 1ab (*WSBY* 24.1ab; see 16 n. 8).

[25] This last paragraph is different in the *BZL:*

All this is just an abbreviated account of their ideas. Yet still one does not know whether these heavens are the same or different, horizontal or vertical, high or low, material or immaterial, or by what kind of practice one can ascend to what kind of level, by what kind of herb one can attain what kind of life. Indeed, I have never heard them propose a proper theory on the gradation of attainment in accordance with the law of cause and effect. Thus, looking at what they give as their cause, observing what they give as their grounds, and inspecting what they give as their basis, I find all they have are just empty and foolish ideas. (T. 2110; 52.545b)

31

Taoist Scriptures: Revealed and As Yet Unrevealed

[151b5]¹ The catalog of scriptures submitted by the Taoists of Mystery Metropolis² quotes Lu Xiujing of the Liu-Song dynasty as saying:³

"Of altogether 186 scrolls of Highest Clarity scriptures, 117 have already been revealed.⁴ Beginning with the *Shiqing jinq* (Scripture of Initial Clarity), sixty-nine scrolls in forty divisions have not yet been revealed to the world."

Examining the present catalogs of Taoist scriptures, we find they all say that these texts are already available.

Lu also says, "Among the scriptures of the Mystery Cavern,⁵ fifteen scrolls are still hidden in the heavenly palaces."⁶ Yet upon examination of today's catalog, it turns out that they, too, are listed as available.

I laugh at this and say:

Lu Xiujing lived under the reign of Emperor Ming of the Liu Song dynasty [r. 465–73 C.E.]. In the seventh year of the reign period Great Beginning [471 C.E.], he compiled the catalog upon imperial order.⁷

---

¹ Kenkyūhan 1988, 619 n. 962. The same section, slightly longer, is also found in *BZL* 8 (T. 2110; 52.545bc).

² The *BZL* refers to this as "the catalog of all scriptures submitted by the Taoists of the Monastery of Mystery Metropolis et al." The monastery was the major Taoist institution of Chang'an at the time (see *Chang'an zhi* 9 [Gazeteer of Chang'an]).

³ Kenkyūhan 1988, 620 n. 964. Lu Xiujing's catalog was the first systematic list of Taoist scriptures. He submitted it to the throne in 471. It survives only in fragments (see *YJQQ* 4.4a; *DJYS* 2.3b–4a). The passage used here is not found among them.

⁴ This refers to the concept that sacred scriptures are originally created and stored in the highest heavens above. They are revealed, that is, translated for the benefit of mortals, in accordance with the rhythm of the kalpas. On the appearance of the Shangqing scriptures, see *Zhengao* 19.9b; *YJQQ* 4.6ab (Kenkyūhan 1988, 620 nn. 965, 967). On their collection and editing, see Strickmann 1978b. For a reconstituted list and analysis, see Robinet 1984.

⁵ These are the Lingbao scriptures, revealed by the Lord of Numinous Treasure (*DJYS* 2.5b–6a; Kenkyūhan 1988, 620 n. 968). For early Lingbao catalogs, see Ōfuchi 1974; Bokenkamp 1983.

⁶ The *BZL* version expands this: "Xiujing's catalog also says, 'The scriptures of the Mystery Cavern consist of thirty-six scrolls. Twenty-one of these have already been revealed to the world, come down during greater and lesser kalpas in eleven sections. Altogether, fifteen scrolls are still hidden in the heavenly palaces and have not yet appeared'" (T. 2110; 52.545b).

⁷ Lu Xiujing (406–77) was an important Taoist of the fifth century, posthumously known as Jianji xiansheng (Master of Simple Serenity). Sick in his youth, he cured himself with the

Here, he says that certain scriptures are "still hidden in the heavenly palaces."

Since then, more than one hundred years have passed. Yet I have not heard that any heavenly being has descended in the meantime.[8] Nor have I seen any Taoist ascend to heaven. Therefore, I do not know from where and how these texts should have appeared.

They must be quite as fraudulent as the trickery of Shaoweng, General of Peaceful Accomplishment, who fed an apparently ancient script to an ox and pretended to speak upon the orders of Madam Wang.[9]

Scriptures such as the *Huangting* (Yellow Court) and the *Yuanyang* (Primordial Yang) substitute the word *Tao* for *Buddha*.[10] Those of the Numinous Treasure were made up by Zhang Ling and first appeared in the reign period Red Bird of the Wu Kingdom [238–51 C.E.].[11] Sim-

---

help of immortality techniques and became an active Taoist. Around 450, he stayed at the court under Emperor Wen for three years, then retired to Mount Lu. In 467, he returned to court where he participated in debates with the Buddhists and compiled an integrated catalog of Taoist scriptures. It was submitted to the emperor in 471, as documented in the *Lingbao shoudu yibiao* (*DZ* 528, fasc. 294). He died at the age of seventy in 477, leaving behind numerous writings. See Yoshioka 1955, 18–44; Ōfuchi 1964, 260–64; Chen 1975, 282–83; Qing 1988, 465–86; Ren 1990, 143–67. A short biography in English is found in Bell 1987.

[8] On the phenomenon of Taoist celestials descending to earth, see Fukunaga 1982. See also Kenkyūhan 1988, 620 n. 965.

[9] Kenkyūhan 1988, 620 n. 973. This refers to two incidents in the time of the Han Emperor Wu. As the *Shiji* records:

Shaoweng by his magical arts succeeded in summoning forth at night the apparition of [the dead favorite] Madam Wang and the god of the stove while the emperor stood within a curtained enclosure and gazed at them from afar. The emperor accordingly honored Shaoweng with the title General of Peaceful Accomplishment and rewarded him with lavish gifts. . . .
Shaoweng wrote a message on a piece of silk and fed it to an ox. Pretending to know nothing of the matter, he announced to the emperor, "There appears to be some strange object in this ox's belly!" The ox was slaughtered and its belly opened, revealing the piece of silk, and the words written on it were exceedingly strange. The emperor, however, recognized the handwriting . . . and had Shaoweng executed. (*Shiji* 28; see Watson 1968b, 2:41–42)

[10] Kenkyūhan 1988, 620 n. 975. The same criticism is also voiced in *Erjiao lun* 10 (T. 2103; 52.141b) and *BZL* 6 (T. 2110; 52.534b). The "Yellow Court" is the *Huangting jing*, contained in *DZ* 331 and 332, fasc. 167 (see Schipper 1975a; Robinet 1979). The "Primal Yang" is the *Yuanyang miao jing*, found in *DZ* 334, fasc. 168–69 (see Maspero 1981, 485). Today, neither shows a particularly strong Buddhist influence, unlike many Lingbao scriptures (see Zürcher 1980). This, of course, may be the result of later editing (see Bokenkamp 1991).

[11] The Lingbao school claims that their sacred texts originated in the kalpa Dragon Country at the beginning of time and flourished first in the kalpa Red Radiance (*YJQQ* 4.4b; Kenkyūhan 1988, 621 n. 976). They were revealed variously on earth, last to Ge Xuan during the reign period Red Bird of the Wu Kingdom (*YJQQ* 3.11b; Kohn 1993a, 47). Historically, the first Lingbao scripture was compiled by Ge Chaofu in the last decade of the fourth century who claimed it originated with his ancestor Ge Xuan. The bulk of the canon was put together by Ge's followers in the early fifth century. The scriptures inherit the Tao of the Celestial Masters but have nothing immediately to do with Zhang Daoling. See Bokenkamp 1983; Kobayashi 1992. On Zhang Daoling, see section 7.

ilarly, the texts of Highest Clarity originated with Ge Xuan and first emerged in the time of the Song and Qi dynasties [420–501 C.E.].[12] Bao Jing, finally, put together the scriptures of the Three Sovereigns. But, in his case, the fake was discovered and he was executed.[13]

Although the trickery of Shaoweng brought him execution in the Han dynasty, some people these days still follow his example. Is this not deplorable, indeed?

In addition, the *Hanshu* states that Zhang Lu's grandfather Zhang Ling, in the time of Emperor Huan [r. 148–69 C.E.], produced talismans to delude the masses.[14] Those who received his Tao paid tribute in the form of five pecks of rice. Thus, people called the Zhangs "rice thieves." Ling passed the leadership to his son Heng, who, in turn, gave it to his son Lu. Together they are called the "three masters;" their wives are the "three ladies." They all are said to have ascended to heaven in broad daylight. Those who first received their Tao were called "demon soldiers." More advanced adherents were known as "libationers."[15]

The whole thing is rather evil and utterly vulgar, uncivilized in the extreme. All these examples show the same basic decrepitude.[16]

[12] The Shangqing scriptures were revealed to Yang Xi in 364–70. See Ch'en 1945, 92; Strickmann 1978b, 1981; Robinet 1984. On Ge Xuan, ancestor of both Ge Hong and Ge Chaofu, see *Shenxian zhuan* 7; Güntsch 1988, 218–25.

[13] Kenkyūhan 1988, 621 n. 978. The *Sanhuang wen* are the texts by which the Three Sovereigns governed the world (see app. 2). Bao Jing was a relative of Ge Hong by marriage. His life is recorded in *Jinshu* 95, but no mention is made of a violent end. See Chen 1975, 76; Robinet 1984, 1:11. Bao Jing is associated with the *Sanhuang wen* in the section on the transmission of Taoist scriptures and rules of the *YJQQ* (see Kenkyūhan 1988, 621 n. 978):

> The time of King Wu of the Jin arrived [265–90 C.E.]. Then there was a man from Jinling by the name of Bao Jing. He was an official who served as the prefect of Nanhai.
>
> From an early age he had been fond of the Tao of immortality, and on the second day of the second month of the second year of Primordial Vigor [292], he withdrew to Mount Songgao. There, in a chamber of rock, he undertook a long pure fast. In the midst of it, suddenly before him there appeared the ancient texts of the Three Sovereigns—characters carved deep into the stone.
>
> At that time Bao did not have a proper teacher, so he relied on his own methods. Pledging four hundred feet of pure silk, he made a formal compact with the gods and so received the texts. Later he transmitted them to Ge Hong and thus they have been handed down from one generation to the next, all the way to the present day. (4.10b–11a)

[14] The *BZL* details this: "The biography of Liu Yan in the *Hanshu* states that Zhang Lu's grandfather Zhang Ling in the reign of Emperor Huan came to visit Shu and studied the Tao on Crane-Cry Mountain. There he produced talismans" (T. 2110; 52.545b). The passage is found in *Hou Hanshu* 65 (see 7 n. 10; Kenkyūhan 1988, 621 n. 980).

[15] With the exception of the "three ladies," all this is standard information on Zhang Ling and the early Celestial Masters. See 7 n. 9.

[16] The *BZL* concludes the section differently:

> Those who first came to study with them were called demon soldiers. More advanced adherents were called libationers. They gathered together a large crowd of followers—

32

Five Hundred Million Layers of Heaven

[151b24] The *Wenshi zhuan* says:[1]

"Heaven consists of 500,055,555 layers. The earth is similarly structured.[2] It is ten thousand miles thick with metal pillars and axletrees in its four corners.[3] It has a circumference of 3,600 miles.

[1] Kenkyūhan 1988, 621 n. 986. This passage is cited in *TPYL* 60.4b as from *Guanling neizhuan*. A similar text, moreover, is cited in the *Daobao jing* (*DZ* 1353, fasc. 1036–37) as from the *Zhenren neizhuan* (Inner Biography of the Perfected):

> The four corners of the vast void are nine times 10^{11} miles from each other. The earth is ten thousand miles thick. Underneath, there is a great void. On the four corners, there are four metal pillars of spontaneity. There are also thirty-six hundred supporting metal axletrees. Each pillar has a circumference of five thousand miles. They are all connected with one another in a network of divine wind. (2.11a)

[2] Kenkyūhan 1988, 622 n. 987. This piece of information is already mentioned in section 10 (10 n. 8), in a citation from the *Duming miaojing*. It is further found in *BZL* 6 (T. 2110; 52.536b) after the *Lingshu jing* (Scripture of Numinous Writings) and in *Tianguan jing* 3b (Scripture of the Heavenly Pass; *DZ* 987, fasc. 628).

[3] The idea that heaven is supported by four pillars in the four far corners of the world is part of ancient Chinese mythology. They were identified as the feet of the turtle that held up the dome of the sky (see Allan 1991). That the earth is similarly upheld above the void is first noted in the *Bowu zhi*, which describes the situation in similar terms (1.11b; see Kenkyūhan 1988, 622 n. 988).

---

how many exactly has never been quite clear. The wives of the three masters were called the three ladies.

In the end, Ling was devoured by a python, and his disciples, too, were eaten by the snake. Yet the texts claim that they ascended to heaven in broad daylight. It is all a big cheat and false enchantment, as the historical chronicles make abundantly clear. The *Yaoshu* (History of the Yao Dynasty) says, "Ever since the dynasties of old down to the present, Buddhist monks have been known as *daoshi*, 'men of the way.' But then, in the time of Emperor Taiwu of Wei [424–52], there was a sorcerer by the name of Kou Qianzhi, who cheated and deluded everyone. Calling himself Celestial Master, he stole the title *daoshi* and used it for his own libationers."

The *Liji* states: "One who is fond of archery must be skilled at making a basket for his arrows; one who is fond of cold weather must be able to make himself a thick furcoat." The affair here is just like this! If the Tao of Zhang Ling was really straight and pure, then how come his descendants have inherited so much delusion and deceit?

Again, the *Sanyuan pin* says, "Those who accumulate goodness will also have descendants born in their families who accumulate goodness. Those who accumulate evil will also have descendants born in their families who accumulate evil." If Zhang Ling indeed ascended to heaven in broad daylight, what did he do that was not good? Yet here are his descendants, full of sorcery and wrong ideas.

It really is uncivilized in the extreme, as all these examples show perfectly clearly. (T. 2110; 52.545bc)

"A divine wind supports it; the four seas furnish its underground arteries. Heaven and earth, mountains and rivers, and the Milky Way in the sky all circulate its energy. Wind and clouds all rise from its mountains."[4]

I laugh at this and say:

The *Santian zhengfa jing* says:[5] "The radiance of heaven was not yet bright. After more than seven thousand kalpas darkness and light first divided. Then the nine energies arose. The Heavenly King of the Nine Perfections[6] and the Heavenly King of Primordial Beginning were endowed with the quality of spontaneity and established the names of the nine heavens.

"An upper, middle, and lower perfection then constituted one prime. Each prime had three heavens. The Palace of Upper Prime became the residence of the Highest Lord of the Tao."[7]

If we now calculate that these heavens are at a distance of 99,990 miles from each other,[8] then the ninth heaven should be 799,920 miles

---

[4] According to traditional Chinese geography, the earth is a living organism that functions in a way similar to the human body. The divine wind of the world thus corresponds to the vital energy (*qi*) in the human body, whereas the four seas and the various natural features are the equivalent of the energy conduits. The well-being of a human being as well as of the earth then depends on the smooth and unhindered flow of energy in all its parts. Mountains in this context serve not only as connecting links with heaven but also as concentration points of energy. Here, clouds, coagulated and visible *qi*, assemble and rain is brought forth. The ancient method of siting human-made objects in accordance with the life-stream of the earth, *fengshui*, is the most obvious expression of this thinking. See Needham 1958, 500–25; Eitel 1973. For Chinese references in the phenomena mentioned, see Kenkyūhan 1988, 622 nn. 990–94.

[5] Kenkyūhan 1988, 622 n. 995. The first paragraph of this passage is close to *Santian zhengfa jing* 1a (*DZ* 1203, fasc. 876) as translated in 1 n. 14. The second paragraph is not found in the *Santian zhengfa jing*, which scarcely mentions the Three Primes. Instead, it speaks of three times three perfections (upper, middle, lower), which make up three main heavens: the Heaven of Clear Tenuity, the Heaven of the Remnants of Yu, and the Heaven of Great Redness (1b).

[6] The *Santian zhengfa jing* has "Perfected King of the Nine Heavens."

[7] The Highest Lord of the Tao, according to the *Santian zhengfa jing*, is the coagulation of the three main heavens. He rules in a jasper palace but is not specifically associated with the highest heaven. In a note, the text describes him.

The Highest Lord of the Tao is the emperor of the host of the perfected. His position is high and his energy extremely pure. Thus, he is called "highest." He is endowed with all the energies and contains the ranks of all the perfected. His name is not the result of the fact that he was raised first in the beginning of heaven and was thus the highest. Rather, he received the title "highest" and duly became the ruler of the myriad gods. (2a)

[8] This information is taken from the *Santian zhengfa jing*, "Each energy is separated from the next by 99,990 miles" (1a). It seems that the citation was cut short here.

from the first. One mile has 300 paces, and 1 pace is 6 feet.[9] The entire distance thus comes to 1,439,856,000 feet.

If we then divide this by those five hundred million layers of heaven, we must conclude that each layer is about two feet away from the next. Just imagine: an earth ten thousand miles thick covered by two feet of heaven. How is it possible?

The *Wenshi zhuan* also says:[10] "Laozi led an enormous army commanded by the Four Heavenly Kings. The soldiers were sixteen feet tall, the shortest among them still rising to twelve feet."

Just think! The people are so big while the heavens are so small! How can they live except by lying on their backs all the time and never getting up? Startling indeed! Such an assembly of weird ideas!

---

[9] Kenkyūhan 1988, 623 nn. 997–98. These measurements are standard, and are found in ancient official documents. See *Guliang zhuan* (Guliang's Commentary [to the *Spring and Autumn Annals*]), Xuan 15; *Guoyu* (Record of the States), Zhouyu 2.

[10] Kenkyūhan 1988, 623 n. 1000. This is not found in the *Wenshi zhuan* as transmitted separately. A similar reference, however, is contained in the *Huahu jing* as cited in *SDZN*. Here, Laozi is angered by the barbarian king's refusal to accept his teaching and sends Yin Xi to heaven to bring down a heavenly army. Millions of troops descend, infantry and cavalry, all of them fourteen feet tall (9.19a). Sixteen feet is the size often used for Buddhist statues at the time. See Matsubara 1961; Ōmura 1972.

33

Taoist Formalities of Entering and Leaving

[151c12] The *Xuanzhong jing* (Scripture of Central Mystery) says:[1]

"The ritual tablet held by Taoists was originally made of gold and jade. It is one inch wide and 5.5 inches long. It is used as a symbol of power.

"In Middle Antiquity, kings held it [when] giving audience to their lords and generals.[2] In Lower Antiquity, however, gold and jade be-

---

[1] This citation is unclear. On the text, see appendix 2.
[2] The royal scepter used in ancient China was the *ruyi*. See Laufer 1912, 335; Yetts 1916, 787.

came scarce, and people used various kinds of wood to make the tablets. Since then, they have been nine inches long and [are] called hand tablets. The purpose of holding them is to ward off other people's scorn. They serve as protection for the Taoist.[3]

"When a Taoist enters the residence of a feudal lord, a manor, or a private home, he should stop ten paces before the dwelling to put on his ceremonial cap and robe and take hold of his ritual tablet. Thus, he may enter. In no case is he to approach sideways or backwards.[4]

"When a Taoist leaves a dwelling, he should take off his cap and robe once outside and put on his plain [undyed] clothes. Then, he may set out on the road. He should never expose himself lest he discredit the Taoist teaching.[5]

"Even when entering the place of a commoner,[6] proper dignity and formality should be observed scrupulously. The Taoist should sit only when he has the tablet in his hands, at the same time making sure the commoners do not think him strange.[7]

"When a Taoist travels for more than one hundred miles, he should

---

[3] The ritual tablet is an indispensable accessory of the formally clad Taoist as depicted in *Fengdao kejie* 5.4a–8b (*DZ* 1125, fasc. 760–61). Yet only one description mentions the tablet specifically: "When attending a ritual, the Taoist must wear his cap, belt, and ceremonial robe. He must hold the ritual tablet and clearly state his name" (5.6a). For more details, see also *WSBY* 41.5a–7a, Lagerwey 1981, 136–38.

[4] There are numerous details regarding Taoist formalities of entering and leaving, of sitting down and getting up. The *Fafu kejie wen* (Rules and Precepts Regarding Ritual Garb; *DZ* 788, fasc. 563) lists forty-six rules on Taoist dress. The fifth states, "Unless attired in a ceremonial robe, no Taoist shall enter or leave a dwelling, walk in public, or be seen by common people" (7a). See also *Laojun yinsong jiejing* 12a (Mather 1979, 113).

[5] Exposure of the body was considered harmful not only to the image of the Taoist teaching but also to the salvation of the Taoist himself. The *Siji mingke* (Illustrious Rules of the Four Ultimates; *DZ* 184, fasc. 77–78) has: "A Taoist shall never expose his bare head by not wearing his ceremonial cap. Taking off one's clothes and exposing the body causes harm to the personal body and the deities residing therein. It will also bring shame to the teaching of perfection" (5.7a).

[6] Kenkyūhan 1988, 624 n. 1017. The distinction between lay followers and commoners or unbelievers as one of purity and defilement is made in Lu Xiujing's *Daomen kelue* 4b (Abbreviated Rules for Taoist Followers; *DZ* 1127, fasc. 761).

[7] Exact rules of etiquette for sitting down or getting up are specified in the *Yaoxiu keyi* (Essential Rules and Observances; *DZ* 463, fasc. 204–7).

When a Taoist enters a superior's hall, he first—well before entering—puts on his formal garb and takes hold of his ritual tablet. He straightens his robe and cloak.

Facing east and with the tablet in the correct position, he then visualizes the people inside, may they be the heavenly venerables of the ten directions, the host of sages and perfected, the present king of the land, the prefect, or the local magistrate. (9.7a)

Even when entering or leaving a common hostel, the proper etiquette must be followed. (9a)

have with him a staff,[8] a ceremonial cap and robe, an incense burner, a brass water pitcher, and an alms bowl.[9]

"He should always have the utensils of houselessness with him and make sure to exhibit the proper dignity and formality. This will bring the ten kinds of merit."[10]

I laugh at this and say:

The *Ziran jing* (Scripture of Spontaneity) states:[11] "Taoists wear ceremonial caps and gowns and preceptors' robes.[12] The gown is 36 feet or 360 inches long, patterned on the 36 weeks or 360 days of the year.[13]

"It is held in two corners by six folds each. Next to these are two sleeves, again with six folds each. Altogether that makes twenty-four folds, corresponding to the twenty-four energies.[14]

---

[8] The *Daoxue keyi* (Rules and Observances for Students of the Tao) (*DZ* 1126, fasc. 761) describes this implement.

> Every student of the Tao must know the staff of nine knots. It is useful in supporting the old and serves as protection in danger. Each knot has its own name. Remember them well. The first is the Great Imperial Star. The second is called Fiery Star. The third is the Horn Star. The fourth is the Equalizer. The fifth is the Long Star. The sixth is the Palace Chamber Star. The seventh is known as the Village Star. The eighth is the East Well Star, and the ninth the Dog Star.
> All knots are named after stars in the sky. Someone under forty who has not yet received the scriptures and the teaching is called "without rank." He must not carry a staff. Similarly, one who has been cured from some disease by means of the staff must not carry one, even if he be in close attendance to a master. (2.9b–10a)

[9] On Taoist ritual implements, such as bells, curtains, incense burners, and garments, various devices for storing scriptures, canopies and carriages, see *Fengdao kejie* 3.1a–6a. They are largely adapted from Buddhist models as described in *Shishi yaolan* (Essential Observations for Buddhist Monks; T. 2127; 54.279c–80a). See Kenkyūhan 1988, 624 n. 1019. For details on contemporary Taoist equipment, see Yoshioka 1979.

[10] This refers to the merit that comes from the ten good deeds or abstention from the ten evil actions. See 3 n. 10; Kenkyūhan 1988, 625 n. 1021.

[11] Kenkyūhan 1988, 625 n. 1022. The *Ziran jing* is lost but cited to similar effect in the *WSBY*:

> The Perfected of Great Ultimate said: "To receive the Tao and handle the scriptures the Taoist must wear proper ritual garb, cap and gown. The gown must be thirty-six feet long and have thirty-two folds. Or he can wear cap and gown made from deer skin, which, in fact, is highly excellent. In that case, the gown has no fixed numbers of folds. The gown should be matched with a yellow lower garment. The feet should be clad in straw sandals, but strong leather sandals can also be worn." (43.1b)

[12] The *Daomen kelue* explains this. "Taoist formal garb . . . consists of a cap, a gown, and a robe. When entering a sacred precinct to worship the Tao, one must wear the gown. For reciting the scriptures, one must don the robe. NOTE: A robe is a cloak. It is fastened at the shoulders and does not reach the ground" (5a).

[13] Kenkyūhan 1988, 625 n. 1023. The same measurements are given in *WSBY* 43.1b and in *Fafu kejie wen* 5b. The latter passage details the differences in clothing between male and female Taoists of various ranks and specifies the exact number of folds in their robes.

[14] *BZL* 9 says that this rule only developed in the sixth century. "Taoists originally wore

"The Taoists' two belts are patterned on yin and yang, just as the two corners of the ceremonial cap are patterned on the two forces of heaven and earth.¹⁵ In addition, the ceremonial cap in its shape corresponds to the lotus."¹⁶

The *Ziran jing* spells out such detailed rules and regulations, so why do Taoists not follow them? Instead, they imitate the garb worn by Zhang Lu and the Yellow Turbans¹⁷—against the rules and without proper awareness!

---

scholars' dress and were no different from lay people. Only in the time of Emperor Wu of Zhou [561–78] did they begin to wrap their robes horizontally and pull them together in twenty-four folds patterned on the twenty-four energies of yin and yang" (T. 2110; 52.529a).

¹⁵ The same description of the gown and belts is also found in *BZL* 6. Here it is introduced as follows: "The Taoists' caps and gowns are just like those worn by the followers of Confucius and Mozi in the old days. Formerly the five emperors wore deer skins, and Xu You [the adviser of Yao] wore a cap of animal hide. So the Taoists dress just like ordinary folk of old" (T. 2110; 52.526b).

¹⁶ More detailed instructions for proper garb, detailing differences according to rank and sex, are found in *WSBY* 43.1a–4b (Lagerwey 1981, 140) and in *Fafu kejie wen* 4b–5a (see Kenkyūhan 1988, 559 n. 325).

¹⁷ A similar criticism is also made in *Erjiao lun* 9 (T. 3103; 52.140ab). The Yellow Turbans wore yellow in accordance with a popular prophecy that the coming dynasty would rule under the phase earth and with the color yellow. Taoists have continued that tradition, giving rise to an association with rebellion. See section 7.

34

Taoists Worship the Buddha

[151c28]¹ The *Huahu jing* says:²

> I pray with an udumbara flower in my hands.
> I pray by burning sandalwood incense.
> I sacrifice to the bodies of a thousand buddhas.
> I knock my head and pay obeisance to Dīpaṃkara.³

¹ Kenkyūhan 1988, 626 n. 1029. This entire section is also contained in *Fayuan zhulin* 55 (T. 2122; 53.705b–06c).

² Kenkyūhan 1988, 626 n. 1030. This citation is not found in any of the extant versions of the *Huahu jing*. It is, however, also contained in *Poxie lun* 1 (T. 2109; 52.477c) and *Guang hongming ji* 11 (T. 2103; 52.162b). Zürcher translates it (1959, 313) and places it among the fragments of the counter*huahu* theory. These were integrated by Zhen Luan into citations of the *Huahu jing* proper, probably with polemic intent.

³ Kenkyūhan 1988, 626 nn. 1031–33. This passage bears a close relationship to the *Lotus Sūtra*. The udumbara flower is mentioned there as a symbol of the continued recurrence of

It also says:[4]

> Why has the Buddha been born so late?
> Why did the nirvāṇa take place so early?
> Since I could not see Śākyamuni,
> My heart is constantly in pain.

And the *Dajie wen* (The Great Precepts) states,[5] "Students of the Tao should visualize themselves wandering to the great palaces of flowing light to pay obeisance to the Buddha."

I laugh at this and say:

The *Fuzhai jing* (Scripture on the Performance of Rites) states:[6] "The Heavenly Venerable ordered the Mysterious Perfected of the Right,[7] 'Śākyamuni transformed the world through his teaching of the continuous transmigration through birth and death. Therefore, I send you, Old Man of Heaven[8] and Mysterious Perfected of the Right, to transform the world with the salvation through immortality[9] and the great teaching of no-death'."

---

buddhas in the world (T. 262; 9.10a); sandalwood incense occurs as one of the fragrances that delight heavenly beings (T. 262; 9.48b); and the Buddha Dīpaṃkara, designated to reach buddhahood when Śākyamuni Buddha in his life as Rutong Bodhisattva offered him five lotus flowers, always appears when a buddha preaches the Lotus. See Getty 1962, 12–14; Nakamura 1981, 746.

[4] This stanza is also cited in *Poxie lun* 1 (T. 2109; 52.477c), *BZL* 5 (T. 2110; 52.522b), and *Gaoseng zhuan* 1 (T. 2059; 50.328c). See Kenkyūhan 1988, 626 n. 1035. For a detailed discussion of its occurrences and variants, see Zürcher 1959, 296.

[5] Kenkyūhan 1988, 626 n. 1038. The same sentence as from the *Zhihui guanshen dajie jing* (Scripture of Great Precepts of Wisdom and Self-observation) is found in *Poxie lun* 1 (T. 52.477c). It is similar to that in the *Dajie wen* (*DZ* 1364, fasc. 1039) except for the reference to the Buddha. "Students of the Tao should visualize themselves wandering to the palaces of flowing light in the great Brahma heavens to pay obeisance to the emperors and kings of the Four Heavens and listen to the chanting of the celestials. It is the most elegant and wondrous thing among the empyreans!" (16a).

[6] The *Fuzhai jing* is an ancient Lingbao scripture still contained in the Taoist canon (*DZ* 532, fasc. 295). This passage, however, is not found there.

[7] Kenkyūhan 1988, 627 n. 1041. This personage and his counterpart, the Mysterious Perfected of the Left, are close attendants of the Highest Venerable Lord. They are mentioned in *Dingzhi jing* 1b (*DZ* 325, fasc. 167) and described in the *Biyao juefa* (Instructions and Methods of Esoteric Essentials), in its section on "Observances for Paying Homage to the Perfected." "Visualize the Highest Venerable Lord wearing a cloak of nine-colored clouds and a cap of the nine virtues. To his left, see the Mysterious Perfected of the Left; to his right, the Mysterious Perfected of the Right. Then see dragon and tiger lords as well as jade lads and maidens standing to his right and left" (*YJQQ* 45.8b).

[8] According to the *Laozi bianhua jing* (S. 2295), this is the name under which Laozi instructed the Yellow Emperor (Seidel 1969b, 65). More generally, "Old Man of Heaven" is an honorary appellation for celestials of high standing.

[9] Kenkyūhan 1988, 627 n. 1044. "Salvation through immortality" is short for "attaining

In addition, the *Laozi xu* has:[10] "Taoism is concerned with life; Buddhism with death. Taoism eschews all defilement; Buddhism does not. Taoism belongs to yang and to life, therefore, it taboos all that is defiling. Buddhism is just the opposite."

According to this, purity and impurity are divided by heaven, life [Taoism] and death [Buddhism] are greatly segregated. Why, then do Taoists not observe the great Tao of purity and emptiness[11] and instead wish to follow Buddhism, the defiled and evil teaching with its emphasis on birth and death?

Formerly, the chief minister of Yin asked Confucius about the sages. Confucius answered: "Neither the Three Sovereigns, the Five Emperors, the Three Kings nor myself are really sages. But among the people of the western regions, there is a sage."[12]

Thus, we know that Confucius considered the Buddha a sage, whereas he did not consider the Tao as specially sagacious.

The *Huahu jing* says,[13] "Of all the great methods in the world, the Buddha's is first."

The *Shengxuan jing* (Scripture of Ascension to the Mystery) states, "My teacher transformed and wandered through India."[14]

In addition, the *Fuzi* (Writings of Fuzi) has,[15] "Laozi's teacher was called Śākyamuni."

---

immortality and reaching salvation [going beyond the world]," a phrase found in *Baopuzi* 13/58/3 (Ware 1966, 217).

[10] A similar passage from the same source is contained in section 8. For a translation and discussion in connection with the conversion of the barbarians, see Zürcher 1959, 306.

[11] Kenkyūhan 1988, 627 n. 1050. "Purity and emptiness" are mentioned as characteristics of the Tao in the bibliographic section of the *Hanshu* (chap. 30).

[12] Kenkyūhan 1988, 627 n. 1052. This passage summarizes a story found in the *Liezi*. The chief minister of Shang asks Confucius who was a sage. Confucius denies that he himself is one, nor would he accept the various sage rulers of antiquity. Pressed relentlessly to name a real sage,

> Confucius grew impatient and changed color. He said nothing for a moment. "Among the people of the western lands," he answered at last, "there is a sage. He does not actively rule, yet there is no disorder. He does not actively teach, yet there is faith in him. He does not actively transform things, yet there is progress. He is so magnificent—people do not have a rightful name to call him. Still, I am not sure that even he is a sage. Really, whether he truly is a sage or not, I cannot tell." (4.4b–5a; see also Graham 1960, 78)

[13] Kenkyūhan 1988, 628 n. 1053. This passage is not contained in any extant versions of the *Huahu jing*, but it is also found in *Erjiao lun* 7 (T. 2103; 52.139c). See also Zürcher 1959, 312.

[14] Kenkyūhan 1988, 628 n. 1055. This citation is also found in *Erjiao lun* 7 (T. 2103; 52.139b) as from the *Xisheng xuanjing* (Mysterious Scripture of Western Ascension) and in *Zhenzheng lun* 2 (T. 2112; 52.564c) as from the *Xisheng jing* (Scripture of Western Ascension; DZ 726, fasc. 449–50). It is found in the latter (1.1a). On both texts, see appendix 2.

[15] Kenkyūhan 1988, 628 n. 1056. The *Fuzi* in twenty scrolls is a philosophical work patterned on the *Zhuangzi* and written by Fu Lang, a local prince of the fourth century (bio. *Jinshu* 114). Listed first in the bibliographic section of the *Suishu* (History of the Sui Dynasty), it is extant in fragments. For details, see Zürcher 1959, 437 n. 124.

A similar statement is also found in the *Daozhai jing* (Scripture of Rites for the Tao),[16] "The immortals are called by the [sounds of the] Brahma Heavens; the Buddhas are called by esoteric formulas."

Now, the sūtras that have come in from abroad in many instances refer to the Brahma Heavens.[17] The "Brahma" that the Taoists are so fond of is, therefore, actually of Buddhist origin. It is only because they have been learning from Buddhism for so long that they speak of Brahma as if it were their own.

Moreover, the *Lingbao* has:[18] "There are secret sounds of great Brahma for all thirty-two heavens. Recite the eight words used for each heaven ten thousand times and you will be able to fly, and your ancestors up to seven generations will ascend to the Southern Palace."

This is more proof that Taoists, in fact, learned their practices from the Buddhists. But they only know how to copy Brahma, they do not have any clue what the Buddhist idea of Brahma really signifies. They just believe in it in utter ignorance! Although that, too, might bring a little good fortune, I cannot but reel in laughter!

[16] This citation is unclear.

[17] The four Brahma heavens are above the Three Worlds and beneath the Three Clarities in the classical scheme of thirty-six heavens (see 27 n. 4). Their sounds are considered part of original creation and, therefore, powerful spells. See *Fayuan zhulin* (T. 2122; 53.576a; Kenkyūhan 1988, 628 n. 1058). Historically, the formulas used to call upon the celestials are adaptations from the Sanskrit. See Bokenkamp 1991.

[18] Kenkyūhan 1988, 628 n. 1059. This passage is found in two separate statements in the *Zhutian neiyin yuzi* (DZ 97, fasc. 49; see also section 15).

> Each of the thirty-two heavens has sounds in eight characters. This makes 256 characters altogether. They are the immeasurably powerful, secret sounds of the great Brahma of the thirty-two heavens. (3.2b)
>
> Recite them ten thousand times, and your Tao will be complete. Then you will be able to fly. This Tao is a most venerable method and a vast teaching. It saves all without limit. Even your ancestors up to the seventh generation will receive good fortune and ascend to the Southern Palace. (3.3b)

35

The Taoist Harmonizing of Energies

[152a2][1] The *Zhenren neichao lü* (Rules of the Perfected for Proper Homage in the Inner Chamber) says:[2]

[1] Kenkyūhan 1988, 628 n. 1061. This entire section, with more extended citations, is also found in *BZL* 8 (T. 2110; 52.545c–46a).

[2] This citation is unclear. The text is also cited in Shi Minggai's refutation of Fu Yi's memorial (T. 2103; 52.172b; see Kenkyūhan 1988, 629 n. 1062).

"The Perfected said: 'As for the proper ritual, at new moon and full moon,[3] all men and women shall fast for three days.[4] They shall then enter their private chambers and emerge only to see the preceptor. To establish proper merit and virtue, both yin and yang should come in together. For all the six periods,[5] during day and night,"[6] and so on. One really should not listen to such base and confused ideas.[7]

Then, again, the *Daolü* (Tao Rules) says:[8] "The practice of energy[9]

[3] Kenkyūhan 1988, 629 n. 1063. Taoist rituals often were scheduled at new or full moon. See *Xuandu lüwen* 16a (Rules of Mystery Metropolis; *DZ* 188, fasc. 78).

[4] Fasting before rituals includes the abstention from meat, wine, and sexual activities as well as purification of the body through fragrant baths and of the mind through meditations. See Saso 1972; Soymié 1977; Malek 1985.

[5] These are the six prescribed daily periods of worship (sunset, early evening, midnight, dawn, morning, and noon), commonly used in Chinese Buddhism but possibly of Greek origin. See Pas 1986; Kenkyūhan 1988, 629 n. 1068.

[6] The passage refers to a rite of sexual intercourse. The *BZL* cites it somewhat differently:

Adepts first pay their respects to the preceptor, then enter their private chambers and emerge only in order to go before him. To establish proper merit and virtue, yin and yang should make their offerings together as ordered. When their merit is accomplished, they leave. For all the six periods, during day and night, they are thus constantly gaining merit. (T. 2110; 52.545c)

Shi Minggai in *Guang hongming ji* 12 details the ritual further, relying on the same text:

During the rituals held at new and full moon, Taoists attend on their preceptor in their private chambers. Feeling and intention are made akin, and men and women engage in joining together. They match their four eyes and two noses, above and below. They join their two mouths and two tongues, one with the other. Once yin and yang have met intimately, essence and energy are exchanged freely. The rites of men and women are performed and the Tao of male and female is harmonized. (T. 52.172b)

[7] The *BZL* does not have this last sentence. Instead, it adds several further citations.

The *Zhenren neili daojia neishi lü* (Esoteric Rites of the Perfected and Rules for Taoists in Attendance in the Inner Chamber) says:

"Do not fail to observe the proper order of attendance in the inner chamber. Do not harbor desire for the ordinary way [of intercourse] or fail to observe the teachings of [sexual] control. Do not lust for relations with outsiders or fail to observe the rituals of the proper nourishing of the inner chamber. Do not lust to be first or fail to observe the rules of cultivation of the inner chamber.

"Laozi says, 'My teacher taught me the *Jindan jing* (Scripture of Gold and Cinnabar). He made me concentrate my mind and nourish my jade stalk [penis], return the yin essence in the rhythm of three, five, seven, and nine. He taught me to regulate my breathing and guide my jade pond fluid [saliva] into my mysterious darkness [abdomen]. Thus, I practiced the Tao of mutual guarding and ascended to Great Clarity.'"

Again, the text has: "Laozi says, 'My teacher taught me to align my essence with his, to join him in the eating of gold and cinnabar and ascend to Great Clarity. I moved according to the three and five and stayed within the limit of the seven and nine. I regulated my breathing in the great mystery and opened the Gate of Life. I strengthened and guarded my jade pond fluid and worshiped Mother Tao'." (T. 2110; 52.545c)

[8] Kenkyūhan 1988, 630 n. 1071. The *BZL* cites this text as *Zhenren neili yishi jiaxing daolü* (Tao Rules of the Perfected for the Practice of Esoteric Rites While Attending on the Preceptor and at Home). The text has not been transmitted otherwise.

[9] The practice of energy (*xingqi*) is a general term for all methods that enhance and guide

has its proper order. You must not willfully avoid the ugly and approach the pretty [females], push ahead or interrupt the process."

In addition, the *Xuanzi* (Writings of the Master of Mystery) has:[10] "Never commit perverse acts, and you can go beyond the world! Never harbor jealousy, and you can leave the world behind! Yin and yang in harmony, you can ascend astride a dragon."[11]

I laugh at this and say:

When I myself was twenty years old, I was fond of Taoist practices and joined an institution to study. The first thing I was taught was the Tao of harmonizing the energies[12] according to the *Huangshu* (Yellow Book),[13] the ritual intercourse of men and women, undertaken in the rhythm of three, five, seven, and nine.[14]

---

the *qi* in the body: gymnastics, breathing exercises, diets, meditations, inner alchemy, and sexual techniques. Here, it seems to refer specifically to the latter. See Maspero 1981, 443–554; Sakade 1983; Engelhardt 1987. For Chinese references, see Kenkyūhan 1988, 630 n. 1072.

[10] Kenkyūhan 1988, 630 n. 1075. This citation is unclear. The bibliographic chapter of the *Suishu* lists a *Xuanzi* in five scrolls. The *BZL* cites this passage as the words of a person Xuanzi quoted in the *Daoshi lilü* (Ritual Rules for Taoists), an otherwise unknown text.

[11] The *BZL* adds a citation of the words of Chisongzi from the same source: "To ascend to heaven and open the Gate of Life, the perfected of the purple halls open the intestinal gateway" (T. 2110; 52.545c–46a). Ascension to heaven on the back of a dragon or in a carriage drawn by dragons is one of the highest forms of immortal transformation. See Kohn 1990b, 18. It is described first in the *Huainanzi* and the *Baopuzi* (Kenkyūhan 1988, 630 n. 1079).

[12] *Heqi*, or harmonizing the energies, is the technical term for sexual practices. On sexual methods among Taoist longevity techniques, see Stein 1963; Maspero 1981, 443–554; Robinet 1991, 67–68. For Chinese sexual methods in general, see van Gulik 1961; Ishihara and Levy 1970; Harper 1987; Ishida 1991; Wile 1992.

[13] The *Huangshu* is an ancient sexual manual revealed to the first Celestial Master Zhang Daoling, later revised and expurged under Shangqing Taoism. The Shangqing version still exists as the *Dongzhen huangshu* (Yellow Book of Perfection Cavern; *DZ* 1343, fasc. 1031); it contains a description of the original revelation (1b–2a and 12b). The ancient work survives only in citations, especially among Buddhist polemics. See appendix 2.

[14] On this expression, see Kobayashi 1990, 199; Kobayashi 1992. The *Dongzhen huangshu* explains it as the basic rhythm of the Tao (1b). It is also the rhythm of ritual intercourse—the three and five being the lower, the seven and nine the upper end of the scale (see Kenkyūhan 1988, 630 n. 1081). The *Dongzhen huangshu* says specifically:

If you wish to pursue the power of life, go well beyond the three and five, but never pass the seven and nine. (1b)

The Tao uses the days after the first ten-day of the month. Its numbers are three, five, seven, and nine. From the tenth to the fifteenth day, practice daily in this rhythm. These days are the six harmonies of heaven, earth, and humanity when the sun and the moon are equally luminous.

Never make it rain wantonly! If you waste your rain, your root will wither and decay. Without proper understanding of the method of the three and five, the practice of the seven and nine, you will perform wantonly. Then, I'm afraid, you will become like a fish out of water, like a man without cosmic energy. (9a)

Never do only the three and five, but always practice the three, five, seven, and nine in conjunction with the twenty-four gods [of the body and the year]. (9b)

The four eyes and two tongues meet each other. Then one practices the Tao in the Cinnabar Field.[15] Through this practice, one supposedly will go beyond all dangers and live forever.[16]

Then they exchange[17] partners and swap the women around, giving themselves over to lustful excitement! Their fathers and elder brothers stand there looking on, yet they know no shame. On the contrary, they praise this as the "perfected technique of equalizing the energies." Even today, Taoists still continue this practice. How they ever succeed in finding the Tao like this remains a mystery to me!

[15] There are three Cinnabar Fields in the body: an upper in the center of the head called the Niwan Palace; a middle one in the solar plexus called the Red Palace; and a lower one in the abdomen often associated if not actually identified with the Gate of Life. See Maspero 1981, 455–59; Porkert 1984, 280; Kohn 1991a. For Chinese references, see Kenkyūhan 1988, 631 n. 1083.

[16] The *BZL* has this somewhat differently.

As the four eyes, four nostrils, two mouths, two tongues, and four hands are clasped together, one concentrates one's mind to make yin and yang join each other—twenty-four times, in accordance with the twenty-four energies of the year. Through this practice you will realize the true formula in the Cinnabar Field. But make sure to keep it to yourself and never let it leak out. Nor must you harbor jealousy. The practice will protect you from all dangers and disasters. You will be called a perfected, go beyond the world, and live forever. (T. 2110; 52.546a)

The same instructions are also found in *BZL* 6 as cited from the *Huangshu* (T. 2110; 52.531c–32a; Kenkyūhan 1988, 630 n. 1081). For a translation, see Maspero 1981, 535–36.

[17] I read *jiao*, "exchange," of the *BZL* version for *jiao*, "teach," in the *XDL* proper.

36

Philosophical Works as Taoist Texts

[152b4][1] The *Xuandu jingmu* (Catalog of Scriptures of Mystery Metropolis) says:[2]

"Of altogether 6,363 scrolls of Taoist scriptures, biographies, talismans, sacred charts, and discussions,[3] 2,040 are available at present.

[1] Kenkyūhan 1988, 631 n. 1089. This entire section, with a detailed list of cataloged scriptures, is also contained in *BZL* 8 (T. 2110; 52.546b–47a).

[2] Kenkyūhan 1988, 632 n. 1090. The *BZL* has the title *Xuandu guan jingmu* (Catalog of Scriptures of the Monastery of Mystery Metropolis). See also section 31. For a general discussion of the understanding of Taoist scriptures in the *XDL,* see Kohn 1992b.

[3] These are four of the twelve divisions of the Taoist canon today. They are: Basic Texts; Divine Talismans; Jade Formulas; Sacred Charts; Genealogical Registers; Rules and Precepts; Rituals and Observances; Techniques and Methods; Secret Arts; Biographies; Hymns of

They make up 40,054 pages altogether. Of these texts, more than 1,100[4] scrolls are scriptures, biographies, talismans, or sacred charts.[5] The remaining 884 scrolls are philosophical discussions.

"Texts in altogether 4,323 were listed by Lu Xiujing.[6] We know their numbers and titles, but they have not yet been revealed and are, therefore, unavailable in earthly editions."[7]

I laugh at this and say:

According to the catalog submitted by the Taoists [of Mystery Metropolis], Lu Xiujing's work listed only 1,228 scrolls of scriptures, including materials on medicines, health practices, talismans, and sacred charts.[8] He had no miscellaneous or philosophical works listed at all.

Yet Taoists now present a list of more than two thousand scrolls of texts.[9] This is because they simply integrated the titles of 884 scrolls

---

Praise; Memorials. On the divisions and development of the Taoist canon, see Liu 1973; Ōfuchi 1979a; Yamada 1984a; Thompson 1985a; Boltz 1987, 4.

[4] The *BZL* specifies the number as 1,156 (T. 2110; 52.546b).

[5] A long list of the different kinds of talismans and charts then current is found in Liang Qiuzi's *Huangting neijing yujing zhu* 3.9ab (Jade Radiant Commentary to the Inner Radiance Scripture of the Yellow Court; *DZ* 402, fasc. 190). See Kenkyūhan 1988, 633 n. 1092.

[6] The *BZL* has a longer version of this sentence. "Texts in altogether 4,323 scrolls were already listed in the catalog that the Taoist Lu Xiujing submitted to Emperor Ming of the Liu-Song. Their titles and editions, however, have not yet appeared today" (T. 52.546b). On Lu Xiujing, see 31 n. 7.

[7] The *BZL* lists these in great detail (see table 2). According to established Taoist tradition, the earliest catalog listed scriptures in eighteen thousand scrolls (see *Daozang quejing mulu* [Catalog of Lost Scriptures in the Taoist Canon]; *DZ* 1430, fasc. 1056). Most of the early texts, however, are lost and are only cited in Buddhist polemics. See also *Falin biezhuan* 3 (T. 2051; 50.209a); *Fayuan zhulin* 55 (T. 2122; 53.704b; Kenkyūhan 1988, 632 n. 1094). Other early sources include Wang Jian's *Qizhi* (Seven Treatises) of the year 473; Meng Fashi's catalog; and Tao Hongjing's list of scriptures. These are lost without a trace. Then there is Ruan Xiaoxu's *Qilu* (Seven Records) of the year 523, which is cited in *Guang hongming ji* 3 (T. 2103; 52.108c). It gives the following list:

Table 2
List: Texts in Four Divisions

Divisions	Texts	Wrappers	Scrolls
Scriptures, precepts	290	311	838
Garb and food	48	52	167
Sexual practices	13	13	38
Talismans, charts	70	76	103
TOTAL	421	452	1,146

In comparison, Buddhist materials consisted of 2,410 texts in 2,595 wrappers and 5,400 scrolls. See Yoshioka 1955, 31–35; Fukui 1964, 164; Chen 1975, 106–12.

[8] The same information is also found in *Fayuan zhulin* 55 (T. 2122; 53.704a).

[9] The *BZL* specifies the number as 2,040 scrolls (T. 2110; 52.546c).

of works in the bibliographic section of the *Hanshu* as Taoist scriptures and treatises.[10] This being so, the entire catalog becomes questionable. How could philosophers like Hanfeizi, Mengzi, or Huainanzi all be talking merely about the Tao?

In addition, they include the [alchemical] methods of yellow and white of the Eight Worthies,[11] the art of metamorphosis according to Tao Zhu,[12] talismans for turning over heaven and toppling earth, and techniques to become immune to weapons and kill demons.[13] Now, if they consider works on pharmacology and casting spells proper Taoist materials, I really cannot understand why they do not also include [texts on divination such as] the *Lianshan* (Connected Mountains), *Guizang* (Safe Repository), *Yilin* (Forest of Changes), and the *Taixuan* (Great Mystery),[14] [texts on medicine such as] the *Huangdi* (Yellow Emperor's [Classic]) and the *Jingui* (Golden Casket),[15] and [texts on military strategy such as] the *Taigong liutao* (Six Tactics of Taigong).[16]

In Lu Xiujing's catalog, the philosophers are not listed. On what

[10] Kenkyūhan 1988, 632 n. 1097. The same sentence is also cited as by Zhen Luan in *Fayuan zhulin* 55 (T. 2122; 53.703b).

[11] The Eight Worthies are the immortality teachers of Liu An. They are described in his Taoist biography.

> One day, eight old men with white beards and eyebrows appeared at his gate. When the gatekeeper saw them, he immediately stole away to inform the prince, who ordered him, as if on his own initiative, to put some difficult questions to the newcomers. . . .
>   Scarcely had he spoken these words, when all eight of them turned into youths of fourteen or fifteen. Their coils of hair became black and silky; their complexions looked rosy like peach blossoms. (*Shenxian zhuan* 4; Giles 1948, 42–43; Güntsch 1988, 121)

The Eight Worthies are also mentioned in the *Soushen ji* and the *Baopuzi* (11/51/9; Ware 1966, 195). See Kenkyūhan 1988, 633 n. 1099.

[12] Tao Zhu or Lord Zhu of Tao was a minister in Yue. He allegedly was the second reappearance of Fan Li, an immortal and student of military strategy. See *Liexian zhuan* (Kaltenmark 1953, 102–4). For more on his story, see 36 n. 23.

[13] On the various magical arts of the immortals, see 22 n. 13. Immunity to weapons is mentioned particularly in *Baopuzi* 6/27/1 (Ware 1966, 115), whereas the elimination of demons is central in the *Shenzhou jing* (on the text, see Mollier 1990). See Kenkyūhan 1988, 634 n. 1102.

[14] Kenkyūhan 1988, 634 nn. 1105–7. These four texts refer to the divination classics of the Xia, Shang, Zhou, and Han dynasties respectively. On the first two, the *Lianshan* and the *Guizang*, lost today, see Imai 1974. On the *Yilin*, see Nylan and Siuin 1988, 48; Morgan 1993, 97. On the *Taixuan* of Yang Xiong of the Han, see Fung and Bodde 1952, 2:36–46; Nylan 1993.

[15] Kenkyūhan 1988, 634 n. 1108. Classics on Chinese traditional medicine frequently have the Yellow Emperor in the title, but there is also a *Jingui lu* listed among medical texts in the bibliographic section of the *Suishu*. For more on medical texts, see Unschuld 1985.

[16] This is a military classic listed in the bibliographic section of the *Suishu* (see Kenkyūhan 1988, 634 n. 1109). On Taigong, see 1 n. 7. The *BZL* continues this enumeration: "and the *Yinfu jing* (Scripture of Hidden Correspondences), works on yin and yang, charts on interpreting names and siting houses, the seventy-two kinds of burials, and more of the like" (T. 2110; 52.546c).

Table 3
Scriptures Listed by Lu Xiujing

Yangsheng jing (Scripture on Nourishing Life), 1/10,[a] edited by Pengzu

Shenxian zhuan (Biographies of Spirit Immortals), 1/10, by Ge Hong

Liexian zhuan (Immortals' Biographies), 1/10, edited by Liu Xiang

Yixia lun (Treatise on Barbarians and Chinese), 1/5, by the Taoist Gu Huan

Zhuangzi (Writings of Zhuangzi), 1/17, by Zhuang Zhou, edited by Ge Hong

Baopuzi (Book of the Master Who Embraces Simplicity), 1/20, by Ge Hong

Guangchengzi (Writings of Guangchengzi), 1/4 edited by Shang Luogong

Yinwenzi (Book of Yinwenzi), 1/2, edited by Liu Xin

Huainanzi (Writings of the Prince of Huainan), 1/20, by Liu An, Prince of Huainan

Wenzi (Writings of Wenzi), 1/11, by Wen Yang

Liezi (Writings of Liezi), 1/8, by Lie Kou

Baopuzi fushi fang (Dietary Methods of the Master Who Embraces Simplicity), 1/4, by Ge Hong

Cuiwenzi (Writings of Cuiwenzi), 1/7, by Cuiwenzi

Guiguzi (Writings of Guiguzi), 1/13, by Master Guigu

Fushi qinji jing (Scripture of Dietary Avoidances), 1/5

Huangdi longshou jing (Dragon Head Scripture of the Yellow Emperor), 1/5, revealed by the Dark Girl

Zhilian wushi (On Refining the Five Minerals), 1/8

Guaiyi zhi (Record of Strange Wonders), 1/12

Xingli zhaishe fa (Methods of Building Houses to Advantage), 1/5

Zhibing jing (Scripture on the Healing of Diseases)

Shuo yinyang jing (Scripture on Yin and Yang)

Riyue mingjing jing (Scripture on the Bright Mirrors of the Sun and the Moon)

Taixuan jing jing (Scripture on the Mirror of Great Mystery)

Anmo jing (Scripture on Massages)

Cuiwenzi zhouhou jing (Cuiwenzi's Scripture on Elbowback [?])

Tao Zhu bianhua shu jing (Tao Zhu's Scripture on the Arts of Transformation)

Pengzu jijing (Scriptural Record of Pengzu)

Yangxing jing (Scripture on Nourishing Inner Nature), 1, Pengzu et al., eds

Dingzhi jing (Scripture on Setting the Will)

Guigu xiansheng bianhua lei jing (Master Guigu's Scripture on Different Kinds of Transformations)

Shiguang wei Xigongzi shouyao jing (Scripture on Medicines Bestowed by Shikuang on Xigongzi)

Jiugong shigui xujing (Scripture on Divination through the Nine Palaces, Milfoil, and Tortoise Shells)

Daoyin tu (Gymnastics Chart)

Hetu wen (River Chart with Text), 1/9, edited by He Chengtian et al.

Zhicao tujing (Illustrated Scripture of Fungi and Herbs)

Zhicao tu (Chart of Fungi and Herbs)

Zouyangzi (Writings of Zouyangzi)

Jiangdu Wang Sisheng (Writings of Wang Sisheng of Jiangdu), 1/2

Daode xuanyi (Mysterious Meaning of the Tao and the Virtue), in 33 scrolls, edited by Meng Zhizhou

Biran lun (On Necessity)[b]

Yingyin lun (On Splendor and Withdrawal)

Suitong lun (On Pervasion)

Guigen lun (To Return to the Root)

Mingfa lun (To Clarify the Law)

Ziran yinyuan lun (On Natural Causation)

Wufu lun (On the Five Talismans)

Sanmen lun (On the Three Gateways)

Source: T. 2110; 52.546bc; Kenkyūhan 1988, 632 n. 1089.

[a]Numbers after the texts indicate the numbers of wrappers (*bu*) and scrolls (*juan*) and are given as, for example, "1/10." No number means that the text consists of only one scroll.

[b]The last eight essays are by Liu Xiujing.

basis are they included today? In the catalog that the Taoists presented in the seventh month of last year [569], only 350 scrolls of philosophical writings were declared as Taoist scriptures. But now they are talking about more than 800 scrolls. Why this discrepancy between then and now?

When people have faults, they are afraid to let others know them; when they have good points, they are anxious lest others overlook them.[17] Now, the Taoists write in their texts, "Who has not received Taoist precepts must not read Taoist scriptures!"[18] Taking this position, are they ashamed to let others know their faults? If, however, they declare the philosophers to be Taoist scriptures, they have to collect and withdraw them all from general circulation. How could they possibly leave them at large?

Again, the Taoists state clearly: "Our Laozi's *Daode jing* was originally among the philosophers, but now it is venerated as scripture. The traditions are so close, so what is wrong about this?" This being so, we know that Laozi and Huangzi belong to the tradition of the philosophers.[19] But, then, why should their tradition be all that different from the seven classics of the Confucians?[20] In addition, Ban Gu places the six classics first, then the two sections.[21] He also lists Laozi among the "medium to higher wise ones."[22] This is a record of fact.

Another point. Tao Zhu actually is Fan Li, a retainer of Gou Jian, the king of Yue. Together they were imprisoned in a stone keep in Wu. Tao Zhu ate excrement and drank urine; he was in an altogether awful

---

[17] This attitude is clearly spelled out in the biography of Hu Zhi in *Sanguo zhi* 27. See Kenkyūhan 1988, 634 n. 1111.

[18] Kenkyūhan 1988, 634 n. 1112. A warning against giving access to sacred materials to the uninitiated is contained in many Taoist texts. A clear rule is stated in the *Laojun jiejing* (Precepts of the Venerable Lord; DZ 784, fasc. 562; on the text, see Kohn 1994): "Only after having received the proper precepts, a man or woman may receive the scriptures and divine methods" (22a).

[19] Kenkyūhan 1988, 635 n. 1117. The name Huangzi is not known outside of Buddhist polemics, where it is found twice more in *Guang hongming ji* 1 (T. 2103; 52.99a, 100a). It might refer to Huangdi, the Yellow Emperor, and the texts associated with him, which in the Han were grouped with the works of Laozi as the tradition of Huang-Lao. See Jan 1978; Murakami 1988; Peerenboom 1991.

[20] Kenkyūhan 1988, 635 n. 1118. The seven classics as listed in *Hou Hanshu* 35 are the *Shijing* (Songs), *Shujing* (History), *Liji* (Rites), *Yuejing* (Music), *Yijing* (Changes), *Chunqiu* (Spring and Autumn Annals), and *Lunyu* (Analects).

[21] Kenkyūhan 1988, 635 n. 1119. This refers to the bibliographic section of the *Hanshu*. The six classics are the ones listed in 36 n. 20, except the *Lunyu*. The two sections are the two parts of the *Daode jing*, that is, the *Daojing* and the *Dejing*.

[22] On Laozi as a sage of medium rank, see 7 n. 15.

state.[23] Still, even today his so-called arts are honored and followed. Is this not utterly incomprehensible?

In addition, Fan Li's son was later killed in Qi.[24] Why ever did he not use his father's "arts" and transform himself [to escape his fate]?

Another story, in the *Zao tiandi jing*,[25] records how Laozi took refuge in the womb of the queen of King You; this means he was King You's son. Then [the text claims] he served as an archivist; this means he was King You's official. Under the Han, moreover, so the *Huahu jing*, Laozi was Dongfang Shuo.[26]

If we look into this, we find that King You was killed by the western barbarians.[27] Why, then, did Laozi not provide his lord and father with a divine talisman to ensure that he would not die?

Moreover, when Emperor Wu of the Han drove the country to exhaustion with his wars, more than half the population perished. Why, if Laozi was Dongfang Shuo, did he bear this and not give the people talismans that made them invulnerable and insensitive to hunger?[28] Why did he not provide them with methods for repelling people and spells against demons[29] and thus save the country? With his own eyes he saw the hardships people were suffering and yet remained too heartless and unmoved to save the people. How could he be anything other than a fraud, a cheat, and a liar?

Finally, the catalog of Taoists scriptures lists more than 6,000 scrolls of texts.[30] Examining this figure closely, it becomes clear that only 2,040 scrolls are actually available today.[31] The remainder[32] are merely

[23] Kenkyūhan 1988, 635 n. 1122. The biography of Gou Jian in *Shiji* 41 mentions Fan Li as his retainer. The specific story referred to here is recorded in *Wu Yue chunqiu* (Spring and Autumn Annals of Wu and Yue) 7.52a.

[24] Kenkyūhan 1988, 636 n. 1125. He was actually killed in Chu. See *Shiji* 41.

[25] This text is the *Chuji*, cited in section 1 (see 1 n. 1).

[26] Kenkyūhan 1988, 636 n. 1129. This information is not found in the *Huahu jing*. Dongfang Shuo, an immortal under the Han Emperor Wu, is identified with the essence of the planet Venus, that is, he was a celestial being of high quality. Like Laozi, he transformed himself. "In the time of the Yellow Emperor, he was the Wind Lord. Under Yao he was the Master of Duty Accomplished. Under the Zhou he was Lao Dan. In Yue he was Fan Li, and in Qi he was Chiyi Zipi" (*Fengsu tongyi* 2). See also Giles 1948, 47–51; Kaltenmark 1953, 93; Seidel 1969b, 68.

[27] The first historical record of these events is found in *Shiji* 4. See Kenkyūhan 1988, 636 n. 1131.

[28] Literally, "able to avoid grains." This refers to the basic method of Taoist dietetics. See 17 n. 12.

[29] Such methods and spells were the pride and joy of Taoists. They are also criticized in *Erjiao lun* 9 (T. 2103; 52.141b). See Kenkyūhan 1988, 637 n. 1137.

[30] The *BZL* specifies this number as 6,363 (T. 2110; 52.547a).

[31] The same information is also found in *Fayuan zhulin* 55 (T. 2122; 53.704b).

[32] The *BZL* gives the exact number of 4,323 (T. 2110; 52.547a).

listed and classified as "not yet revealed." Should it be that lead and ink were not being prepared so that the worldly editions of the texts could not yet be written?[33]

Well, here's enough now of these incoherent tangles! I will not spread them any further!

[33] The *BZL* cites this differently: "The remaining texts in 4,323 scrolls, as indicated in Lu Xiujing's catalog, do not yet have a proper edition. What terrible falsehood! Already Lu's catalog was a great fake, but now the list of Mystery Metropolis really is the fake of a fake!" (T. 2110; 52.547a).

Appendixes

The Texts of the Medieval Debates

This appendix provides summaries of the major texts on the debates among Buddhists and Taoists in the Six Dynasties and early Tang, as they are found in the Taishō canon and the dynastic histories. It is arranged in chronological order and combines texts on one subject into a set group. Each entry is introduced with title, author, author's dates and biography (if available), edition, and scholarly references.

1. The Debate on Zhang Rong's *Menlü* (465)
2. The Debate on Gu Huan's *Yixia lun* (467)
3. The *Bianhuo lun* (ca. 500)
4. The Debate on the *Sanpo lun* (ca. 500)
5. The Debate on Chronology (520)
6. The Debates under the Northern Zhou (567–570)
7. The Debate Surrounding Fu Yi (621–623)
8. The Debate Surrounding Li Zhongqing (626)

1. The Debate on Zhang Rong's *Menlü* (465)

Menlü (Instructions to My Followers), by Zhang Rong (444–97, biog. *Nan Qishu* 41, *Nanshi* 33), ed. *Hongming ji* 6 (T. 2102; 52.38c). Kenkyūhan 1975, 3:358–60; Schmidt-Glintzer 1976, 113–14; Lai 1979, 28–29.

The official Zhang Rong was influenced by both his father's adherence to Buddhism and his mother's veneration for the Tao. The letter is addressed to his followers (two brothers He, two brothers Kong, and Zhou Yong) and explains his religious position.

Taoism and Buddhism are ultimately one and the same. Their "root" or fundamental principle is the same, but their "traces" or appearances in the world and formal practices are different. Like music and rites, they have a true original form yet develop differently over time. Like a wild goose flying high might appear to be a duck or swallow, the teachings seem different but are ultimately identical.

Da Zhang shu bing wen Zhang (Answering Zhang's Letter and Posing Questions to the Author), by Zhou Yong (biog. *Nan Qishu* 41), ed. *Hong-*

ming ji 6 (T. 2102; 52.38c–39b). Kenkyūhan 1975, 3:360–63; Schmidt-Glintzer 1976, 114–16; Lai 1979, 29–31.

Zhou Yong counters Zhang's position. All agree that the Confucian principles are highest and universally accepted. Yet what in this context is "root"? Where should one look for an ultimate identity?

The root of Taoism is the *Daode jing,* that of Buddhism, the *Mahā prajñāpāramitā-śāstra.* The former focuses on empty nonbeing; the latter centers on dharma nature. Both—however identical in some vague origin —really differ in description and application.

Zhang admits that the teachings are different in their traces. Zhou adds that they are not only different but contradictory. Among all the different traces, where can a root be found? Is there really an identity among all the opposition and controversy?

If so, if the teachings indeed have a common root, why can one not follow the traces of Buddhism and yet stick to the root of the Tao? This is what he would prefer to do.

Da Zhou Yong shu bing da suowen (Reply to Zhou Yong's Letter and Answer to His Questions), by Zhang Rong, ed. *Hongming ji* 67 (T. 2102; 52.39b–40b). Kenkyūhan 1975, 3:363–70; Schmidt-Glintzer 1976, 116; Lai 1979, 31–34.

Replying to Zhou's suggestions, Zhang argues that the root can be found by searching for the essence of a teaching with one's own mind and spirit. Anything visible is accessible to knowledge, and indeed the Buddhists claim that truth is matter and matter is truth.

By studying what is there, it can be known. By analyzing it further in the depth of one's own spirit, one can pursue it to the root. The root, however manifold its traces, is only one. Because there is only one spirit within the self, there can be only one Tao—just as there was only one true spirit even among the Five Emperors of antiquity and never more than one Tao among the Three Sovereigns of old.

The same principle also applies to the empty nonbeing of the Tao and the dharma nature of Buddhism. When examined in the spirit of purity and serenity, they are recognized as having one essence. All practical differences are marginal in comparison.

Zhou chong dashu bing wen chongwen (Zhou's Counterreply Asking Further Questions), by Zhou Yong, ed. *Hongming ji* 6 (T. 2102; 52.40b–41b). Lai 1979, 34–38.

Zhou Yong replies again. When truth is matter and matter is truth, one should look at the actual appearance of the teachings in the world and not some elusive "root." Examining the two teachings from this perspective, however, Buddhism emerges as the more sage.

In addition, the ultimate goal of the Taoists in the *Daode jing* proves elusive. The Buddhists, however, provide a clear goal and practical methods of meditation to attain it. The spirit when pure and serene may indeed be only one, yet the two teachings create two different forms of purity and serenity. Thus, there are definitely two different "Tao." Zhang defines Tao as the unknowable and ineffable, to be found only in an emptied soul. Zhou, on the contrary, understands Tao as the practical way of cleaning the mind, as the path to serenity. Tao, he claims, has to be the practical application because otherwise truth could only exist in the serenity of the spirit and would be lost in the actual world.

The practical teaching of dharma nature can, of course, be understood as a trace of the original essence of Buddhism. Yet it is still easily accessible. The practical instructions and explanations that should go with the *Daode jing*, however, are hard to find. Besides, if one took the underlying essence of the two teachings as a separate entity, one would end up with three teachings altogether: Taoism, Buddhism, and ultimate oneness. The discrepancies would still remain unresolved.

2. The Debate on Gu Huan's *Yixia lun* (467)

Yixia lun (Treatise on Barbarians and Chinese), by Gu Huan (420–83), ed. *Nanshi* 75, *Nan Qishu* 54. Kenkyūhan 1975, 3:370–76; Schmidt-Glintzer 1976, 100–103; Tang 1981, 462; Chen 1952, 169–72; Liebenthal 1955, 82–83; Yoshikawa 1984, 492–99; Nakajima 1985, 244–51.

The main argument of this treatise is the fundamental identity of Taoism and Buddhism. Their sageness is the same, as expressed in the story of Laozi becoming the Buddha (cited after the *Xuanmiao neipian*) and in the Buddha's repeated role as teacher of dynasties and helper of the world (after the *Taizi ruiying benqi jing*). Both teachings, moreover, seek to convert the people and strive for the same things—nirvāṇa and immortality, as reached through true spirituality and perfect oneness.

Although identical in their foundations, the teachings differ considerably in their traces. To compare:

Taoism	Buddhism
China	Central Asia
Civilized	Barbarian
Expressed in Chinese	Expressed in barbarian babble

Formal court robes	Shaved heads, wide garments
Greeting by kneeling	Greeting by crawling on the floor
Burial in tombs	Cremation or water burial
Continuity through rites	Development through many life forms
Upholding of marriage	Renunciation of family
Ancestral rites	No ancestor worship
Filial piety	No filiality
Based on rites	No rites
Aims for no more death	Aims for no more life
Simple and straightforward	Fanciful and complex
Concrete and practicable	Abstruse and strange
True and easy words	Elaborate language
Few, esoteric scriptures	Numerous, trivial writings
Difficult to access	Easy to access
Used to develop the good	Used to limit evil
Spontaneity	Fearless courage
Traces subtle and hidden	Traces large and obvious
Superior	Inferior

Shu yu Gu daoshi (**Letter to Taoist Gu**), by Xie Zhenzhi, ed. *Hongming ji* 6 (T. 2102; 52.41b–42b). Kenkyūhan 1975, 3:376–82; Schmidt-Glintzer 1976, 108–11; Hurvitz 1961, 35; Yoshikawa 1984, 500–502.

Xie Zhenzhi criticizes Gu Huan's thesis. There are three forces—heaven, earth, and humanity—that make up the cosmos everywhere whether Chinese or not. Human inclinations—love, greed, veneration—are the same all over the world. Why, then, should the saving grace of the Buddha not apply equally to all humankind?

The origins of both teachings follow the universal pattern, yet Buddhism is superior. It is powerful and radiant and increasingly reaches out toward China. Indeed, China has entered an age of Buddhism. Practiced here in three different vehicles, it leads people to the ultimate goal.

Gu Huan may list many differences. Yet all these outer formalities, behavioral codes, rites, and common practices are not valid criteria for judging the fundamental quality of the teachings. They represent instead the concrete customs of a specific time and place and are not part of the highest principle of the religion.

Taoism is not made superior because of the rites. Rather, the goal of Buddhism, the attainment of ultimate purity, is superior. For this, one must leave all rites and social codes behind. Shaving one's head, one is free from hair styles; wearing loose robes, one is free from the restriction of court garments; fasting and eating simple fare, one is free from hankering after fancy tastes. Nor are few and esoteric scriptures better than numerous and outspoken ones. Buddhism is superior because its teaching is easy to access and its writings are extensive and clear.

Chong shu yu Gu daoshi (Second Letter to Taoist Gu), by Xie Zhenzhi, ed. Hongming ji 6 (T. 2102; 52.42b–43a). Kenkyūhan 1975, 3:382–88; Hurvitz 1961, 34; Yoshikawa 1984, 504–6.

The three forces make up the cosmos everywhere and different local customs do not diminish the underlying unity of humankind. The Great Ultimate divides everywhere into yin and yang; the human body grows under the influence of the five phases. Cultures develop: at first people are primitive, lack proper government, live on trees, and eat wild animals; later, the sages give them rules and set up proper relationships. None of this has anything to do with Taoism or Buddhism.

The sage is in true harmony with universal essence. He represents highest goodness and can pervade all; he accords with all beings, and all forms of life return to him. The Buddha was such a sage. Whoever, independent of country or race, follows the right way can become like him. Just as right and left make no difference to the balance of heaven, so noble and humble, Chinese or barbarian make no difference to the True Way.

The Tao is one; its shapes are two. Truth is only one; its appearance is twofold. Thus, whatever shape one accepts, whatever practices one follows, one is bound to return to original oneness. To make the goal more accessible, practices can be unified. This is what the Buddha did.

If, then, Confucius and Laozi were identical with the Buddha, they would be inferior manifestations of him because the doctrines they preach are so limited. Taoism, for example, teaches only how to lengthen one's life, whereas Buddhism teaches the necessity and means to leave life and death entirely. In addition, Taoist scriptures are crude concoctions, not only false in content but frequently plagiarizing Buddhist sūtras. The only Taoist book of any value is the Daode jing, and even this contains no doctrine of liberation from life and death. Thus, by any standard of comparison, Buddhism emerges as superior.

Nan Gu daoshi Yixia lun (In Critique of Taoist Gu's Treatise on Barbarians and Chinese), by Zhu Zhaozhi (biog. see Nan Qishu 55), ed. Hongming ji 7 (T. 2102; 52.43a–44b). Kenkyūhan 1975, 3:389–400; Hurvitz 1961, 35; Yoshikawa 1984, 503.

Zhu Zhaoshi also finds fault with Gu Huan's ideas. If the two teachings are basically one, their various forms must point to this underlying oneness. What good does it do to argue one against the other?

More specifically, the Tao of the sages encompasses all and is originally nameless. It matches the myriad beings in all situations. Sage wisdom is equally encompassing; it is true awakening or the complete realization of the Tao. This was attained by the Buddha.

Barbarians and Chinese have different life styles and customs, so the sages set up different teachings for them; for some people they created three hundred rules, for others, three thousand. The same holds true for rituals, attire, and codes of behavior. In all cases, however, the rules of the sages bring out the best in people, and the deepest essence of the teachings goes beyond them.

In Chinese antiquity, the Confucian sages set up the rites for the people, but they have been in serious disarray since the Han. Buddhism at this time arrived to supplement and replace the earlier order.

The sage takes care of the people like a mother of her children. He feeds them first and gives them the best morsels to strengthen their bodies. Confucius did this in his time and way, and so did the Buddha. Their teachings may not be quite the same, but Buddhism is the one active at present and best suited for this time.

If Buddhists relinquish their families and do not bow to their worldly superiors, this is the way of the spiritual. Did not Confucius himself admit that the ways of the supernatural were wondrous and could not be known? Enlightenment may be solitary and the four karmic fruits highly personal, yet they are not asocial. There are different vehicles for different people, and Buddhism is certainly not in all cases a solitary teaching.

Buddhism supposedly focuses on limiting evil, whereas Taoism develops the good. This seems to indicate that the Chinese are inherently good. Still, this goodness is not obvious and, in view of the existence of atrocious punishments in China, rather difficult to prove.

Yi Yixia lun zi Gu daoshi (Doubts about the Treatise on Barbarians and Chinese, addressed to Taoist Gu), by Zhu Guangzhi (biog. see *Nanshi* 75), ed. *Hongming ji* 7 (T. 2102; 52.44b–45b). Kenkyūhan 1975, 3:400–10; Hurvitz 1961, 35–36.

Zhu Guangzhi voices an overall disagreement, then deals with specific points. The Buddhist teaching accounts for cultural and individual differences by proposing three vehicles and six forms of salvation and different explanations of the sūtras and discourses. Cultural diversity takes on many forms. Buddhism and Taoism have different styles of greeting, which reflect cultural variations and should be accepted as such. The two teachings are, thus, not really incompatible. Religious rules and methods reflect cultural variance and are the result of specific situations; this is not a fundamental and irrevocable state.

Gu says that Buddhists reject their families and do not bow to worldly authority. This, however, is part of Buddhist culture, which strives for liberation from all ties. To free oneself from one's inferiors means that one also has to be independent of one's superiors.

Gu claims that there is a fundamental difference between the pure Tao and the vulgar customs of the people. Indeed, the Tao is perfect; there can be no essential difference between one Tao and another. Similarly, all common practices are equally vulgar and encumbered. One must see beyond them and recognize the saving message of the Buddha. Then the petty distinctions are mere trifles.

For Gu, Buddhism represents the state of no life, Taoism that of no death. In fact, thinking about the two, one finds they are ultimately the same. Without life, there is no death; without death, there can be no life. Because they are the same, one is just as good as the other.

Gu finds Buddhist writings extensive, flowery, and complex, whereas Taoist texts are essential, simple, and esoteric. This may be so, but ultimately it is advantageous to have broader explanations than merely brief and obscure formulas.

Gu states that Buddhism serves to limit evil; Taoism develops the good. If, however, the nature of the barbarians were wholly evil, no amount of chastising would help. If they were wholly good, no encouragement would be necessary. Really, the notion is absurd. Obviously, good and evil exist in varying proportions in all human beings and societies, regardless of nationality. If the good of the Chinese and the good of the barbarians are intrinsically different, then why call them both good or evil in the same words?

To Gu, the barbarian language sounds like the twitter of birds and the grunting of animals. Well, to hear what sounds like gibberish, a Chinese need not leave his own country at all. Some of China's own dialects are mutually unintelligible. Is one to say that one dialect is "right" while the rest are "wrong"? Besides, if Sanskrit sounds like nonsense to Gu, how does he suppose Chinese sounds to Indian ears? Clearly, the underlying principle of the teaching is essential, and any word in any language that conveys the principle is as good as another.

Bo Yixia lun (**Disputing the Treatise on Barbarians and Chinese**), by Yuan Can (420–77, biog. *Songshu* 89), ed. *Nan Qishu* 54. Schmidt-Glintzer 1976, 103; Hurvitz 1961, 36.

Yuan Can disputes Gu Huan's claim to Taoist superiority. The Buddha, he states, lived before Laozi, so all Chinese texts have only appeared after Buddhism. The teachings, moreover, are not only different on the surface but even in their roots. Taoism and Confucianism are primarily concerned with the affairs of the world; Buddhism centers fundamentally on the escape from all sensual existence. Nirvāṇa and immortality are not the same thing at all. Nirvāṇa is the purification of spirit; immortality is the transformation of the body. Nirvāṇa means true permanence in freedom from all mundane concerns; immortality is just a hoax achieved by a few men who add black dye to their graying temples. There is no identity of Taoism and Buddhism.

Da Yuan Can bo Yixia lun (**In Answer to Yuan Can's Criticism**), by Gu Huan, ed. *Nan Qishu* 54, *Quan Qiwen* 44. Schmidt-Glintzer 1976, 104–5.

Gu Huan defends his position by turning the chronology around. Laozi was a man of the Eastern Zhou, yet Buddhist scriptures only appeared under the Later Han. There is an eight-hundred-year gap between the two. In addition, the teachings may be different, but Taoism is still superior. Buddhism originated in the barbarian west and was originally an instrument to correct and control the immoral ways and loose customs of the area. Taoism, emerging in China, the place of civilization as codified in the rites, is naturally superior. The two teachings are different in origin and cultural setting. They are not made for each other's cultural spheres, which remain as separate as the habitats of birds and fish.

The most fundamental difference between the teachings lies in their continuity. True permanence is only found in the Tao. The ascent to immortality is an increasing purification and growth in serenity, nonaction, and namelessness.

Zhengyi lun (**On True Oneness**), by Meng Jingyi (dated after 470), ed. *Nanshi* 75, *Quan Qiwen* 22. Schmidt-Glintzer 1976, 106.

Meng Jingyi came from the same district as Gu Huan. He does not defend the *Yixia lun* in particular, but his treatise presents the same outlook.

Buddha and Laozi both emphasize oneness as the ultimate goal. Oneness is different from all concrete phenomena; it is mysterious, empty, and hidden. Oneness underlies all existence and brings forth all beings in endless transformation. Yet in itself it remains utterly free from activity and involvement. The Buddhists call it "fundamental reality," for the Taoists it is the "mysterious female." It is the "great emblem" of the Taoists and the "dharmakāya" of the Buddhists reached by the very same practice of nonpractice, through the attainment of noncultivation.

Concrete rules and behavioral patterns of both teachings are numerous, yet they all lead to ultimate oneness, to goodness, to truth. Taoism and Buddhism were not originally separate; they were interpreted differently only in later erroneous views.

Zheng erjiao lun (**Correcting the Position of the Two Teachings**), by Ming Sengshao (d. 483, biog. *Nanshi* 50), ed. *Nan Qishu* 54, *Hongming ji* 6 (T. 2102; 52.37b–38c). Kenkyūhan 1975, 3:348–57; Schmidt-Glintzer 1976, 107–8; Hurvitz 1961, 38–39.

Ming Sengshao takes up specific points in Gu Huan's treatise. First, he discusses the narration of the *Xuanmiao neipian,* according to which Laozi became the Buddha. Striding on the essence of the sun, he entered the mouth of Queen Māyā and was born nine months later through her armpit. This is spurious. The true teaching of Taoism is Laozi's *Daode jing* and not the various later texts claiming Taoist origin. Moreover, it is neither natural to make a woman pregnant by riding on the energy of the sun and entering her mouth, nor is it proper to be born from an armpit. How, if the doctrines are so confused, can the teaching stand up to scrutiny?

Second, the Buddha's service as dynastic teacher over several generations. The essence of the Buddhist teaching is enlightenment, and there is no need for an extended life span. Rather than for prolonged years, it aims at true permanence.

Third, compatibility of the teachings. Taoism comes in different forms. Laozi's *Daode jing* concentrates on nonaction; later movements aim at an illusory immortality and stir up rebellion among the people. There is no such division in Buddhism. In addition, Laozi remained limited in his wisdom; the Buddha developed much higher spirituality. There can be no true identity of Taoism and Buddhism.

Bo Gu daoshi Yixia lun (**Disputing Taoist Gu's Treatise on Barbarians and Chinese**), by Shi Huitong (biog. *Gaoseng zhuan* 7, T. 2059; 50.374c–75a), ed. *Hongming ji* 7 (T. 2102; 52.45b–47a). Kenkyūhan 1975, 3:410–26.

To Shi Huitong, Gu is a "blind man who is trying to distinguish pearls from red berries," a "deaf person who tries to distinguish music from a donkey's braying." The *Daode jing* is obscure and confused, inaccessible to people, and no measure for Buddhism.

Gu claims that Laozi was the Buddha. In fact, Laozi was Kāśyapa and Confucius was Prince Purelight; both were attendants of the Buddha and neither was the enlightened one himself. Life in antiquity was uncivilized. The sages changed that with their establishment of rites and laws. Taoists reject these with their proposal of nonaction and their criticism of Confucian virtues. Moreover, Buddhist rules are superior because India is the center of the world and, thus, the Buddhist teaching is of a central quality unattainable by either Confucius or Laozi.

Nevertheless, Buddhism and Taoism are ultimately not incompatible. Their essential teachings are free from personality and their virtue is not one-sided. They are like the sun that shines equally on everyone, like the wind that blows over all.

Gu equates Buddhism with no life and Taoism with no death. Yet even the *Daode jing* acknowledges the essential value of death: to be ready for life one has to obtain a position of death, it says, and states that heaven and earth live forever because they do not give life to themselves. Moreover, what is wrong with death? After all, all the great sages of China died and have tombs in well-known places. In fact, even the *Daode jing* supports the Buddhist position. Buddhists supposedly destroy their bodies. But does not the *Daode jing* say that "having a body is a great affliction?" Well, the Buddhists, at least, are doing something about this.

***Ronghua lun* (On Barbarians and Chinese)**, by Shi Sengmin, ed. *Hongming ji* 7 (T. 2102; 52.47a–48a). Kenkyūhan 1975, 3:426–34.

Gu Huan's argument lacks logic. On the one hand, he claims that Buddhism and Taoism are the same; on the other hand, he pits them against each other. In fact, the two teachings are fundamentally different.

Buddhism represents enlightenment and true numen; Taoism is a mere assembly of "ways," methods for long life, confused and insignificant. Buddhism is universal and the true ancestor of the myriad gods and teachings. It goes beyond life and death, leading to eternal bliss, whereas Taoism just seeks an immortality in the heavens, which are still part of the life-and-death cycle.

Buddhism is the only true teaching of the world. Laozi appeared as Kāśyapa, a disciple of the Buddha. He brought the *Daode jing* to China upon the Buddha's orders so that there would be at least a semblance of Buddhist doctrine in this country. Then he returned to India. This is the truth behind Laozi's emigration, not the distorted tales of the conversion of the barbarians. In addition, all other Chinese sages from the Duke of Zhou to Confucius and Zhuangzi are, in fact, appearances of the Buddha. They all taught a doctrine of high morality and culture, a limited form of Buddhism that the Chinese could comprehend.

Gu Huan claims that there are massive cultural differences between the Chinese and their Central Asian neighbors. This is true, but the distinction is not only between east and west but also between north and south and center. Everywhere customs and cultures differ. Yet Gu does not see that far; he is rather like a frog in a deep well who has never glimpsed the vastness of rivers and lakes. Thus, he cannot know that the Buddhist teaching originated in the very center of the universe, that in fact India is the center of a much larger world of which China occupies only a marginal portion.

Gu also claims that Buddhist habits and rites are not suited for China. This is not true. Because Buddhism is the true teaching of the center, its rules, too, are universal and its law will never change. Although local customs may differ, the law of the sage must not be altered, otherwise the true numen will be lost.

Taoist scriptures, Gu notes, are few and rare, mysterious and obscure. In fact, however, it is much better to have broad and clear documents, numerous and ample explanations of the teaching!

Taoist garb, although the teaching claims to represent the height of Chinese culture, is that of the Yellow Turbans. Instead of showing the high style of ancient China, Taoists associate themselves with rebels, peasants, and scum. They have no grounds to complain about Buddhist fashion.

3. The *Bianhuo lun* (ca. 500)

Bianhuo lun (**To Discriminate Errors**), by Shi Xuanguang (biog. unclear), ed. *Hongming ji* 8 (T. 2102; 52.48a–49c). Kenkyūhan 1975, 3:435–48.

Among the early texts, the *Bianhuo lun* is most concrete because it deals with the actual situation of Taoism at the time. Attacking Taoist longevity techniques and popular talismanic practices, the text is divided into two main sections.

I. The five rebellious acts of Taoists

   1. They give highest value to prohibited scriptures.
   2. They falsify the true Tao.
   3. They engage in sin by harmonizing the energies.
   4. They cause rebellions in the name of the Tao.
   5. They demean virtue in their petition prayers.

II. The six extreme characteristics of Taoists

   1. Extreme lawlessness: They awe demons by wearing talismans.
   2. Extreme artfulness: They control the people by cowing them into submission.
   3. Extreme inhumanity: They hold banquets at the gates of tombs.
   4. Extreme fraudulence: They claim to have the means of overcoming dangers and the hardships of life.
   5. Extreme craziness: They delude themselves that they commit sins.
   6. Extreme murderousness: They make light of warmth and cold [life and death].

The Tao originally is pure and clear and has been part of the Chinese tradition since High Antiquity. Taoists use this Tao and distort it into something utterly strange.

They create esoteric scriptures, pursue filthy practices, and cheat emperors into searching for immortals (I.1); they plot rebellion and fake evidence that their leaders have ascended to heaven (I.2); they engage in lascivious orgies as part of ritual (I.3); they rise in rebellion, fight against the established mandate of heaven, worship demons, and put about empty lies and fantasies (I.4); they act in the name of virtue but, in fact, engage in drunken assemblies and claim to influence the course of nature (I.5).

Their bad character becomes further evident in their belief that they have absolute power over demons with the help of talismans and petition prayers. This delusion leads them to rise in rebellion (II.1). In addition, their religious organization and public display of fancy rituals are geared toward awing the people into submission. Especially the first Celestial Master claimed to be inspired by heaven and wrote talismans to subdue the people. Later Taoists engaged in so-called rites of mud and ashes, rolling in the dirt like donkeys, hanging themselves head-down, and exciting themselves into a fever. All these are barbarian practices, not worthy of China (II.2).

Parties held near their relatives' tombs show the deep moral depravity of the Taoists. To give them credit, criticism of the noisy singing and brawling was voiced and attempts were made to limit the amount of alcohol per person to three pints. However, even this "liquor control" could not prevent the Taoists' immoral nature from bursting forth (II.3). Another delusion Taoists engage in is that they have power over the ups and downs of life. The fact, however, is that life moves on as it will, that sickness and disease, weakness and misfortune come of their own accord and will not obey any odd talisman with drawings of the stars or written in fancy cinnabar ink (II.4).

The worst craziness of all is that they believe they are responsible for whatever happens in the world. Believing that they can summon demon servants and have the natural world under their thumb, they claim that all events are the result of their own sinfulness. What nonsense! The fact is that when a body dies, it decays and feeds the plants of the earth; its flesh turns into soil, its moisture into rivers. All life is, thus, part of an integrated cosmic process; it cannot be controlled or influenced through demons and sin (II.5).

The same arrogance leads Taoists to assume they have power over life and death. They produce talismans and petitions and hang them over doors or stick them on windows—all to keep out and kill demons. Worse than that, they also have the "All-Overcoming Yellow Spirit Seal," which kills people. They take away life without so much as a second thought. Life, however, is not so easily destroyed. People after death suffer punishment in the hells then emerge anew to life to again grow deaf and mute with their bones decaying unto death from which the rebirth cycle starts once more (II.6).

4. The Debate on the *Sanpo lun* (ca. 500)

Sanpo lun (**On the Threefold Destruction Caused by Buddhism**), by an unknown Taoist of the Liang, lost, cited in the *Miehuo lun* (see next). Schmidt-Glintzer 1976, 117.

Buddhism wreaks threefold destruction: on the state, the family, and the individual. It destroys the state by upsetting the population and wasting economic resources because it tempts people away from productive work and into monastic communities. It destroys the family by making different members follow different rules, causing unhappiness and a loss of harmony. It destroys the individual by making him injure his body and commit unfilial acts. More specifically, the Buddha failed as a royal prince, and Buddhist customs are utterly barbarian.

Miehuo lun (**To Dispel Errors**), by Liu Xie (biog. *Liangshu* 50, *Nanshi* 72), ed. *Hongming ji* 8 (T. 2102; 52.49c–51c). Kankyūhan 1975, 3:448–60. Hurvitz 1961, 29–30.

This refutes nine passages from the *Sanpo lun*.

1. Taoism reaches for eternal life, Buddhism strives for the end of all life in a state of nirvāṇa, which is death.

Answer. The opposite is true. Buddhism refines the spirit, whereas Taoism only cares for the body. The spirit is immortal and limitless and can reach beyond the Six Harmonies. Bright people stick to what is truly immortal; only fools deal with what decays. Through meditation and absorption one attains permanence of spirit, the wondrous state of nirvāṇa, which is much superior to the fancy bodily states reached through immortality techniques and drugs. One cannot find eternity in the body, and what good is it to fly up into the heavens? Only nirvāṇa holds true permanence.

2. The Buddha was born a prince, but princes do not shave their heads or abandon their families. This shows that Buddhism is a destructive and evil teaching. The body is the sacred inheritance from one's parents and must not be harmed; one must not leave one's kin. Buddhism violates the most basic rules of filial piety.

Answer. Buddhist filial piety lies in the heart, not in the hair. Even in Chinese antiquity, sages cut their hair and tattooed their bodies, yet they are still praised as virtuous. They could explain high principles very clearly. How much more should the Buddha be able to do so, with his attainment of true wisdom?

3. The first destruction: Buddhism enters the state and destroys it by upsetting the population. Monks do not weave, yet wear clothes; they do

not plant, yet eat food. The state is impoverished, subject to the five disasters, and eventually destroyed.

Answer. The Mahāyāna teaching in its various doctrines is great and lofty. The establishment of temples and monasteries bears witness to its growth and importance. To build and live in them creates merit that will benefit a thousand generations. In addition, there were countless disasters and rebellions in Chinese antiquity; the state now is in no greater jeopardy than before.

4. The second destruction: Buddhism enters a family and destroys it by upsetting its harmony. Different members will follow different rules and life styles; there is no more filial piety, only unhappiness and distrust.

Answer. Should one give up eternal bliss for the Confucian rites? Is not the pursuit of karmic fruits a great merit that benefits the family? In addition, filial piety in its present form is a later development. The Three Sovereigns and Five Emperors of antiquity did not follow this system. They had their own way to transform the people, just as Buddhism has its own path to liberation.

5. The third destruction: Buddhism enters an individual and destroys him by causing injury to the body, unfilial conduct, and an unnatural preference for death. It even teaches mothers to bow to their children.

Answer. Whether one becomes a monk or stays lay depends on one's karma. Never at any time or place has an entire population renounced the world. There were always only a select few, since everyone's condition is different. Thus, the teaching is divided into monastic and lay. For the former, family relations are an emotional bond that harms the spirit; hair is a sensual gratification that hinders progress. To practice properly, both must be abandoned. One does not kneel before one's parents because the teaching is more venerable. Any son who has become a representative of the teaching reaches beyond the Three Worlds. So he should receive homage from his mother.

6. Kumārajīva became a Buddhist follower because he realized his own evil nature. So did all the barbarians. In addition, Laozi says that to improve people one need not harm their bodies. How evil must the Buddhists be if they injure themselves? Moreover, they call themselves *sangmen* (*śramaṇa*), which means "gate of mourning," indicating their preference for death; they call their leader *foutu* (*buddha*), which is "floating butcher." Only later, when they were criticized for this, did they change the words to the more innocuous *sāngmen, shamen,* and *fotu.*

Answer. The first Buddhist texts were translated under Emperor Ming of the Han. At that time, people tried to find the right Chinese words to transliterate Sanskrit. Later, they adapted them to improve understanding.

This editing process is natural; it happens to ancient Chinese texts all the time. Are not Confucian writings glossed and given commentaries? Are there not difficult terms in the *Yaodian* (Book of Yao), which have explanations?

7. Buddhism originated in the west and is unfit for China. The barbarians are cruel, lack rites, and live like animals. Laozi left China to civilize them.

Answer. Laozi left China not to cultivate the barbarians but because the morals of the Chinese had sunk so low. Nobody knows what became of him. Still, his emigration made it possible for Wang Fou to compile the *Huahu jing,* which gives an utterly unreasonable account. Buddha and Laozi could never be the same person.

8. The rulers of High Antiquity never heard of Buddhism.

Answer. All these rulers were, in fact, bodhisattvas, but they taught a religion that was suited to China at that time. Their teachings were basically Buddhist, valuing morality and virtue. None of them did anything even remotely like Taoist practice today.

9. Taoism is centered on primordial cosmic energy and on attaining the One. All Chinese share this belief. Those who do not are barbarians.

Answer. The ultimate of Buddhahood is the One, too. It is formless and without personal consciousness, capable of infinite responses. Once objects and their names came into being, Buddhahood, too, was named *bodhi,* or Tao. Its appearances in the world—be they the dream of Emperor Ming, the birth of the Buddha as a prince, the teaching formulated in different scriptures, or the four noble truths—are expressions of its underlying oneness. The Buddha's message, preached in different places, languages, and forms, is always one. It may appear in Confucian garb here and in Buddhist garb elsewhere. It is not alien to China but merely appears in its appropriate form.

Da Sanpo lun (In Response to the "Threefold Destruction"), by Shi Sengshun, ed. *Hongming ji* 8 (T. 2102; 52.51c–53c). Kenkyūhan 1975, 3:461–74.

Refutation of the *Sanpo lun* in nineteen sections.

1. Nirvāṇa is death and does not lead to long life.

Answer. All power of life comes from a force that is not alive itself. Thus, Confucius, Laozi, and Zhuangzi all valued death. Life is suffering; to end rebirth and transmigration is, therefore, bliss.

2. A prince should not give up his family.

Answer. This prince wished to show that human relations are bondage.

All beings have Buddha nature. To develop it one must be free from bondage. Thus, his behavior.

3. A prince should not cut off his hair.

Answer. To show love for one's family, one keeps one's hair. To show respect for one's teacher, one cuts it off. It is a sign of surrender to the teaching, of giving up all inner bonds of love. Hair is light but the teaching is serious; give importance to what is important.

4. Mothers should not bow to their sons, even if they are monks.

Answer. Whoever is sworn to the monastic life is at-one with the highest Tao and, therefore, takes precedence. Similar cases of position taking precedence over family relation are known from China.

5. To shave the head means to become a "floating image" (*foutú*).

Answer: "Floating image" is the transliteration of "Buddha," and this means the enlightened one. One shaves the head to demonstrate one's distance from the world.

6. *Sangmen* (*śramaṇa*) means "gate of mourning."

Answer. *Men* means "gate," and gate means the entrance and the place of origin. Both Buddhism and Taoism call their teachings "gates." *Sang* means "mourning," and mourning indicates death and destruction. Here, it means the end of all impurities necessary for the liberation of the spirit.

7. The barbarians are ignorant. Laozi went west, manifested his image in a statue, and converted them.

Answer. Images and statues are not erected while someone is alive. Thus, the Buddha was worshiped with flowers and incense only after he had entered nirvāṇa. Not all barbarians are ignorant. Kumārajīva, for example, was born in Central Asia yet was widely educated and translated many Buddhist scriptures. There is a difference between true and ordinary people, those who have attained higher levels and those who have not— whether in China or elsewhere.

8. Shaving the head was a measure to subdue the barbarians.

Answer. The various tribes on China's periphery do not have organized kingship. Without Buddhism, they would not be much different from animals. The benefit of the Buddhist teaching, however, also applies to China.

9. *Shamen* (*śramaṇa*) means "to sift and cleanse" (*shatai*).

Answer. The expression may mean "to sift and cleanse," but what is cleansed? The impurities of the mind. Thus, *shamen* means to calm the mind and attain the source. It is an expression for spiritual cultivation.

10. When Buddhism enters a state, it destroys it.

Answer. On the contrary, Buddhism helps the people become better and more civilized. It eliminates the need for cruel punishments and raises the overall level of morality.

11. When Buddhism enters a family, it destroys it.

Answer. Buddhism teaches loving kindness and compassion for all life and prepares people for higher states. Taoists with their strange exorcistic rites are doing much worse.

12. When Buddhism enters a person, it destroys him.

Answer. The personal body, even Laozi agrees, is a hindrance to cultivation. Likewise, the Buddha described the Three Worlds as a house on fire. Those who wish to attain truth thus leave the world with its luxury and splendor, gain and fame, and attain perfect serenity. They become complete as human beings, they are not destroyed.

13. Buddhists do not differentiate between songs and laments.

Answer. Laments are sung for mourning, but songs also can express sadness. Even Confucius passed someone singing near a grave and did not criticize him.

14. Buddhists do not bow to their superiors.

Answer. Even within society, people of a certain rank do not bow to others. How much more so the monks who are outside social bonds?

15. To shave the head is evil and harmful.

Answer. This has already been answered. It is an expression of service for the teacher, of one's willingness to wander through the ten directions for guidance, of one's membership in the community of heavenly beings.

16. To leave the household means to avoid one's duty.

Answer. Ha, ha! These are but empty words! To leave the household means to establish oneself in the original ground. One cultivates the spirit, attains truth, and goes beyond the world. This duty and merit is much greater than what one leaves behind.

17. One can never be free from causation.

Answer. To be free from causation means to be free from the karma that leads to further rebirth. It is quite possible.

18. Taoism enhances virtue and supports the state.

Answer. Among the ninety-six different teachings, Buddhism is foremost. It makes the gods of rivers and mountains produce the right weather and appreciate the sacrifices made to them. The Taoist ways, on the contrary, are just some fancy rites like that of mud and ashes. Buddhist activities are more powerful and older, going back to the times when the Great Ultimate divided into yin and yang. All deviations of the proper ways have always been rectified by Buddhism.

19. The Tao has primordial energy as its center.

Answer. "Tao" means a way, a method to get somewhere. Therefore, the *śramaṇas* are also called *daoren,* or "men of the way." Buddhism contains the original essence of the way, whereas Taoism only represents its far ends. Thus, the doctrine of primordial energy is just a manner of expressing the continuity of rebirth: energy comes and there is life; it leaves and there is death. Taoism is nothing but a teaching about continued life-and-death. In addition, Zhuangzi says, the Tao is even in excrement. Is it that kind of Tao they get by "harmonizing the energies"?

5. The Debate on Chronology (520)

Jiang Bin versus Tanmuzui, summary ed. *Fodao lunheng* (T. 2105; 52.403a–4a). Wang 1934, 44–45; Tang 1938, 535–38; Ch'en 1964, 184–86; Kusuyama 1976; Kusuyama 1979: 373–81; Lai 1986, 67–71.

There are no specific texts concerning this debate. It is included in this appendix because of the important changes it wrought in polemic style, arguments, and Taoist texts.

The confrontation took place in front of Emperor Ming of the Northern Wei. The main contestants were the Taoist Jiang Bin and the Buddhist Tanmuzui. The topic of debate was the seniority of the teachings as evident in the chronology of their respective founders.

Originally, Laozi was considered a contemporary of Confucius, who left for the west around 479 B.C.E., the year of Confucius's death and the beginning of the Warring States period. The birth of the Buddha, independent of Taoist competition, was dated to 689 B.C.E. owing to a *Zuozhuan* record of a wondrous sighting in the western sky.

The theory that Laozi became the Buddha necessitated an earlier dating of his life. In the *Santian neijie jing* of the early fifth century, he was first described as having left China under King You of the Zhou, that is, around 770 B.C.E. This gave him enough time to cross the desert, convert the thirty-six barbarian countries, return to heaven, and be born again as the Buddha.

In 520, the Buddhists bettered their position. Using a miraculous occurrence described in the *Mu tianzi zhuan* as the sign of the Buddha's birth, they dated it to 1029 B.C.E. or the twenty-fourth year of King Zhao of Zhou. Some texts also placed the event two years later.

The Taoist countermove consisted of dating the emigration to 1030 B.C.E. (Zhao 23). They documented this in a text called *Kaitian jing,* which presumably contained an account of Laozi creating the world, followed by his various transformations, especially emphasizing his role as the "teacher of Zhou," and his exploits in the western lands.

The debate of 520 went against the Taoists, whose scripture was proven a forgery. The *Kaitian jing* was destroyed. In the aftermath, a new version of Laozi's activities in the early Zhou was written, which dated the events with fictitious reign titles, such as Highest Sovereign and Nonultimate, and had Yin Xi become the Buddha. This is the *Wenshi zhuan,* of which fragments are still extant (see app. 2).

The orthodox birth date of Laozi today is the ninth year of King Wuding of Shang or 1316 B.C.E. This is 287 years before the assumed emigration and eighty years after the conception in Yangjia 17 (1392 B.C.E.). This dating is found in the literature since the Tang and probably goes back to the Laozi hagiography written by Yin Wencao in the late seventh century.

6. The Debates under the Northern Zhou (567–570)

Wei Yuansong's Memorial on How to Reform Buddhism, summary ed. *Guang hongming ji* 7 (T. 2103; 52.131c–32b). Tsukamoto 1974, 2:547–50; Ch'en 1964, 187–90; Magnin 1979, 160–62; Kamata 1984, 434–38.

The memorial by Wei Yuansong set in motion the events that led to the compilation of the *Xiaodao lun* in 569 and the persecution of Buddhism in 574. It proposed an integrated lay Buddhist theocracy, based on the principles of the sage rulers of old.

Translation. Under the rule of Yao and Shun, there was no Buddha to order the country, yet the country was at peace. Under the Qi and Liang, there were temples and lodges to govern the people, yet the people did not flourish and there was no harmony with the Tao. Even if one accepts that the people were not spoiled by the temples and lodges, how can the order of the land lie with the Buddha?

The only thing necessary is to teach the people to join their hearts with the Tao. Once the people are in harmony with the Tao, there is peace. When the Tao nourishes the people, good order will naturally be established.

The Qi and Liang contended for Buddha images and extensive constructions of nine-storied buildings that reached into the clouds. Yao and Shun, on the contrary, sympathized with the commoner's lot and built low structures of pounded earth. Although the Qi and Liang were not without merit toward the temples and lodges, they were yet cheated and lasted only for a short period. How, then, could Yao and Shun have served the Buddha and ruled for such a long time?

To benefit the people and increase the wealth of the country—this is truly to develop the Buddha mind. The Buddha mind most basically consists of great compassion, of harboring all living beings in peace and happiness, and of never letting the masses suffer. Devotion toward mud and wood [images], on the contrary, lessens this true consciousness and enhances being without feelings.

Now, the ruler of our Great Zhou [dynasty] vastly connects succeeding generations and in constancy encompasses the Six Harmonies. In his single mind, he combines the twofold radiance of the sun and the moon, nourishes the four kinds of living beings, and supports the myriad families like the solid earth. Equal to mysterious heaven, he truly represents the glory of the Three Sovereigns of old.

Indeed! When the people first encountered him, it was as if the Five Emperors had come back to rule again. Blessed is the time when the common people find such a ruler! How can they not long for the superior reign of Yao and Shun? How can they not wish to rid themselves of the apocalyptic rule of the Qi and Liang?

I, therefore, propose that a great and encompassing Buddhist church be established, which includes all people under heaven. I do not mean the establishment of a narrow, prejudiced institution that does nothing but keep the two divisions and five sections of the sūtras. In the encompassing church I envision, there is no difference between laity and clergy or between those well-versed and ignorant in the teaching. It will serve to love and benefit the common people equally and without harm.

Let the city-god temples be turned into Buddhist temples and pagodas! Let the great ruler of the Zhou be the Tathāgata! Use the suburbs and towns as monks' living quarters, and harmonize the relations between husbands and wives to form the basis of the sage congregation. Let them toil in sericulture to fill the households with prosperity, and let them communally use this prosperity to recompense the government's grace.

The virtuous shall be officers of three ranks: the elders shall be abbots; the benevolent and wise shall be administrators; and the brave and courageous, preceptors. All shall practice the ten good deeds to subdue what is not yet at peace; they will be free from greed and thus end all robbery and theft. The cold and bare shall be clothed, and the lonely and helpless nurtured. The widowed shall be remarried, and the single be matched. The old and the sick shall be cared for, and the destitute be supported. All those loyal and filial will be amply rewarded, the bad and rebellious will be vigorously chastised. All pure and straightforward administrators will be promoted in rank, the flattering and cheating among ministers will be removed.

Then throughout the Six Harmonies, there will be no cry against the tyranny of Shang; all over the Eight Wilds there will be songs praising the just rule of Zhou. Even birds and fishes will rest peacefully in their nests and hollows, and all creatures of water and land will attain long life.

Xiaodao lun (**Laughing at the Tao**), by Zhen Luan (dat. 570), ed. *Guang hongming ji* 9 (T. 2103; 52.143c–152c).

This contains a polemical attack against the mythology and practices of Taoism, contending its suitability to serve as the encompassing orthodoxy of China. The thirty-six sections of the text imitate the division of the Taoist canon. The title is a pun on the *Daode jing:* "When an inferior person hears the Tao, he laughs out loud." For more, see the translation.

Erjiao lun (**On the Two Teachings**), by Shi Daoan (dat. 570), ed. *Guang hongming ji* 8 (T. 2103; 52.136b–143c). Hachiya 1982; Tsukamoto 1974, 2:566–69.

There are two kinds of religion: outer and inner. The outer cares for the body, serves the state, and harmonizes society. The inner delivers the spirit, goes beyond society, and transcends life and death. In the current situation, Confucianism is the outer, Buddhism the inner.

The Confucian tradition is clearly described in the bibliographic section of the *Hanshu*. It consists of nine distinct traditions: the Confucians, Taoists, Yin-Yang cosmologists, Legalists, Nominalists, Mohists, political theorists, miscellaneous thinkers, and agriculturists. Their documents are part of the order of the state; the emperor himself stands at the pinnacle of this teaching. Their various thinkers, with or without official position, serve as advisers to the ruler. Among them, Confucius was the greatest. He was a real sage, but even he did not have an official rank. Laozi, by comparison, was secondary, a mere worthy.

The outer teaching keeps the state together and the country at peace. Without it disorder and instability arise. Lack of veneration for the outer teaching caused the Han dynasty to end and China to be conquered by the western peoples.

Religious Taoism must not be mistaken for the Taoism that is part of the Confucian tradition because it is very different from the teachings of Laozi. In fact, it is only concerned with talismans, demonology, and ascent to the immortals. It has nothing to do with emptiness and nonbeing, with modesty, virtue, and seemly seclusion.

Religious Taoism is most clearly represented by the movement of the Three Zhangs. They cheat the people, steal their rice, lead them into delusion, and exploit them. Even their successor Kou Qianzhi, so highly thought of by the Northern Wei, is no better. Religious Taoists claim that their spells and exorcisms can prolong life and create political stability. Why then do not all Taoists live to a hundred? It really is beneath the emperor's dignity to even listen to their shamanistic and superstitious nonsense.

In addition, they rely on a large canon of Taoist texts to support their claims. But these texts are not at all like the *Daode jing* and the *Zhuangzi*. They are later forgeries—the Lingbao canon by Zhang Daoling, the Shangqing scriptures by Ge Xuan, and the Sanhuang texts by Bao Jing—or mere plagiarisms of Buddhist sūtras. Religious Taoism has, thus, nothing to do with the outer religion, the proper teaching for the state.

With Confucianism on the outside, Buddhism is the inner teaching, the spiritual dimension of life. Not for use within society, it is made for recluses and goes beyond life and death. It reaches depths entirely unknown to any thinker of the outer tradition, penetrating the source of all. It is higher and better and deeper than the six classics and nine traditions. Especially in conjunction with the latter, it has its proper place in civilized society.

In particular the inner and outer teachings can be evaluated under twelve headings:

1. Return to the origins, clarify the roots.
2. Confucianism and Taoism rise and fall.
3. The ruler is the head of all religion.
4. Examine body and mind.
5. Immortality is different from nirvāṇa.
6. Laozi's Tao is superior to immortality.
7. Neither Laozi nor Confucius are the Buddha.
8. Buddhism is not an offspring of Taoism.
9. Taoist garb and methods are not of Laozi.
10. Sacred texts can be genuine or fake.
11. Religious doctrines influence politics.
12. Rely on the Law and give up all doubts.

7. The Debate Surrounding Fu Yi (621–623)

Jiansheng sita sengni yikuo limin shi (**Memorial on Reducing Buddhist Institutions and Recluses to Enhance the State and Benefit the People**), by Fu Yi (555–639), ed. *Guang hongming ji* 7 (T. 2103; 52.134a–35b); *Jiu Tangshu* 79. Wright 1951; Wright 1990, 112–23; De Groot 1903, 39–41; Yoshikawa 1984, 535–39.

Fu Yi harshly criticizes Buddhism and its role in the Chinese state, taking up many arguments from earlier debates. Buddhists lack loyalty and filial piety as expressed in their refusal to bow to the emperor and kneel before their parents; they avoid taxation and military service; they scrounge on the productivity of the common people. Ever since Buddhism was introduced, the state has suffered from corruption, rebellions, and natural disasters. Buddhism is a barbarian teaching unfit for the Chinese.

To remedy this situation, all monks and nuns should be returned to the laity and work for production. That would stop their hypocrisy of being without desires yet eating and wearing clothes. They should also follow the natural interaction of yin and yang, marry and multiply as do the Taoists. That would keep them from committing the grave sin of being without descendants. Monks and nuns should further be forced to bow to the ruler because the great sages of old never hesitated to do so. If they refuse, they should be shipped off to the barbarians where their fanciful ideas came from in the first place.

Fu Yi specifies his argument in eleven points:

1. Two hundred thousand monks and nuns are too many. If they married, the state could have one hundred thousand new subjects every year. The women could weave; the men could plant and serve in the army. They would strengthen the state, not exploit it. Moreover, it would destroy the Buddhist church organization, which is a state within the state, refuses to accept secular authority, and even participates in rebellions.

2. Monasteries, temples, and stūpas are fancy buildings, eighty-four thousand of them are a great deal too many. In antiquity, rulers built simple structures of pounded earth with thatched roofs and no more than ten or so at a time, and even those were condemned by the historians as luxury and detrimental to virtue. All the people's labor that goes into these building projects could be directed more usefully elsewhere.

3. With Buddhist institutions and buildings destroyed, the country would be well ordered and the people at peace. This would mean real happiness and prosperity, not the artificial good fortune promised by the Buddhists. Temples and monasteries, for example, could be put to excellent use as garrisons for the army. Nor would there be an entire segment of the population beyond the arm of the law; nobody could get away with lax morals and corruption any longer.

4. Buddhists refuse to kill silkworms to make cloth, yet they wear silk. They sit in meditative solitude, doing nothing, yet let the country feed and clothe them. If everyone did that, where would our food and clothes come from?

5. Reintegrating the monks and nuns into the working populace would benefit the people in their labor and make the country more prosperous.

6. Governments without Buddhism provide perfect order and last a long time. Governments with Buddhism are tyrannical and short-lived.

7. One should return to the principles of Confucius and the Duke of Zhou and send the alien teachings back to the western regions. Barbarian practices should not be followed.

8. Buddhist ideas are hollow and fanciful. They have little substance.

9. When the population, the farmers and artisans, have a good life and decent income, the country is prosperous, and the people are happy.

10. When emperors and kings receive the mandate of Heaven, it is in all cases because they overcome the previous government.

11. Straight words and loyal remonstration have been uttered since antiquity and have often caused harm to their speakers.

Poxie lun (**To Destroy Heresy**) in two scrolls, by Shi Falin (572–640; biog. T. 2051), ed. T. 2109; 52.474c–89c.

This work summarizes many arguments of earlier debates. It often seems more a history of past debates than an argument against Fu Yi.

1. Buddhism goes beyond the world. As documented in the *Liezi*, Confucius himself denied the rulers of China's golden age sage status and accepted only "the sage in the west." Even Confucius recognized the superiority of Buddhism. Thus, its followers do not remain householders but live as recluses. Fu Yi in his blind fury goes even against the words of China's greatest master.

2. Taoism is merely a form of Buddhism. All Taoist revelations, even those followed by Zhang Daoling and his group, were ultimately inspired by Buddhism. Taoists believe in Buddhist heavens and follow the doctrine of karma and retribution. They have many rituals and prayers to ensure that their ancestors can ascend to the Buddhist heavens. Even Laozi himself was a disciple of the Buddha, sent to China to propagate the true teaching. Thus, all forms of Taoism, ancient and recent, go back to Buddhism.

3. The classics mention Buddhism. The *Zhoushu* and the *Liezi* contain various references to the Buddha as the great sage in the west.

4. The Buddha sent Laozi, Confucius, and Yan Hui to spread his teaching in China. All ancient Chinese philosophies are, therefore, inspired by Buddhism. The texts agree that the Buddha was Laozi's teacher.

5. Buddhism holds the true key to eternity. The spirit survives forever, while the body falls away and rots. Only through the purification of the spirit in nirvāṇa can true immortality be found.

6. Taoists plagiarize Buddhist sūtras for their own scriptures. Most texts listed in Taoist catalogs are stolen from Buddhist works. Buddhist doctrine is an essential part of Taoism.

7. Buddhism is senior. As proven conclusively in the debates of 520, the Buddha was born under the Shang and reached nirvāṇa even before Laozi ever appeared.

Falin then summarizes Fu Yi's arguments and refutes them. He emphasizes repeatedly that rebellions and cases of corruption have not increased significantly since the introduction of Buddhism. Monks and nuns serve to raise the spiritual merit and well-being of the country. Monasteries and temples are signs of prosperity and the spread of the teaching; they are good for the state.

Juedui Fu Yi feifo faseng shi (**Strong Rebuttal of Fu Yi's Proposal to Abolish Buddhist Teachings and Recluses**), by Shi Minggai, ed. *Guang hongming ji* 12 (T. 2103; 52.168b–75c).

Since Buddhism was introduced under the Han, the country has been flourishing as never before. More people have become enlightened, and the population as a whole has been happier. Fu Yi's most basic criticism is, therefore, not justified.

Divided then into eight sections, the text takes up the main arguments of Fu Yi's memorial:

1. Defrock monks to strengthen the army.
2. Build simple buildings instead of fancy monasteries to boost the country's virtue.
3. Destroy all temples or use them for better purposes.
4. Take away the monks' robes, which rob the country of silk.
5. Return the recluses to the productive population.
6. The country is better off without Buddhism.
7. Let the barbarians learn Confucianism and Taoism.
8. Buddhist doctrine is fanciful and not practical.

The argument repeats the standard defense of Buddhism. It is otherworldly and thus its practitioners stay free from society; nevertheless, the splendor of its institutions and representatives documents the prosperity of the state.

Neide lun (**On Inner Virtue**), by Li Shizheng, ed. *Guang hongming ji* 14 (T. 2103; 52.187b–95a).

This, too, contends Fu Yi's position with traditional arguments.

I. To correct the following errors:
1. The Buddha came from the western barbarians.
2. The Duke of Zhou and Confucius never spoke of him.
3. One can denigrate Buddhism in favor of Taoism.
4. One can relate Buddhism to sorcery and magic.
5. In antiquity there were rebellious monks.
6. Monks are like owls that discard their kin.
7. The monks' hair style is ridiculous.

8. People made from mud serve images made from mud.
9. Buddhism causes rebellion and destruction.
10. Without Buddhism the people have peace.

II. To clarify [the teaching of] life
III. [To understand] emptiness and existence

8. The Debate Surrounding Li Zhongqing (626)

Shiyi jiumi lun (**The Ten Differences and Nine Errors**), by Li Zhongqing
(Taoist of Qingxu guan, friend of Fu Yi, see T. 2104; 52.382b), lost, cited in
Bianzheng lun 6 (T. 2110; 52.526c–37a).

A shorter version is found in *Guang hongming ji* 13 (T. 2103; 52.175c–87b).

The ten differences between Buddhism and Taoism are

1. Their sages are born to the right and left.
2. They have different teachings about life and death.
3. Their positions are those of high and low, east and west.
4. The Chinese converted the barbarians.
5. Taoists favor long life, Buddhists prefer early death.
6. They are different according to first and second born.
7. Divine immortals return to the void.
8. Divine marks and signs indicate the true sages.
9. Chinese rank higher than barbarians.
10. Some obey, some violate the prohibitions.

Buddhist counterarguments are

1. The sage's birth can be high or low.
2. The teaching can be profound or shallow.
3. The position of virtue can be noble or humble.
4. Cultural improvements can be wide or narrow.
5. Life spans can be long or short.
6. Historical appearances can be early or late.
7. Ways to salvation can be bright or obscure.
8. Auspicious bodily marks can be few or many.
9. Ritual observances can be the same or different.
10. Gates to the Law can be sudden or gradual.

Replies to the nine supposed faults of Buddhists:

1. The Zhou knew nothing of the Buddha.
2. Buddhists erect statues and pagodas.
3. Buddhists have strange observances, garments, and implements.

4. They reject agriculture and military service.
5. They claim their teaching is the foundation of the state.
6. They do not care about loyalty and filial piety.
7. There is no real translation for the Three Jewels.
8. They apply the same system for different areas.
9. They deny that Laozi became the Buddha.

Bianzheng lun **(In Defense of What Is Right)**, by Shi Falin (572–640), ed. T. 2110; 52.489c–550c, in eight chapters and twelve sections.

This is the longest and most involved of all the texts of the debates. It contains the arguments of most earlier texts, including selections from the *Xiaodao lun*.

Chapter 1 (490b–97a)

Section 1: "The Three Teachings Represent the Tao" (pt. 1).

Chapter 2 (497a–502b)

Section 1: "The Three Teachings Represent the Tao" (pt. 2).
Overall philosophical exposition of the various aspects of the three teachings and their unity and diversity in relation to the unifying Tao of heaven, earth, and humanity.

Chapter 3 (502c–09c)

Section 2: "Ten Dynasties of Buddhist Worship" (pt. 1).

Chapter 4 (510a–20c)

Section 2: "Ten Dynasties of Buddhist Worship" (pt. 2).
Historical exposition of the imperial support of Buddhism since its introduction during the Han. The ten dynasties are the Eastern Jin, followed by the four southern (Liu-Song, Southern Qi, Liang, and Chen) and three northern dynasties (Wei, Zhou, and Qi), plus the Sui and Tang.

Chapter 5 (520c–24c)

Section 3: "Priorities of Buddhism versus Taoism."
Summary of the arguments on dating the lives of the Buddha versus Laozi, on the impact of Buddhism on ancient history, and on fictional reign titles.

Section 4: "Buddha or Laozi as the Teacher of Dynasties"
On the role of the two competing sages in ancient history, under the Three Sovereigns, the Five Emperors, and Three Kings.

Chapter 6 (524c–37a)

Section 5: "The Ten Differences between Buddhism and Taoism."

Section 6: "The Nine Faults of Buddhism."
Summary of the debate with Li Zhongqing.

Section 7: "Primordial Energy as the Foundation of the Tao."
Refutation of the claim to Taoist superiority based on the doctrine of primordial energy. It repeats the argument of the *Bianhuo lun*.

Chapter 7 (537b–42c)

Section 8: "Mutual Interaction between the Teachings."
Historical instances of victory and/or defeat of the various factions.

Section 9: "Scriptural Composition and the Number of Scriptures."
Repetition of the argument that Buddhist sūtras are more numerous, more original, and better written than Taoist scriptures.

Chapter 8 (542c–50c),

Section 10: "Calling out Taoist Lies."
Citation of various sections of the *Xiaodao lun*:

1. Numinous scriptures spontaneously distributing themselves
2. The Highest Lord of Numinous Treasure arising and dying with the kalpas (*XDL* 27)
3. Plagiarizing Buddhist sūtras for Taoist scriptures (*XDL* 29)
4. Imitating the Buddhist system of the four karmic fruits and ten bodhisattva stages (*XDL* 30)
5. Taoist Scriptures: revealed and as yet unrevealed (*XDL* 31)
6. The Taoist harmonizing of energies (*XDL* 35)
7. Establishing the Heavenly Venerable and falsifying his deeds
8. Philosophical writings as Taoist works (*XDL* 36)

Section 11: "The Heritage of History."
Discussion of the differences between the two teachings in various concrete areas: appearance and garb of their sages, festivals and fast days, implements and terminology, and so on.

Section 12: "Where the Heart Returns."
A concluding eulogy on Buddhism.

Taoist Texts Cited in the *Xiaodao lun*

In the following list, all texts cited in the *Xiaodao lun* (*XDL*), except historical materials such as the *Hanshu* or the *Chunqiu*, are discussed in terms of provenance, dates, editions, contents, and *XDL* citations.

A numbered overview of these texts precedes the actual list (table 4). Each text is referred to by the title most commonly used in the *XDL*. This is followed by the full title of the text as extant in the Taoist canon or among Dunhuang manuscripts, listed under "Full" and given with English translation. The location of the citation in the *XDL* appears under the abbreviation *XDL*, then approximate dates (Date), extant editions of the text (Eds.), and references in secondary literature (Refs.) are given.

In the discussion, I describe as much of the history and content of each text as is known from extant editions and discussions in scholarly analyses and summarize the content of the passages cited in the *XDL*.

The *XDL* is referred to by section numbers. "A" indicates the "Presumption," or first part of the section; "B" denotes its "Challenge," or second part, beginning with "I laugh at this and say."

For citations of the texts in other Taoist materials, see the reference work by Ōfuchi and Ishii (1988).

Table 4
Texts Cited in the *XDL*

1. *Chuji*	15. *Huangshu*	28. *Shenxian jinye jing*
2. *Dajie wen*	16. *Jiku jing*	29. *Shenxian zhuan*
3. *Daolü*	17. *Jiutian shengshen*	30. *Shijie jing*
4. *Daozhai jing*	*zhangjing*	31. *Wenshi zhuan*
5. *Dayou jing*	18. *Laozi baibashi jie*	32. *Wufu jing*
6. *Dongxuan dongfang*	19. *Laozi xiaobing jing*	33. *Wulian jing*
qingdi song	20. *Laozi xujue*	34. *Xuandu jingmu*
7. *Du guowang pin*	21. *Miaozhen jing*	35. *Xuanmiao neipian*
8. *Duming miaojing*	22. *Nanji zhenren wenshi*	36. *Xuanzhong jing*
9. *Duren benxing jing*	*pin*	37. *Xuanzi*
10. *Duren miaojing*	23. *Nüqing wen*	38. *Youwu shengcheng pin*
11. *Dushen pin*	24. *Sanhuang jing*	39. *Zhenren neichao lü*
12. *Fuzhai jing*	25. *Santian zhengfa jing*	40. *Zhutian neiyin*
13. *Guangshuo pin*	26. *Sanyuan pin*	41. *Ziran jing*
14. *Huahu jing*	27. *Shengxuan jing*	42. *Zuigen pin*

1. *Chuji* (Record of Beginnings)

Full   *Taishang laojun zaoli tiandi chuji* (Record of the Beginnings of
       Heaven and Earth as Created by the Highest Venerable Lord)
XDL 1A, 1B, 24A, 36B
Date   Sixth century
Eds.   Lost
Refs. Kusuyama 1979, 430–32

According to Kusuyama, this text was a fabrication of Zhen Luan based
on various other Taoist texts to show the absurdities of the Taoist teaching
(1979, 432).

If genuine, the *Chuji* might be related to the *Kaitian jing*, not extant,
which was used by Jiang Bin in the debate of 520. The latter presumably
contained an account of Laozi creating the world (like today's *Kaitian jing*
in *DZ* 1437, fasc. 1059; *YJQQ* 2; trans. in Kohn 1993a, 35–43), followed by
his transformations and his exploits in the west. Jiang Bin used it to argue
that Laozi went west to convert the barbarians before the birth of the
Buddha in 1029 B.C.E. and then became the Buddha (see Kusuyama 1976;
Kusuyama 1979, 373). During the debate, the text was found a forgery and
banned. Later, the *Wenshi zhuan* was compiled to take its place (see app. 1;
Fukui 1962, 282). Like the *Kaitian jing*, the *Chuji* might have been an
account of Laozi's activities and his role in the creation and development of
the world.

Most *XDL* citations of the *Chuji* refer to Laozi's conversion of the barbarians. The largest reference occurs in section 1, with later sections repeat-
ing the same information. Two cosmological parts are found: Laozi's creation of the cosmos (1A) and the height and structure of Mount Kunlun
(1B).

2. *Dajie wen* (The Great Precepts)

Full   *Shangqing dongzhen zhihui guanshen dajie wen* (The Great Precepts of
       Wisdom and Self-observation from the Truth Cavern of Highest
       Clarity)

XDL 8B, 20B, 22B, 24B, 34A
Date   Sixth century
Eds.   *DZ* 1364, fasc. 1039; *WSBY* 54
Refs. Schmidt 1985; Ren and Zhong 1991, 1078–79

The great precepts originally were floating rays of light, diffused and overflowing, radiating through the great void. After three thousand kalpas, they assembled into this text. The Heavenly King of Primordial Beginning transmitted it to the Lord of the Tao, highest of the great sages. Together they ascended to the Hall of Pervasive Perfection to recite and chant the precepts. Later, they passed them on to the Heavenly Emperor of Great Tenuity and to the Heavenly King, the Elevated Immortal of Great Ultimate. All this was done only by word of mouth; never had the text been written down. (1ab)

The *Dajie wen* contains the Shangqing version of the formal Taoist precepts. The Lingbao version is the *Sanyuan pin,* that of the Celestial Masters, the *Laozi baibashi jie,* both cited in the *XDL* and discussed in this appendix.

The text as we have it today consists of twenty-four pages, and divides the precepts according to the Three Primes. It begins with 180 elementary and strictly prohibitive precepts ("Students of the Tao! Do not——") for those ranking in the Lower Prime (1a–10b). Next, it lists thirty-six partly prohibitive, partly prescriptive precepts for followers ranking in Middle Prime (10b–12b). They include rules of social politeness and tranquility of mind. The last division contains eighty-four precepts for advanced disciples of Higher Prime (12b–17b). They are prescriptions of certain thoughts to keep in mind, for example, "May I be at peace in poverty and recite the scriptures of the Tao without slackening." They also include reminders about ecstatic excursions and the various celestial regions to be visited, for example, "May I wander to the palaces and residences in the various heavens to ask about the Tao and discuss the scriptures with the perfected." Altogether, the *Dajie wen* contains three hundred precepts.

The last pages of the text contain comments and admonitions on the precepts by their three divine recipients, the Heavenly King of Primordial Beginning (17b–19b), the Heavenly Emperor of Great Tenuity (19b–22a) and the Elevated Immortal of Great Ultimate (22a–24b). They each recount their experiences in receiving and following the precepts, show in glowing vivacity the delights that come from obeying them scrupulously, and picture the gory details of the failure to do so. Powers and ranks transferred with each level are detailed.

The text has a Lingbao format yet presents a definite predilection for Shangqing. It says, in the words of the Heavenly King of Primordial Beginning:

All those who recite the [Shangqing scripture] *Dadong zhenjing* (Perfect Scripture of Great Pervasion) ten thousand times will be received into heaven by a cloud chariot. Those who practice according to the scriptures of the Mystery Cavern of Numinous Treasure, the writings that have persisted for many kalpas, will not all become immortal. Worse, those who take elixirs of gold and potent fluids will never reach the goal. Why is this? It is because they do not properly practice and venerate these precepts of wisdom and self-observation. (18a)

The effort to combine the various strands of Taoist teachings while putting Shangqing first places the text in the context of the integration of Taoist teachings that began with Lu Xiujing in the late fifth century. Nevertheless, with the exception of the *XDL* and the *WSBY* (chap. 45), the *Dajie wen* is not cited before the seventh century when it appears in the *SDZN, Yaoxiu keyi, Xuanmen dayi,* and the works of Zhang Wanfu. It can be dated to the sixth century.

The *XDL* refers to various precepts from this text: Taoists should not consume wine or meat (8A); they must not worship ghosts and popular deities (20B); they should not harbor an evil heart (22B, 24B); they should visualize themselves wandering up to heaven to pay obeisance to the Buddha (34A).

3. *Daolü* (Tao Rules)

Full   *Zhenren neili yishi jiaxing daolü* (Tao Rules of the Perfected for the Practice of Esoteric Rites While Attending on the Teacher and at Home)

In both the *XDL* (35A) and the *BZL* (T. 2110; 52.545), the *Daolü* is cited in the context of sexual rituals. Such practices, the text states, must be undertaken only in the proper environment and by following the proper rules. The text does not survive elsewhere. Nothing else is known about this scripture.

4. *Daozhai jing* (Scripture on Rites for the Tao)

The *XDL* cites this text once (34B): "One speaks of the immortals in the Brahma heavens and of the Buddha as not yet revealed." It is otherwise unknown.

5. *Dayou jing* (Scripture of Great Existence)

Full   *Dongzhen taishang suling dongyuan dayou miaojing* (Wondrous scrip-
        ture of Great Existence of Simple Numen and Pervading Prime, Con-
        tained in Highest Perfection Cavern)
XDL   17B
Date   Fifth century
Eds.   *DZ* 1314, fasc. 1026
Refs.   Robinet 1984, 2:285–302; Ren and Zhong 1991, 1035–17

The text contained in the Taoist canon and analyzed by Robinet is not the
text cited in the *XDL* but the *Suling jing* (Scripture of Immaculate Numen;
DZ 1314, fasc. 1026), an important scripture of Shangqing Taoism. Attached
to the name of Su Lin and his master Yuanzi, the scripture contains a
mixture of texts of different origins. It is arranged in nine divisions but
might be better divided into five sections: the Three Caverns (1a–12b); the
Nine Palaces (12b–24b); the Three Ones (24b–41a); the words of the Three
and Nine Simplicities (41a–43b); and the clear ordinances of the Nine
Perfected (43b–68b).

The text used in the *XDL,* however, also found in *SDZN* 3.1b and in
Wufu xu 3.22a, is a "Verse on Great Existence" that goes back to the fourth
century. The *XDL* cites it once in connection with the *Wufuxu* (17B). The
passage describes the destruction of life through the five grains and ad-
monishes practitioners to keep their bowels free from excrement.

6. *Dongxuan dongfang qingdi song* (Eulogy for the Green Emperor of the East, Contained in Mystery Cavern)

Full   In *Shangqing zhuzhen zhangsong* (Eulogy Verses for the Assembled
        Perfected of Highest Clarity)
XDL   26A
Date   Fifth century
Eds.   *DZ* 608, fasc. 334
Refs.   Ren and Zhong 1991, 438

The *XDL* uses this text in its Dongxuan (Lingbao) version. This has not
survived, but the same verses are found in a collection of Shangqing chants
of praise and protection, which were sung during religious services and
ordination ceremonies. The collection divides into five kinds according to
different melodies used.

The passage on the Green Emperor of the East focuses on the kalpa cycles (26A). It claims that a kalpa lasts as long as a chun tree before it gives way to a new cycle.

7. *Du guowang pin* (Chapter on Saving the Kings)

The first citation of this text (22A) deals with the Eastern Lord of Opening Light, a celestial who summons the perfected and gods. He is clad in black and devours countless demons. The second reference (30A) discusses the different ways in which people attain the Tao. Some move along fast and go right to the top; others have to make their way through the ten stages. The material is not known independently.

8. *Duming miaojing* (Wondrous Scripture on the Salvation of Life)

Full   *Taishang zhutian lingshu duming miaojing* (Wondrous Scripture on the Salvation of Life in the Numinous Writing of the Various Heavens)
XDL   27A
Date   Fifth century
Eds.   *DZ* 23, fasc. 26; *WSBY* 4; *SDZN* 8
Refs.   Ōfuchi 1974, 51; Bokenkamp 1983, 483; Ren and Zhong 1991, 23

The *Duming miaojing* of nineteen pages is part of the ancient Lingbao corpus (no. 16). The Heavenly Venerable of Primordial Beginning addresses the Lord of the Tao and other high Taoist deities in a celestial hall. Explaining the nature of the paradises in the five directions, he emphasizes that "there is no sound of crying or lament but only the expression of happiness and joy" (1b). All paradise residents have attained their blissful state because they possess the perfected writings of Numinous Treasure.

Next follow verses on the salvation of life in five sections, arranged again after the five directions (1b–19b). These were chanted by successful practitioners now in the paradises. Believers will benefit from them even on earth: "They uphold the spirit, calm the energy, and harmonize body and soul" (18a).

In addition, the Heavenly Venerable relates the genesis of Numinous Treasure in the beginning of the world and its subsequent end in a variety of kalpic disasters.

The *XDL* cites the *Duming miaojing* once in reference to the end of a kalpa cycle (27A). The passage classifies the scriptures: handbooks on techniques and methods will be destroyed even in a minor kalpa cycle; lesser scriptures, such as the *Taiping jing*, will survive that but end with a big kalpa; only the perfected writings of Numinous Treasure will survive forever on the Mountain of Jade Capital.

9. *Duren benxing jing* (Scripture of the Original Endeavor of Universal Salvation)

Full   *Taishang dongxuan lingbao zhenwen duren benxing miaojing* (Scripture of the Original Endeavor of Universal Salvation, Perfected Writing of Highest Numinous Treasure Contained in Mystery Cavern)

XDL   3B, 10B, 27B

Date   Fifth century

Eds.   P. 3022, repr. Ōfuchi 1979, 54–55; see also *WSBY* 47.41–5b; *YJQQ* 101.2a–3a

Refs.   Fukui 1952, 54; Ōfuchi 1974, 50; Bokenkamp 1983, 482

The *Duren benxing jing*, part of the Lingbao corpus (no. 13), has only survived in fragments. It deals with the appearances of the Lord of the Tao during the various ages of the world and his continued effort to save humanity.

The *XDL* contains the same citation three times (3B, 10B, 27B), once slightly more extensive (27B). In the passage, the Lord of the Tao recounts his adventures, emphasizing that he continues to "go along with the kalpas, saving innumerable people."

10. *Duren miaojing* (Wondrous Scripture of Universal Salvation)

Full   *Lingbao wuliang duren shangpin maiojing* (Superb and Wondrous Scripture of Universal Salvation of Numinous Treasure)

XDL   10B, 20A

Date   Fifth century

Eds.   *DZ* 1, fasc. 1–13; P. 2606, repr. Ōfuchi 1979, 64–69; with commentaries, *DZ* 87–95, fasc. 38–48

Refs.   Ōfuchi 1974, 50–51; Chen 1975, 70–71; Strickmann 1978a; Fujiwara 1980b; Bokenkamp 1983, 482; Sunayama 1984; Sunayama 1990, 272–304; Kobayashi 1990, 473–74; Robinet 1991, 163; Ren and Zhong 1991, 3–4

The *Duren jing* as we have it today consists of two parts. The first scroll of the *DZ* edition belongs to the ancient Lingbao corpus (no. 15). It survives in Dunhuang and has been commented on variously. The remaining sixty scrolls were compiled under the auspices of Divine Empyrean (Shenxiao) Taoism in the early twelfth century (see Strickmann 1978a).

The old *Duren jing* was revealed by the Heavenly Venerable of Primordial Beginning for the sake of humankind. It contains the inner names of the lords of the heavens, the esoteric names of the demon kings, and the hidden appellations of the host of spirits. By reciting this text, one can join the celestial crowd. In fact, the Heavenly Venerable himself recited the scripture and thereby summoned the gods to do his bidding. The sacred utterances are in the original language of the heavens, written in Brahma script, and concealed in a heavenly palace in Mystery Metropolis. The text gives these "inner sounds" and furnishes an explanation, not unlike the *Zhutian neiyin*.

Recognized as a powerful means toward salvation, the *Duren jing* was honored from early on. The first commentaries, contained in *DZ* 87, were written already in the Six Dynasties by Yan Dong of the Southern Qi (ca. 479–93) and by Li Shaowei of the sixth century (see Sunayama 1984). During the Tang, the text was used in the imperial examination for Taoist priests. Further commentaries were written of a more philosophical nature: one by Cheng Xuanying of the midseventh century, another by Xue Youlou of the year 754.

Cheng Xuanying in particular is a senior thinker of the Chongxuan (Twofold Mystery) school of Taoist thought. He uses Li Shaowei's work, allowing the conclusion that Li also belonged to this school. On this commentary, see especially Fujiwara 1980b. For a general discussion of Chongxuan thought, see Robinet 1977; Fujiwara 1980a, 1980c; Zhao 1982; Sunayama 1980, 1980a, 1990; Kohn 1991a, 189–200; Kohn 1991b, 139–46.

The *XDL* cites the *Duren jing* twice: once about the Heaven of Grand Network where no disaster ever reaches (10B), then again with an incantation of the demon kings of the Three Worlds (20A).

11. *Dushen pin* (Chapter on Saving Oneself)

XDL   30A

According to the single *XDL* citation (30A), this is the Taoist adaptation of a Buddhist text: "When the mendicant heard the Heavenly Venerable preach the teaching, he immediately attained the stage of stream enterer." The text is not known separately.

12. *Fuzhai jing* (On the Performance of Rites)

Full   *Taiji zhenren fu lingbao zhaijie weiyi zhujing yaojue* (Essential Formulas of the Various Numinous Treasure Scriptures on the Majestic Observances of Rites and Precepts, Distributed by the Perfected of Great Ultimate)

XDL   34B

Date   Fifth century
Eds.   *DZ* 532, fasc. 295; *SDZN* 7
Refs.   Ōfuchi 1974, 54; Lagerwey 1981, 123, 127; Bokenkamp 1983, 484;
        Kobayashi 1990, 344; Sunayama 1990, 55–66; Ren and Zhong 1991,
        386–87

The *Fuzhai jing* is twenty-four pages long and belongs to the ancient Lingbao corpus (no. 24). It was transmitted by the Perfected of Great Ultimate, Xu Laile, and written by the Master of the Southern Peak, Zheng Yin, upon inspiration from Immortal Duke Ge.

It is a ritual text that specifies the exact times and procedures of Lingbao rites. How to burn incense and what prayers to chant; how to pay homage to the gods of the ten directions and when to light the lamps; how to call on the preceptors and which titles to use; what food to eat and where to live. It also details rituals for textual transmission and ordination, instructions pertaining to the meditation chamber, and the roles and tasks of various Taoist masters.

The text emphasizes the centrality of three texts: the *Daode jing*, the *Dadong zhenjing*, and the *Lingbao jing*. The latter indicates the *Wupian zhenwen chishu* (Five Sections of Perfect Texts in Red Characters), first text of the Lingbao canon, today contained in *DZ* 22, fasc. 26. The second is the highest text of Shangqing Taoism. The *Daode jing* is ranked highest: by reciting it faithfully one can live a long life, ascend to heaven as an immortal, and have one's ancestors up to seven generations transferred to the heavens.

The *XDL* cites the *Fuzhai jing* once (34B). According to this passage, not contained in the *DZ* today, the Heavenly Venerable ordered the Mysterious Perfected of the Right to go down and transform the world with the Tao of immortality.

13. *Guangshuo pin* (Chapter of Broad Explanations)

The *XDL* cites this text twice, once (1B) on the distance between heaven and earth, and again (5B) on the King of Original Longevity who ascended to the Brahma Heaven and whose wife went to the Miaofan Heaven and later became Buddha. The work is otherwise unknown.

14. *Huahu jing* (Scripture of the Conversion of the Barbarians)

Full   *Laozi xisheng huahu jing* (Scripture of Laozi's Western Ascension and
        Conversion of the Barbarians)

XDL   2B, 9B, 12A, 14A, 17A, 18B, 19A, 19B, 21A, 34A, 34B
Date   Fourth century, sixth century, eighth century
Eds.   Preface = P. 4502; repr. Fukui 1952, 279; Yoshioka 1959, 73–74;
    chap. 1 = S. 1857; repr. T. 54.1266a–67b; Ōfuchi 1979b, 656–59; trans.
    in Kohn 1993a, 71–80
    chap. 2 = S. 6963; repr. Yoshioka 1959, 473–81; Ōfuchi 1979b, 659–67;
    chap. 8 = P. 3404; repr. Yoshioka 1959, 484–90; Ōfuchi 1979b, 668–74;
    chap. 10 = P. 2004; repr. T. 54.1267c–70b; Ōfuchi 1979b, 674–80;
    chap. 10 = P. 2360, excerpt; Ōfuchi 1979b, 680–81;
    chap. 10 = S. 2081; repr. Yoshioka 1959, 493–96; Ōfuchi 1979b, 681–
    85, also known as *Taishang lingbao laozi huahu miaojing*, trans. in
    Seidel 1984a.
    For long citations, see also *SDZN* 9.14b–20b; *Youlong zhuan* 4 (*DZ*
    774, fasc. 555); *Hunyuan shengji* 4–5 (*DZ* 770, fasc. 551–53)
Refs.   Pelliot 1903, 325–27; Wang 1934; Ch'en 1945; Fukui 1952; Zürcher 1959,
    288–320; Yoshioka 1959; Ōzaki 1976; Kusuyama 1979, 437–73; Stein
    1979, 547; Seidel 1984a; Qing 1988, 439; Kohn 1989a; Kohn 1991a, 60–
    70; Reiter 1990b

The earliest traces of the "conversion of the barbarians" can be found in
Xiang Kai's memorial of the year 166 C.E. Here, he mentions that "some
people say that Laozi has gone into [the region of] the barbarians and has
become the Buddha" (Zürcher 1959, 291). Next, there are several passages
of the *Xirong zhuan* of the *Weilue* cited by Pei Songzhi in his commentary
to the *Sanguo zhi* and by Falin in the *BZL*.

A full-length scripture entitled *Huahu jing* is reported to have been first
compiled by Wang Fou around the year 300. As Zürcher has shown, this
Huahu jing was "well-known and exerted some influence . . . among the
numbers of the highest classes in Chang'an" around the year 385 (1959,
297). Gradually, the text grew, especially within Louguan Taoism in the
north, until by the middle of the Tang dynasty—despite proscriptions in
668 and 705—it had grown to ten chapters.

There are three main versions of the text recognized today: the earliest
of the fourth century, now lost; the second of the sixth century, cited in the
XDL and the *SDZN;* and the third of the eighth century, surviving partly
in Dunhuang.

Among the remaining fragments, the *SDZN* version and chapter 1 contain the classical Laozi hagiography; chapter 2 deals with demonological
and theoretical problems of the religion. In chapter 8, Laozi meets an interested but somewhat unwilling barbarian king with whom he has a long
scholastic discussion on the question of good government in harmony
with the Tao.

Chapter 10 describes Laozi's exploits, including his appearances, wanderings, and the conversion. The Dunhuang fragment of the text (P. 2360)

is largely cosmological and concentrates on transformations of Laozi. The Lingbao version (trans. in Seidel 1984a) connects cosmology with the conversion in the style of a Buddhist sūtra, introducing passages with "the Heavenly Venerable said."

The *Huahu jing* came to the fore again during the debates among Buddhists and Taoists under the Yuan (see Ch'en 1945; Thiel 1961). It disappeared from circulation after Emperor Shizu ordered all copies burned in 1281, but a version of the scripture from that time, published in the Ming, still survives and has been reedited and translated (Reiter 1990b). It consists of eighty-one illustrations that are accompanied by short textual explanations.

The *XDL* cites the *Huahu jing* with eleven passages. Two are identified in extant versions: the list of Laozi's transformations (2B), which also appears in the *SDZN;* Laozi's report on his activities in Kapilavastu (19A), which is found in chapter 10 of the Dunhuang manuscripts.

Four further passages fit in with the *Huahu jing* as now known: the cosmological comparison of Buddhist heavens with the layers of Mount Kunlun (9B); the interpretation of *nanwu fo* as "No higher Buddha south" (12A); the development of culture under the guidance of Laozi (17A); and a comparison of Taoism and Buddhism in terms of east and west (21A), which possibly formed part of the earliest conversion polemics (Zürcher 1959, 305).

The remainder seem to belong to the Buddhist counter*huahu* scripture. Passages of this kind extol the activities of Kāśyapa in his role as Laozi (14A) and as a preserver of the Buddha's bones (18B, 19B); they also contain explicit praise of the Buddhist teaching (34A, 34B).

15. *Huangshu* (Yellow Book)

Full   *Dongzhen huangshu* (Yellow Book of Perfection Cavern)
XDL   8B, 35B
Date   Third century, sixth century
Eds.   *DZ* 1343, fasc. 1031
Refs.   Rao 1956, 104; Maspero 1981, 536; Kobayashi 1990, 203–4; Ren and Zhong 1991, 1061–62

The *Huangshu* is an ancient sexual manual that was revealed to the first Celestial Master Zhang Daoling in 142 C.E. The old text, eight scrolls in all, survives only in citations, especially in Buddhist polemics. Besides the *XDL,* it is cited in *Hongming ji* 7 (T. 2102; 52.46c, 47c) and 8 (48b, 53c); *Guang hongming ji* 5 (T. 2103; 52.117c), 6 (126b), 8 (140c), and 13 (184b); and in *BZL* 6 (T. 2110; 531c–532a). The text seems to have been a manual of sexual practices with detailed instructions and cosmological explanations.

A later version of the text was adapted by Shangqing Taoism. Known as *Dongzhen huangshu*, this is still extant. It claims to go back to Zhang Daoling (1b–2a; 12b) yet expunges the more open sexual descriptions of the earlier text, revealing a pervasive ambivalence of Shangqing Taoists toward the sexual practices of the Celestial Masters (see Kobayashi 1992).

The *Dongzhen huangshu* in fifteen pages consists for the most part of charts and lists of auspicious dates for the consummation of sexual intercourse. It explains the relationship of yin and yang in terms of the stems and branches of the traditional Chinese calendar (especially the six *jia*); the five phases and twenty-four energies of the year; the nine palaces in the sky and the eight trigrams of the *Yijing*; and the various gods residing in the human body. In addition, the text specifies gymnastics, massages, concentration exercises, and visualizations to be undertaken before sexual practice and emphasizes the efficacy of the techniques to dissolve bad fortune and extend life. Another Shangqing manual of the same type is the *Shangqing huangshu guodu yi* (Highest Clarity Observances for Salvation through the Yellow Book; *DZ* 1294, fasc. 1009).

The *XDL* does not cite the *Huangshu* as such but only refers to it as the sexual manual revealed to the first Celestial Master.

16. *Jiku jing* (Scripture of Rescue from Suffering)

Full   *Taishang dongxuan lingbao tianzun shuo jiku jing* (Scripture of Rescue from Suffering Revealed by the Heavenly Venerable and Contained in the Mystery Cavern of Highest Numinous Treasure)

XDL   9A, 10B, 15B, 25B
Date   Sixth century (?)
Eds.   *DZ* 375, fasc. 181; S. 793, repr. Ōfuchi 1979, 217–18
Refs.   Ren and Zhong 1991, 281

All *XDL* citations of the *Jiku jing* are in fact found in the *Yundu jieqi jing* (Scripture on Kalpa Revolutions):

Full   *Dongxuan lingbao benxiang yundu jieqi jing* (Scripture on Kalpa Revolutions in their Original Appearance, Contained in the Mystery Cavern of Numinous Treasure)

Date   Sixth century
Eds.   *DZ* 319, fasc. 165
Refs.   Yoshioka 1955, 192; Ren and Zhong 1991, 239

The *Jiku jing* as it has survived in the Taoist canon is a short text of only three pages. Placed in the mouth of the Heavenly Venerable, it discusses ways of attaining the Tao, salvational activities of the deity, and the importance of precepts and formal rites. It also speaks of various methods to worship the Tao, including sacrifices for the ten directions, the recollection of sins, recitation and copying of the scriptures, the creation of images, and the offering of flowers.

Proper practice helps in sickness and drives out demons, protects women in childbirth, and guards homes against evil. By reciting this scripture three times a day after proper purification, all sins and suffering are driven out.

All *XDL* citations under the title *Jiku jing* are, in fact, found in a text today transmitted as *Yundu jieqi jing*. This work has fifteen pages and consists of a dialogue between the Heavenly Venerable of Numinous Treasure and the Taoist Yanming on Mount Dongfou. It focuses on the events during a major kalpa revolution, detailing the cosmology and sacred geography of the world and calculating the kalpa cycles. It also deals with various ways to avoid the ill effects of cosmic disasters, using the words "rescue from suffering" that make up the title used in the *XDL*.

On pages 4b–5a, the text specifies the *Shenzhou jing* (Scripture of Divine Incantations; *DZ* 335, fasc. 170–73) as the most powerful means to hold kalpic demons and illnesses at bay. It summarizes especially the second scroll of this text, which goes back to a separate group within the organization of the Celestial Masters (see Mollier 1990). The combination of the *Shenzhou jing* tradition with Lingbao cosmology dates the text to the sixth century. Although used in the *XDL,* the work is not cited in other Taoist sources of the time and only listed in Du Guangting's *Huanglu dazhai yi* (Observances of the Great Yellow Register Rite; *DZ* 508, fasc. 278–90).

The *XDL* cites this text four times. Its first citation refers to the height of Mount Kunlun (9A). In the other three instances, the same passage on the events at the end of a kalpa is cited, sometimes longer (10B), sometimes shorter (15B, 25B).

17. *Jiutian shengshen zhangjing* (Stanzas of the Vital Spirit of the Nine Heavens)

Full   *Dongxuan lingbao ziran jiutian shengshen zhangjing* (Scripture of Stanzas of the Vital Spirit of the Nine Heavens of Spontaneity, Contained in the Mystery Cavern of Numinous Treasure)

XDL   16B

Date   Fifth century

Eds.   *DZ* 318, fasc. 165; *DZ* 396, fasc. 186; *DZ* 197, fasc. 187; *DZ* 398, fasc. 188; P. 4659, repr. Ōfuchi 1979b, 8–9; *YJQQ* 16

Refs.   Fukui 1952, 193; Ōfuchi 1974, 47; Bokenkamp 1983, 480; Mollier 1990, 24; Kobayashi 1990, 217–40; Ren and Zhong 1991, 237–38

The Lord of Heavenly Treasure is the venerable god of Great Cavern. The Elder of Heavenly Treasure is the ancestral energy of this lord, the energy of Jade Emptiness. Originally, he resided in chaos and great non-being and rested in primordial loftiness. After 99,990 billion transformations of energy, in the first year of Dragon Country, he brought forth the Lord of Heavenly Treasure and revealed his sacred scriptures. Since then, he has been called the Highest Palace of Great Existence in Jade Clarity. (1a)

The *Jiutian shengshen zhangjing,* also known as *Sanbao dayou jinshu* (Book on the Three Treasures in Golden [Characters] Stored in [the Palace of] Great Existence), goes back to the early fifth century. It outlines the classical Taoist myth on the creation of the world. The three energies—mysterious, beginning, and primordial—combined to form a heavenly sound. This sound coagulated into the numinous writings of the heavens, which, in turn, took shape as the Three Elders. They brought forth the Three Treasures, lords of the world who were at the same time heavenly palaces.

The text presents the numinous stanzas of the Lords of the Three Treasures and their Nine Heavens. Pure powers of creation, these stanzas incorporate the "vital spirit" of the universe. Demons or numinous forces by reciting them can ascend to heaven; ordinary people attain great longevity.

The world was created with the help of the Nine Heavens and their esoteric verses, yet it will be destroyed. The *Jiutian shengshen zhangjing* predicts the imminence of a great kalpic transformation during which a deluge will sweep away all sinners. Only the initiates of the Celestial Masters will be saved and, with the help of the stanzas contained here, recreate the world.

The text as known today was put together from two parts. The first consists of the original stanzas to the gods of the Nine Heavens (9b–14a) and their introduction (5a–8a). This was compiled around 420 C.E. by a member of the Ge-family tradition and formed part of the original Lingbao canon (no. 5).

The second part, the stanzas to the Lords of the Three Treasures (8a–9b), the first part of the introduction (1a–4b), and the two poems in praise of the Perfected of Great Ultimate (14ab), were added around 430 by a member of the Celestial Masters. The text was thereby transformed from a Lingbao scripture into a document accessible not only to the Celestial Masters but—because of the theory of the Three Caverns prominent in the text—to all Taoist schools of the time (Kobayashi 1990, 236).

The *XDL* cites the text once (16B) in reference to the ranking of the gods, giving a short summary of what today appears in the first few paragraphs.

18. *Laozi baibashi jie* (The Hundred and Eighty Precepts of Laozi)

Full   *Laojun shuo yibai bashi jie* (The One Hundred and Eighty Precepts Revealed by the Venerable Lord)

XDL   22A

Date   Fifth century

Eds.   P. 4731, P. 4562, repr. Ōfuchi 1979b, 685; *YJQQ* 39.1a–14b; see also *DZ* 786, fasc. 562; *DZ* 463, fasc. 204–7, 5.14a–19a

Refs.   Yoshioka 1970, 70; Schmidt 1985; Maeda 1985a; Kobayashi 1990, 341–46

This is the Celestial Masters version of the formal Taoist precepts. Hagiographically traced back to Zhang Daoling, the text was compiled in the early fifth century to reorganize the Taoist church and improve the morals of its representatives.

The preface, fully reconstituted from the various editions, can be divided into three parts. The first recounts the early appearances of the Tao of Great Peace and Laozi's exploits during his western journeys. The second consists of a dialogue between Laozi and Gan Ji, the alleged recipient of the *Taiping jing*. The third, the preface proper, introduces the value of the precepts in the words of the Venerable Lord. Whereas the third part belonged to the text from its very beginning, the first and second were added in the sixth century to establish a link of the text with the then newly reedited *Taiping jing* (see Maeda 1985a).

The bulk of the text consists of the 180 precepts. They regulate Taoist life, placing a high emphasis on the honesty and propriety of community life, forbidding theft, adultery, killing, and the like. Many rules also concern the waste of food and the proper behavior toward community members, outsiders, slaves, and animals. To gang up with brigands and soldiers is formally forbidden—a reminder of the unfortunate rebellion of Sun En (see Kobayashi 1990).

The *XDL* cites the text only once (22A) with a claim that Laozi's precepts will cause trees to wither when they are pronounced over them. Such a passage is not found in the text as transmitted separately.

19. *Laozi xiaobing jing* (Laozi's Scripture of Melting Ice)

Full   same

XDL   5B, 24A

Date   Fourth century

Eds.   Lost

Refs.   Fukui 1952, 290; Zürcher 1959, 302

This scripture is only known from its two *XDL* citations. In the first case (5B), it is cited in conjunction with the *Huahu jing,* of which it may have been a variant. In the second case (24A), a longer passage deals with the severing of family attachments. The *BZL* contains a similar citation as from the *Huahu jing,* again indicating the close relation between the two texts.

20. *Laozi xu* (Introduction to the *Laozi*)

Full   *Daode zhenjing xujue* (Introductory Explanation to the Perfect Scrip-
        ture of the Dao and the Virtue)
XDL   2A, 8A, 34B
Date   Six Dynasties
Eds.   S. 75, P. 2370; repr. Yoshioka 1959, 40–45; Ōfuchi 1964, 344–51;
        Ōfuchi 1979, 509–11; Takeuchi 1978, 6:220–23; Yan 1983, 265, 273
Refs.   Yoshioka 1959, 40; Ōfuchi 1964, 344–434, Takeuchi 1978, 6:220;
        Kusuyama 1979, 134–37; Kobayashi 1990, 269–95

This text consists of five sections, dated differently.

Section 1 is a eulogy on the cosmic Laozi. It claims to go back to the third century and, in the view of most scholars, might indeed come from the environment of Ge Xuan.

Kobayashi, however, believes that sections 1, 3, 4, and 5 all go back to the Celestial Masters of the fifth century. In particular, he notes the use of Buddhist terms, such as "ten directions," "various heavens," "ninefold darkness," and so on, which did not appear in Taoist materials before the late Eastern Jin. Moreover, Laozi is said to have originated "without cause," a definitely Buddhist notion. To him, the text is close to the *Santian neijie jing* of the year 420. The latter documents the newly defined orthodoxy of the Celestial Masters, legitimizing their organization under the newly founded Liu-Song dynasty and in the face of the recent Taoist rebellion of Sun En.

Section 2 tells the legend of Heshang gong, the Master on the River (for more details on this, see Kusuyama 1979; Chan 1991). The text here is closely related to Ge Hong's *Shenxian zhuan,* which has led Ōfuchi to date it to the fourth century. Fukui and Kusuyama, on the other hand, have connected it with the emerging link between the Heshang gong commentary to the *Daode jing* and the Heshang gong legend in the mid- to late Six Dynasties and thus dated it later. Kobayashi compares it carefully with the *Shenxian zhuan* and finds it much later. He dates it to the midsixth century, also in connection with the emerging Heshang gong legend.

Section 3 is a summary of Laozi's conversion of the barbarians, placed in the mouth of Ge Xuan, the legendary transmitter of the Lingbao scriptures. Ōfuchi sees it in connection with the *Huahu jing* and dates it to the late fourth or early fifth century. Fukui recognizes certain correspondences of the text to the conversion story as told in the *Wenshi zhuan* and dates it to the midsixth century.

Kobayashi disagrees with both. Emphasizing that the text establishes a link between the *Daode jing* and Ge Xuan and shows distinct signs of Celestial Masters cosmology, he places it around the year 420. The *Wenshi zhuan*, in his view, is an expansion of the *Laozi xu*.

Section 4 praises the *Daode jing* in the words of Zheng Siyuan, a student of Ge Xuan. Such encomia were added to Taoist texts first in the Lingbao scriptures. This, according to Ōfuchi, shows the affiliation of the text with this movement and allows a dating to the early fifth century. Kobayashi again places the text in a Celestial Masters environment. He emphasizes the ritual nature of the text, which consists of an incantation of praise chanted after the recitation of the text. The recitation of the *Daode jing* is particularly known among the Celestial Masters. Furthermore, the text also shows signs of Celestial Masters thinking.

Section 5 contains instructions for visualization and meditation practice to be undertaken in conjunction with the recitation of the *Daode jing*. The practice looks Lingbao to Ōfuchi and Celestial Masters to Kobayashi. In either case, it dates the text to the fifth century.

The combination of these various heterogeneous parts into one text, according to Kobayashi, has to do with the compilation of the *Heshang zhenren zhangju* (Verses and Sayings of the Perfected on the River) and its development into the *Heshang gong zhangju* (Verses and Sayings of the Master on the River) as one of the major *Daode jing* commentaries of the time. This occurred toward the end of the reign of Emperor Wu of the Liang, which allows a dating of the entire *Laozi xu* to approximately 540 C.E.

The first *XDL* citation of the *Laozi xu* deals with Laozi's emigration (2A). It is found in the third section of the text. The two others (8A, 34B) deal with the cosmological and practical contrasts between Taoism and Buddhism. They are not contained in the manuscript as it has survived in Dunhuang and have not been considered in any discussion of the text.

If accepted as part of an earlier edition of the *Laozi xu*, they would belong to the third section on the conversion. The passage cited in 34B, in particular, is reminiscent of a *Huahu jing* citation in 21A, which Zürcher thinks was part of the original *Huahu jing* of 300 C.E. The passage found in 8A, however, has some affinity with the *Santian neijie jing* and would substantiate Kobayashi's claim of a Celestial Masters origin of the text.

21. *Miaozhen jing* (Scripture of Wondrous Perfection)

Full   *Laozi miaozhen jing* (Laozi's Scripture of Wondrous Perfection)
XDL   29A
Date   Fifth century
Eds.   Lost; fragments collected in Maeda 1987, 27–32
Refs.   Maeda 1987; Qing 1988, 440; Sunayama 1990, 194; Kobayashi 1990,
        347–50

Not mentioned at all since the Song and reduced to one scroll under the Tang, the *Miaozhen jing* had two scrolls in the late Six Dynasties. At this time, it was listed together with the *Daode jing*, the *Xisheng jing*, and other texts associated with Laozi as one of the scriptures given to a "Master of High Mystery" (*Fengdao kejie* 4.7a).

The text is cited eleven times in the *WSBY* in close connection with the ancient philosophical tradition. Topics of fragments include the proper morality in government and self-cultivation (including the Confucian virtues); right accordance with the rhythm of the times; the way to lead an orderly family and community life; how to be careful in speech and avoid overstimulating the five senses; how to understand the spontaneity of nature and be equally soft and yielding; how to cultivate oneself, maintain good health, and keep the spirit(s) at peace in the body.

The idyllic vision of a traditional Lao-Zhuang scripture, however, is disturbed by two earlier references to the text. First, around the year 470, Xie Zhenzhi in an answer to Gu Huan's anti-Buddhist *Yixia lun* insists that "texts like the *Lingbao* and the *Miaozhen* are just imitations of the *Lotus Sūtra*" (T. 2102; 52.42c). Then, one hundred years later, the *XDL* cites a *Miaozhen ge* (Song of Wondrous Perfection; 29A), which indeed is an almost verbatim adaptation of the *Lotus Sūtra* that only alters "Buddha" to "Tao."

Based on these two citations, Kobayashi dates the text before Xie's letter around 470 and after Kumārajīva's translation of the *Lotus Sūtra* in 406. In addition, he adduces three reasons why the text should be placed closer to 470 than 406: (1) Songs, analogous to Buddhist *gāthā*, were attached to Taoist scriptures only from the Liu-Song onward, that is, after 420. (2) The *Miaozhen jing* presents Taoism as superior to Buddhism. It was thus written in a competitive but not yet polemical environment, which arose only after Liu Yu esatblished the Liu-Song. (3) The text introduces its sections with the words "The Tao said" rather than using "Laozi" or "the Venerable Lord." This indicates a thorough identity of the deity with the cosmic power, which is not found before the midfifth century (Kobayashi 1990, 347–50).

This still leaves the discrepancy between later citations and early references unexplained. One solution is to ignore the Buddhist references, interpreting the mention in Xie's letter as meaning "all those wondrous perfection texts of the Numinous Treasure" and charging Zhen Luan with making up his own materials. This would leave the *Miaozhen jing* an intact Lao-Zhuang philosophical text written in the wake of the *Xisheng jing*, which it cites, and imitating it (Maeda 1987, 26).

It is, however, also possible to assume that the *Miaozhen jing* underwent a thorough editing process in the sixth century. Stimulated by the Taoist defeat in the debate of 520, the *Kaitian jing* was destroyed (see app. 1) and various other texts were massively cleansed of offending Buddhist imitations (see Bokenkamp 1990). The *Miaozhen jing*, then, originally an adaptation of the *Lotus Sūtra*, was turned into a rather harmless philosophical work, as which it is cited in the *WSBY*. Zhen Luan, writing around the same time, knew of the text yet could come up only with its final *gāthā* to use for his argument. This would also explain why the text increasingly lost impact until it vanished altogether toward the end of the Tang.

22. *Nanji zhenren wenshi pin* (Chapter of Questions Asked by the Perfected of South Culmen)

XDL   13B

The *XDL* uses this text once (13B) with a passage on the eternity of the Mountain of Jade Capital. The text is not otherwise known.

23. *Nüqing wen* (Nüqing's Writ)

Full   *Nüqing guilü* (Nüqing's Statutes against Demons)
XDL   6A
Date   Fourth century
Eds.   *DZ* 790, fasc. 563; *SDZN* 6; *YJQQ* 40
Refs.   Kobayashi 1990, 376–78, 415–19; Mollier 1990, 22; Ren and Zhong 1991, 569

In the beginning of the world, there were no adverse forces or nasty demons. Men obeyed their parents and women were chaste. Rulers observed the rites and ministers behaved loyally. The six harmonies were joined in unity; there was no distress nor harm. Since the first year of Highest Sovereign, however, people have turned to manifold trickery and no longer believed in the Great Tao. (1.1a)

Then there were bad energies in all the five directions, innumerable predators and reptiles; demons began to fly about everywhere, many people died, and the good order of the world disintegrated. By now, the time of the Celestial Masters, demons number in the billions and nobody is safe any more. More drastic measures have to be taken.

The *Nüqing guilü* solves this problem by giving detailed instructions on how to keep demons at bay. It lists the names, appearances, and exact location of demons. For example,

> The third elder demon of Southvillage is called Che with the first name Ni. He presides over the records of the dead and counts the sins of the living. His location is to the northwest of Mount Tai (1.2a).
>
> The demon of Great Harmony has a head but no body. His head is three feet long. His eyes are three inches big; his ears, seven inches wide. His eyebrows are five inches long; his mouth opens as far as three inches. His nose is two inches long; his whiskers measure three. His hair reaches as far as ten feet. He breathes the energy of heaven; as he exhales, it turns into clouds. If you want to practice seeing him, his name is Zibei. Call him three times and his shape will appear. (2.6a)

Calling out the names of the demons when in need will keep them away or force them to appear in their true shapes. Reciting lists of names in a formal liturgy over a period of time will ensure good fortune and freedom from their nasty impact.

As the world approaches its end, those who do not know the names of the demons and do not practice Taoism will be exterminated through war, starvation, and disease. Eventually, the world will be cleansed and the new era of the Tao can begin. Then, Great Peace will rule everywhere and the faithful will return to their country of origin (Mollier 1990, 22).

The date of the *Nüqing guilü* is controversial. Its eschatological vision is inspired by Buddhism, and it refers to the chosen as the "seed people." Both characteristics do not appear in Taoist literature before 360 C.E. At the same time, the *Nüqing guilü* does not mention the doctrine of the Three Heavens, central to the Celestial Masters of the Liu-Song. This may date it to the Eastern Jin (Kobayashi 1990, 377).

Yet the text might also have originated in the north and thus not received any Liu-Song Taoist impact. In that case, it would be placed in the environment of Kou Qianzhi in the early fifth century (Ren and Zhong 1991, 569).

The *XDL* cites the text once (6A) with a passage that is found in the *Wulian jing*. It describes how the souls of one's ancestors up to the ninth generation can be transferred to the heaven of radiant light and will be reborn after thirty-two years.

24. *Sanhuang jing* (Scripture of the Three Sovereigns)

Full   *Dongshen sanhuang wen* (Writ of the Three Sovereigns of Spirit Cavern)

XDL   13A

Date   Third century, sixth century

Eds.   See *WSBY* 43.1a; *DJYS* 2.3a; *YJQQ* 6.5b

Refs.   Ōfuchi 1964, 277–343; Chen 1975, 71–78; Kobayashi 1990, 223–25, 371–73

The *XDL* citation of the *Sanhuang jing* is, in fact, found in the *Badi jing* (Scripture of the Eight Emperors)

Full   *Dongshen badi miaojing jing* (Scripture on the Wondrous Essence of the Eight Emperors, Contained in Spirit Cavern)

Date   Sixth century

Eds.   *DZ* 640, fasc. 342

Refs.   Ren and Zhong 1991, 459

The *Sanhuang jing,* or *Sanhuang wen,* is a collection of ancient talismans believed to have been used by the Three Sovereigns to govern the world in perfect harmony. They were first revealed to Bo He in the third century as writings in a cave after three years of wall-gazing (see *Shenxian zhuan* 7; Güntsch 1988, 214–16; Petersen 1990, 177–82). Later, the texts were found by Bao Jing, Ge Hong's father-in-law, in a grotto on Mount Song. From him they passed down to Ge Hong, who mentions them in the same breath as the *Wuyue zhenxing tu* (Chart of the True Shape of the Five Sacred Mountains; see Schipper 1967) and notes that they consisted of three scrolls. With him they became part of the Ge-family tradition.

In the fifth century, further explanations were added and the texts grew to four scrolls. Called the *Dongshen jing* (Scriptures of Spirit Cavern), the *Sanhuang wen* were integrated as the lowest of the Three Caverns into the newly devised arrangement of Taoist scriptures.

Through yet more additions, the texts developed into eleven scrolls by the midsixth century. They then contained the writings of the Three Sovereigns together with those of the Eight Divine Emperors (*Badi jing*). Three further scrolls on the ritual application of the talismans and explanations of the texts completed the collection by the end of the Six Dynasties. For more details and a full list of scriptures, see Chen 1975, 71.

Even in the time of Ge Hong, the texts had contained both talismans and explanations. Later, through the gradual addition of further commentary and various ritual formulas, the collection of the Dongshen group came into being. It remains unclear, however, whether Ge Hong's text was transmitted intact throughout the Six Dynasties or whether the process of addition also changed the nature of the original scriptures.

The position of the *Sanhuang wen* among Taoist scriptures in general is twofold. On the one hand, they were placed lowest among the Three Caverns, and they certainly are the smallest collection. On the other hand, they contributed significantly to the concept of the Three Caverns as the Three Sovereigns were identified with the Three Lords ruling them (Kobayashi 1990, 371).

The single *XDL* citation of this text (13A) deals with the West Country Immortal who says that august writing is based on birds' tracks and that the Three Sovereigns rule over all. It is found in the *Badi jing*. This text, of twenty-nine pages, begins with a description of the nine sovereigns, i.e., the Three Sovereigns linked with the Three Ones and the three primordial energies. The gods are half-animal, with either bodies or heads of birds or snakes. To maintain good relations with them, Taoists have to obey certain precepts and perform proper ceremonies, including the correct writing of their talismans. Detailed instructions are included.

25. *Santian zhengfa jing* (Scripture of the Proper Law of the Three Heavens)

Full   *Taishang santian zhengfa jing* (Highest Scripture of the Proper Law of the Three Heavens)
XDL   1B, 3B, 4A, 32B
Date   Fifth century, seventh century
Eds.   *DZ* 1203, fasc. 876
Refs.   Ōzaki 1974; Robinet 1984, 2:87–91; Kobayashi 1990, 433–45; Ren and Zhong 1991, 949

This text is listed in Shangqing catalogs yet is not an original Shangqing scripture. It belongs to the tradition of the Celestial Masters, whose typical cosmology and general terminology are clearly in evidence. According to Ōzaki, the first part (1a–5b) goes back to the fifth century, whereas the second part can be divided into six distinct sections that were added in the sixth and seventh centuries.

The *Santian zhengfa* is cited variously, but only few passages, notably those in the *WSBY*, are actually found in today's text. Others occur in the *Jiuwei badao jing* (Scripture of the Nine Tenuities and Eight Ways; *DZ* 1395, fasc. 1048), a text assembled on the basis of original Shangqing documents but dated considerably later. The creation cosmology does not conform to Shangqing concepts, and the dialogue between the Highest Lord and the Latter-Day Sage is not in Shangqing format. Only few sections

(4ab, 8b–9b) are similar to the classical scriptures of Highest Clarity (Robinet 1984, 2:87).

During the Six Dynasties, several versions of the text existed, one called *Shangqing santian zhengfa jing,* another known as *Dongzhen santian zhengfa jing* (Perfection Cavern Scripture, Highest Clarity Scripture of the Proper Law of the Three Heavens). Both are cited with similar passages in late Six Dynasties materials. Together with selections from the *Siji mingke* (Illustrious Rules of the Four Quarters; *DZ* 184, fasc. 77–78; see Ōzaki 1977) and the *Jiuwei badao jing,* these texts were integrated into the *Taishang santian zhengfa jing* now contained in the Taoist canon (Kobayashi 1990, 444).

The earliest version of the text goes back to the Eastern Jin and is known as *Chu liutian zhiwen santian zhengfa jing* (Scripture of the Proper Law of the Three Heavens that Abolishes the Writ of the Six Heavens). This was an eschatological text describing kalpa revolutions and the events at the end of a cycle. It contained the basic eschatology of Shangqing Taoism.

The *XDL* cites the *Santian zhengfa jing* three times with the same passage on the creation of the world and the first separation of the light and the turbid (1B, 3B, 32B). In addition, it refers to the text with regard to the first human beings and their creation from earth (4A). For a detailed comparison of these *XDL* passages with their counterparts in the Taoist canon, see Ōzaki 1974, 14.

26. *Sanyuan pin* (Precepts of the Three Primes)

Full   *Taishang dongxuan lingbao sanyuan pinjie gongde qingzhong jing* (Scripture on the Weight of Merit and Virtue As Based on the Precepts of the Three Primes Contained in the Mystery Cavern of Highest Numinous Treasure)

XDL   3A, 3B, 4B, 6B, 25A

Date   Fourth century

Eds.   *DZ* 456, fasc. 202; *DZ* 36, fasc. 28; *DX* 2850, repr. Ōfuchi 1979b, 903; *WSBY* 34, 66

Refs.   Ōfuchi 1974, 52; Bokenkamp 1983, 483; Maeda 1985, 87; Schmidt 1985; Ren and Zhong 1991, 338–39

This is the ancient Lingbao version of the formal Taoist precepts (no. 18). Spoken by the Highest Venerable of Primordial Beginning for the sake of the Lord of the Tao, the text first describes the offices of the Three Primes, that is, the three central bureaus of Heaven, Earth, and Water that are in charge of life and death. Each bureau has specific administrative responsibilities and an extensive staff of 120 officials, named in each case with proper title and relevant duties.

Then the text lists sixty sins each under the jurisdiction of the Three Primes. The Highest Prime is concerned with the proper transmission of scriptures, relationship to the masters and preceptors, and harmony within the religious community. The text here only lists forty-three precepts, yet it says,

> These sixty precepts are supervised by the Twelve Officials of the Central Administrative Section of the First Office of the Department of Heaven; by the Fourteen Officials of the Central Administrative Section of the First Office of the Department of Earth; and by the Fourteen Officials of the Central Administrative Section of the First Office of the Department of Water. (24b)

The Middle Prime punishes jealousy, greed, nasty schemes, and improper relations with women, outsiders, slaves, and animals. The Lower Prime is concerned with basic social politeness and respect among community members, punishing theft, slander, gossip, laziness, lack of filial piety and loyalty, and other egoistic faults. For a translation of the precepts, see Kohn 1993a, 100–6.

The *XDL* uses the text mainly in connection with cosmology, about the talisman that creates the world (25A) and the offices of the Three Primes (3B, 6B). In addition, it cites a passage on the responsibility of the individual for his fate (4B).

27. *Shengxuan jing* (Scripture of Ascension to the Mystery)

Full	*Taishang dongxuan lingbao shengxuan neijiao jing* (Scripture of the Esoteric Teaching on Ascension to the Mystery Contained in the Mystery Cavern of Highest Numinous Treasure)
XDL	34B
Date	Sixth century
Eds.	Yamada 1992; Ōfuchi 1979b, 151–90; *WSBY* 34, 46
Refs.	Sunayama 1990, 227–29; Ren and Zhong 1991, 867–68

The one *XDL* citation of the *Shengxuan jing* is, in fact, found in the *Xisheng jing* (Scripture of Western Ascension)

Full	Laozi xisheng jing (Scripture of Laozi's Western Ascension)
Date	Fifth century
Eds.	*DZ* 726, fasc. 449–50; *DZ* 666, fasc. 346–47; Fujiwara 1983; Kohn 1991a, 257–73
Refs.	Fujiwara 1983, 1985; Maeda 1989, 1990a, 1990b; Sunayama 1990, 330–46; Ren and Zhong 1991, 474–75, 519; Kohn 1991a

The Tao said:

To honor the teaching and practice the Tao, you must

> diligently cultivate yourself,
> firmly set your will on progress,
> always uphold the precepts,
> strongly concentrate your thoughts,
> strictly stick with reality in your imagination!

In addition, always visualize the Tao and abandon all falsehood and doubts, enticements and wrong, unchastity and passion. As you give up all bad deeds and depraved thoughts, you can truly embrace perfection.

Thus, by first laboring hard, then being rewarded, you can go beyond your self and ascend to the immortals. Just relax and allow it to happen; never impatiently glance ahead! (chap. 9; Yamada 1992, 23; *WSBY* 46.2b)

First compiled in the sixth century, the *Shengxuan jing* was expanded under the Sui and Tang. It survives today in citations and fragments from Dunhuang. Chapters 5 to 10 are complete; chapter 7 is also contained in the Taoist canon (*DZ* 1122, fasc. 759); a complete collation is found in Yamada 1992.

The text is an offshoot of the Lingbao scriptures and, in content, a Mahāyāna-style exposition of the Taoist teaching by the Highest Venerable Lord to Zhang Daoling, the first Celestial Master. It emphasizes the philosophical dimension of the Tao and the systematic and gradual practice necessary to attain it. In that, it is closely related to the *Benji jing*, the *Xuanmen dayi*, and the *DJYS* of the early Tang.

Its system consists of three ranks of attainment: higher, medium, and lower. Those reaching a higher level are spirit immortals; they ascend to heaven in broad daylight, are served by jade maidens and pure lads, and transform physically into diamond bodies and radiant beings. Medium-level practitioners are finders of nirvāṇa; they serve as celestial officers of slightly lower rank but still attain residence in the heavenly halls. Those on the lower level are practitioners of longevity; they follow diets and practice gymnastics to extend their years and eventually become officers of the earth who sit in judgment over the souls of the dead. To reach each level, one has to follow a specific set of practices and code of behavior. The *Shengxuan jing* thus integrates various kinds of Taoist teaching and practice into an organized whole.

The *XDL* cites it once (34B) with a passage that is actually from the *Xisheng jing*. This work, dated to the fifth century, is first mentioned in connection with the conversion of the barbarians and as such is cited in Buddhist polemics. Except the first section, however, which mentions

Laozi setting out for the west, the text today is a mystical exposition of the Tao spoken by Laozi for the sake of Yin Xi.

The thirty-nine sections of the text can be roughly divided into five parts. The first part establishes the general setting, outlines Yin Xi's practice, and expostulates on some fundamental problems of speaking about the ineffable. The second part describes the immanence of the Tao in the world and outlines the way of accessing it. The third part provides a more concrete explanation of theory and practice and refers to the practice of meditation. The fourth part deals with the life of the sage. Part five, finally, discusses the return of everything to its origins and includes Laozi's return to heaven.

Five commentaries contained in the Song-dynasty edition (*DZ* 726) are by Wei Jie (497–559), a scholar-official who retired to Taoism; by Xu Miao from Qurong, the home of Shangqing Taoism, of the early Tang; by Chongxuanzi, unknown; by Li Rong of the seventh century, famous philosopher of the Chongxuan school and defender of Taoism in the debates among Buddhists and Taoists; and by Liu Renhui of the middle to late Tang.

Like most Buddhist polemics, the *XDL* (34B) cites the *Xisheng jing* with the first section, where Laozi leaves China and speaks of his teacher as being in India. This has been taken as a reference to the Buddha and proof that Laozi not only knew of him but even served him as his teacher. Zhen Luan cites the passage as from the *Shengxuan jing*, a confusion not uncommon in the literature.

28. *Shenxian jinye jing* (The Spirit Immortals' Scripture on the Golden Fluid)

Full   *Baopuzi shenxian jinzhuo jing* (The Spirit Immortals' Scripture on the Golden Fluid as Transmitted by the Master Who Embraces Simplicity)

XDL   28A, 28B

Date   Han, Six Dynasties

Eds.   *DZ* 917, fasc. 593

Refs.   Wang 1964; Needham 1976, 88–90; Chen 1983a, 27; Chen 1983b; Meng 1984, 79–80; Ren and Zhong 1991, 680–81; Pregadio 1991, 574–78

Grind the gold to powder and cast it into the mercury so that the two substances join. Wash the amalgam in pure water more than ten times, then add two ounces each of realgar and salpeter. (1a)

The *Jinye jing* in three scrolls is a technical treatise on alchemical methods, especially on the concoction and ingestion of the golden fluid. It is closely related in style and content to the *Baopuzi* of Ge Hong (see Ware 1966; Sailey 1978).

Divided into text and commentary, the text proper—based on changes in weight systems between the Han and the Jin—can be dated to the Han. The commentary was written during the late Six Dynasties. As it stands, the scripture can be divided into five parts: the preparation of the golden fluid; the preparation of reverted cinnabar; the application of reverted cinnabar; the properties of the golden fluid; and the preparation of an elixir for immortality. Most methods described in the text proper are also found in the *Baopuzi*. For more details on the text and on its relation to other alchemical sources, see Pregadio 1991.

The *XDL* cites the *Jinye jing* twice in the same section (28) with similar passages, a mixture of what appears as text and commentary in the Taoist canon.

29. *Shenxian zhuan* (Biographies of Spirit Immortals)

Full	same
XDL	2B, 16B
Date	Fourth century
Eds.	*Daozang jinghua* 5.11; *Han Wei congshu*; see also *YJQQ* 109; *Taiping guangji* 5
Refs.	Fukui 1951; Kominami 1974; Shimomi 1974; Yamada 1974, 1977, 1983; Güntsch 1988, 9; Petersen 1990, 173

Originally written by Ge Hong (261–341), the alchemist known as the "Master Who Embraces Simplicity," this text was rearranged, if not reassembled, in the Tang and Song. Today's version, contained in various collections and cited frequently, does not match the citations of the text from before the Tang, such as those found in Pei Songzhi's commentary to the *Sanguo zhi* and the *SDZN*. Rather, in the early literature, the *Shenxian zhuan* is often confused with the *Baopuzi* and the *Liexian zhuan*, originally compiled by Liu Xiang under the Han but also reassembled later (see Kaltenmark 1953).

The *Shenxian zhuan* as known now is derived from the *Taiping guangji* collection of the early Song. A critical edition is found in the *Siku quanshu*. The standard version contains ten scrolls and ninety-four biographies of spirit immortals of different type and stature. Several of Ge Hong's close relations and teachers are included as are sages of old, such as Laozi, Guangchengzi, and Lu Ao. In addition, there are Ge Hong's contemporaries, such as Guo Pu; the founder of religious Taoism, Zhang Daoling; and several greater and lesser immortal personalities. For a study of Li Babai's biography, for example, see Yamada 1977. A complete translation of the text is found in Güntsch 1988.

The *XDL* refers to the *Shenxian zhuan* twice, in both instances using Ge Hong's opinion and narration as a common-sense reference point against confused Taoist worldview. The first instance (2B) deals with the repeated appearances of Laozi in the world, a notion that Ge Hong finds rather strange. The second instance (16B) invokes the biography of Shen Xi in reference to the ranks of the highest heavenly deities.

30. *Shijie jing* (The Ten Precepts)

Full   *Dongxuan lingbao tianzun shuo shijie jing* (Scripture of Ten Precepts As Revealed by the Heavenly Venerable and Contained in the Mystery Cavern of Numinous Treasure)

XDL   23A

Date   Fifth century

Eds.   *DZ* 459, fasc. 203; S. 645, P. 2347, 2350, 3770; repr. Ōfuchi 1979b, 97–100

Refs.   Fukui 1952, 197; Bokenkamp 1989; Sunayama 1990, 142; Ren and Zhong 1991, 341

There are many different sets of ten precepts in Taoism. Those in the *Shijie jing* appear first in the *Dingzhi jing* (Scripture on Setting the Will toward Wisdom; *DZ* 325, fasc. 167), of the ancient Lingbao corpus (no. 12; Bokenkamp 1983, 481). They are later cited in *WSBY* 46, *YJQQ* 38, and the *Yaoxiu keyi* (Yoshioka 1961; Kusuyama 1982, 56).

The ten precepts here begin with the classic five rules of Buddhism: do not kill, steal, lie, commit adultery, or submit to intoxication. Then they add five more: maintain harmony with the family, rejoice in the goodness of others, assist the unfortunate, refrain from revenge when harmed, and never strive to attain the Tao ahead of others.

The *XDL* cites the text only once under the title *Shijie shisi chishen jing* (23A). The *shisi chishen* of the title, "fourteen principles of self-control," are rules of social politeness. They appear first in the *Zuigen pin* of the Lingbao corpus (see app. 2) and are part of the *DZ* and Dunhuang versions of the *Shijie jing*. The actual *XDL* passage on the priority of the north in worship, however, does not appear in the text.

31. *Wenshi zhuan* (Biography of Master Wenshi)

Full   *Wenshi xiansheng wushang zhenren guanling neizhuan* (The Inner Biography of Master Wenshi, the Highest Perfected and Guardian of the Pass)

XDL   2B, 5A, 5B, 8B, 9A, 10A, 16A, 23B, 25B, 28B, 30A, 32A; 3B, 4B (cited as *Yuanshi zhuan*)

Date   Sixth century

Eds.   *SDZN* 9.8b–14b; fragments in *Taiping yulan, Yiwen leiju, Chuxue ji*

Refs.   Fukui 1962; Yamada 1982; Zhang 1990, 1991

Listed in the bibliographical section of the *Suishu, Tangshu,* and *Jiu Tang-shu,* this text was compiled by Louguan Taoists to popularize a new version of the conversion, according to which Yin Xi became the Buddha. This version was necessary after the debate of 520 when the *Kaitian jing,* which first dated Laozi's emigration to the early Zhou and identified him with the Buddha, was destroyed. The *Wenshi zhuan* succeeded it, giving an exposition of the creation of the world and the exploits of Laozi. Shifting the emphasis from Laozi to Yin Xi, it established the Buddha as an independent figure and Laozi's partner, if originally his disciple (see Fukui 1962).

The text has nothing to do with the philosophical *Wenshi zhenjing* (Perfect Scripture of Master Wenshi; *DZ* 667, fasc. 347; *DZ* 727, fasc. 450–52). As the *neizhuan* or inner biography of Yin Xi, the Guardian of the Pass, it rather belongs to a genre of biography that emerged as a new type of religious literature in the fifth century. The biographies served to give adepts the proper guidance in their pursuit of the Tao. Famous examples are the *Huangdi neizhuan* (Esoteric Biography of the Yellow Emperor; lost) and the *Ziyang zhenren neizhuan* (Esoteric Biography of Ziyang the Perfected; *DZ* 303, fasc. 152) on the Shangqing practitioner Zhou Ziyang (Porkert 1979).

Technical texts on meditation and physical practices, such as the *Huangting jing* (Yellow Court Scripture) or the *Dantian jing* (Cinnabar Field Scripture), were then appended to the great hagiographies. Inner biographies linked the lives of the saints with the original cosmology of the Tao, just as the adept's daily life of aspiration was filled with the ritual and meditation of the Tao (Mugitani 1982, 32). Thus, the *Wenshi zhuan* was probably the leading exposition of a religious practice that visualized or ritually imitated the exploits of Laozi and Yin Xi.

The *XDL* cites the *Wenshi zhuan* fourteen times. Two passages appear twice: the description of the kalpic deluge and fire (10A, 25B) and the narrative of Laozi and Yin Xi traveling to heaven (16A, 23B). Three citations on the conversion of the barbarians can roughly be identified with passages now contained in the *SDZN* (5A, 30A) or with remaining *Huahu jing* fragments (8B). Another, on the size of heaven and earth, is found in the *TPYL* (9A).

The remaining six passages are unidentified. Three deal with cosmological themes: the location of heaven and hell (3B); the sins that merit punishment in hell (4B); and the various layers of heaven (32A). The first two are cited as from the *Yuanshi zhuan,* an alternative title of the *Wenshi zhuan;* the last appears again as from the *Duming miaojing* (10B).

Three further passages, finally, speak of Laozi as the Tao: his transformations (2B); his relation to the Great One (28B); and his leadership of the heavenly kings (32B).

32. *Wufu jing* (Scripture of the Five Talismans)

Full	*Taishang lingbao wufuxu* (Explanation of the Five Talismans of Highest Numinous Treasure)
XDL	11A, 17B
Date	Fourth century
Eds.	*DZ* 388, fasc. 183
Refs.	Ōfuchi 1974, 53; Ishii 1981, 1984; Kaltenmark 1960, 1981; Chen 1975, 62–66; Bokenkamp 1983, 483; Bokenkamp 1986; Yamada 1984b, 1987a, 1989b; Kobayashi 1990, 45–104; Ren and Zhong 1991, 287–89; Kohn 1993a, 43–48

The *Wufuxu* originally consisted of only one scroll. The oldest version of this was compiled by Emperor Yu of the Xia dynasty on the basis of the revealed Lingbao scriptures. After he finished [ordering the world], he hid it on the north side of Mount Laosheng. Later Lezichang received the sacred scripture from the immortal Huolin and made it known to the world. The version that the immortal Ge Xuan obtained in his lifetime consisted of two scrolls. Since then, the text has grown to the size of three scholls. (Lu Xiujing's catalog; Ōfuchi 1979b, 727)

An ancient Lingbao scripture (no. 20) and one of the most important texts of early religious Taoism, the *Wufuxu* has received much scholarly attention. In its present form, in three scrolls, it is a composite text that consists of several distinct parts.

First, there are the five ancient Lingbao talismans. The first scroll contains their myth, telling how they served the Three Sovereigns and Five Emperors and were hidden by Di Ku in the Kunlun mountains. Later, they were recovered, used, and hidden again by the flood hero, Yu, to be acquired a millennium later with improper means by King Helü of Wu, who duly lost his kingdom. Finally, they were made accessible to Taoists of the Later Han, notably Ge Xuan. From him the text was transmitted into the Ge-family tradition and thence into the Lingbao canon. The talismans themselves with illustrations and explanations are contained in the third scroll. Kaltenmark (1981) and Kobayashi (1990) see the talismans as the oldest part of the text. All scholars agree that members of the Ge family played a central role in compiling the scripture (Ren and Zhong 1991).

Next, there are descriptions of the techniques and lineages of certain

Han-dynasty immortals or magicotechnicians, people who specialized in longevity and cosmology and whose ideas survive in Han apocrypha. Here, in particular, are the ways of Lezichang and Huaziqi, both practitioners of the Later Han, who ingested sesame and the five sprouts and worked on expelling the three worms from the body. They are described in the first scroll. Yamada considers their methods and lineage crucial for the development and compilation of the *Wufuxu* (1984b, 1987a, 1989b).

The entire second scroll, moreover, is dedicated to dietary methods, including many detailed recipes for the concoction of immortality drugs. This is an extension of the magicotechnician's ways described in the first scroll. It also goes together well with Ge Hong's *Baopuzi;* thus, some scholars date it to the fourth century. Kobayashi thinks it forms part of the latest level of the text and dates from around the year 410.

In addition, the first scroll contains specific meditation instructions on the ingestion of solar and lunar essences and the visualization of the gods of the body. Although similar to the *Taiping jing* and thus possibly fairly early, these represent a different tradition, which is more focused on religious visions and ritual. Rather than to the magicotechnicians, this part goes back to the early Taoist movements (Yamada 1989b).

The third scroll, finally, has a number of additional talismans and spells with specific explanations. They serve to protect the active adept from serpents, dragons, tigers, panthers, and other nasty creatures of the wild. In this, they are close to the magical charms described in the *Baopuzi* and might again be rather early. The more formal ritual, however, also found in the third scroll, belongs to a later phase of editing.

For an overview of the various sources on and citations of the *Wufuxu,* see Ishii 1981 and 1984. On the *Wufuxu* in the Lingbao catalog, see Ōfuchi 1974 and Bokenkamp 1983. A translation of the myth in the first scroll is found in Bokenkamp 1986, and the meaning of the talismans and the cosmic implications of the terms *ling* and *bao* are discussed in Kaltenmark 1960.

The *XDL* cites the text twice, first from the first scroll in regard to the human body and the deities residing therein (11A), then again from the second scroll on the qualities of Yellow Essence, an immortality herb that prolongs life (17B).

33. *Wulian jing* (Scripture of Fivefold Purification)

Full   *Taishang dongxuan lingbao miedu wulian shengshi miaojing* (Wondrous Scripture of Salvation from Extinction through Fivefold Purification for Reviving the Dead, Contained in the Mystery Cavern of Highest Numinous Treasure)

XDL   6A

Date   Fifth century
Eds.   *DZ* 369, fasc. 181; P. 2865, S. 298, repr. Ōfuchi 1979, 70–77
Refs.   Ōfuchi 1974, 51–52; Bokenkamp 1983, 483; Ren and Zhong 1991,
        277–78

To put at rest the bodies of the dead and all those under the administration of Earth, to console and cherish them, to make them reach a swift return, a new birth in a world of good fortune, in a prosperous family and with ample emoluments, to ensure their fortune continues forever from generation to generation—use these Ordinances of the Luminous Perfected. (18b–19a)

Part of the ancient Lingbao corpus (no. 17), the *Wulian jing* details the necessary rituals to protect the bodies and souls of the dead and help them toward easy and fortunate rebirths, preferably in the heavens. The rites, based on the esoteric sounds of the thirty-two heavens found in the *Duren jing* and the *Zhutian neiyin*, are linked to the five phases and thus to the Five Emperors and the five directions. For each direction, the text spells out exact procedures, specifying the materials and amounts to be used for people of different social ranks. Prayers for the good fortune of the dead and to banish their wrath along the lines of the *Nüqing guilü* are appended.

The *XDL* cites the text once (6A) on instructions how to bury the dead with dyed silk and pieces of colored stone inscribed with the pure jade characters of the heavens.

34. *Xuandu jingmu* (Catalog of Scriptures of Mystery Metropolis)

Full   *Xuandu guan jingmu* (Catalog of Scriptures of the Monastery of
        Mystery Metropolis)
XDL   31A, 36A
Date   570
Eds.   Lost
Refs.   Yoshioka 1955, 30–37; Ōfuchi 1964, 164; Chen 1975, 106–12

This list of Taoist scriptures, compiled in the same year as the *XDL,* is the fifth among early Taoist catalogs. They are known mostly from Buddhist sources.

The oldest is Lu Xiujing's *Sandong jingshu mulu* (Catalog of Scriptures and Texts of the Three Caverns), dated to 471. It lists Taoist sacred texts, talismans, and works on methods in altogether 1,228 scrolls (see *XDL* 31A). Next are two lists of scriptures, the *Yuwei qibu jing mulu* (Catalog of Scriptures and Texts of the Jade Warp in Seven Divisions) by Preceptor Meng (Fashi) and the *Jingmu* (Catalog of Scriptures) by Tao Hongjing. Only their titles have survived. The fourth early catalog is Ruan Xiaoxu's *Qilu xiandao lu* (Record of the Way of the Immortals in Seven Sections) that lists texts in altogether 1,138 scrolls. The contents are known from citations in Buddhist sources.

The *Xuandu guan jingmu* was compiled by the Taoists of the Monastery of Mystery Metropolis in Chang'an upon imperial suggestion. A further list of scriptures, similarly sponsored by Emperor Wu at the time of his persecution of Buddhism, was put together by the Louguan Taoist Wang Yan in 572–78 (see *YJQQ* 85.18b–20a; Qiug 1988, 435; Ren 1990, 224; Zhang 1991, 81). It was called the *Sandong zhunang* (Pearly Bag of the Three Caverns) or the *Zhunang jingmu* (Catalog of the Pearly Bag) and consisted of seven scrolls. This text is lost, too. It should not be confused with Wang Xuanhe's *SDZN* in ten scrolls of the seventh century.

The *XDL* uses the *Xuandu jingmu* twice (31A, 36A). In both cases it compares it with Lu Xiujing's work and gives the numbers of scrolls listed as Taoist texts.

35. *Xuanmiao neipian* (Esoteric Record of Mystery and Wonder)

Full *Xuanmiao yunü yuanjun neipian* (Esoteric Record of the Goddess Jade Maiden of Mystery and Wonder)

XDL 5B, 18A, 18B

Date Fifth century

Eds. Lost; fragments in *Yixia lun* (467 C.E.); *SDZN* 8.4a; *Miaomen youqi* 7b; *Yongcheng jixian lu* 1.2ab (*DZ* 783, fasc. 560–61); *Daode zhenjing guangsheng yi* 2.20b (*DZ* 725, fasc. 440–48)

Refs. Yoshioka 1959, 17; Zürcher 1959, 301–3; Fukui 1964; Kohn 1989c; Kobayashi 1990, 382–85

The *Xuanmiao neipian* is closely related to the *Santian neijie jing* (*DZ* 1205, fasc. 876) of 420 C.E., which refers to Laozi's mother as the Jade Maiden of Mystery and Wonder. In 469, it is cited in Gu Huan's *Yixia lun* (see app. 1) among various Buddhist scriptures. The text was, therefore, certainly extant in the fifth century, but might even predate the *Santian neijie jing*.

A citation that survived in Dunhuang (S. 4226; Ōfuchi 1979b, 704) contains a criticism of Buddhism and also of the Celestial Masters, the Way of Great Peace, and Highest Clarity. From this reference, the author of the *Xuanmiao neipian* most probably belonged to the Ge-family tradition and Numinous Treasure (Kobayashi 1990, 384).

The *Xuanmiao neipian* survives only in citations. Taking them together, it appears that it was a hagiography of Laozi that emphasized the career of his mother. The expression *xuanmiao* (mystery and wonder), however, is used in the first section of the *Daode jing* in reference to the Tao in general. Thus, *Xuanmiao neipian* might also be read in the plural and indicate a collection of Taoist scriptures.

The *XDL* cites the text three times about Laozi's birth as the Buddha. This passage is commonly found in other fragments of the text.

36. *Xuanzhong jing* (Scripture of Central Mystery)

The *XDL* cites this text twice: Once (20A) on the precepts, talismans and registers Taoists receive and on their practice of erecting altars in the direction of the five sacred mountains, worshiping them by offering wine and meat; then again (33A) on the ritual tablet of the Taoists, their garb, and their proper way of entering and leaving residences and places of worship. From these citations it seems that the text was a practical manual, a book of rules. It is otherwise unknown.

37. *Xuanzi* (Writings of the Master of Mystery)

A text *Xuanzi* in five scrolls is mentioned in the bibliographic chapter of the *Suishu*. The *XDL* cites it once (35B) with an admonition not to commit perverse acts and never to harbor jealousy.

The *BZL* cites the same passage as the words of a person called Xuanzi quoted in the *Daoshi lilü* (Ritual Rules for Taoists), an otherwise unknown text.

38. *Youwu shengcheng pin* (Chapter on Being and Nonbeing, Birth and Completion)

The *XDL* cites this text once (3B) with a philosophical statement that "emptiness is the mother of the myriad beings; the Tao is their father." The text is not known otherwise.

39. *Zhenren neichao lü* (Rules of the Perfected for Proper Homage in the Inner Chamber)

The *XDL* cites this text once (35A) in the context of sexual rituals. These are celebrated at new and full moon, after participants have purified themselves for three days. They enter the chamber, pay homage to the master, and commence the rites. The *BZL* gives a similar reference. Otherwise, the text has not been transmitted.

40. *Zhutian neiyin* (Esoteric Sounds of All Heavens)

Full *Taishang lingbao zhutian neiyin ziran yuzi* (Esoteric Sounds and Spon-
      taneous Jade Characters of All Heavens of Highest Numinous Trea-
      sure)
XDL 7B, 15A, 34B
Date Fifth century
Eds. *DZ* 97, fasc. 49; P. 2431, repr. Ōfuchi 1979b, 23–30
Refs. Ōfuchi 1974, 48; Bokenkamp 1983, 486; Bokenkamp 1991, 59–60; Ren
       and Zhong 1991, 74

This text is an ancient Lingbao scripture in four scrolls (no. 7). It contains the esoteric sounds of the thirty-two heavens—eight heavens in each of the four directions—which are also contained in the *Duren jing*. The text adds a detailed explanation by the Sovereign of Heavenly Perfection (Tianzhen huangren).

Each of the thirty-two heavens has one eight-character verse, totaling 256 characters of the sacred "hidden script of Great Brahma." These characters formed at the first beginning of the universe directly from primordial energy. They contain the power of life and death and reappear at the beginning of each new age to reconstitute heaven and earth.

The first scroll sets out the 256 characters in heavenly writing. Scroll two is dedicated to a list of the spirits in the thirty-two heavens and furnishes the celestial location of each word with a description of its talismanic efficacy. Scrolls three and four translate the verses into the language of mortals and give an explanation.

The *XDL* cites the text three times (7B, 15A, 34B), mostly from the third scroll, explaining the esoteric sounds and thereby referring to the structure and organization of the heavens.

41. *Ziran jing* (Scripture of Spontaneity)

Full *Zhenyi ziran jingjue* (Scriptural Instructions of Spontaneity of Perfect
      Unity)
XDL 33B
Date Fifth century
Eds. P. 2356, P. 2403, P. 2452; repr. Ōfuchi 1979b, 116–18; *WSBY* 43.
Refs. Ōfuchi 1974, 53; Bokenkamp 1983, 484

A technical text on Taoist conduct and garb, this text belongs to the ancient Lingbao corpus (no. 23) and has survived in Dunhuang fragments. The *XDL* uses it once (33B) with a lengthy description of Taoist garb.

42. *Zuigen pin* (The Roots of Sin)

Full   *Taishang dongxuan lingbao zhihui zuigen shangpin dajie jing* (Great Precepts of the Upper Section Regarding the Roots of Wisdom and Sin, Contained in the Mystery Cavern of Highest Numinous Treasure)

XDL   2B, 3B, 21B, 29B
Date   Fifth century
Eds.   *DZ* 457, fasc. 202; P. 2461, repr. Ōfuchi 1979b, 30–37; *WSBY* 47
Refs.   Ōfuchi 1974, 48; Bokenkamp 1983, 481; Ren and Zhong 1991, 340

This scripture, in two scrolls, is part of the old Lingbao corpus (no. 8) and represents one Lingbao version of the precepts and statutes. It is set in a formal audience in the heavens. The Lord of the Tao sees the Heavenly Venerable of Primordial Beginning and asks him for an explanation of the laws governing karma and destiny. "The Heavenly Venerable thereupon summoned the spirit immortals and flying celestials of the ten directions. He opened the wrapper of long night, contained in the jade casket of ninefold darkness. From this, he took the register of sins of the living and the dead where evils as well as the seeds of purity are recorded" (1.2a).

He then proceeds to explain his salvational activities during the four major phases, or kalpas, of the universe. They are

1. Dragon Country (Longhan). People were very pure and free from evil and led a simple life. The Heavenly Venerable descended to help them live in perfect accordance with the Law. There was no sin. At the end of this kalpa the world collapsed.

2. Red Radiance (Chiming). There was a trace of impurity and evil among living beings, karma and retribution first began. The Heavenly Venerable saved as many as he could and established the first colonies of celestials above. Again, the kalpa ended with the complete destruction of everything.

3. Opening Sovereign (Kaihuang). People were still living simply, but there were the beginnings of culture and civilization as exemplified in the knotting of cords for reckoning. Because the minds of people were simple and still largely unconscious, their life spans were as long as thirty-six thousand years. Again, the Heavenly Venerable supported the age.

4. Highest Sovereign (Shanghuang). Culture developed fully and the world declined in earnest. Strife and jealousy, hatred and war were

bringing about the dark age of humanity, which still continues. Ever since, the Heavenly Venerable has handed down precepts and rules to ensure the survival and salvation of at least a few. (1.2a–3a)

The scripture then gives several sets of precepts as spoken by the Heavenly Venerable. First are the ten good deeds: Taoists should guard the lives of all beings, help the sick, support those in need, serve their teacher, pay obeisance to the scriptures, maintain the fasts, be withdrawing and yielding, teach the ignorant, spread the teaching, and always remain within the rules of the teaching (4ab).

Then, there are the fourteen principles of self-control, also part of the *Shijie jing*. They specify detailed rules of social politeness in various situations. Next, 180 precepts arranged according to three levels are mentioned but not spelled out. They presumably refer to the precepts of the *Sanyuan pin*.

Furthermore, there are the ten precepts and twelve resolutions already contained in the *Chishu yujue* (*DZ* 352, fasc. 178), the second text of the ancient Lingbao canon. They contain the five precepts of Buddhism, encourage Taoists to keep a calm mind, and spell out the mental attitude favored by the faithful (see Bokenkamp 1990). For example, "I will delight in the scriptures and teachings. I will study them widely to let my understanding deepen and to make my determination firm and enlightened. I will liberate and transform all those in ignorance and darkness" (1.6a).

The ten good deeds are, moreover, contrasted with the ten evils, whose dire consequences in the hells are spelled out. The first scroll concludes with the Lord of the Tao pleading for a moment of divine insight into the actual workings of karma on earth. The Heavenly Venerable agrees, and for an instant all mundane fates are laid open to the brilliance of heavenly light, startling people into spiritual awareness (1.10a). The attending immortals and celestials sing a song of praise.

In the second scroll, the Highest Lord speaks with the representatives of twelve countries about ways to help the hell prisoners held there to a speedy rebirth.

The *XDL* cites the Heavenly Venerable's recollection of his experiences during the first kalpas of the universe (2B, 21B) and his explanation of the precepts (3B, 23B) in the beginning of the scripture.

Titles of Texts Cited

Apitan piposha lun   Abhidharma-vibhāsā-śāstra
Ayu wang jing   Aśokarāja sūtra

Badi jing   Scripture of the Eight Emperors
Baopuzi   Book of the Master Who Embraces Simplicity
Baopuzi shenxian jinzhuo jing   The Spirit Immortals' Scripture on the Golden Fluid as
     Transmitted by the Master Who Embraces Simplicity
Benji   Original Record
Benji jing   Scripture of Original Time
Bianhuo lun   To Discriminate Errors
Bianzheng lun   In Defense of What Is Right
Biyao juefa   Instructions and Methods of Esoteric Essentials
Bo Gu daoshi Yixia lun   Disputing Taoist Gu's Treatise on Barbarians and Chinese
Bowu zhi   Record of Ample Things
Bo yixia lun   Disputing the Treatise on Barbarians and Chinese

Chang'an zhi   Gazetteer of Chang'an
Chishu yujue   Jade Instructions in Red Characters
Chong shu yu Gu daoshi   Second Letter to Taoist Gu
Chuci   Songs of the South
Chuji   Record of Beginnings
Chu liutian zhiwen santian zhengfa jing   Scripture of the Proper Law of the Three Heavens
     that Abolishes the Writ of the Six Heavens
Chunqiu   Spring and Autumn Annals
Chunqiu fanlu   Variegated Remarks on the *Spring and Autumn Annals*
Chu sanzang jiji   Collected Records from the Tripitaka
Chuyao jing   Dharmapada

Daban niepan jing   Mahāparinirvāṇa sūtra
Dadai liji   Historical Record of the Elder Dai
Dadong yin zhujing   Annotated Scripture of the Secrets of Great Pervasion
Dadong zhenjing   Perfect Scripture of Great Pervasion
Dafang guangfo huayan jing   Buddha avataṁsaka Sūtra (Garland Sūtra)
Dajie wen   The Great Precepts
Danshu lingbao zhenwen wupian   Perfect Text of Numinous Treasure in Cinnabar Writing
     and Five Tablets
Dantian jing   Cinnabar Field Scripture
Daobao jing   Scripture of the Treasure of the Tao

Daode jing   Scripture of the Tao and the Virtue

Daode jing kaiti xujue yishu   Supplementary Commentary and Topical Introduction to the
      Daode jing

Daode zhenjing guangsheng yi   Wide Sage Meaning of the Perfect Scripture of the Tao and
      the Virtue

Daode zhenjing xujue   Introductory Explanation to the *Daode jing*

Daojiao sandong zongyuan   The Ancestral Origin of the Three Caverns of the Taoist
      Teaching

Daojiao yishu   The Pivotal Meaning of the Taoist Teaching

Daolü   Tao Rules

Daomen jingfa   Scriptural Methods for Taoist Followers

Daomen kelue   Abbreviated Rules for Taoist Followers

Daoshi lilü   Ritual Rules for Taoists

Daoxue keyi   Rules and Observances for Students of the Tao

Daoyuan jing   Scripture of the Prime of the Tao

Daozang jinghua   Blossoms of the Taoist Canon

Daozang quejing mulu   Catalog of Lost Scriptures in the Taoist Canon

Daozhai jing   Scripture on Rites for the Tao

Da Sanpo lun   In Response to the "Threefold Destruction"

Da Tang xiyu ji   Record of Western Regions of the Great Tang Dynasty

Dayou jing   Scripture of Great Existence

Da Yuan Can bo Yixia lun   In Answer to Yuan Can's Criticism

Da Zhang shu bing wen Zhang   Answering Zhang's Letter and Posing Questions to the
      Author

Da zhidu lun   Mahāprajñāpāramitā-śāstra

Da Zhou Yong shu bing da suowen   Reply to Zhou Yong's Letter and Answer to His
      Questions

Dingzhi jing   Scripture on Setting the Will

Diwang shiji   Chronological Record of Emperors and Kings

Dongshen badi miaojing jing   Scripture on the Wondrous Essence of the Eight Emperors,
      Contained in Spirit Cavern

Dongshen jing   Scripture of Spirit Cavern

Dongxuan dongfang qingdi song   Eulogy for the Green Emperor of the East, Contained in
      Mystery Cavern

Dongxuan lingbao benxiang yundu jieqi jing   Scripture on Kalpa Revolutions in their Orig-
      inal Appearance, Contained in the Mystery Cavern of Numinous Treasure

Dongxuan lingbao tianzun shuo shijie jing   Scripture of Ten Precepts As Revealed by the
      Heavenly Venerable and Contained in the Mystery Cavern of Numinous Treasure

Dongxuan lingbao ziran jiutian shengshen zhangjing   Scripture of Stanzas of the Vital Spirit
      of the Nine Heavens of Spontaneity, Contained in the Mystery Cavern of Numinous
      Treasure

Dongzhen huangshu   Yellow Book of Perfection Cavern

Dongzhen taishang suling dongyuan dayou miaojing   Wondrous Scripture of Great Exis-
      tence of Simple Numen and Pervading Prime, Contained in Highest Perfection
      Cavern

Du guowang pin   Chapter on Saving the Kings

Duming miaojing   Wondrous Scripture on the Salvation of Life

Duren benxing jing   Scripture of the Original Endeavor of Universal Salvation
Duren jing   Scripture of Universal Salvation
Duren miaojing   Wondrous Scripture of Universal Salvation
Dushen pin   Chapter on Saving Oneself

Erjiao lun   On the Two Teachings
Erjiao yaolu   Essential Record of the Two Teachings

Fafu kejie wen   Rules and Precepts Regarding Ritual Garb
Fahua yishu   Commentary to the Lotus Sūtra
Falin biezhuan   Special Biography of the Monk Falin
Fanyi mingyi ji   Collection of Translated Terms and Meanings
Fayuan zhulin   Pearl Garden of the Dharma Forest
Fengdao kejie   Rules and Precepts for Worshiping the Tao
Fengfa yao   Essentials in Worshiping the Dharma
Fengsu tongyi   General Account of Popular Customs
Foban nihuan jing   Mahāparinirvāṇa sūtra
Fodao lunheng   Balanced Discussion of the Buddhist Way
Fo suoxing zan   Buddhaćarita
Fozu lidai tongzai   Comprehensive Account of Buddhist Patriarchs through the Ages
Fozu tongji   Comprehensive Record of Buddhist Patriarchs
Fuzhai jing   On the Performance of Rites

Gaoseng zhuan   Biographies of Eminent Monks
Gaoshi zhuan   Biographies of Eminent Men
Guang hongming ji   Expanded Record to Spread and Clarify [Buddhist Doctrine]
Guangshuo pin   Chapter of Broad Explanations
Guanling neizhuan   Inner Biography of the Guardian of the Pass
Guanshen dajie   Great Precepts of Self-observation
Guishan xuanlu   Mysterious Record of Turtle Mountain
Guizang   Safe Repository
Guliang zhuan   Guliang's Commentary [to the *Spring and Autumn Annals*]
Guoqu xianzai yinguo jing   Sūtra on Cause and Effect in Past, Present, and Future
Guoyu   Record of the States

Hanshu   History of the Han Dynasty
Han Wei congshu   Collected Works of the Han and Wei Dynasties
Heshang gong zhangju   Verses and Sayings of the Master on the River
Heshang zhenren zhangju   Verses and Sayings of the Perfected on the River
Hetu   River Chart
Hetu guadi xiang   River Chart Patterns of the Earth
Hongming ji   Record to Spread and Clarify [Buddhist Doctrine]
Hou Hanshu   History of the Later Han Dynasty
Huahu jing   Scripture of the Conversion of the Barbarians
Huainanzi   Writings of the Prince of Huainan
Huangdi neijing taisu   The Yellow Emperor's Classic on Internal Medicine, Great
    Simplicity

Huangdi neizhuan   Inner Biography of the Yellow Emperor
Huanglu dazhai yi   Observances of the Great Yellow Register Rite
Huangshu   Yellow Book
Huangting jing   Yellow Court Scripture
Huangting neijing jing   Inner Radiance Scripture of the Yellow Court
Huangting neijing yujing zhu   Jade Radiance Commentary to the Inner Radiance Scripture of the Yellow Court
Huangting waijing jing   Outer Radiance Scripture of the Yellow Court
Huayan jing   Avatamsaka Sūtra (Garland Sūtra)
Hunyuan benji   Original Record of Chaos Prime
Hunyuan shengji   Sage Record of Chaos Prime
Hunyuan zhenlu   Perfect Account of Chaos Prime

Jiansheng sita sengni yiguo limin shi   Memorial on Reducing Buddhist Institutions and Recluses in Order to Enhance the State and Benefit the People
Jiku jing   Scripture of Rescue from Suffering
Jindan jing   Scripture of Gold and Cinnabar
Jinglü yixiang   The Extraordinary World of Sūtras and Rules
Jingmu   Catalog of Scriptures
Jinkui lu   Record of the Golden Casket
Jinshi cuibian   Collected Items on Metal and Stone
Jinshi zalu   Miscellaneous Records of the Age of Jin
Jinshu   History of the Jin Dynasty
Jiuku jing   Scripture of Salvation from Suffering
Jiu Tangshu   Old History of the Tang Dynasty
Jiutian shengshen zhangjing   Stanzas of the Vital Spirit of the Nine Heavens
Jiuwei badao jing   Scripture of the Nine Tenuities and Eight Ways
Jiuzhang suanshu   Mathematical Arts in Nine Sections
Juedui Fu Yi feifo faseng shi   Strong Rebuttal of Fu Yi's Proposal to Abolish Buddhist Teachings and Recluses

Kaitian jing   Scripture on Opening the Cosmos
Kongzi jiayu   Kong Family Annals

Lao Dan fei daxian lun   Lao Dan Was Not a Great Worthy
Laojun bashiyi hua tushuo   Illustrated Explanations of the Eighty-One Transformations of the Venerable Lord
Laojun benqi jing   Scripture of the Original Endeavor of the Venerable Lord
Laojun jiejing   Precepts of the Venerable Lord
Loajun jinglü   Scriptural Rules of the Venerable Lord
Laojun nianpu   Chronology of the Venerable Lord
Laojun shuo yibai bashi jie   The One Hundred and Eighty Precepts Revealed by the Venerable Lord
Laojun yinsong jiejing   Scripture of Precepts Recited by the Venerable Lord
Laozi baibashi jie   The Hundred and Eighty Precepts of Laozi
Laozi bianhua jing   Scripture of the Transformations of Laozi

Laozi fushi jingshuo   Mr. Fu's Explanation to the *Laozi*

Laozi huahu ge   Song on Laozi Converting the Barbarians

Laozi miaozhen jing   Laozi's Scripture of Wondrous Perfection

Laozi shilue   Brief History of Laozi

Laozi xiaobing jing   Laozi's Scripture of Melting Ice

Laozi xisheng huahu jing   Scripture of Laozi's Western Ascension and Conversion of the Barbarians

Laozi xu   Introduction to the *Laozi*

Laozi yiwen fanxun   A Critical Examination of Doubtful Questions about Laozi

Laozi zhongjing   Central Scripture of Laozi

Liangshu   History of the Liang Dynasty

Lianshan   Connected Mountains

Lidai sanbao ji   Record of the Three Jewels through the Ages

Liexian zhuan   Immortals' Biographies

Liezi   Writings of Liezi

Liji   Book of Rites

Lingbao jing   Scripture of Numinous Treasure

Lingbao shoudu yibiao   Memorial on Transmission [of Scriptures] and Ordination in Numinous Treasure

Lingbao wuliang duren shangpin miaojing   Superb and Wondrous Scripture of Universal Salvation of Numinous Treasure

Lingbao zuigen pin   Numinous Treasure Scripture on the Roots of Sin

Lingshu jing   Scripture of Numinous Writings

Lishi apitan lun   Lokaprajñāpty-abhidharma

Lishi zhenxian tidao tongjian   Comprehensive Mirror through the Ages of Perfected Immortals and Those Who Embody the Tao

Louguan benji   Original Record of Louguan

Lunheng   Balanced Discussions

Lunyu   Analects of Confucius

Luoshu   Writ of the Luo River

Lüshi chunqiu   Spring and Autumn Annals of Mr. Lü

Mengzi   Writings of Mencius

Menlü   Instructions to My Followers

Miaofa hualian jing   Saddharmapuṇḍarīka Sūtra (Lotus Sūtra)

Miaomen youqi   Entrance to the Gate of All Wonders

Miaozhen ge   Song of Wondrous Perfection

Miaozhen jing   Scripture of Wondrous Perfection

Miehuo lun   To Dispel Errors

Mingfo lun   To Clarify Buddhism

Mingzhen ke   Rules for the Illustrious Perfected

Mohe moye jing   Mahāmāyā Sūtra

Mohe zhiguan   Great Treatise of Śamatha-Vipaśyanā

Mouzi lihuo lun   Mouzi's Correction of Errors

Mozi   Writings of Mozi

Mu tianzi zhuan   Biography of King Mu of Zhou

Nan Gu daoshi Yixia lun   In Critique of Taoist Gu's Treatise on Barbarians and Chinese
Nanjing   Classic of Difficult Issues
Nanji zhenren wenshi pin   Chapter of Questions Asked by the Perfected of South Culmen
Nan Qishu   History of the Southern Qi Dynasty
Nanshi   History of the Southern Dynasties
Neide lun   On Inner Virtue
Neidian beiming jixu   Introduction to the Palace Collection of Steles and Inscriptions
Neiguan jing   Scripture on Inner Observation
Niepan jing   Nirvāṇa Sūtra
Nüqing guilü   Nüqing's Statutes against Demons
Nüqing wen   Nüqing's Writ

Poxie lun   To Destroy Heresy

Qilu   Seven Sections
Qilu xiandao lu   Record of the Way of the Immortals in Seven Sections
Qingjing faxing jing   Sūtra on Practicing the Dharma in Purity and Clarity
Qizhi   Seven Treatises
Quan Qiwen   Complete Qi Literature
Quan Tangwen   Complete Tang Literature

Ronghua lun   On Barbarians and Chinese

Sanbao dayou jinshu   Book on the Three Treasures in Golden [Characters] Stored in [the
    Palace of] Great Existence
Sandong jingmu   Catalog of Scriptures in the Three Caverns
Sandong jingshu mulu   Catalog of Scriptures and Texts of the Three Caverns
Sandong zhunang   Bag of Pearls from the Three Caverns
Sanfu huangtu   Yellow Chart of the Three Mainstays
Sanguo zhi   Record of the Three Kingdoms
Sanhuang jing   Scripture of the Three Sovereigns
Sanhuang wen   Text of the Three Sovereigns
Sanlun xuanyi   Mysterious Meaning of the Three Treatises
Sanpo lun   On the Threefold Destruction Caused by Buddhism
Santian neijie jing   Scripture on the Esoteric Explanation of the Three Heavens
Santian zhengfa jing   Scripture of the Proper Law of the Three Heavens
Santu wuku jing   Scripture of the Three Bad Rebirths and Five Sufferings
Sanwu liji   Chronological Record of the Three and Five
Sanyuan pin   Precepts of the Three Primes
Shangqing dongzhen zhihui guanshen dajie wen   The Great Precepts of Wisdom and Self-
    Observation from the Truth Cavern of Highest Clarity
Shangqing huangshu guodu yi   Highest Clarity Oberservances for Salvation through the
    Yellow Book
Shangqing zhuzhen zhangsong   Eulogy Verses for the Assembled Perfected of Highest
    Clarity
Shangshu kao lingyao   Numinous Radiance in Analyzing the Book of History
Shanhai jing   Classic of Mountains and Seas

Shengxuan jing Scripture of Ascension to the Mystery
Shenxian jinye jing The Spirit Immortals' Scripture on the Golden Fluid
Shenxian zhuan Biographies of Spirit Immortals
Shenzhou jing Scripture of Divine Incantations
Shier shangpin quanjie Twelve High-Level Precepts
Shier youjing Sutra of the Twelve Wanderings
Shiji Historical Records
Shijia fangzhi Record of Śākya
Shijie jing The Ten Precepts
Shijie shisi chishen jing Scripture of the Ten Precepts and Fourteen Principles of Self-control
Shijing Book of Songs
Shiqing jing Scripture of Initial Clarity
Shi sanshijiu zhangjing Explanations to the Scripture in Thirty-nine Sections
Shishi yaolan Essential Observations for Buddhist Monks
Shisong lü Sarvāstivāda vinaya
Shiyi ji Collected Records of Things Inherited
Shiyi jiumi lun The Ten Differences and Nine Errors
Shizhou ji Record of the Ten Continents
Shuijing zhu Annotated River Classic
Shuji Record of Shu
Shujing Book of History
Shuowen jiezi zhu Annotated Character Dictionary
Shuoyuan Garden of Stories
Shushu jiyi Record of Mathematical Arts
Shuyi ji Record of Marvels
Shu yu Gu daoshi Letter to Taoist Gu
Siji mingke Illustrious Rules of the Four Ultimates
Siku quanshu Complete Books in the Four Storehouses
Sishier zhangjing Sūtra in Forty-Two Sections
Songshu History of the [Liu] Song Dynasty
Soushen ji In Search of the Supernatural
Suishu History of the Sui Dynasty
Suling jing Scripture of Immaculate Numen

Taidan yinshu Great Cinnabar Secret Writings
Taigong liutao Six Tactics of Taigong
Taiji zhenren fu lingbao zhaijie weiyi zhujing yaojue Essential Formulas of the Various Numinous Treasure Scriptures on the Majestic Observances of Rites and Precepts, Distributed by the Perfected of Great Ultimate
Taiping guangji Expansive Record of the Taiping Era
Taiping jing Scripture of Great Peace
Taiping yulan Imperial Encyclopedia of the Taiping Era
Taiqing zhonghuang zhenjing Perfect Scripture of Central Yellow of Great Clarity
Taishang dongxuan lingbao miedu wulian shengshi miaojing Wondrous Scripture of Salvation from Extinction through Fivefold Purification for Reviving the Dead, Contained in the Mystery Cavern of Highest Numinous Treasure

Taishang dongxuan lingbao sanyuan pinjie gongde qingzhong jing   Scripture on the Weight of Merit and Virtue As Based on the Precepts of the Three Primes Contained in the Mystery Cavern of Highest Numinous Treasure

Taishang dongxuan lingbao shengxuan neijiao jing   Scripture of the Esoteric Teaching on Ascension to the Mystery Contained in the Mystery Cavern of Highest Numinous Treasure

Taishang dongxuan lingbao tianzun shuo jiku jing   Scripture of Rescue from Suffering Revealed by the Heavenly Venerable and Contained in the Mystery Cavern of Highest Numinous Treasure

Taishang dongxuan lingbao zhenwen duren benxing miaojing   Scripture of the Original Endeavor of Universal Salvation, Perfected Writing of Highest Numinous Treasure Contained in Mystery Cavern

Taishang dongxuan lingbao zhihui zuigen shangpin dajie   Great Precepts of the Upper Section Regarding the Roots of Wisdom and Sin, Contained in the Mystery Cavern of Highest Numinous Treasure

Taishang laojun zaoli tiandi chuji   Record of the Beginnings of Heaven and Earth as Created by the Highest Venerable Lord

Taishang lingbao wufuxu   Explanation of the Five Talismans of Highest Numinous Treasure

Taishang lingbao zhutian neiyin ziran yuzi   Esoteric Sounds and Spontaneous Jade Characters of All Heavens of Highest Numinous Treasure

Taishang zhutian lingshu duming miaojing   Wondrous Scripture on the Salvation of Life in the Numinous Writing of the Various Heavens

Taixuan   Great Mystery

Taizi ruiying benqi jing   Sūtra of the Original Endeavor of the Prince in Accordance with All Good Omens

Tangji   Tang Record

Tangshu   History of the Tang Dynasty

Tiandi yundu jing   Scripture on the Revolutions of Heaven and Earth

Tianguan jing   Scripture of the Heavenly Pass

Tianguan santu   Three Ways to Go beyond the Heavenly Pass

Weigui ke   Observances to Scare off Demons

Weilue   Short Record of the Wei Dynasty

Weimo jing   Vimalakīrti nideśa sūtra

Wenshi xiansheng wushang zhenren guanling neizhuan   The Inner Biography of Master Wenshi, Highest Perfected and Guardian of the Pass

Wenshi zhenjing   Perfect Scripture of Master Wenshi

Wenshi zhuan   Biography of Master Wenshi

Wufu jing   Scripture of the Five Talismans

Wujing suanshu   Calculation Arts of the Five Classics

Wulian jing   Scripture of Fivefold Purification

Wupian zhenwen chishu   Five Sections of Perfect Texts in Red Characters

Wuqian wen   Text in Five Thousand Words

Wushang biyao   Esoteric Essentials of the Most High

Wuxing dayi   Great Meaning of the Five Phases

Wu Yue chunqiu   Spring and Autumn Annals of Wu and Yue
Wuyue zhenxing tu   Chart of the True Shape of the Five Sacred Mountains

Xiangfa jueyi jing   Sūtra to Allay Doubts during the Age of Semblance Dharma
Xiaodao lun   Laughing at the Tao
Xiaojing   Classic of Filial Piety
Xichuan qingyang gong beiming   Inscription of the Black Sheep Temple in Sichuou
Xinlun   New Discussions
Xirong zhuan   Chronicle of the Western Barbarians
Xisheng jing   Scripture of Western Ascension
Xiyu zhuan   Chronicle of Western Regions
Xuandu guan jingmu   Catalog of Scriptures of the Monastery of Mystery Metropolis
Xuandu jingmu   Catalog of Scriptures of Mystery Metropolis
Xuandu lüwen   Rules of Mystery Metropolis
Xuange   Song of Mystery
Xuanmen dayi   Great Meaning of the Gate of All Wonders
Xuanmiao neipian   Esoteric Record of Mystery and Wonder
Xuanmiao yunü yuanjun neipian   Esoteric Record of the Goddess Jade Maiden of Mystery
    and Wonder
Xuanyan xinji minglao bu   Illuminated and Venerable Sections in the New Record of
    Mysterious Words
Xuanzhong jing   Scripture of Central Mystery
Xuanzi   Writings of the Master of Mystery
Xu gaoseng zhuan   Further Biographies of Eminent Monks
Xunzi   Writings of Xunzi

Yaodian   Book of Yao
Yaoshu   History of the Yao Dynasty
Yaoxiu keyi   Essential Rules and Observances
Yijiao jing   Scripture of Testamentary Teachings
Yijing   Book of Changes
Yilin   Forest of Changes
Yinfu jing   Scripture of Hidden Correspondences
Yiwen leiju   Classified Collection of Artistic Writings
Yixia lun   Treatise on Barbarians and Chinese
Yi Yixia lun zi Gu Daoshi   Doubts about the Treatise on Barbarians and Chinese, Ad-
    dressed to Taoist Gu
Yizhou ji   Record of Yi Province
Yongcheng jixian lu   Record of the Assembled Immortals in the Heavenly Walled City
Youlong zhuan   Like onto a Dragon
Youming lu   Record of Darkness and Light
Youwu shengcheng pin   Chapter on Being and Nonbeing, Birth and Completion
Yuanqi lun   On Primordial Energy
Yuanshi zhuan   Biography of Master Yuanshi
Yuanyang jing   Scripture of Primordial Yang
Yudao lun   To Illustrate the Way

Yuejing   Book of Music
Yundu jieqi jing   Scripture on Kalpa Revolutoins
Yunji qiqian   Seven Tablets in a Cloudy Satchel
Yuwei qibu jing mulu   Catalog of Scriptures and Texts of the Jade Warp in Seven Divisions

Za ahan jing   Samyuktāgama
Zao tiandi ji   Record of the Creation of Heaven and Earth
Zengyi ahanjing   Ekottarāgama
Zhaolun   Treatises of Sengzhao
Zhengao   Declarations of the Perfected
Zheng erjiao lun   Correcting the Position of the Two Teachings
Zhengwu lun   Rectification of Unjustified Criticism
Zhengyi lun   On True Oneness
Zhengyi yuelu yi   Arranged Observances of Orthodox Unity
Zhenren neichao lü   Rules of the Perfected for Proper Homage in the Inner Chamber
Zhenren neili daojia neishi lü   Esoteric Rites of the Perfected and Rules for Taoists in Attendance in the Inner Chamber
Zhenren neili yishi jiaxing daolü   Tao Rules of the Perfected for the Practice of Esoteric Rites While Attending on the Preceptor and at Home
Zhenshu   Bood of the Perfected
Zhenyi ziran jingjue   Scriptural Instructions of Spontaneity of Perfect Unity
Zhenzheng lun   To Examine What Is Right
Zhidu lun   Prajñāpāramitā-śāstra
Zhihui guanshen dajie jing   Scripture of Great Precepts of Wisdom and Self-observation
Zhongxian ji   Collection of the Host of Immortals
Zhou chong dashu bing wen chongwen   Zhou's Counterreply Asking Further Question
Zhougui jing   Scripture of Spells against Demons
Zhouli   Rites of the Zhou
Zhoushu   History of the Northern Zhou Dynasty
Zhuangzi   Writings of Zhuangzi
Zhuanxing jiku jing   Scripture on Rescue from Suffering in the Rebirth Cycle
Zhunang jingmu   Catalog of the Pearly Bag
Zhutian neiyin   Esoteric Sounds of All Heavens
Zhutian neiyin bazi wen   Esoteric Sounds of All Heavens in Eight Character Verses
Zhutian neiyin yuzi   Esoteric Sounds and Spontaneous Jade Characters of All Heavens
Ziran jing   Scripture of Spontaneity
Ziyang zhenren neizhuan   Inner Biography of Ziyang the Perfected
Zuigen pin   The Roots of Sin
Zuozhuan   Mr. Zuo's Commentary to the *Spring and Autumn Annals*

GLOSSARY

An Lushan 安錄山
Anmo jing 安摩經
Apitan piposha lun 阿毘曇毘婆沙論
Ayu wang jing 阿育王經

Badi jing 八帝經
Baishi xiansheng 白石先生
Bao Jing 鮑靚
Baopuzi 抱朴子
Baopuzi fushi fang 抱朴子服食方
Baopuzi shenxian jinzhuo jing
　　抱朴子神仙金汋經
Benji 本紀
Benji jing 本際經
Bianhuo lun 辯惑論
Bian Shao 邊韶
Bianzheng lun 辨正論
Biran lun 必然論
Biyao juefa 秘要訣法
Bo He 帛和
Bowuzhi 博物志
Bo Yi 伯夷
Bo Yixia lun 駁夷夏論
Buzhou 不州

Cangjie 蒼頡
Cao Zhi 曹植
Chang'an zhi 長安志
Cheng Xuanying 成玄英
Che Ni 車匿
Chen Jiao 陳焦
Chen Jingyuan 陳京元
Chen Tuan 東搏
chi 尺
Chiming 赤明
Chishu yujue 赤書玉訣

Chiyou 蚩尤
Chong shu yu Gu daoshi 重書與顧道士
Chongxuan 重玄
Chongxuanzi 沖玄子
Chongxu guan 崇虛觀
Chuci 楚辭
Chuji 初記
Chu liutian zhi wen santian zhengfa jing
　　除六天之文三天正法經
chun 椿
Chunqiu 春秋
Chunqiu fanlu 春秋繁露
Chu sanzang jiji 出三藏記集
Chuyao jing 出曜經
Cui Hao 崔浩
Cuiwenzi 崔文子
Cuiwenzi zhouhou jing 崔文子肘後經
cun 寸

Daban niepan jing 大般涅槃經
Dadai liji 大戴禮記
Dadong yin zhujing 大洞隱注經
Dadong zhenjing 大洞眞經
Dafang guangfo huayan jing
　　大方廣佛華嚴經
Dajie wen 大戒文
Danshu lingbao zhenwen wupian
　　丹書靈寶眞文五篇
Dantian jing 丹田經
Danyuan zhenren 丹元眞人
Daobao jing 道寶經
Daode jing 道德經
Daode jing kaiti xujue yishu
　　道德經開題序訣義疏
Daode xuanyi 道德玄義
Daode zhenjing guangsheng yi
　　道德眞經廣聖義

Daode zhenjing xujue 道德眞經序訣

Daojiao sandong zongyuan
道敎三洞宗元

Daojiao yishu 道敎義樞

Daoli tian 忉利天

Daolü 道律

Daomen jingfa 道門經法

Daomen kelue 道門科略

daoren 道人

daoshi 道士

Daoshi lilü 道士禮律

Daoxue keyi 道學科儀

Daoyin tu 導引圖

Daoyuan jing 道元經

Daozang jinghua 道藏精華

Daozhai jing 道齋經

Da Sanpo lun 答三破論

Da Tang xiyu ji 大唐西域記

Dayou jing 大月經

Da Yuan Can bo Yixia lun
答袁粲駁夷夏論

Da Zhang shu bing wen Zhang
答張書幷問張

Da zhidu lun 大智度論

Da Zhou Yong shu bing da suowen
答周顒書幷答所問

Di 狄

Di Ku 帝嚳

Dingxin jing 定心經

Dingzhi jing 定志經

Diwang shiji 帝王世紀

Dongshen jing 洞神經

Dongxuan dongfang qingdi song
洞玄東方青帝頌

*Dongxuan lingbao benxiang yundu jieqi
jing* 洞玄靈寶本相運度劫期經

Dongxuan lingbao tianzun shuo shijie jing
洞玄靈寶天尊說十戒經

*Dongxuan lingbao ziran jiutian shengshen
zhangjing* 洞玄靈寶自然九天生神
章經

Dongzhen huangshu 洞眞黃書

*Dongzhen taishang suling dongyuan dayou
miaojing* 洞眞太上素靈洞元大有
妙經

Du Guangting 杜光庭

Du guowang pin 度國王品

Duming miaojing 度命妙經

Dunhuang 敦煌

Duren benxing jing 度人本行經

Duren miaojing 度人妙經

Dushen pin 度身品

Du Yu 杜預

Erjiao lun 二敎論

Erjiao yaolu 二敎要錄

Fafu kejie wen 法服科戒文

Fahua yishu 法華義疏

Falin biezhuan 法琳別傳

Fan Li 范蠡

Fanyi mingyi ji 翻譯名義集

Fayuan zhulin 法苑珠林

Fengdao kejie 奉道科戒

Fengfa yao 奉法要

fengshui 風水

Fengsu tongyi 風俗通義

Foban nihuan jing 佛般泥洹經

Fodao lunheng 佛道論衡

Fo suoxing zan 佛所行讚

fotu 佛圖

Fotudeng 佛圖澄

foutu 浮屠

foutú 浮圖

Fozu lidai tongzai 佛祖歷代通戴

Fozu tongji 佛祖通紀

Fudaogai 扶刀蓋

Fuligai 扶力蓋

Fushi qinjijing 服食禁忌經

Fu Xi 伏羲

Fu Yi 傅弈

Fu Yue 傅說

Fuzhai jing 敷齋經

Fuzi 符子

Gan Ji 干吉
Gan Shi 干室
Gaoseng zhuan 高僧傳
Gaoshi zhuan 高士傳
Ge Chaofu 葛巢甫
Ge Hong 葛洪
Ge Xuan 葛玄
Gonggong 共工
Gou Jian 句踐
Guaiyi zhi 怪異志
Guangchengzi 廣成子
Guang hongming ji 廣弘明記
Guangshuo pin 廣說品
Guanling neizhuan 關令內傳
Guanshen dajie 觀身大戒
Guanyin 觀音
Gu Huan 顧歡
Guigen lun 歸根論
Guigu xiansheng bianhua lei jing
　　鬼谷先生變化類經
Guiguzi 鬼谷子
Guishan xuanlu 龜山玄錄
Guizang 歸藏
Guliang zhuan 穀梁傳
Guo Pu 郭璞
Guoqu xianzai yinguo jing
　　過去見在因果經
Guoshuzi 郭叔子
Guoyu 國語

Han Pingzi 韓平子
Hanshu 漢書
Han Wei congshu 漢魏叢書
Han Zhong 韓終
Helü 闔閭
Heshang gong 河上公
Heshang zhenren zhangju
　　河上眞人章句
Hetu 河圖
Hetu guadi xiang 河圖括地象
Hongming ji 弘明記
Hou Hanshu 後漢書

Hu 胡
Huahu jing 化胡經
Huainanzi 淮南子
huangdi 皇帝
Huangdi 黃帝
Huangdi longshou jing 黃帝龍首經
Huangdi neijing taisu 黃帝內經太素
Huangdi neizhuan 黃帝內傳
huangjing 黃精
Huang Jinghua 黃景華
Huanglu dazhai yi 黃籙大齋儀
Huangshu 黃書
Huangting nei/wai jing jing 黃庭內 /
　　外景經
Huan Tan 桓譚
Huan Xuan 桓玄
Huayan jing 華嚴經
Huaziqi 華子期
Huhai 胡亥
Huilin 慧琳
Huiyuan 慧遠
Huizong 徽宗
Hulao 虎牢
Hunyuan benji 混元本紀
Hunyuan shengji 混元聖紀
Hunyuan zhenlu 混元眞錄
Huolin 霍林
Hu Zhi 古質

ji 跡
jia 甲
Jiang Bin 姜斌
Jiangdu Wang Sisheng 江都王思聖
Jian Pingzi 建平子
Jiansheng sita sengni yiguo limin shi
　　減省寺塔僧尼益國利民事
jiao 醮
Jiku jing 濟苦經
Jindan jing 金丹經
Jinglü yixiang 經律異相
Jingmu 經目
Jingui lu 金匱錄

Jinshi cuibian 金石萃編
Jinshi zalu 晉世雜錄
Jinshu 晉書
Jiugong shigui xujing 九宮蓍龜序經
Jiuku jing 救苦經
Jiu Tangshu 舊唐書
Jiutian shengshen zhangjing
　　九天生神章經
Jiuwei badao jing 九微八道經
Jiuzhang suanshu 九章算術
Jizang 吉藏
Juedui Fu Yi feifo faseng shi
　　決對傅奕廢佛法僧事
Juling 巨靈

Kaihuang 開皇
Kaitian jing 開天經
Kang Shao 康邵
Kongzi jiayu 孔子家語
Kou Qianzhi 寇謙之
Kunlun 崑崙
Kunwu 昆吾

Lao Dan 老聃
Lao Dan fei daxian lun 老聃非大賢論
Laojun bashiyi hua tushuo
　　老君八十一化圖說
Laojun benqi jing 老君本起經
Laojun jiejing 老君戒經
Laojun jinglü 老君經律
Laojun nianpu 老君年譜
Laojun shuo yibai bashi jie
　　老君說一百八十戒
Laojun yinsong jiejing 老君音誦誡經
Laozi 老子
Laozi baibashi jie 老子百八十戒
Laozi bianhua jing 老子變化經
Laozi miaozhen jing 老子妙眞經
Laozi ming 老子銘
Laozi shilue 老子史略
Laozi xiaobing jing 老子消冰經
Laozi xisheng huahu jing
　　老子西昇化胡經

Laozi xu 老子序
Laozi yiwen fanxun 老子疑問反訊
Laozi zhongjing 老子中經
Le Penggui 樂朋龜
Lezichang 樂子長
Liang Qiuzi 梁邱子
Liangshu 梁書
Lianshan 連山
Li Babai 李八百
Lidai sanbao ji 歷代三寶記
Liexian zhuan 列仙傳
Liezi 列子
Liji 禮記
Lingbao 靈寶
Lingbao chishu yujue 靈寶赤書玉訣
Lingbao shoudu yibiao 靈寶授度儀表
Lingbao wuliang duren shangpin miaojing
　　靈寶無量度人上品妙經
Lingshu jing 靈書經
Lin Lingsu 林靈素
Li Rong 李榮
Li Shaowei 李少微
Lishi apitan lun 立世阿毘曇論
Li Shizheng 李師政
Lishi zhenxian tidao tongjian
　　歷世眞仙體道通鑑
Liu Gen 劉根
Liu-Han 劉漢
Liu Ji 劉基
Liu Renhui 劉仁會
Liu Xiang 劉向
Liu Xie 劉勰
Liu Yan 劉焉
Liu Yu 劉裕
Li Ying 李膺
Li Zhongqing 李仲卿
Longhan 龍漢
Louguan benji 樓觀本記
Lu Ao 盧敖
Lunheng 論衡
Lunyu 論語
Luoshu 洛書
Lüshi chunqiu 呂氏春秋

Lu Wan 盧綰
Lü Wang 呂王
Lu Xiujing 陸修靜

Man 蠻
Meng Fashi 孟法師
Meng Jingyi 孟景翼
Mengzi 孟子
Menlü 門律
Miaofa lianhua jing 妙法蓮華經
Miaomen youqi 妙門由起
Miaozhen ge/jing 妙眞歌 / 經
Miehuo lun 滅惑論
Mingfa lun 明法論
Mingfo lun 明佛論
Ming Sengshao 明僧紹
Mingzhen ke 明眞科
Mohe moye jing 摩訶摩耶經
Mohe zhiguan 摩訶止觀
Mouzi lihuo lun 牟子理惑論
Mozi 墨子
Murong 墓容
Mu tianzi zhuan 穆天子傳

Nan Gu daoshi Yixia lun
    難顧道士夷夏論
Nanjing 難經
Nanji zhenren wenshi pin
    南極眞人問事品
Nan Qishu 南齊書
Nanshi 南史
nanwu 南無
Neide lun 內德論
Neidian beiming jixu 內典碑銘集序
Neiguan jing 內觀經
neizhuan 內傳
Niepan jing 涅槃經
Nügua 女媧
Nüqing guilü 女青鬼律
Nüqing wen 女青文

Pangu 盤古
Pei Songzhi 裴松之

Pei Ziye 裴子野
Pengzu jijing 彭祖記經
pi 匹
Poxie lun 破邪論

qi 氣
Qilu 七錄
Qilu xiandao lu 七錄仙道錄
Qingjing faxing jing 清淨法行經
qingxin dizi 清信弟子
Qingyang gong 靑羊宮
Qin Shi 秦失
Qizhi 七志
Quan Qiwen 全齊文
Quan Tangwen 全唐文

Riyue mingjing jing 日月明鏡經
Rong 戎
Ronghua lun 戎華論
Ruan Xiaoxu 阮孝緒
Rutong 儒童

Sanbao dayou jinshu 三寶大有金書
Sandong jingmu 三洞經目
Sandong jingshu mulu 三洞經書目錄
Sandong zhunang 三洞珠囊
Sanfu huangtu 三輔黃圖
sāngmen 桑門
sangmen 喪門
Sanguo zhi 三國志
Sanhuang jing/wen 三皇經 / 文
Sanlun xuanyi 三論玄義
Sanmen lun 三門論
Sanpo lun 三破論
Santian neijie jing 三天內解經
Santian zhengfa jing 三天正法經
Santu wuku jing 三途五苦經
Sanwu liji 三五曆紀
Sanyuan pin 三元品
Sengyou 僧祐
Sengzhao 僧肇
shamen 沙門
Shanghuang 上皇

Shangqing 上清

*Shangqing dongzhen zhihui guanshen dajie
wen* 上清洞眞智慧觀身大戒文

Shangqing huangshu guodu yi
上清黃書過度儀

Shangqing zhuzhen zhangsong
上清諸眞章頌

Shangshu kao lingyao 尙書考靈曜

Shanhai jing 山海經

shanxin nan/nü 善信男 / 女

Shaoweng 少翁

shatai 沙汰

Shengxuan jing 昇玄經

Shennong 神農

Shenshu 神荼

Shen Xi 沈羲

Shenxian jinye jing 神仙金液經

Shenxian zhuan 神仙傳

Shenxiao 神霄

Shenzhou jing 神咒經

Shi Daoan 釋道安

Shier shangpin quanjie 十二上品權戒

Shier youjing 十二遊經

Shi Falin 釋法琳

Shiguang wei Xigongzi shouyao jing
師曠爲西宮子授藥經

Shi Hu 石虎

Shi Huitong 釋惠通

Shiji 史記

Shijia fangzhi 釋迦方志

Shijie jing 十誡經

Shijie shisi chishen jing 十誡十四持身經

Shijing 詩經

Shi Le 石勒

Shi Minggai 釋明槪

Shiqing jing 始清經

Shi sanshijiu zhangjing 釋三十九章經

Shi Sengmin 釋僧敏

Shi Sengshun 釋僧順

Shishi yaolan 釋氏要覽

shisi chishen 十四持身

Shisong lü 十誦律

Shi Xuanguang 釋玄光

Shiyi ji 拾遺記

Shiyi jiumi lun 十異九迷論

Shizhou ji 十洲記

Shuijing zhu 水經註

Shuji 蜀記

Shujing 書經

Shun 舜

Shuowen jiezi zhu 說文解字注

Shuo yinyang jing 說陰陽經

Shuoyuan 說苑

Shuqi 叔齊

Shushu jiyi 數術記遺

Shuyi ji 述異記

Shu yu Gu daoshi 書與顧道士

Shuzun 叔遵

Siji mingke 四極明科

Siku quanshu 四庫全書

Siku tiyao 四庫提要

Sishier zhangjing 四十二章經

Songgao shan 嵩高山

Songshu 宋書

Soushen ji 搜神記

Suishu 隋書

Suitong lun 遂通論

Su Lin 蘇林

Suling jing 素靈經

Sun Chuo 孫卓

Sun En 孫恩

Sun Zheng 孫盛

Taidan yinshu 太丹隱書

Taigong liutao 太公六韜

Taigong wang 太公王

*Taiji zhenren fu lingbao zhaijie weiyi zhu-
jing yaojue* 太極眞人敷靈寶齋戒威
儀諸經要訣

Taiping guangji 太平廣記

Taiping jing 太平經

Taiping yulan 太平御覽

Taiqing zhonghuang zhenjing
太清中黃眞經

Taishang 太上

Taishang dongxuan lingbao miedu wulian

shengshi miaojing 太上洞玄靈寶滅度五煉生尸妙經

Taishang dongxuan lingbao sanyuan pinjie gongde qingzhong jing 太上洞玄靈寶三元品戒功德輕重經

Taishang dongxuan lingbao shengxuan neijiao jing 太上洞玄靈寶昇玄內教經

Taishang dongxuan lingbao tianzun shuo jiku jing 太上洞玄靈寶天尊說濟苦經

Taishang dongxuan lingbao zhenwen duren benxing miaojing 太上洞玄靈寶真文度人本行妙經

Taishang dongxuan lingbao zhihui zuigen shangpin dajie jing 太上洞玄靈寶智慧罪根上品大戒經

Taishang laojun zaoli tiandi chuji 太上老君造立天地初記

Taishang lingbao wufuxu 太上靈寶五符序

Taishang lingbao zhutian neiyin ziran yuzi 太上靈寶諸天內音自然玉字

Taishang zhutian lingshu duming miaojing 太上諸天靈書度命妙經

Taixuan 太玄

Taixuan jing jing 太玄鏡經

Taiyi 太一

Taizi ruiying benqi jing 太子瑞應本起經

Tangji 唐紀

Tangshu 唐書

Tanmuzui 曇漠最

Tanyao 曇曜

Tao Hongjing 陶弘景

Tao Zhu bianhua shu jing 陶朱變化術經

Tiandi yundu jing 天地運度經

Tianguan jing 天關經

Tianguan santu 天關三圖

Tianlao 天老

Tianshi 天師

Tianzhen huangren 天真皇人

Tongdao guan 通道觀

Tudigong 土地公

Tujue 突厥

Wang Bi 王弼

Wang Fangping 王方平

Wang Fou 王浮

Wang Gongqi 王公期

Wang Mingguang 王明光

Wang Xizhi 王羲之

Wang Xuanhe 王懸河

Wang Yan 王延

Wang Yuan 王遠

Wang Yuanzhi 王遠知

Wei Jie 韋節

Weilue 魏略

Weimo jing 維摩經

Wei Wangzhi 衛王直

Wei Yuansong 衛元嵩

Wenshi xiansheng wushang zhenren guanling neizhuan 文始先生無上真人關令內傳

Wenshi zhenjing 文始真經

Wenshi zhuan 文始傳

Wenxuan 文選

Wufu jing/xu 五符經／序

Wujing suanshu 五經算術

Wulian jing 五鍊經

wuming shi 無名氏

Wupian zhenwen chishu 五篇真文赤書

Wuqian wen 五千文

Wushang biyao 無上祕要

Wuxing dayi 五行大義

Xianbi 鮮卑

Xiangfa jueyi jing 相法決疑經

Xiang Kai 襄楷

Xianyang 咸陽

Xiaodao lun 笑道論

Xiao Ji 蕭吉

Xiaojing 孝經

Xi Chao 郤超

Xichuan qingyang gong beiming
西川青羊宮碑銘
Xie Shouhao 謝守灝
Xieyizi 爕邑子
Xie Zhenzhi 謝鎮之
Xingli zhaishe fa 興利宅舍法
xingqi 行氣
Xinlun 新論
Xiongnu 匈奴
Xirong zhuan 西戎傳
Xisheng jing 西昇經
Xishouzi 錫壽子
Xiwangmu 西王母
Xiyu zhuan 西域傳
Xizezi 錫則子
Xuandu (guan) jingmu 玄都(觀)經目
Xuandu lüwen 玄都律文
Xuange 玄歌
Xuanmen dayi 玄門大義
Xuanmiao neipian 玄妙內篇
Xuanmiao yunü yuanjun neipian
玄妙玉女元君內篇
Xuanyan xinji minglao bu
玄言新記明老部
Xuanzhong jing 玄中經
Xuanzi 玄子
Xuanzong 玄宗
Xuchengzi 續成子
Xue Youlou 薛幽樓
Xu gaoseng zhuan 續高僧傳
Xu Jia 徐甲
Xu Laile 徐來勒
Xu Miao 徐邈
Xunzi 荀子

Yan Dong 嚴東
Yangsheng jing 養生經
Yang Xi 楊羲
Yangxing jing 養性經
Yang Xiong 楊雄
Yan Hui 顏回
Yanming 炎明
Yao 堯

Yaodian 堯典
Yaoshu 姚書
Yaoxiu keyi 要修科義
Yi 夷
Yijiao jing 遺教經
Yijing 易經
Yinfu jing 隱符經
Yin Gui 尹軌
Yingyin lun 榮隱論
Yin Wencao 尹文操
Yinwenzi 尹文子
Yin Xi 尹喜
Yiwen leiju 藝文類聚
Yixia lun 夷夏論
Yi Yixia lun zi Gu Daoshi
疑夷夏論諮顧道士
Yizhou ji 益州記
Yongcheng jixian lu 墉城集仙錄
Youlong zhuan 猶龍傳
Youming lu 幽明錄
youpose 憂婆塞
youpoyi 憂婆夷
Youwu shengsheng pin 有無生成品
Yu 禹
Yuan Can 袁粲
Yuande 元德
Yuanqi lun 元氣論
Yuanshi zhuan 元始傳
Yuanyang jing 元陽經
Yuanzi 肙子
Yudao lun 喻道論
Yuejing 樂經
Yulu 鬱壘
Yundu jieqi jing 運度劫期經
Yunji qiqian 雲笈七籤
Yunmeng shan 雲夢山
Yuwei qibu jing mulu 玉緯七部經目錄
Yuwen Hu 宇文護
Yuwen Tai 宇文泰
Yuwen Yong 宇文雍

Za ahan jing 雜阿含經
Zao tiandi ji 造天地記

ze luo jue pu tai yuan da luo qian
　澤落覺菩臺緣大羅千

Zengyi ahan jing 增一阿含經

Zhang Bin 張賓

Zhang Daoling 張道陵

Zhang Heng 張衡

Zhang Liang 張良

Zhang Lu 張魯

Zhang Qian 張騫

Zhang Rong 張融

Zhang Wanfu 張萬福

Zhang Yuezhi 張說之

Zhang Zhan 張湛

Zhaolun 肇論

Zhen Dan 甄亶

Zhengao 眞誥

Zheng erjiao lun 正二敎論

Zheng Siyuan 鄭思遠

Zhengyi (lun) 正一（論）

Zheng Yin 鄭隱

Zhengyi yuelu yi 正一閱籙儀

Zhen Luan 甄鸞

Zhenren neichao lü 眞人內朝律

Zhenren neili daojia neishi lü
　眞人內禮道家內侍律

Zhenren neili yishi jiaxing daolü
　眞人內禮詣師家行道律

Zhenxingzi 鎭行子

Zhenyi ziran jingjue 眞一自然經訣

Zhenzheng lun 甄正論

Zhibing jing 治病經

Zhicao tujing 芝草圖經

Zhidu lun 智度論

Zhihui dingzhi jing 智慧定志經

Zhihui guanshen dajie 智慧觀身大戒

Zhilian wushi 治練五石

Zhishi 智實

Zhongxian ji 衆仙集

Zhou chong dashu bing wen chongwen
　周重答書幷問重問

Zhougui jing 咒鬼經

Zhouli 周禮

Zhoushu 周書

Zhou Yong 周顒

Zhou Ziyang 周紫陽

Zhuangzi 莊子

Zhuanxing jiku jing 轉形濟苦經

Zhuan Xu 顓頊

Zhu Guangzhi 朱廣之

Zhunang jingmu 珠囊經目

Zhutian neiyin (yuzi) 諸天內音（玉字）

Zhu Zhaozhi 朱昭之

Zhuzi jicheng 諸子集成

Zibei 子碑

Ziran jing 自然經

Ziran yinyuan lun 自然因緣論

Ziyang zhenren neizhuan 紫陽眞人內傳

Zouyangzi 鄒陽子

Zuigen pin 罪根品

Zuozhuan 左傳

Akizuki Kan'ei. 1964. "Rikuchō dōkyō ni okeru ōhōsetsu no hatten." *Jimbun shakai* 33:25–60.

———. 1965. "Sairon sangen shisō no keisei." *Hirosaki daigaku bunkei ronsō* 1:437–56.

———. 1983. "Dōkyō shi." In *Dōkyō,* edited by Fukui Kōjun, Yamazaki Hiroshi, Kimura Eiichi, and Sakai Tadao, 1:31–57. Tokyo: Hirakawa.

Allan, Sarah. 1972. "The Identities of T'ai-kung-wang in Chou and Han Literature." *Monumenta Serica* 29:57–99.

———. 1981. *The Heir and the Sage: A Structural Analysis of Ancient Chinese Dynastic Legends.* San Francisco, Calif.: Chinese Materials Center.

———. 1984. "Drought, Human Sacrifice and the Mandate of Heaven in a Lost Text from the *Shang shu.*" *Bulletin of the School of Oriental and African Studies* 47:523–39.

———. 1991. *The Shape of the Turtle: Myth, Art and Cosmos in Early China.* Albany: State University of New York Press.

Andersen, Poul. 1980. *The Method of Holding the Three Ones.* London: Curzon Press.

———. 1990. "The Practice of *Bugang.*" *Cahiers d'Extrême-Asie* 5:15–53.

Asano Yūichi. 1982. "Taiheikyō ni okeru kyūkyokusha." *Tōhōshūkyō* 60:1–22.

Aspinwall, Marguerite. 1927. *Jataka Tales out of Old India.* New York: G. P. Putnam's Sons.

Bareau, André. 1955. *Les premiers concils bouddhiques.* Paris: Annales du Musée Guimet, no. 60.

Bauer, Wolfgang. 1956. "Der Herr vom gelben Stein." *Oriens Extremus* 3:137–52.

Baxter, William H. 1983. "A Look at the History of Chinese Color Terminology." *Journal of the Chinese Language Teachers Association* 19, no. 1:1–25.

Beal, Samuel. 1871. *A Catena of Buddhist Scriptures from the Chinese.* London: Trubner.

Bell, Catherine. 1987. "Lu Hsiu-ching." In *Encyclopedia of Religion.* Edited by Mircea Eliade, 9:50–51. New York: Macmillan.

Benn, Charles D. 1987. "Religious Aspects of Emperor Hsüan-tsung's Taoist Ideology." In *Buddhist and Taoist Practice in Medieval Chinese Society,* edited by David W. Chappell, 127–45. Honolulu: University of Hawaii Press.

———.1991. *The Cavern Mystery Transmission: A Taoist Ordination Rite of A.D. 711.* Honolulu: University of Hawaii Press.

Bennett, Stephen. 1978. "Patterns of the Sky and Earth: A Chinese Science of Applied Cosmology." *Chinese Science* 3:1–26.

Bhandarkar, D. R. 1955. *Aśoka.* Calcutta: Calcutta University Press.

Bilsky, Lester J. 1975. *The State Religion of Ancient China.* 2 vols. Taipei: Chinese Folklore Association.

Bodde, Derk. 1975. *Festivals in Classical China.* Princeton: Princeton University Press.

Bokenkamp, Stephen. 1983. "Sources of the Ling-pao Scriptures." In *Tantric and Taoist Studies,* edited by Michel Strickmann, 2:434–86. Brussels: Institut Belge des Hautes Etudes Chinoises.

———. 1986. "The Peach Flower Font and the Grotto Passage." *Journal of the American Oriental Society* 106:65–79.

———. 1989. "Death and Ascent in Ling-pao Taoism." *Taoist Resources* 1, no. 2:1–20.

———. 1990. "Stages of Transcendence: The *Bhūmi* Concept in Taoist Scripture." In *Chinese Buddhist Apocrypha,* edited by Robert E. Buswell, 119–46. Honolulu: University of Hawaii Press.

———. 1991. "Taoism and Literature: The *Pi-lo* Question." *Taoist Resources* 3, no. 1:57–72.

Boltz, Judith M. 1987. *A Survey of Taoist Literature: Tenth to Seventeenth Centuries.* Berkeley: University of California, China Research Monograph 32.

Buswell, Robert E., ed. 1990. *Chinese Buddhist Apocrypha.* Honolulu: University of Hawaii Press.

Cahill, Suzanne. 1993. *Transcendence and Divine Passion: The Queen Mother of the West in Medieval China.* Stanford, Calif.: Stanford University Press.

Chamberlagne, J. H. 1962. "The Development of Kuan Yin: Chinese Goddess of Mercy." *Numen* 9:44–52.

Chan, Alan. 1990. "Goddesses in Chinese Religion." In *Goddesses in Religions and Modern Debate,* edited by Larry W. Hurtado, 9–81. Atlanta, Ga.: Scholars Press.

———. 1991. *Two Visions of the Way: A Study of the Wang Pi and the Ho-shang-kung Commentaries on the Laozi.* Albany: State University of New York Press.

Chan Hok-lam. 1968. "Liu Chi and His Models: The Image-Building of a Chinese Imperial Adviser." *Oriens Extremus* 15:34–55.

Chan, Wing-tsit. 1964. *A Source Book in Chinese Philosophy.* Princeton, N.J.: Princeton University Press.

Chavannes, Edouard. 1910. *Le T'ai Chan.* Paris: Annales de Musée Guimet.

———. 1919. "Le jet des dragons." *Mémoires concernant l'Asie Orientale* 1919:55–214.

Chaves, Jonathan. 1977. "The Legacy of Ts'ang Chieh: The Written Word as Magic." *Oriental Art* 23, no. 2:200–215.

Chen Guofu. 1975. *Daozang yuanliu kao.* Taipei: Guting.

———. 1983a. *Daozang yuanliu xukao.* Taipei: Mingwen.

———. 1983b. *Daozangjing zhong waidan huanbaifa jingjue.* Shanghai: Guji.

Ch'en, Kenneth. 1945. "Buddhist-Taoist Mixtures in the *Pa-shih-i-hua t'u.*" *Harvard Journal of Asiatic Studies* 9:1–12.

———. 1952. "Anti-Buddhist Propaganda during the Nan-ch'ao." *Harvard Journal of Asiatic Studies* 15:166–92.

———. 1954. "On Some Factors Responsible for the Anti-Buddhist Persecution under the Pei-ch'ao." *Harvard Journal of Asiatic Studies* 17:261–73.

———. 1963. "A Propos the *Feng-fa-yao* of Hsi Ch'ao." *T'oung-pao* 50:79–92.

———. 1964. *Buddhism in China.* Princeton, N.J.: Princeton University Press.

Chen, William Y. 1987. *A Guide to Tao-tsang chi yao*. Stony Brook, N.Y.: Institute for the Advanced Study of World Religions.

Creel, Herrlee G. 1949. *Confucius: The Man and the Myth*. New York: John Day.

Crespigny, Ralph de. 1976. *Portents of Protest in the Later Han Dynasty: The Memorials of Hsiang K'ai to Emperor Huan*. Faculty of Asian Studies, Oriental Monograph series, no. 19. Canberra: Australian National University Press.

De Groot, J. J. M. 1903. *Sectarianism and Religious Persecution in China*. Amsterdam: Johannes Müller.

DeWoskin, Kenneth J. 1977. *Six Dynasties Chih-kuai and the Birth of Fiction*. Princeton, N.J.: Princeton University Press.

Dien, Albert E., ed. 1991. *State and Society in Early Medieval China*. Stanford, Calif.: Stanford University Press.

Doré, Henri. 1914–38. *Researches into Chinese Superstitions*, translated by M. Kennelly. 13 vols. Shanghai: Tusewei Press.

Dull, Jack. 1966. *A Historical Introduction to the Apocryphal (ch'an-wei) Texts of the Han Dynasty*. Ph.D. diss., University of Washington, Seattle.

Dutoit, Julius. 1906–21. *Jatakam: Das Buch der Erzählungen aus früheren Existenzen Buddhas*. Munich: Oskar Schloss Verlag.

Dutt, Sukumar. 1962. *Buddhist Monks and Monasteries of India: Their History and Contribution to Indian Culture*. London: Allen and Unwin.

Eberhard, Wolfram. 1942a. *Die Lokalkulturen des Nordens und des Westens*. Leiden: T'oung-pao Supplement 37.

———. 1942b. *Die Lokalkulturen des Südens und des Ostens*. Peking: Monumenta Serica Monograph 3.

———. 1949. *Dao Toba-Reich Nordchinas*. Leiden: E. Brill.

———. 1965. *Conquerors and Rulers*. Leiden: E. Brill.

Eberhard, Wolfram, and Alide Eberhard. 1946. *Die Mode der Han- und Chin-Zeit*. Antwerpen: De Sikkel.

Eichhorn, Werner. 1954–55. "Description of the Rebellion of Sun En and Earlier Taoist Rebellions." *Mitteilungen des Instituts für Orientforschung* 2, no. 2:232–52, and 2, no. 3:463–76.

———. 1955. "Bemerkungen zum Aufstand des Chang Chio und zum Staate des Chang Lu." *Mitteilungen des Instituts für Orientforschung* 3:291–327.

———. 1957. "T'ai-p'ing und T'ai-p'ing Religion." *Mitteilungen des Instituts für Orientforschung* 5:113–40.

———. 1976. *Die alte chinesische Religion und das Staatskultwesen*. Leiden: E. Brill.

Eitel, E. J. [1873] 1973. *Feng-shui or The Rudiments of Natural Science in China*. Cambridge: Coleaygue.

Eliade, Mircea. 1961. *Images and Symbols: Studies in Religious Symbolism*. London: Harvill Press.

Engelhardt, Ute. 1987. *Die klassische Tradition der Qi-Übungen: Eine Darstellung anhand des Tang-zeitlichen Textes Fuqi jingyi lun von Sima Chengzhen*. Wiesbaden: Franz Steiner.

Erkes, Eduard. 1931. "Spuren chinesischer Weltschöpfungsmythen." *T'oung-pao* 28:355–68.

———. 1942. "Eine P'an-ku Mythe der Hsia-Zeit." *T'oung-pao* 36:159–74.

Forke, Alfred. [1907] 1972. *Lun-Heng: Wang Ch'ung's Essays.* 2 vols. New York: Paragon.

Fracasso, Ricardo. 1988. "Holy Mothers of Ancient China." *T'oung-pao* 74:1–46.

Franke, Otto. 1930. *Geschichte des chinesischen Reiches.* Vol. 1 of 4 vols. Berlin: Walter de Gruyter.

———. 1936. *Geschichte des chinesischen Reiches.* Vol. 2 of 4 vols. Berlin: Walter de Gruyter.

Fujiwara Takao. 1962. "Kō Kan Rōshi chū kō." *Kangibunka* 3:19–29.

———. 1980a. "Dōtokukyō hachijūichō no chōjiron ni tsuite." *Kagawa daigaku kyōiku gakubu kenkyū hōkoku* 49:1–36.

———. 1980b. "Genshi muryō dojin jōhin myōkyō Shi Gen'ei chū." *Kagawa daigaku kyōiku gakubu kenkyū hōkoku* 49:37–60.

———. 1980c. "Ryu Shinki, Sai Shikō, Sha Genbi no Dōtokukyō chū ni tsuite." *Kagawa daigaku kyōiku gakubu kenkyū hōkoku* 49: 61–77.

———. 1983. "'Saishōkyō' Ri Ei chū." *Kagawa daigaku ippan kyōiku kenkyū* 23:117–50.

———. 1985. "Dōshi Ri Ei no Saishōkyō chū ni tsuite." *Kagawa daigaku kikubun kenkyū* 10:616.

Fukui Kōjun. 1951. "Shinsenden kō." *Tōhōshūkyō* 1:1–21.

———. 1952. *Dōkyō no kisoteki kenkyū.* Tokyo: Risōsha.

———. 1962. "Bunshi naiden kō." *Tōhōgaku ronshū* (fifteenth anniversary volume): 276–89.

———. 1964. "Genmyō naihen ni tsuite." In *Iwai hakase koki kinen rombunshū,* 565–75. Tokyo.

Fukui Kōjun, Yamazaki Hiroshi, Kimura Eiichi, and Sakai Tadao, eds. 1983. *Dōkyō.* 3 vols. Tokyo: Hirakawa.

Fukunaga, Mitsuji. 1969. "'No-Mind' in *Chuang-tzu* and Ch'an Buddhism." *Zimbun* 12:9–45.

———. 1982. "Dōkyō ni okeru tenshin no kōrin jukai." In *Chūgoku chūsei no shūkyō to bunka,* edited by Fukunaga Mitsuji, 1–46. Kyōto: Kyōto University, Jimbun kagaku kenkyūjo.

———. 1987a. "Kidō to shindō to shindō to shōdō." In *Dōkyō shisōshi kenkyū,* edited by Fukunaga Mitsuji, 413–36. Tokyo: Iwanami.

———. 1987b. "Kōten jōtei to Tennō taitei to Genshi tenson." In *Dōkyō shisōshi kenkyū,* edited by Fukunaga Mitsuji, 123–56. Tokyo: Iwanami.

Fung Yu-lan and Derk Bodde. 1952. *A History of Chinese Philosophy.* 2 vols. Princeton, N.J.: Princeton University Press.

Geiger, Wilhelm. 1925. *Samyutta-Nikaya aus dem Pali-Kanon der Buddhisten.* Munich: Oskar Schloss Verlag.

Gernet, Jacques. 1956. *Les aspects économiques du Bouddhisme dans la société chinoise du Ve au Xe siècle.* Paris: Publications de l'Ecole Française d'Extrême-Orient 39.

Getty, Alice. [1914] 1962. *The Gods of Northern Buddhism.* Tokyo: Tuttle.

Giles, Lionel. 1948. *A Gallery of Chinese Immortals.* London: John Murray.

Girardot, Norman. 1983. *Myth and Meaning in Early Taoism.* Berkeley: University of California Press.

Goodrich, Anne S. 1981. *Chinese Hells.* St. Augustin: Monumenta Serica Monograph.

Graham, A. C. 1960. *The Book of Lieh-tzu.* London: A Murray.

————. [1981] 1990. "The Origins of the Legend of Lao Tan." In *Studies in Chinese Philosophy and Philosophical Literature,* edited by A. C. Graham, 111–24. Albany: State University of New York Press.

Granet, Marcel. 1918. *Universismus.* Leiden: E. Brill.

————. 1926. *Danses et légendes de la Chine anciénne.* 2 vols. Paris: F. Alcan.

————. [1892–1910] 1964. *The Religious System of China.* 6 vols. Taipei: Chengwen.

Grube, Wilhelm. 1896. "Taoistischer Schöpfungsmythos." *Bastian Festschrift,* 447–57. Berlin.

Gu Jiegang. 1936. *Sanhuang kao.* Beijing: Yenching Journal of Chinese Studies Monograph no. 8.

————, ed. 1963. *Gushi bian.* 7 vols. Hongkong: Taiping.

Gulik, Robert H. van. 1961. *Sexual Life in Ancient China.* Leiden: E. Brill.

Güntsch, Gertrud. 1988. *Das Shen-hsien-chuan und das Erscheinungsbild eines Hsien.* Frankfurt: Peter Lang.

Hachiya Kunio. 1982. "Hokushū Dōan nikyōron chūshaku." *Tōyōbunka* 62:175–212.

Hackmann, Heinrich. 1920. "Die Mönchsregeln des Klostertaoismus." *Ostasiatische Zeitschrift* 8:141–70.

Haloun, Gustav. 1925. "Die Rekonstruktion der chinesischen Urgeschichte durch die Chinesen." *Japanisch-deutsche Zeitschrift für Wissenschaft und Technik* 3, no. 7:243–79.

Harada Jirō. 1984. "Taiheikyō no seimeikan, chōseisetsu ni tsuite." *Nippon chūgoku gakkaihō* 36:71–83.

Harada, Yoshito. 1937. *Chinese Dress and Personal Ornaments in the Han and Six Dynasties.* Tokyo: Tōyōbunko.

Harper, Donald. 1987. "The Sexual Arts of Ancient China as Described in a Manuscript of the Second Century B.C." *Harvard Journal of Asiatic Studies* 47:459–98.

Hawkes, David. 1959. *Ch'u Tz'u: The Songs of the South.* Oxford: Clarendon Press.

Henderson, John B. 1984. *The Development and Decline of Chinese Cosmology.* New York: Columbia University Press.

Hendrischke, Barbara. 1991. "The Concept of Inherited Evil in the *Taiping Jing.*" *East Asian History* 2:1–30.

————. 1993. "Der Taoismus in der Tang-Zeit." *Minima sinica* 1993/1:110–43.

Hirth, Friedrich. 1917. "The Story of Chang K'ien: China's Pioneer in Western Asia." *Journal of the American Oriental Society* 37:89–152.

Holmgren, Jennifer. 1981. "Seeds of Madness: A Portrait of Kao Yang, First Emperor of Northern Ch'i, A.D. 530–60." *Papers on Far Eastern History* 24:99–107.

————. 1982. "Family, Marriage and Political Power in Sixth Century China: A Study of the Kao Family of the Northern Ch'i, c. 520–50." *Journal of Asian History* 16:1–16.

————. 1991. "Politics of the Inner Court under the Hou-chu (Last Lord) of the Northern Ch'i (ca. 565–73)." In *State and Society in Early Medieval China,* edited by Albert E. Dien, 269–330. Stanford, Calif.: Stanford University Press.

Homann, Rolf. 1971. *Die wichtigsten Körpergottheiten im Huang-t'ing-ching.* Göppingen: Alfred Kümmerle.

Hou Ching-lang. 1975. *Monnaies d'offrande et la notion de trésorerie dans la réligion chinoise.* Paris: Mémoirs de l'Institut des Hautes Etudes Chinoises 1.

————. 1979. "Physiognomie d'après le teint sous la dynastie des Tang." In *Contributions aux études de Touen-houang,* edited by Michel Soymié, 2:55–70. Paris-Geneva: Ecole Française d'Extrême-Orient.

Hucker, Charles O. 1985. *A Dictionary of Official Titles in Imperial China.* Stanford, Calif.: Stanford University Press.

Hurvitz, Leon. 1956. *Wei Shou on Buddhism and Taoism.* Kyōto: Kyōto University, Institute for Research in Humanities.

————. 1961. "Additional Observations on the 'Defense of Faith'." In *Tsukamoto Zenryū hakase soshu kinen Bukkyō shigaku ronshū,* 28–41. Kyōto.

————. 1962. *Chih-i (538–597): An Introduction to the Life and Ideas of a Chinese Buddhist Monk.* Brussels: Institut Belge des Hautes Etudes Chinoises.

————. 1976. *Scripture of the Lotus Blossom of the Fine Dharma.* New York: Columbia University Press.

Ikeda On. 1981. "Chūgoku rekidai mokuken rakukō." *Tōyō bunka kenkyūjo kiyō* 86:193–278.

Imai Usaburō. 1974. "Renzan kizō no nieki ni tsuite." In *Uno Tetsuto sensei hakuju shukuga kinen Tōyōgaku Ronsō,* 211–25. Tokyo: Uno Tetsuto sensei hakuju shukuga kinenkai.

Imbault-Huart, M. C. 1884. "La légende du premier pape des taoïstes." *Journal Asiatique* 8, no. 4:389–461.

Ishibashi Nariyasu. 1991. "Shinshutsu Nanatsudera zō 'Seijō hōgyō kyō' kō." *Tōhōshūkyō* 78:69–87.

Ishida Hidemi. 1987. *Ki: Nagareru shintai.* Tokyo: Hirakawa.

————. 1989. "Body and Mind: The Chinese Perspective." In *Taoist Meditation and Longevity Techniques,* edited by L. Kohn, 41–70. Ann Arbor: University of Michigan, Center for Chinese Studies Publications.

————. 1991. "Shoki no bōchū yōsei shisō to sensetsu." *Tōhōshūkyō* 77:1–21.

Ishihara, Akira, and Howard S. Levy. 1970. *The Tao of Sex.* New York: Harper and Row.

Ishii Masako. 1980. *Dōkyōgaku no kenkyū.* Tokyo: Kokusho kankōkai.

————. 1981. "Reihō gofukyō no ikkōsatsu." *Sōka daigaku ippan kyōikubu ronshū* 5:1–20.

————. 1983. "Dōkyō no kamigami." In *Dōkyō,* edited by Fukui Kōjun, Yamazaki Hiroshi, Kimuru Eiichi, and Sakai Tadao, 1:121–88. Tokyo: Hirakawa.

————. 1984. "Taijō reihō gofujo no ikkōsatsu." In *Makio Ryōkai hakase shōju kinen ronshū Chūgoku no shūkyō to kagaku,* 13–32. Tokyo: Kokusho kankōkai.

Jan Yun-hua. 1978. "The Silk Manuscripts on Taoism." *T'oung-pao* 63:65–84.

Jenner, W.J.F. 1981. *Memories of Lo-yang: Yang Hsüan-chih and the Lost Capital, 493–534.* Oxford: Clarendon Press.

Kalinowski, Marc. 1985. "La transmission du dispositif des Neuf Palais sous les Six-dynasties." In *Tantric and Taoist Studies,* edited by Michel Strickmann, 3:773–811. Brussels: Institut Belge des Hautes Etudes Chinoises.

————. 1991. *Cosmologie et divination dans la Chine ancienne: Le compendium des Cinq Agents.* Paris: Publications de l'Ecole Française d'Extrême-Orient, no. 166.

Kaltenmark, Maxime. [1953] 1988. *Le Lie-sien tchouan.* Paris: Ecole Française d'Extrême-Orient.

———. 1960. "Ling-pao: Note sur un terme du taoïsme religieux." *Mélanges publiés par l'Institut des Hautes Etudes* 2:559–88.

———. 1969. *Lao-tzu and Taoism.* Stanford, Calif.: Stanford University Press.

———. 1979. "The Ideology of the *T'ai-p'ing-ching.*" In *Facets of Taoism,* edited by Holmes Welch and Anna Seidel, 19–52. New Haven, Conn.: Yale University Press.

———. 1980. "Chine." *Dictionnaire des Mythologies,* 1–75. Paris: Flammarion.

———. 1981. "Quelques remarques sur le 'T'ai-shang Ling-pao wou-fou siu'." *Zimbun* 18:1–10.

Kamata Shigeo. 1963. "Dōkyō kyōri no keisei ni oyoboshita bukkyō shisō no eikyō." *Tōyō bunko kenkyūjo kiyō* 31:165–240.

———. 1966. "Dōsei shisō no keisei katei." *Tōyō bunko kenkyūjo kiyō* 4:61–154.

———. 1968. "Genshutoku no arawareru bukkyō shisō." *Chūgoku gakushi* 5: 119–44.

———. 1984. *Chūgoku bukkyō shi.* Vol. 3. Tokyo: Tokyo University.

———. 1986. *Dōzō nai bukkyō shisō shiryō shūsei.* Tokyo: Daizō shuppansha.

Kamitsuka Yoshiko. 1986–87. "Shinkō ni tsuite." *Nagoya daigaku kyōyōbu kiyō* 30: 175–219 and 31:1–62.

———. 1988a. "Kaigō dojin setsu no seisei (I)." *Tōyō gakujutsu kenkyū* 27:35–53.

———. 1988b. "Taiheikyō no shōfu to taihei no riron ni tsuite." *Nagoya daigaku kyōyōbu kiyō* 32:41–75.

———. 1990. "Hōsho seitōkun o megutte: Rikuchō jōseiha dōkyō no ikkōsatsu." *Tōhōshūkyō* 76:1–23.

———. 1992a. "Kaigō dojin setsu no seisei (II)." *Nagoya daigaku kyōikubu kiyō* 36:1–32.

———. 1992b. "Ma no kannen to shōma no shisō." In *Chūgoku ko dōkyō shi kenkyū,* edited by Yoshikawa Tadao, 89–144. Kyōto: Dōhōsha.

———. 1992c. "Dōkyō girei to ryu." *Nihon bunka kenkyū* 3:126–34.

———. 1993. "Nanbokuchō jidai no dōkyō sōzō." In *Chūgoku chūsei no bunbutsu,* edited by Tonami Mamoru, 225–89. Kyōto: Kyōto University, Jimbun kagaku kenkyūjo.

Kanaoka Shōkō, ed. 1983. *Tonkō to Chūgoku dōkyō.* Tokyo: Daitō.

Kandel, Barbara. 1973. "Der Versuch einer politischen Restauration: Liu An, der König von Huai-nan." *Nachrichten der Gesellschaft für Natur- und Völkerkunde Ostasiens* 113:58–82.

———. 1979. *Taiping jing: The Origin and Transmission of the 'Scripture on General Welfare'—The History of an Unofficial Text.* Hamburg: Gesellschaft für Natur- und Völkerkunde Ostasiens.

Kao, George, ed. [1946] 1974. *Chinese Wit and Humor.* New York: Sterling Publishing.

Karetzky, Patricia E. 1992. *The Life of the Buddha: Ancient Scriptural and Pictorial Traditions.* Lanham, Md.: University Press of America.

Karlgren, Bernhard. 1946. "Legends and Cults in Ancient China." *Bulletin of the Museum of Far Eastern Antiquities* 18:199–365.

Kenkyūhan, ed. 1975. *Gumyōshū kenkyū.* 3 vols. Translated by the Chūsei shisōshi kenkyūhan. Kyōto: Kyōto University, Jimbun kagaku kenkyūjo.

———. 1988. "Shōdōron shakuchū." Translated by the Rikuchō Zui Tō jidai no dōbutsu ronsō kenkyūhan. *Tōhōgakuhō* 60:481–680.

Kern, Fritz. 1956. *Aśoka: Kaiser und Missionar*. Bern: Francke Verlag.

Kern, Hendrik. 1963. *Saddharma-puṇḍarīka or the Lotus of the Wonderful Law*. New York: Dover.

Kimura Eiichi. 1962. *Eon kenkyū*. 2 vols. Kyōto: Hōsōkan.

Knaul, Livia. 1981. *Leben und Legende des Ch'en T'uan*. Frankfurt: Peter Lang.

———. 1986. "Chuang-tzu and the Chinese Ancestry of Ch'an Buddhism." *Journal of Chinese Philosophy* 13, no. 3:411–28.

Kobayashi Masayoshi. 1990. *Rikuchō dōkyōshi kenkyū*. Tokyo: Sōbunsha.

———. 1992. "The Celestial Masters under the Eastern Jin and Liu-Song Dynasties." *Taoist Resources* 3, no. 2:17–45.

Kohn, Livia. 1988. "Mirror of Auras: Chen Tuan on Physiognomy." *Asian Folklore Studies* 47, no. 2:215–56.

———. 1989a. "Die Emigration des Laozi: Mythologische Entwicklungen vom 2. bis 6. Jahrhundert." *Monumenta Serica* 38:49–68.

———. 1989b. "Guarding the One: Concentrative Meditation in Taoism." In *Taoist Meditation and Longevity Techniques*, edited by Livia Kohn, 123–56. Ann Arbor: University of Michigan, Center for Chinese Studies Publications.

———. 1989c. "The Mother of the Tao." *Taoist Resources* 1, no. 2: 37–113.

———. 1989d. "Taoist Insight Meditation: The Tang Practice of *Neiguan*." In *Taoist Meditation and Longevity Techniques*, edited by Livia Kohn, 191–222. Ann Arbor: University of Michigan, Center for Chinese Studies Publications.

———, ed. 1989e. *Taoist Meditation and Longevity Techniques*. Ann Arbor: University of Michigan, Center for Chinese Studies Publications.

———. 1990a. "Chen Tuan in History and Legend." *Taoist Resources* 2, no. 1:8–31.

———. 1990b. "Transcending Personality: From Ordinary to Immortal Life." *Taoist Resources* 2, no. 2:1–22.

———. 1991a. *Taoist Mystical Philosophy: The Scripture of Western Ascension*. Albany: State University of New York Press.

———. 1991b. "Taoist Visions of the Body." *Journal of Chinese Philosophy* 18:227–52.

———. 1992a. *Early Chinese Mysticism: Philosophy and Soteriology in the Taoist Tradition*. Princeton, N.J.: Princeton University Press.

———. 1992b. "Philosophy as Scripture in the Taoist Canon." *Journal of Chinese Religions* 20:61–76.

———, ed. 1993a. *The Taoist Experience: An Anthology*. Albany: State University of New York Press.

———. 1993b. "Taoist Scriptures as Mirrored in the *Xiaodao lun*." *Taoist Resources* 4, no. 1:47–69.

———. 1994. "The Five Precepts of the Venerable Lord." *Monumenta Serica* 42.

———. Forthcoming (a). "Laozi: Ancient Philosopher, Master of Longevity, and Taoist God." In *Religions in China*, edited by Donald Lopez. Princeton, N.J.: Princeton University Press.

———. Forthcoming (b). "Zur Symbolik des Bösen im alten China." In *Verschiedenheit und Einheit: Studien zum Geist in China und im Abendland. Festschrift für Rolf Trauzettel*, edited by Ingrid Krüssmann, Hans-Georg Müller, and Wolfgang Kubin. St. Augustin: Academia Verlag.

Kominami Ichirō. 1974. "Shisenden no fukugen." In *Iriya kyōju taikan kinen Gengogaku ronsō*, 30–114. Tokyo.

————. 1984. *Chūgoku no shinwa to monogatari—Ko shōsetsushi no tenkai.* Tokyo: Iwanami.

————. 1991. *Seiōbō to tanabata denshō.* Tokyo: Heibonsha.

Kroll, Paul W. 1985. "In the Halls of the Azure Lad." *Journal of the American Oriental Society* 105:75–94.

Kubo Noritada. 1986. *Dōkyō no kamigami.* Tokyo: Hirakawa.

Kubota Ryō'on. 1943. *Shina judōbutsu kōshōshi.* Tokyo: Daitō.

Kusuyama Haruki. 1976. "Rōkunden to sono nendai." *Tōhōshūkyō* 47:12–30.

————. 1978. "Seiyōshi densetsu kō." *Tōhōshūkyō* 52:1–14.

————. 1979. *Rōshi densetsu no kenkyū.* Tokyo: Sōbunsha.

————. 1982. "Dōkyō ni okeru jūkai." *Bungaku kenkyūka kiyō* 28:55–72.

————. 1983. "Jukyō to dōkyō." In *Dōkyō,* edited by Fukui Kōjun, Yamazaki Hiroshi, Kimura Eiichi, and Sakai Tadao, 2:49–94. Tokyo: Hirakawa.

————. 1992. *Dōka shisō to dōkyō.* Tokyo: Hirakawa.

Lagerwey, John. 1981. *Wu-shang pi-yao: Somme taoïste du VIe siècle.* Paris: Publications de l'Ecole Française d'Extrême-Orient.

————. 1987. *Taoist Ritual in Chinese Society and History.* New York: Macmillan.

Lai, Whalen. 1979. "Chou Yong vs. Chang Jung (On Śūnyatā); The Pen-wu Yu-wu Controversy in Fifth-Century China." *Journal of the International Association of Buddhist Studies* 1, no. 2:23–44.

————. 1986. "Dating the *Hsiang fa chüeh i ching.*" *Annual Memoirs of the Otani University Shin Buddhist Comprehensive Research Institute* 4:61–91.

————. 1987. "The Earliest Folk Buddhist Religion in China: *T'i-wei Po-li Ching* and Its Historical Significance." In *Buddhist and Taoist Practice in Medieval Chinese Society,* edited by David W. Chappell, 11–35. Honolulu: University of Hawaii Press.

————. 1990. "Society and the Sacred in the Secular City: Temple Legends of the *Lo-yang Ch'ieh-lan-chi.*" In *State and Society in Early Medieval China,* edited by Albert E. Dien, 229–68. Stanford, Calif.: Stanford University Press.

————. 1993. "The Three Jewels in China." In *Buddhist Spirituality: Indian, Southeast Asian, Tibetan, and Early Chinese,* edited by Takeuchi Yoshinori, 275–42. New York: Crossroad.

Lamotte, Etienne. 1958. *Histoire du bouddhisme indien: Des origins à l'ère Śaka.* Louvain: Publications universitaires.

————. 1987. *History of Indian Buddhism: From the Orgins to the Śaka Era.* Translated by Sara Webb-Boin. Louvain: Peeters Press.

Larre, Claude, Isabelle Robinet, and Elisabeth Rochat de la Vallée. 1993. *Les grands traités du Huainan zi.* Paris: Editions du Cerf.

Lau, Joseph D. C. 1982. *Chinese Classics: Tao Te Ching.* Hong Kong: Hong Kong University Press.

Lauffer, Berthold. 1912. *Jade: A Study in Chinese Archaeology and Religion.* Chicago: Field Museum of Natural History.

Le Blanc, Charles, and Rémi Mathieu, eds. 1992. *Mythe et philosophie a l'aube de la Chine impérial: Etudes sur le Huainan zi.* Montreal: Les Presses de l'Université de Montréal.

Lévi, Jean. 1983. "L'abstinence des céréals chez les taoïstes." *Etudes Chinoises* 1:3–47.

Levy, Howard S. 1956. "Yellow Turban Rebellion at the End of the Han." *Journal of the American Oriental Society* 76:214–27.

Lewis, Mark E. 1990. *Sanctioned Violence in Early China*. Albany: State University of New York Press.

Li Bincheng. 1981. "Tangdao fodao zhi zheng yanjiu." *Shijie zongjiao yanjiu* 1981, no. 2:99–108.

Liebenthal, Walter. 1950. "Shih Hui-yüan's Buddhism." *Journal of the American Oriental Society* 70:243–59.

———. 1952. "The Immortality of the Soul in Chinese Thought." *Monumenta Nipponica* 8:327–92.

———. 1955. "Chinese Buddhism during the Fourth and Fifth Centuries." *Monumenta Nipponica* 11:44–83.

———. 1968. *Chao-Lun, the Treatise of Seng-chao*. Hong Kong: Hong Kong University Press.

Link, Arthur E. 1961. "Cheng-wu lun: The Rectification of Unjustified Criticism." *Oriens Extremus* 8:136–65.

Link, Arthur E., and Timothy Lee. 1966. "Sun Ch'o's *Yü-tao-lun:* A Clarification of the Way." *Monumenta Serica* 25:169–96.

Liu Chenghuai. 1988. *Zhongguo shanggu shenhua*. Shanghai: Wenyi.

Liu, Ts'un-yan. 1973. "The Compilation and Historical Value of the *Tao-tsang*." In *Essays on the Sources of Chinese History*, edited by Donald Leslie, 104–20. Canberra: Australian National University Press.

Loewe, Michael. 1979. *Ways to Paradise: The Chinese Quest for Immortality*. London: Allen and Unwin.

McGovern, William M. 1939. *The Early Empires of Central Asia*. Chapel Hill: University of North Carolina Press.

Maeda Shigeki. 1985a. "Rikuchō jidai ni okeru Kan Kichi den no hensen." *Tōhōshūkyō* 65:44–62.

———. 1985b. "Rōkun hyakuhachijū kaijo no seiritsu ni tsuite." *Tōyō no shisō to shūkyō* 2:81–94.

———. 1987. "Rōshi myōshinkyō shōkō." *Waseda daigaku daigakuin bungaku kenkyūka kiyō* 14:21–32.

———. 1988. "Rōshi chūkyō oboegaki." In *Chūgoku kodai yōsei shisō no sōgōteki kenkyū*, edited by Sakade Yoshinobu, 474–502. Tokyo: Hirakawa.

———. 1989. "Rōshi saishōkyō no tekisto ni tsuite." *Yamamura joshi tanki daigaku kiyō* 1:1–30.

———. 1990a. "Butsudō ronsō ni okeru Rōshi saishōkyō." *Tōhōshūkyō* 75:61–77.

———. 1990b. "Rōshi saishōkyō kō." *Nihon chūgoku gakkai hō* 42:77–90.

Magnin, Paul. 1979. *La vie et l'œuvre de Huisi (515–577)*. Paris: Ecole Française d'Extrême-Orient.

Major, John S. 1978. "Myth, Cosmology, and the Origins of Chinese Science." *Journal of Chinese Philosophy* 5:1–20.

———. 1984. "The Five Phases, Magic Squares, and Schematic Cosmography." In *Explorations in Early Chinese Cosmology*, edited by Henry Rosemont, 133–66. Chico: Scholars Press.

———. 1993. *Heaven and Earth in Early Han Thought: Chapters Three, Four, and Five of the Huainanzi*. Albany: State University of New York Press.

Malek, Roman. 1985. *Das Chai-chieh-lu*. Frankfurt: Peter Lang, Würzburger Sino-Japonica 14.

Mansvelt-Beck, B. J. 1980. "The Date of the *Taiping jing*." *T'oung-pao* 66:149–82.

Maruyama Hiroshi. 1986. "Shōitsu dōkyō no jōshō girei ni tsuite." *Tōhōshūkyō* 68:44–64.

———. 1987. "Jōshō girei yori mitaru shōitsu dōkyō no tokushoku." *Bukkyō shigaku kenkyū* 30:56–84.

———. 1991. "Gyokutan happyō kagi kō." *Tōhōshūkyō* 77:50–79.

Maspero, Henri. 1924. "Légendes mythologiques dans le Chou King." *Journal Asiatique* 20:1–101.

———. 1937. "Les dieux taoïstes: comment on communique avec eux." *Comptes-rendus de l'Academies Inscriptions et Belles-Lettres* 1937:362–74.

———. 1981. *Taoism and Chinese Religion*. Translated by Frank Kierman. Amherst: University of Massachusetts Press.

Mather, Richard B. 1979. "K'ou Ch'ien-chih and the Taoist Theocracy at the Northern Wei Court 425–451." In *Facets of Taoism*, edited by Holmes Welch and Anna Seidel, 103–33. New Haven, Conn.: Yale University Press.

Mathieu, Rémi. 1983. *Etude sur la mythologie et l'ethnologie de la Chine anciénne*. 2 vols. Paris: Collège du France.

Matsubara Sangwrō. 1961. *Chūgoku bukkyō chōkokushi kenkyū*. Tokyo: Yoshikawa Kōbunkan.

Matsumoto Kōichi. 1983. "Dōkyō to shūkyō girei." In *Dōkyō*, edited by Fukui Kōjun, Yamazaki Hiroshi, Kimura Eiichi, and Sakai Tadao, 1:189–230. Tokyo: Hirakawa.

Meng Naichang. 1984. "Zhongguo liandao shu." *Shijie zongjiao yanjiu* 1984, no. 4:72–84.

Michaud, Paul. 1958. "The Yellow Turbans." *Monumenta Serica* 17:47–127.

Michihata Ryōshu. 1957. *Tōdai bukkyō no kenkyū*. Kyōto: Heirakuji Shorten.

Mitarai Masaru. 1971. "Shinnō to Chiyo." *Tōhōshūkyō* 41:1–15.

———. 1987. "Shirei ni tsuite." *Hiroshima daigaku daigakubu kiyō* 46:38–45.

Miura Kunio. 1983. "Dōten fukuchi ron." *Tōhōshūkyō* 61:1–23.

Miyakawa Hisayuki. 1954. "Dōkyō kyōten no genryu." *Tōhōshūkyō* 4/5:41–122.

———. 1974. *Rikuchōshi kenkyū: Shūkyō hen*. Kyōto: Heirakuji shoten.

———. 1979. "Local Cults around Mount Lu at the Time of Sun En's Rebellion." In *Facets of Taoism*, edited by Holmes Welch and Anna Seidel, 83–102. New Haven, Conn.: Yale University Press.

———. 1980. "Chō Ryō to Chō Kaku." In *Ikeda Suetoshi hakase koki kinen Tōyōgaku ronshū*, 535–50. Tokyo: Meisō.

———. 1991. "Ten chi sui sankan to dōten." *Tōhōshūkyō* 78:1–22.

Miyazawa Masayori. 1986. "Dōkyō tenseki ni mieru shūshin bubun no meishō ni tsuite." *Tōhōshūkyō* 67:22–37.

Mochizuki Shinkō. 1933–36. *Mochizuki bukkyō daijiten*. 10 vols. Tokyo: Sekai seiten kankō kyōkai.

Mollier, Christine. 1990. *Une apocalypse taoïste du Ve siècle: Le livre des incantations divines des grottes abyssales*. Paris: Collège du France, Publications de l' Institut des Hautes Etudes Chinoises no. 31.

Morgan, Carole. 1993. "An Introduction to the *Lingqi jing.*" *Journal of Chinese Religions* 21:97–120.

Morgan, Evan. 1934. *Tao, the Great Luminant.* Shanghai: Kelly and Walsh.

Mugitani Kunio. 1976. "Tō Kōkei nenpu kōryaku." *Tōhōshūkyō* 47:30–61, 48:58–83.

———. 1982. "Kōtei naikeikyō shiron." *Tōyō bunka* 62:29–61.

———. 1985. "Rōshi sōjichū ni tsuite." *Tōhō gakuhō* 57:75–109.

Murakami Yoshimi. 1956. *Chūgoku no sennin.* Kyōto: Heirakuji shoten.

———. 1983. "Renkin jutsu." In *Dōkyō,* edited by Fukui Kōjun, Yamazaki Hiroshi, Kimura Eiichi, and Sakai Tadao, 1:285–328. Tokyo: Hirakawa.

———. 1988. "Kōtei naikyō taiso to dōka shisō." *Tōhōshūkyō* 71:1–19.

Murano, Senchu. 1974. *The Lotus Sūtra.* Tokyo: Nichiren shū Headquarters.

Nakajima Ryuzō. 1982. "Rikuchō kohan yori Zui Tō shoki ni itaru dōka no shizensetsu." *Tōyōbunka* 62:139–74.

———. 1985. *Rikuchō shisō no kenkyū.* Kyōto: Heirakuji shoten.

Nakamura Hajime. [1975] 1981. *Bukkyōgo daijiten.* Tokyo: Tōkyō shoseki.

Needham, Joseph. 1958. *Science and Civilisation in China.* Vol. 3, *Mathematics and the Sciences of the Heavens and the Earth.* Cambridge: Cambridge University Press.

———. 1974. *Science and Civilisation in China.* Vol. 5, *Part II: Spagyrical Discovery and Invention: Magistries of Gold and Immortality.* Cambridge: Cambridge University Press.

———. 1976. *Science and Civilisation in China.* Vol. 5, *Part III: Spagyrical Discovery and Invention: Historical Survey, from Cinnabar Elixir to Synthetic Insulin.* Cambridge: Cambridge University Press.

———. 1980. *Science and Civilisation in China.* Vol. 5, *Part IV: Spagyrical Discovery and Invention: Apparatus, Theories and Gifts.* Cambridge: Cambridge University Press.

———. 1983. *Science and Civilisation in China.* Vol. 5, *Part V: Spagyrical Discovery and Invention: Physiological Alchemy.* Cambridge: Cambridge University Press.

Nylan, Michael. 1993. *The Canon of Great Mystery.* Albany: State University of New York Press.

Nylan, Michael, and Nathan Sivin. 1988. "The First Neo-Confucian: An Introduction to Yang Xiong's *Canon of Supreme Mystery.*" In *Chinese Ideas About Nature and Society: Studies in Honor of Derk Bodde,* edited by Charles LeBlanc and Susan Blader, 41–100. Hong Kong: Hong Kong University Press.

Ochiai, Toshinori. 1991. *The Manuscripts of Nanatsudera.* Kyōto: Italian School of East Asian Studies.

O'Flaherty, Wendy D. 1975. *Hindu Myths: A Sourcebook Translated from the Sanskrit.* Baltimore, Md.: Penguin.

Ōfuchi Ninji. 1964. *Dōkyōshi no kenkyū.* Okayama.

———. 1974. "On Ku Ling-pao ching." *Acta Asiatica* 27:33–56.

———. 1979a. "The Formation of the Taoist Canon." In *Facets of Taoism,* edited by Holmes Welch and Anna Seidel, 252–68. New Haven, Conn.: Yale University Press.

———. 1979b. *Tonkō dōkei.* Tokyo: Kokubu shoten.

———. 1983. *Chūgokujin no shūkyō girei.* Tokyo: Shukubu.

———. 1985a. "Dōkyō ni okeru sangensetsu no seisei to tenkai." *Tōhōshūkyō* 66: 1–21.

———. 1985b. "Gokan matsu gotō beidō no soshiki ni tsuite. *Tōhōshūkyō* 65:1–19.

———. 1991. *Shoki no dōkyō.* Tokyo: Sōbunsha.

Ōfuchi Ninji, and Ishii Masako. 1988. *Dōkyō tenseki mokuroku, sakuin.* Tokyo: Kokusho kankōkai.

Ōmura Seigai. 1972. *Shina bijutsushi chōsohen.* Tokyo: Kokusho kankōkai.

Onozawa Seiichi, ed. 1978. *Ki no shisō.* Tokyo: Tokyo University.

Overmyer, Daniel L. 1990. "Attitudes toward Popular Religion in Ritual Texts of the Chinese State: *The Collected Statutes of the Great Ming.*" *Cahiers d'Extrême-Asie* 5:191–221.

Ōzaki Masaharu. 1974. "Taijō santen seihōkyō seiritsu kō." *Tōhōshūkyō* 43:13–29.

———. 1976. "Rikuchō kodōkyō ni kansuru ikkōsatsu." *Shūkan Tōhōgaku* 36: 99–124.

———. 1977. "Shikyoku meika shomondai." In *Dōkyō kenkyū ronshū,* 341–64. Tokyo: Kokusho kankōkai.

———. 1979. "Kō Kenshi no shinsen shisō." *Tōhōshūkyō* 54:52–69.

———. 1983. "Dōkyō kyōten." In *Dōkyō,* edited by Fukui Kōjun, Yamazaki Hiroshi, Kimura Eiidi, and Sakai Tadao, 1:73–120. Tokyo: Hirakawa.

———. 1984. "The Taoist Priesthood," In *Religion and Family in East Asia,* edited by G. DeVos and T. Sofue, 97–109. Ōsaka: National Museum of Ethnology.

Pas, Julian F. 1986. "Six Daily Periods of Worship: Symbolic Meaning in Buddhist Liturgy and Eschatology." *Monumenta Serica* 37:49–82.

Peerenboom, R. P. 1990. "Cosmogony, the Taoist Way." *Journal of Chinese Philosophy* 17:157–74.

———. 1991. *Law and Morality in Ancient China: The Silk Manuscripts of Huang-Lao.* Albany: State University of New York Press.

Pelliot, Paul. 1903. "Les Mo-ni et le *Houa-hu king.*" *Bulletin de l'Ecole Française d'Extrême-Orient* 3:318–27.

———. 1906. "Response a Ed. Chavannnes, 'Les pays d'Occident d'après le Wei Lio'." *Bulletin de l'Ecole Française d'Extrême-Orient* 6:361–400.

Penny, Benjamin. 1990. "A System of Fate Calculation in *Taiping jing.*" *Papers on Far Eastern History* 41:1–8.

Petersen, Jens O. 1989. "The Early Traditions Relating to the Han-dynasty Transmission of the *Taiping jing.*" *Acta Orientalia* 50:133–71.

———. 1990a. "The Anti-Messianism of the *Taiping jing.*" *Journal of the Seminar for Buddhist Studies* 3:1–36.

———. 1990b. "The Early Traditions Relating to the Han-dynasty Transmission of the *Taiping jing.*" *Acta Orientalia* 51:173–216.

———. 1992. "The *Taiping jing* and the A.D. 102 Clepsydra Reform." *Acta Orientalia* 53:122–58.

Pokora, Timotheus. 1975. *Hsin Lun (New Treatise) and Other Writings by Huan T'an.* Ann Arbor: University of Michigan Press.

Porkert, Manfred. 1961. "Untersuchungen einiger philosophisch-wissenschaftlicher Grundbegriffe und -beziehungen im Chinesischen." *Zeitschrift der deutschen morgenländischen Gesellschaft* 110:422–52.

———. 1974. *The Theoretical Foundations of Chinese Medicine: Systems of Correspondence.* Cambridge, Mass.: MIT Press.

———. 1979. *Biographie d'un taoïste légendaire: Tcheou Tseu-yang.* Paris: Collège de France, Mémoirs de l'Institut des Hautes Etudes Chinoises 10.

Pregadio, Fabrizio. 1991. "The *Book of the Nine Elixirs* and Its Tradition." In *Chūgoku kodai kagaku shiron, zokuhen,* edited by Yamada Keiji and Tanaka Tan, 543–639. Kyōto: Kyōto University, Jimbun kagaku kenkyūjo.

Qing Xitai. 1988. *Zhongguo daojiao shi.* Chengdu: Sichuan renmin.

Rao Zongyi. 1956. *Laozi xiang'er zhu xiaojian.* Hong Kong: Tong Nam Printers.

Reiter, Florian C. 1988. "The Visible Divinity: The Sacred Image in Religious Taoism." *Nachrichten der deutschen Gesellschaft für Natur- und Völkerkunde Ostasiens* 144:51–70.

———. 1990a. *Der Perlenbeutel aus den drei Höhlen: Arbeitsmaterialien zum Taoismus der frühen T'ang-Zeit.* Wiesbaden: Otto Harrassowitz.

———, ed. 1990b. *Leben und Wirken Lao-Tzu's in Schrift und Bild: Lao-chün pa-shih-i-hua t'u-shuo.* Würzburg: Königshausen and Neumann.

Ren Jiyu. 1990. *Zhongguo daojiao shi.* Shanghai: Renmin.

Ren Jiyu, and Zhong Zhaopeng, eds. 1991. *Daozang tiyao.* Beijing: Zhongguo shehui kexue chubanshe.

Rhys-Davids, Caroline A. F. 1950. *The Book of Kindred Sayings: Samyutta Nikaya.* London: Pali Text Society.

Robinet, Isabelle. 1976. "Les randonées extatiques des taoïstes dans les astres." *Monumenta Serica* 32:159–273.

———. 1977. *Les commentaires du Tao to king jusqu'au VIIe siècle.* Paris: Collège du France, Mémoirs de l'Institute des Hautes Etudes Chinoises 5.

———. 1979a. *Méditation taoïste.* Paris: Dervy Livres.

———. 1979b. "Metamorphosis and Deliverance of the Corpse in Taoism." *History of Religions* 19:37–70.

———. 1984. *La révélation du Shangqing dans l'histoire du taoïsme.* 2 vols. Paris: Publications de l'Ecole Française d'Extrême-Orient.

———. 1986. "The Taoist Immortal: Jester of Light and Shadow, Heaven and Earth." *Journal of Chinese Religions* 13–14:87–106.

———. 1989. "Visualization and Ecstatic Flight in Shangqing Taoism." In *Taoist Meditation and Longevity Techniques,* edited by Livia Kohn, 157–90. Ann Arbor: University of Michigan, Center for Chinese Studies Publications.

———. 1990. "The Place and Meaning of the Notion of *Taiji* in Taoist Sources prior to the Ming Dynasty." *History of Religions* 29:373–411.

———. 1991. *Histoire du taoïsme: Des origins au XIVe siècle.* Paris: Editions Cerf.

———. 1993. *Taoist Meditation.* Translated by Norman Girardot and Julian Pas. Albany: State University of New York Press.

Robinson, Richard. 1959. "Mysticism and Logic in the Thought of Seng Chao, Fifth Century Thinker." *Philosophy East and West* 8:99–120.

———. 1967. *Early Mādhyamika in India and China.* Madison: University of Wisconsin Press.

Rosemont, Henry, ed. 1984. *Explorations in Early Chinese Cosmology.* Chico: Scholars Press.

Sailey, Jay. 1978. *The Master Who Embraces Simplicity: A Study of the Philosophy of Ko Hung (A.D. 283–343).* San Francisco, Calif.: Chinese Materials Center.

Sakade Yoshinobu. 1983. "Chōsei jutsu." In *Dōkyō,* edited by Fukui Kōjun, Yamazaki Hiroshi, Kimura Eichii, and Sakai Tadao, 1:239–84. Tokyō: Hirakawa.

———, ed. 1988. *Chūgoku kodai yōsei shisō no sōgōteki kenkyū.* Tokyo: Hirakawa.

Sargent, Galen E. 1957. "T'an-yao and His Time." *Monumenta Serica* 16:363–96.

Saso, Michael. 1972. *Taoism and the Rite of Cosmic Renewal.* Seattle: Washington University Press.

———. 1978. "What is the Ho-t'u?" *History of Religions* 17:399–416.

Saunders, J. J. 1971. *The History of the Mongol Conquests.* New York: Barnes and Noble.

Schafer, Edward H. 1955. "Notes on Mica in Medieval China." *T'oung-pao* 43: 165–286.

———. 1973. *The Divine Woman.* Berkeley: University of California Press.

———. 1977. *Pacing the Void.* Berkeley: University of California Press.

Schipper, Kristofer M. 1965. *L'Empereur Wou des Han dans la légende taoïste.* Paris: Publications de l'Ecole Française d'Extrême-Orient 58.

———. 1967. "Gogaku shingyōzu no shinkō." *Dōkyō kenkyū* 2:114–62.

———. 1975a. *Concordance du Houang-t'ing king.* Paris: Publications de l'Ecole Française d'Extrême-Orient.

———. 1975b. *Concordance du Pao-p'u-tzu nei/wai-p'ien.* Paris: Publications de l'Ecole Française d'Extrême-Orient.

———. 1975c. *Concordance du Tao Tsang: Titres des ouvrages.* Paris: Publications de l'Ecole Française d'Extrême-Orient.

———. 1978. "The Taoist Body." *History of Religions* 17:355–87.

———. 1979. "Le Calendrier de Jade: Note sur le *Laozi zhongjing.*" *Nachrichten der deutschen Gesellschaft für Natur- und Völkerkunde Ostasiens* 125:75–80.

———. 1980. *Concordance du Yun ki ki kian.* 2 vols. Paris: Publications de l'Ecole Française d'Extrême-Orient.

———. 1982. *Le corps taoïste: Corps physique—corps social.* Paris: Fayard.

———. 1985a. "Taoist Ordination Ranks in the Tunhuang Manuscripts." In *Religion und Philosophie in Ostasien: Festschrift für Hans Steininger,* edited by G. Naundorf, K. H. Pohl, and H. H. Schmidt, 127–48. Würzburg: Königshausen and Neumann.

———. 1985b. "Taoist Ritual and Local Cults of the T'ang Dynasty." In *Tantric and Taoist Studies,* edited by Michel Strickmann, 3:812–34. Brussels: Institut Belge des Hautes Etudes Chinoises.

———. 1985c. "Vernacular and Classical Ritual in Taoism." *Journal of Asian Studies* 65:21–51.

Schmidt, Hans-Hermann. 1985. "Die hundertachtzig Vorschriften von Lao-chün." In *Religion und Philosophie in Ostasien: Festschrift für Hans Steininger,* edited by G. Naundorf, K. H. Pohl, and H. H. Schmidt, 151–58. Würzburg: Königshausen and Neumann.

Schmidt-Glintzer, Helwig. 1976. *Das Hung-ming-chi und die Aufnahme des Buddhismus in China.* Wiesbaden: Franz Steiner.

Seidel, Anna. 1969a. "The Image of the Perfect Ruler in Early Taoist Messianism." *History of Religions* 9:216–47.

———. 1969b. *La divinisation de Lao-tseu dans le taoïsme des Han.* Paris: Ecole Française d'Extrême Orient.

———. 1978a. "Buying One's Way to Heaven: The Celestial Treasury in Chinese Religions." *History of Religions* 17:419–32.

———. 1978b. "Das neue Testament des Tao." *Saeculum* 29:147–72.

————. 1978c. "Der Kaiser und sein Ratgeber." *Saeculum* 29:18–50.

————. 1981. "Kokuhō—Note à propos du terme 'trésor nationale' en Chine et au Japon." *Bulletin de l'Ecole Française d'Extrême-Orient* 69:229–61.

————. 1982. "Tokens of Immortality in Han Graves." *Numen* 29:79–122.

————. 1983. "Imperial Treasures and Taoist Sacraments: Taoist Roots in the Apocrypha." In *Tantric and Taoist Studies*, edited by Michel Strickmann, 2:291–371. Brussels: Institut Belge des Hautes Etudes Chinoises.

————. 1984a. "Le sūtra merveilleux du Ling-pao suprême, traitant de Lao tseu qui convertit les barbares." In *Contributions aux études du Touen-houang*, edited by Michel Soymié, 3:305–52. Paris-Geneva: Ecole Française d'Extrême-Orient.

————. 1984b. "Taoist Messianism." *Numen* 31:161–74.

————. 1985. "Geleitbrief an die Unterwelt: Jenseitsvorstellungen in den Graburkunden der Späteren Han Zeit." In *Religion und Philosophie in Ostasien: Festschrift für Hans Steininger*, edited by G. Naundorf, K. H. Pohl, H. H. Schmidt, 161–84. Würzburg: Königshausen and Neumann.

————. 1987a. "Post-Mortem Immortality: The Taoist Resurrection of the Body." In *Gilgul: Essays on Transformation, Revolution, and Permanence in the History of Religions*; edited by S. Shaked, D. Shulman, G. G. Stroumsa, 223–37. Leiden: E. Brill.

————. 1987b. "Traces of Han Religion in Funeral Texts Found in Tombs." In *Akizuki Kan'ei hakase taikan kinen ronshū Dōkyō to shūkyō bunka*, 714–33. Tokyo: Hirakawa.

————. 1988. "Review of *Das Ritual der Himmelsmeister im Spiegel früher Quellen*, by Ursula-Angelika Cedzich." *Cahiers d'Extrême-Asie* 4:199–204.

————. 1990. *Taoismus: Die inoffizielle Hochreligion Chinas*. Tokyo: Deutsche Gesellschaft für Natur- und Völkerkunde Ostasiens.

Shchutskii, Iulian. [1960] 1979. *Researches on the I-ching*. Princeton, N.J.: Princeton University Press, Bollingen Series 62.

Shimomi Takao. 1974. "Katsu Kō 'Shinsen den' ni tsuite." *Fukuoka joshi tandai kiyō* 8:57–75.

Sivin, Nathan. 1968. *Chinese Alchemy: Preliminary Studies*. Cambridge, Mass.: Harvard University Press.

————. 1969. "Cosmos and Computation in Early Chinese Mathematical Astronomy." *T'oung-pao* 55:1–73.

————. 1988. *Traditional Medicine in Contemporary China*. Ann Arbor: University of Michigan, Center for Chinese Studies Publications.

————. 1991. "Change and Continuity in Early Cosmology: *The Great Commentary to the Book of Changes*." In *Chōgoku kodai kagaku shiron, zokuhen*, edited by Yamada Keiji and Tanaka Tan, 3–43. Kyōto: Kyōto University, Jimbun kagaku kenkyūjo.

Smith, Thomas E. 1990. "The Record of the Ten Continents." *Taoist Resources* 2, no. 2:87–119.

————. 1992. "Ritual and the Shaping of Narrative: The Legend of the Han Emperor Wu." Ph.D. diss., University of Michigan, Ann Arbor.

Sōfukawa Hiroshi. 1981. *Konronzan e no shōsen*. Tokyo: Chūōkōron sha.

Soothill, William E. 1987. *The Lotus of the Wonderful Law.* London: Curzon Press.

Soothill, William E., and Lewis Hudous. 1937. *A Dictionary of Chinese Buddhist Terms*. London: Kegan Paul.

Soper, Alexander. 1959. *Literary Evidence for Early Buddhist Art in China.* Ascona: Artibus Asiae Publishers.

Soymié, Michel. 1977. "Les dix jours du jeune taoïste." In *Yoshioka Yoshitoyo hakase kanri kinen Dokyo kenkyū ronshū,* 1–21. Tokyo: Kokusho kankōkai.

———. 1979. *Contributions aux etudes du Touen-houang.* Vol. 1. Geneva: Ecole Française d'Extrême-Orient.

Spiro, Melford. 1970. *Buddhism and Society: A Great Tradition and Its Burmese Vicissitudes.* New York: Harper and Row.

Stein, Rolf A. 1963. "Remarques sur les mouvements du taoïsme politico-religieux au IIe siècle ap. J.-C." *T'oung-pao* 50:1–78.

———. 1971a. "La légende du foyer dans le monde chinois." In *Exchanges et communications: Mélanges offerts a Claude Lévi-Strauss,* edited by J. Pouillon and P. Miranda. The Hague: Mouton.

———. 1971b. "Les fétes de cuisine du taoisme religieux." *Annuaire du Collège de France* 71:431–40.

———. 1979. "Religious Taoism and Popular Religion from the Second to Seventh Centuries." In *Facets of Taoism,* edited by Holmes Welch and Anna Seidel, 53–81. New Haven, Conn.: Yale University Press.

———. 1986. "Avalokiteśvara/Kuan-yin: Un exemple de transformation d'un dieu à une déesse." *Cahiers d'Extrême-Asie* 2:17–77.

———. 1990. *The World in Miniature: Container Gardens and Dwellings in Far Eastern Religious thought.* Translated by Phyllis Brooks. Stanford, Calif.: Stanford University Press.

Strickmann, Michel. 1978a. "The Longest Taoist Scripture." *History of Religions* 17:331–54.

———. 1978b. "The Mao-Shan Revelations: Taoism and the Aristocracy." *T'oung-pao* 63:1–63.

———. 1978c. "A Taoist Confirmation of Liang Wu-ti's Suppression of Taoism." *Journal of the American Oriental Society* 98:467–74.

———. 1979. "On the Alchemy of T'ao Hung-ching." In *Facets of Taoism,* edited by Holmes Welch and Anna Seidel, 123–92. New Haven, Conn.: Yale University Press.

———. 1980. "History, Anthropology, and Chinese Religion." *Harvard Journal of Asiatic Studies* 40:201–48.

———. 1981. *Le taoïsme du Mao chan; Chronique d'une révélation.* Paris: Collège du France, Institut des Hautes Etudes Chinoises.

———, ed. 1983. *Tantric and Taoist Studies.* Vol. 2. Brussels: Institut Belge des Hautes Etudes Chinoises.

———, ed. 1985a. *Tantric and Taoist Studies.* Vol. 3. Brussels: Institut Belge des Hautes Etudes Chinoises.

———. 1985b. "Therapeutische Rituale und das Problem des Bösen im frühen Taoismus." In *Religion und Philosophie in Ostasien: Festschrift für Hans Steininger,* edited by G. Naundorf, K. H. Pohl, and H. H. Schmidt, 185–200. Würzburg: Königshausen and Neumann.

Strong, John. 1983. *The Legend of King Aśoka: A Study and Translation of the Aśokavadāna.* Delhi: Motilal Barnasidass.

Stuart, G. A. [1911] 1976. *Chinese Material Medica: Vegetable Kingdom.* Taipei: Southern Materials Center.

Sunayama Minoru. 1980a. "Dōkyō chūgenha hyōi." *Shūkan tōyōgaku* 43:31–44.

———. 1980b. "Sei Gen'ei no shisō ni tsuite." *Nihon chūgoku gakkai hō* 32:125–39.

———. 1984. "Lingbao duren jing sizhu daji." *Shijie zongjiao yanjiu* 1984, no. 2: 30–48.

———. 1990. *Zui Tō dōkyō shisōshi kenkyū.* Tokyo: Hirakawa.

Suzuki, Daisez T. 1978. *The Lankāvatāra Sūtra.* Boulder, Col.: Prajna Press.

Takeuchi Yoshio. 1978. *Takeuchi Yoshio zenshū.* Tokyo: Kadokawa.

Tambiah, S. J. 1976. *World Conqueror and World Renouncer.* Cambridge: Cambridge University Press.

Tanaka Fumio. 1984. "Taiheikyō no kanshinhō ni tsuite." In *Chūgoku no shūkyō to kagaku,* 291–304. Tokyo: Kokusho kankōkai.

Tang Yongtong. [1938] 1981. *Han Wei liang Jin nanbei chao fojiao shi.* Beijing: Zhonghua.

Tay, C. N. 1976. "Kuan-Yin: The Cult of Half Asia." *History of Religions* 16:147–77.

Teiser, Stephen. 1985. "T'ang Buddhist Encyclopedias: An Introduction to *Fa-yüan chu-lin* and *Chu-ching yao-chi.*" *T'ang Studies* 3:109–28.

Tetsui Yoshinori. 1990. *Chūgoku shinwa no bunka jinruigaku teki kenkyū.* Edited by Ikeda Suetoshi. Tokyo: Hirakawa.

Thiel, Josef. 1961. "Der Streit der Buddhisten und Taoisten zur Mongolenzeit." *Monumenta Serica* 20:1–81.

Thompson, Laurence. 1985a. *Chinese Religion in Western Languages: A Comprehensive and Classified Bibliography . . . through 1980.* Phoenix: University of Arizona Press.

———. 1985b. "Taoism: Classic and Canon." In *The Holy Book in Comparative Perspective,* edited by Frederick M. Denny and Rodney F. Taylor, 204–23. Columbus: University of South Carolina Press.

Tonami Mamoru. 1982. "Tōchūki no bukkyō to kokka." In *Chūgoku chūsei no shūkyō to bunka,* edited by Fukunaga Mitsuji, 589–651. Kyōto: Kyōto University, Jimbun kagaku kenkyūjo.

———. 1986. *Tōdai seiji shakaishi kenkyū.* Kyoto: Dōhōsha.

———. 1988. "Policy towards the Buddhist Church in the Reign of T'ang Hsüan-tsung." *Acta Asiatica* 55:27–47.

———. 1992. "Hōrin no jiseki ni mieru tōsho no bukkyō, dōkyō to kokka." In *Chūgoku ko dōkyō shi kenkyū,* edited by Yoshikawa Tadao, 243–74. Kyōto: Dōhōsha.

Trauzettel, Rolf. 1992. "Chinesische Reflexionen über Furcht und Angst: Ein Beitrag zur Mentalitätsgeschichte Chinas im Mittelalter und in der frühen Neuzeit." *Saeculum* 43.4:307–24.

Tsukamoto Zenryū. 1942. *Shina bukkyōshi kenkyū: Hokugihen.* Tokyo: Kōbundō.

———. 1948. "Hokushū no haibutsu ni tsuite. *Tōhōgakuhō* 16:29–101, and 18: 78–111.

———. 1949. "Hokushū no shūkyō haiki seisaku no hōkai." *Bukkyō shigaku* 1:3–31.

———, ed. 1955. *Jōron kenkyū.* Kyōto: Hōzōkan.

———. 1961. *Gisho shakurōshi no kenkyū.* Tokyo: Bukkyō bungaku kenkyūjo.

———. 1974. *Tsukamoto Zenryū chōsakushū.* 7 vols. Tokyo: Daitō.

Tsukamoto Zenryū, and Leon Hurvitz. 1985. *A History of Early Chinese Buddhism.* 2 vols. Tokyo: Kodansha.

Twitchett, Dennis, ed. 1989. *The Cambridge History of China.* Vol. 3, *Sui and T'ang China, 589–906.* Pt. 1. Cambridge: Cambridge University Press.

Uehara Jundō. 1951. "Shinshu, Gorō ni tsuite." *Tōhōshūkyō* 1:75–81.

Unschuld, Paul. 1985. *Medicine in China: A History of Ideas*. Berkeley: University of California Press.

———. 1986. *Nan-ching: The Classic of Difficult Issues*. Berkeley: University of California Press.

Vandermeersch, Léon. 1980. *Wangdao ou la voie royale: Recherches sur l'ésprit des institutions de la Chine archaïque*. Vol. 2. Paris: Publications de l'Ecole Française d'Extrême-Orient, no. 113.

———. 1985. "Genèse et signification de la théorie des Cinq-Agents dans le Confucianisme ancien." Paper Presented at the Quatrième Colloque Pluri-disciplinaire Franco-Japonais. Paris.

Wang Ka. 1989. "Yuanshi tianzun yu Pangushi kaitian gundi." *Shijie zongjiao yanjiu* 1989, no. 3:61–69.

Wang Kuike. 1964. "Zongguo liandanshu zhongdi jinyi he huachi." *Kexueshi jikan* 7:53–62.

Wang Ming. 1960. *Taiping jing hejiao*. Beijing: Zhonghua.

———. 1982. "Lun Taiping jing de chengshu shidai he zuozhe." *Shijie zongjiao yanjiu* 1982, no. 2:17–26.

Wang Weicheng. 1934. "Laozi huahu shuo kaozheng." *Guoxue jikan* 4, no. 2:1–122.

Wang Yi-t'ung. 1984. *A Record of Buddhist Monasteries in Lo-yang*. Princeton, N.J.: Princeton University Press.

Warder, A. K. 1970. *Indian Buddhism*. Delhi: Motilal Barnasidass.

Ware, James R. 1933. "The *Wei-shu* and the *Sui-shu* on Taoism." *Journal of the American Oriental Society* 53:215–50.

———. 1966. *Alchemy, Medicine and Religion in the China of AD 320*. Cambridge, Mass.: MIT Press.

Watson, Burton. 1968a. *The Complete Works of Chuang-tzu*. New York: Columbia University Press.

———. 1968b. *Records of the Grand Historian of China*. 2 vols. New York: Columbia University Press.

———. 1974. *Courtier and Commoner in Ancient China: Selections from the History of the Former Han by Pan Ku*. New York: Columbia University Press.

Wechsler, Howard. 1985. *Offerings of Jade and Silk*. New Haven, Conn.: Yale University Press.

Weinstein, Stanley. 1987. *Buddhism under the T'ang*. Cambridge: Cambridge University Press.

Wei Qipeng. 1981. "Taiping jing yu Dong Han yixue." *Shijie zongjiao yanjiu* 1981, no. 1:101–9.

Welch, Holmes, and Anna Seidel, eds. 1979. *Facets of Taoism*. New Haven, Conn.: Yale University Press.

White, David Gordon. 1991. *Myths of the Dog-Men*. Chicago: University of Chicago Press.

Wijayaratna, Mohan. 1990. *Buddhist Monastic Life*. Cambridge: Cambridge University Press.

Wile, Douglas. 1992. *Art of the Bedchamber: The Chinese Sexology Classics Including Women's Solo Meditation Texts*. Albany: State University of New York Press.

Wilhelm, Hellmut. 1977. *Heaven, Earth and Man in the Book of Changes*. Seattle: Washington University Press.

Wilhelm, Richard. 1950. *The I Ching or Book of Changes*. Translated by Cary F. Baynes. Princeton, N.J.: Princeton University Press, Bollingen Series 19.

Wright, Arthur F. 1948. "Fo-t'u-teng, a Biography." *Harvard Journal of Asiatic Studies* 11:321–71.

———. 1951. "Fu I and the Rejection of Buddhism." *Journal of the History of Ideas* 12:33–47.

———. 1973. "T'ang T'ai-tsung and Buddhism." In *Perspectives on the T'ang*, edited by Arthur F. Wright and Dennis Twitchett, 239–63. New Haven, Conn.: Yale University Press.

———. 1990. *Studies in Chinese Buddhism*. Edited by Robert M. Somers. New Haven, Conn.: Yale University Press.

Yamada Keiji, and Tanaka Tan, eds. 1991. *Chūgoku kodai kagaku shiron, zokuhen*. Kyoto: Kyoto University, Jimban kagaku kenkyūjo.

Yamada Takashi. 1992. *Kōhon Shōgenkyō*. Sendai: Tōhoku University.

Yamada Toshiaki. 1974. "Taihei kōki shinsenrui kandai hairetsu no ikkōsatsu." *Tōhōshūkyō* 43:30–50.

———. 1977. "Shinsenden Ri Happyaku denkō." In *Yoshioka Yoshitoyo hakase kenri kinen Dōkyō kenkyū ronshū*, 145–63. Tokyo: Kokusho kankōkai.

———. 1982. "Bunshi sensei mujō shinjin kanrei naiden no seiritsu ni tsuite." In *Rekishi ni okeru minshū to bunka*, 221–35. Tokyo: Kokusho kankōkai.

———. 1983. "Shinsendō." In *Dōkyō*, edited by Fukui Kōjun, Yamazaki Hiroshi, Kimura Eiichi, and Sakai Tadao, 1:319–71. Tokyo: Hirakawa.

———. 1984a. "Dōzō junirui seiritsu ni kansuru shiryō no haikei." In *Chūgoku no shūkyō to kagaku*, 519–38. Tokyo: Kokusho kankōkai.

———. 1984b. "Reihō gofu no seiritsu to sono fuzuiteki seikaku." In *Shin'i shisō no sōgōteki kenkyū*, edited by Yasui Kōzan, 165–96. Tokyo: Kokusho kankōkai.

———. 1987a. "Futatsu no shinfu." *Tōyōgaku ronsō* 12:147–65.

———. 1987b. "Gofujo keiseikō: Rakushichō o megutte." In *Akizuki Kan'ei hakase taikan kinen ronshū Dōkyō to shūkyō bunka*, 122–35. Tokyo: Hirakawa.

———. 1989. "Dōbō shinson shikō." *Tōhōshūkyō* 74:20–38.

———. 1989a. "Longevity Techniques and the Compilation of the *Lingbao wufuxu*." In *Taoist Meditation and Longevity Techniques*, edited by L. Kohn, 97–122. Ann Arbor: University of Michigan, Center for Chinese Studies.

Yamazaki, Hiroshi. 1979. "Hokushū no tōdōkan ni tsuite." *Tōhōshūkyō* 54:1–13.

Yang Kuan. 1963. "Huangdi yu huangdi." In *Gushi bian*, edited by Gu Jiegang, 7:189–209. Hongkong: Taiping.

Yang Liansheng. 1956. "Laojun yinsong jiejing jiaoshi." *Zhongyang yanjiu yuan, Lishi yanyu yanjiu suo jikan* 28, no. 1:17–54.

Yan Lingfeng. 1983. *Jingzi congzhu*. Taipei: Xuesheng.

Yasui Kōzan. 1958. "Dōzō ni okeru kōteiden no kōsatsu." *Tōhōshūkyō* 13/14:49–65.

———. 1966. *Isho no kisōteki kenkyū*. Tokyo: Kangi bunka kenkyūkai.

———. 1979. *Isho no seiritsu to sono tenkai*. Tokyo: Kokusho kankōkai.

Yasui Kōzan, and Nakamura Chōhachi. [1960] 1972. *Isho shūsei*. 6 vols. Mimeographed.

Yetts, Percifal. 1916. "The Eight Immortals." *Journal of the Royal Asiatic Society*: 772–807.

Yoshikawa Tadao. 1984. *Rikuchō seishinshi kenkyū*. Kyōto: Dōhōsha.

———. 1987. "Seishitsu kō." *Tōhōgakuhō* 59:125–62.

————. 1988. *Chūgoku kodaijin no yume to shi.* Tokyo: Heibonsha.

————. 1990. "Ō Enchi kō." *Tōhō gakuhō* 62:69–98.

————, ed. 1992a. *Chūgoku ko dōkyō shi kenkyū.* Kyoto: Dōhōsha.

————. 1992b. "Nichichū muei: Shikaisen kō." In *Chūgoku ko dōkyō shi kenkyū,* edited by Yoshikawa Tadao, 175–216. Kyoto: Dōhōsha.

Yoshioka Yoshitoyo. 1955. *Dōkyō kyōten shiron.* Tokyo: Dōkyō kankōkai.

————. 1959. *Dōkyō to bukkyō.* Vol. 1. Tokyo: Kokusho kankōkai.

————. 1961. "Bukkyō jūkai shisō no chūgoku teki shūyō." *Shūkyō kenkyū* 35, no. 1:51–72.

————. 1970. *Dōkyō to bukkyō.* Vol. 2. Tokyo: Kokusho kankōkai.

————. 1976. *Dōkyō to bukkyō.* Vol. 3. Tokyo: Kokusho kankōkai.

————. 1979. "Taoist Monastic Life." In *Facets of Taoism,* edited by Holmes Welch and Anna Seidel, 220–52. New Haven, Conn.: Yale University Press.

Yü Chün-fang. 1990. "Feminine Images of Kuan-Yin in Post-T'ang China." *Journal of Chinese Religions* 18:61–89.

Yu Jiaxi. 1931. "Bei Zhou huifo zhumou zhen Wei Yuansong." *Furen xuezhi* 2, no. 2:1–25.

Yuan Ke. 1954. *Zhongguo gudai shenhua.* Shanghai: Shangwu.

————. 1960. *Zhongguo gudai shenhua.* Beijing: Zhonghua shuju.

————. 1979a. *Gu shenhua yishi.* Beijing: Renmin.

————. 1979b. *Shenhua gushi xinbian.* Beijing: Zhongguo qingnian.

————. 1982. *Shenhua lun wenji.* Shanghai: Wenyi.

————. 1984. *Zhongguo shenhua chuanshuo.* Beijing: Zhongguo minjian wenyi.

————. 1985. *Zhongguo shenhua chuanshuo cidian.* Shanghai: Wenyi.

Yūsa Norboru. 1986. "Seito seiyōkyu seijōsan oyobi shisen ni okeru dōkyō kenkyū no genshō." *Tōhōshūkyō* 68:86–98.

Yü Ying-shih. 1964. "Life and Immortality in the Mind of Han-China." *Harvard Journal of Asiatic Studies* 25:80–122.

Zhang Jiyu. 1990. *Tianshi dao shilue.* Beijing: Huawen.

Zhang Weiling. 1990. "Guanling Yin Xi shenhua yanjiu." *Daojiao xue tansuo* 3:21–74.

————. 1991. "Beichao zhi qian louguan daojiao xiuxingfa de lishi kaocha." *Daojiao xue tansuo* 4:67–117.

Zhao Zongcheng. 1982. "Shilun Cheng Xuanying de Chongxuan zhi dao." *Zongjiao xue yanjiu* 1982:8–15.

Zürcher, Erik. 1959. *The Buddhist Conquest of China: The Spread and Adaptation of Buddhism in Early Medieval China.* 2 Vols. Leiden: E. Brill.

————. 1980. "Buddhist Influence on Early Taoism." *T'oung-pao* 66:84–147.

————. 1982. "Prince Moonlight: Messianism and Eschatology in Early Medieval Buddhism." *T'oung-pao* 68:1–75.

Livia Kohn, Associate Professor of Religion at Boston University, is the author of *Early Chinese Mysticism* (Princeton).